THE OXFORD BOOK OF VILLAINS

John Mortimer is a QC, novelist, and playwright, many of whose works have been televised. His plays include *A Voyage Round my Father*, and his books, *Summer's Lease*, *Paradise Postponed*, *Titmuss Regained*, and *Rumpole of the Bailey* and its sequels. His autobiography, *Clinging to the Wreckage*, won the *Yorkshire Post* Book of the Year Award in 1982, and he won the British Film Academy Writers Award in 1979. John Mortimer holds honorary degrees from five universities in Britain and America, and he is currently Chairman of the Royal Court Theatre, of the Royal Society of Literature, and of the Howard League for Penal Reform.

THE OXFORD BOOK OF VILLAINS

EDITED BY
JOHN MORTIMER

OXFORD NEW YORK
OXFORD UNIVERSITY PRESS
1993

Oxford University Press, Walton Street, Oxford OX2 6DP
Oxford New York Toronto
Delhi Bombay Calcutta Madras Karachi
Kuala Lumpur Singapore Hong Kong Tokyo
Nairobi Dar es Salaam Cape Town
Melbourne Auckland Madrid
and associated companies in
Berlin Ibadan

Oxford is a trade mark of Oxford University Press

First published 1992
First issued as an Oxford University Press paperback 1993

British Library Cataloguing in Publication Data
Data available

Library of Congress Cataloging in Publication Data
The Oxford book of villains / edited by John Mortimer.
p. cm.
Includes indexes.
1. *Villains in literature.* I. *Mortimer, John Clifford,* 1923–
PN56.5.V5095 1992 808.8'03520692—dc20 91-41750
ISBN 0-19-282277-2

1 3 5 7 9 10 8 6 4 2

Printed in Great Britain by
Clays Ltd.
Bungay, Suffolk

CONTENTS

INTRODUCTION

THE anthologist compiling, let us say, a book of nineteenth-century dramatic criticism, or Celtic verse in translation, has a task which is reasonably defined. The difficulties of preparing a book of villains is that the field stretches towards infinity. The world may be short of many things, rain forests, great politicians, black rhinos, saints and caviare, but the supply of villains is endless. They are everywhere, down narrow streets and in brightly lit office buildings and parliaments, dominating family life, crowding prisons and law courts, and providing plots for most of the works of fiction that have been composed since the dawn of history. Faced with the immensity of this material what can the anthologist do? To represent the world's villainy adequately would be impossible. What I have done is to assemble some of the pieces of writing which I think do most to illuminate this dark subject. Most of these extracts are European or American and the majority depict villainy from a Christian point of view. This, I hope, is no discourtesy to the many great civilizations and literatures not here represented; their omission doesn't mean that they are short of villains and I intend no offence. They could form the subject of many other books.

What entered the Almighty's mind when he put the serpent into the Garden of Eden he alone knows, and by now he may well have forgotten. The existence of villainy in a world under divine supervision is a question which has long troubled humanity. It is not the purpose of this introduction, nor indeed of this anthology, to attempt an answer. All that can be said is that, so far as writers of fiction are concerned, the serpent's presence was an unmixed blessing, as was the gift of free will and the power of the individual to choose the path of unrighteousness. If villainy hadn't existed it would have been necessary for the creators of the world's literature to invent it. In most stories villains provide the plot and make virtue interesting. *Hamlet* without the Prince would be difficult, but *Hamlet* without Claudius would be impossible. Imagine the tedium of *Snow White* without the witch or *Little Red Riding Hood* without the wolf, the story of Robin

Hood without the Sheriff of Nottingham or *Cinderella* without the Ugly Sisters. If God, as Malcolm Muggeridge once suggested, is the great dramatist, he knew that the serpent and his descendants were essential characters, and the cast list would be incomplete without them.

Fiction has become, perhaps, over subtle and the frontiers of villainy have become blurred. Heroes are now anti-heroes and since Henry James few writers have been gifted with a true sense of evil. Villainy found its most vivid and full-blooded personification in the Elizabethan theatre and the Victorian novel. There are no two ways about Goneril and Quilp, Lady Macbeth and Uriah Heep. They don't try and explain their immorality, they don't blame their parents or put it all down to premature weaning. They come into their stories not only accepting their moral deficiencies but positively enjoying them. This, and the fact that even the greatest writers find it easier to write about villains than saints, or even ordinarily good people, is what gives them their enormous vitality. Actors often feel that they need to be loved by audiences and play sympathetic characters, but an entertaining villain is always a better part than a dull hero. Richard III comes on to the stage and behaves appallingly, but there can be few better roles for an actor. Who would take on Othello if they had the chance of Iago? The villains have always been the great entertainers, making the spectators feel safe in their comparative decency, enthralled by the wicked machinations on the stage and grateful that nothing like that is happening to them.

So the fictional villains, even if you stick to those well enough written to be included in such a book as this, are innumerable and I could only hope to make a small selection. But what about real life villainy? Once again it is impossible to do justice to the criminals of the world and the field had to be greatly restricted. Fortunately the British have an insatiable appetite for reading about crime; detective stories and the *News of the World* on Sundays are sucked in together and fact and fiction become inextricably mixed so that it is difficult for us to remember that Bill Sikes didn't really kill anyone, but that George Joseph Smith really brought himself to tug the legs of his wives and watch them drown in their bath water. The old murderers, Dr Crippen and Al Capone and Armstrong the poisoner, have become legendary figures, although their crimes were real enough. Billy the Kid was a ruthless killer who didn't even bother to count the Mexicans among his victims, but his name now sounds like that of an attractive cowboy adventurer; time has awarded him a white hat and he has vanished into the safe world of fiction.

Murderers form a long section in this book and I would recommend you not to read it all at once but to vary it, perhaps with an occasional con man or a few seducers and cads. It is a gloomy subject, and yet the murderers I had to deal with as a barrister were easy clients to get on with, usually polite and grateful for whatever you could do for them. I am not speaking of gang killers, or those who robbed with violence, but most murders go on, like Christmas, in the family circle. They take place between husbands and wives or lovers, or between best friends, and these criminals seemed to have reached a certain peace by murdering the one person in life they felt they had to kill. Sitting with them in cells, discussing the case, perhaps joking about the witnesses, it often seemed extraordinary that such apparently calm and reasonable people could break through the great safety barrier of inhibition which prevents us from taking another person's life. It was said of Dr Crippen that he was a kindly, modest, and hospitable little man, endlessly tolerant of his impossible wife. He behaved with great dignity at his trial, only concerned for the acquittal of his mistress, and he faced death with quiet courage. And yet he brought himself to kill his wife, dismember her body, and bury it under the cellar floor.

Armstrong was a gentle lawyer from the little town of Hay-on-Wye who not only murdered his wife but attempted to do in a rival solicitor. His manners were so good that when he passed his intended victim a poisoned scone at tea-time he uttered the immortal words, 'Excuse fingers'. Terrible moments of inhumanity are surrounded by the quiet and casual concerns of everyday life. 'Most of the interest and part of the terror of crime', wrote Filson Young in his introduction to the Crippen trial, 'are not due to what is abnormal but to what is normal in it; what we have in common with the criminal, rather than that subtle insanity which differentiates him from us, is what makes us view with so lively an interest a fellow being who has wandered into these tragic and fatal fields.'

The word 'villain' has many meanings, from the condemnation of the most serious offender to a term of endearment. Sir Toby Belch in *Twelfth Night* not only calls Maria his 'metal of India' but 'the little villain'. The police call anyone with a criminal record a villain, so the word can be applied to the steadiest and most skilled of safe-blowers, the sort of man who votes Conservative, organizes seaside trips for deprived children, and wouldn't hurt a fly. The world of the small-time thief, the burglar and the cut-purse doesn't seem to have changed much since the Elizabethan villains invented their strange and secret language, or Charles Peace showed himself so uncannily adept at entering premises by night and making friends with guard dogs. Such men are not really the enemies of society, and nor do they seek to overturn the social order. They wish society to prosper, live by strong monetarist principles, and are certainly against the closed shop because they want all shops to be open, preferably by jemmy. They believe, in their old-fashioned way, that a woman's place is in the home and that robbing banks is a man's job. For this reason there are few women in the ranks of professional small-time villains, the Elizabethan 'Moll Cutpurse', perhaps an early feminist, being a remarkable exception to this rule.

One argument which will never be satisfactorily resolved concerns the rival claims of nature and nurture as causes of villainy. Are villains, like poets, born and not made? Unemployment, poverty, lack of education or being born into a faithless age cannot account for that extraordinary moment when Dr Crippen became a monster. Those young murderers-for-kicks, Leopold and Loeb, came from the most affluent families and were well educated and intelligent. Racing in stolen cars may be attributed to the hopelessness of a jobless life in an inner city, but bank frauds which ruin thousands are perpetrated by well-off and hard-working men. However, I can imagine that a child born to a family of South London villains, with one uncle in Brixton Prison, another enjoying a holiday in Torremolinos on the Costa Brava (known to villains as the 'Costa del Crime') and a father planning raids on various warehouses, might feel it natural to follow in his family's footsteps. In the same way a child who came from a long line of judges could easily be persuaded to read for the Bar.

Nature and nurture must both have a part to play, and there are no doubt other elements at work. One of the villains interviewed by Professor Laurie Taylor describes the excitement of robbing a bank, the flood of adrenalin and the high-risk intoxication shared by skiers and those who ride to hounds. I have no doubt that it is this excitement which makes some people prefer robbing banks to working behind their counters, even though the glorious moment of exhilaration may well be followed by many tedious years under lock and key.

I also think that villains are those who have been cursed with an unreasonably high degree of optimism. Deterrent sentences have little effect because the true villain never thinks he's going to be caught. In the days when you could be hanged for stealing a handkerchief, handkerchiefs were hardly safe in anyone's pocket. It is a form of insane optimism, the strongly held belief that the day of reckoning will never come, which persuades financiers that frauds will never be discovered. A lot of nonsense is talked about the complexity of fraud cases, and it is said that they are far too difficult for the average jury to understand. In fact such cases are surprisingly simple: the defrauder simply buys goods on credit, or raises money, without the slightest intention of paying it back. The optimistic con man lives forever in the present, when he can take his girlfriends on board his yacht, drink his champagne and smoke his cigars. The bill is never going to be presented and the future is simply not going to happen.

The connection between the law and morality is always tenuous and much villainy is perfectly legal. The domestic tyrant who makes family life intolerable, the sadistic judge and the uncaring sexual manipulator commit no crimes, nor does the man, like Gilbert Osmond in *The Portrait of a Lady*, whose aloof and negative attitude to life can amount to a positive evil. All these have their place in a book of villains.

I have decided, rather than trudge through a chronological history of villainy, to group this rogues' gallery in various categories, so that the reader can select which brand of malefactor he or she wishes to hiss at. As I have already said, what follows is but a drop in the ocean of bad behaviour and no doubt worse is happening around us every day, for villainy is, in many ways, a commonplace thing. As Auden wrote in a memorable poem not quoted elsewhere in this book:

> Evil is unspectacular and always human,
> And shares our bed and eats at our own table,
> And we are introduced to good men every day . . .
> It is the evil that is helpless like a lover
> And has to pick a quarrel and succeeds,
> And both are openly destroyed before our eyes.
>
> 'Herman Melville'

I owe thanks to many people who have helped in the preparation of this anthology. First to Patricia Craig, editor of *The Oxford Book of English Detective Stories*, who found much material unknown to me, gave me constant help and advice and wrote many of the introductory notes. Judith Luna, my editor at the Oxford University Press, asked me to take on this task and, during the many hours when I felt daunted by it, encouraged me to proceed and gave me advice that was always helpful. Jackie Pritchard copy-edited the book with great care and skill, and my daughter Emily Mortimer gave up part of what should have been a holiday to chase dates and references. My greatest gratitude is due to the authors here represented, many of whom have turned the follies, felonies, and weaknesses of mankind into great literature.

JOHN MORTIMER

Turville Heath
September 1991

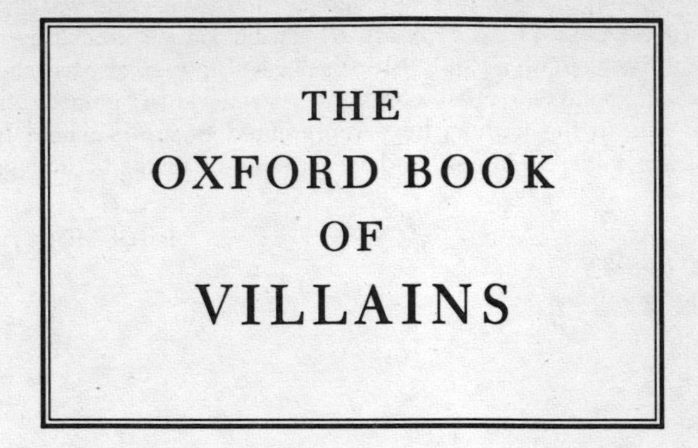

THE OXFORD BOOK OF VILLAINS

I

THE SPIRIT OF EVIL

THE Devil, I safely can aver,
Has neither hoof, nor tail, nor sting;
Nor is he, as some sages swear,
A spirit, neither here nor there,
In nothing—yet in everything.

He is—what we are; for sometimes
The Devil is a gentleman;
At others a bard bartering rhymes
For sack; a statesman spinning crimes;
A swindler, living as he can;

A thief, who cometh in the night,
With whole boots and net pantaloons,
Like some one whom it were not right
To mention;—or the luckless wight,
From whom he steals nine silver spoons.

PERCY BYSSHE SHELLEY, from *Peter Bell the Third*, 1819

'Is this the region, this the soil, the clime,
Said then the lost Arch-angel, 'this the seat
That we must change for heav'n? this mournful gloom
For that celestial light? be it so, since He,
Who now is Sov'reign, can dispose and bid
What shall be right: farthest from Him is best,
Whom reason hath equalled, force hath made supreme
Above His equals. Farewell happy fields,
Where joy for ever dwells! hail horrors! hail
Infernal world; and thou profoundest hell.
Receive thy new possessor; one who brings
A mind not to be changed by place or time.
The mind is its own place, and in itself
Can make a heav'n of hell, a hell of heav'n.
What matter where, if I be still the same,
And what I should be, all but less than He

Whom thunder hath made greater? Here at least
We shall be free; th' Almighty hath not built
Here for His envy, will not drive us hence:
Here we may reign secure, and in my choice
To reign is worth ambition, though in hell:
Better to reign in hell, than serve in heav'n.
But wherefore let we then our faithful friends,
Th' associates and copartners of our loss,
Lie thus astonished on the oblivious pool,
And call them not to share with us their part
In this unhappy mansion; or once more
With rallied arms to try what may be yet
Regained in heav'n, or what more lost in hell?'

JOHN MILTON, *Paradise Lost*, 1667

LUCIFER BROODS

'It was quite simple—
If God could be god
Why couldn't I?

All I asked for
Was equality and independence,
Primus inter pares—
With not too many *pares*.
A rotating chairmanship
Might have been the answer.

What happened to the question?

Better to reign in hell than serve in heav'n—
But better still to reign in both.

What, you might ask, is the point of it all?
Seduction, corruption, ruination—
All this hard labour I put in,
Day after night after day

—The solace of having companions . . .

Companions! Do these lost souls
Imagine they're as good as me?
Damn their eyes!

So I am the Spirit who always says No?
Once I was ready to say Oh yes!'

*

'I do wish he would stop brooding in my head . . .
Where are the aspirins?' Mephisto whispered.
'God knows!' yelled Meretrix.

D. J. ENRIGHT, *A Faust Book*, 1979

FAUSTUS. But may I raise up spirits when I please?
MEPHASTOPHILIS. I Faustus, and do greater things then these.
FAUSTUS. Then theres inough for a thousand soules.
Here Mephastophilis receive this scrowle.
A deede of gift of body and of soule:
But yet conditionally, that thou performe
All articles prescrib'd betweene us both.
MEPHASTOPHILIS. Faustus, I sweare by hel and *Lucifer*
To effect all promises betweene us made.
FAUSTUS. Then heare me reade them: on these conditions following.
First, that Faustus may be a spirit in forme and substance.
Secondly, that Mephastophilis shall be his servant, and at his command.
Thirdly, that Mephastophilis shall do for him, and bring him whatsoever.
Fourthly, that hee shall be in his chamber or house invisible.
Lastly, that hee shall appeare to the said John Faustus, at all times, in what forme or shape soever he please.
I John Faustus of Wertenberge, Doctor, by these presents, do give both body and soule to Lucifer prince of the East, and his minister Mephastophilis, and furthermore graunt unto them, that 24. yeares being expired, the articles above written inviolate, full power to fetch or carry the said John Faustus body and soule, flesh, bloud, or goods, into their habitation wheresoever.

By me John Faustus.

MEPHASTOPHILIS. Speake *Faustus*, do you deliver this as your deede?

FAUSTUS. I, take it, and the divell give thee good on't.

MEPHASTOPHILIS. Now Faustus aske what thou wilt.

FAUSTUS. First will I question with thee about hell,
Tel me, where is the place that men call hell?

MEPHASTOPHILIS. Under the heavens.

FAUSTUS. I, but where about?

MEPHASTOPHILIS. Within the bowels of these elements,
Where we are tortur'd and remaine for ever.
Hell hath no limits, nor is circumscrib'd
In one selfe place, for where we are is hell,
And where hell is, must we ever be:
And to conclude, when all the world dissolves,
And every creature shalbe purified,
All places shall be hell that is not heaven.

FAUSTUS. Come, I thinke hell's a fable.

MEPHASTOPHILIS. I, thinke so still, till experience change thy minde.

FAUSTUS. Why? thinkst thou then that Faustus shall bee damn'd?

MEPHASTOPHILIS. I, of necessitie, for here's the scrowle,
Wherein thou hast given thy soule to *Lucifer*.

FAUSTUS. I, and body too, but what of that?
Thinkst thou that Faustus is so fond, to imagine,
That after this life there is any paine?
Tush, these are trifles and meere olde wives tales.

MEPHASTOPHILIS. But Faustus, I am an instance to prove the contrary,
For I am damnd, and am now in hell.

FAUSTUS. How? now in hell? nay and this be hell,
Ile willingly be damnd here: what walking, disputing, &c.
But leaving off this, let me have a wife, the fairest maid in *Germany*, for I am wanton and lascivious, and can not live without a wife.

MEPHASTOPHILIS. How, a wife? I prithee *Faustus* talke not of a wife.

FAUSTUS. Nay sweete *Mephastophilis* fetch me one, for I will have one.

MEPHASTOPHILIS. Well thou wilt have one, sit there till I come,
Ile fetch thee a wife in the divels name. [*Exit*

CHRISTOPHER MARLOWE, *The Tragicall History of Dr Faustus*, 1588

THE WITCH. Ow! ow! ow! ow!
The damnéd beast—the curséd sow!
To leave the kettle, and singe the Frau!
Accurséd fera!
[*Perceiving Faust and Mephistopheles.*
What is that here?
Who are you here?
What want you thus?
Who sneaks to us?
The fire pain
Burn bone and brain!

[*She plunges the skimming-ladle in the caldron, and scatters flames towards Faust, Mephistopheles, and the Animals. The Animals whimper.*

MEPHISTOPHELES [*reversing the brush, which he has been holding in his hand, and striking among the jars and glasses*].
In two! in two!
There lies the brew!
There lies the glass!
The joke will pass,
As time, foul ass!
To the singing of thy crew.
[*As the Witch starts back, full of wrath and horror:*
Ha! knows't thou me? Abomination, thou!
Knows't thou, at last, thy Lord and Master?
What hinders me from smiting now
Thee and thy monkey-sprites with fell disaster?
Hast for the scarlet coat no reverence?
Dost recognise no more the tall cock's-feather?
Have I concealed this countenance?—
Must tell my name, old face of leather?

THE WITCH. O pardon, Sir, the rough salute!
Yet I perceive no cloven foot;
And both your ravens, where are *they* now?

MEPHISTOPHELES. This time, I'll let thee 'scape the debt;
For since we two together met,
'Tis verily full many a day now.
Culture, which smooth the whole world licks,
Also unto the Devil sticks.
The days of that old Northern phantom now are over;

Where canst thou horns and tail and claws discover?
And, as regards the foot, which I can't spare, in truth,
'Twould only make the people shun me;
Therefore I've worn, like many a spindly youth,
False calves these many years upon me.

THE WITCH [*dancing*]. Reason and sense forsake my brain,
Since I behold Squire Satan here again!

MEPHISTOPHELES. Woman, from such a name refrain!

THE WITCH. Why so? What has it done to thee?

MEPHISTOPHELES. It's long been written in the Book of Fable;
Yet, therefore, no whit better men we see:
The Evil One has left, the evil ones are stable.
Sir Baron call me thou, then is the matter good;
A cavalier am I, like others in my bearing.
Thou hast no doubt about my noble blood:
See, here's the coat-of-arms that I am wearing!
[*He makes an indecent gesture.*

THE WITCH [*laughs immoderately*]. Ha! ha! That's just your way, I know:
A rogue you are, and you were always so.

MEPHISTOPHELES [*to Faust*]. My friend, take proper heed, I pray!
To manage witches, this is just the way.

JOHANN WOLFGANG VON GOETHE, *Faust*, 1801, trans. Bayard Taylor

† *Three of Shakespeare's villains attempt to explain themselves.*

EDMUND. This is the excellent foppery of the world, that, when we are sick in fortune,—often the surfeit of our own behaviour,—we make guilty of our disasters the sun, the moon, and the stars: as if we were villains by necessity; fools by heavenly compulsion; knaves, thieves, and treachers, by spherical predominance; drunkards, liars, and adulterers, by an enforced obedience of planetary influence; and all that we are evil in, by a divine thrusting on: an admirable evasion of whoremaster man, to lay his goatish disposition to the charge of a star! My father compounded with my mother under the dragon's tail; and my nativity was under *ursa major*; so that it follows, I am rough and lecherous.—Fut, I should have been that I am, had the maidenliest star in the firmament twinkled on my bastardizing.—Edgar! pat he comes like the catastrophe of the old comedy: my cue is villainous melancholy, with a sigh like Tom o' Bedlam.

WILLIAM SHAKESPEARE, *King Lear*, 1605/6

GLOSTER. Now is the winter of our discontent
Made glorious summer by this sun of York;
And all the clouds that lour'd upon our house
In the deep bosom of the ocean buried.
Now are our brows bound with victorious wreaths;
Our bruised arms hung up for monuments;
Our stern alarums chang'd to merry meetings,
Our dreadful marches to delightful measures.
Grim-visag'd war hath smooth'd his wrinkled front;
And now—instead of mounting barbed steeds
To fright the souls of fearful adversaries—
He capers nimbly in a lady's chamber
To the lascivious pleasing of a lute.
But I, that am not shap'd for sportive tricks,
Nor made to court an amorous looking-glass;
I, that am rudely stamp'd, and want love's majesty
To strut before a wanton ambling nymph;
I, that am curtail'd of this fair proportion,
Cheated of feature by dissembling nature,
Deform'd, unfinish'd, sent before my time
Into this breathing world, scarce half made up,
And that so lamely and unfashionable
That dogs bark at me as I halt by them;—
Why, I, in this weak piping time of peace,
Have no delight to pass away the time,
Unless to spy my shadow in the sun,
And descant on mine own deformity:
And therefore, since I cannot prove a lover,
To entertain these fair well-spoken days,
I am determined to prove a villain,
And hate the idle pleasures of these days.
Plots have I laid, inductions dangerous,
By drunken prophecies, libels, and dreams,
To set my brother Clarence and the king

In deadly hate the one against the other:
And, if King Edward be as true and just
As I am subtle, false, and treacherous,
This day should Clarence closely be mew'd up,
About a prophecy, which says that G
Of Edward's heirs the murderer shall be.
Dive, thoughts, down to my soul:—here Clarence comes.

WILLIAM SHAKESPEARE, *Richard III*, 1592/3

IAGO. That Cassio loves her, I do well believe it;
That she loves him, 'tis apt, and of great credit:
The Moor—howbeit that I endure him not—
Is of a constant, loving, noble nature;
And I dare think he'll prove to Desdemona
A most dear husband. Now, I do love her too;
Not out of absolute lust,—though peradventure
I stand accountant for as great a sin,—
But partly led to diet my revenge,
For that I do suspect the lusty Moor
Hath leapt into my seat: the thought whereof
Doth, like a poisonous mineral, gnaw my inwards;
And nothing can or shall content my soul
Till I am even'd with him, wife for wife;
Or failing so, yet that I put the Moor
At least into a jealousy so strong
That judgement cannot cure. Which thing to do,
If this poor trash of Venice, whom I trash
For his quick hunting, stand the putting on,
I'll have our Michael Cassio on the hip;
Abuse him to the Moor in the rank garb,—
For I fear Cassio with my night-cap too;
Make the Moor thank me, love me, and reward me,
For making him egregiously an ass,
And practising upon his peace and quiet
Even to madness. 'Tis here, but yet confused:
Knavery's plain face is never seen till used.

WILLIAM SHAKESPEARE, *Othello*, 1604

† *In Verdi's opera* Otello *Iago has a creed of evil.*

IAGO. Yes, I believe in God who has created
Me like himself, cruel and vile he made me.
Born from some spawn of nature or from an atom,
Born into vileness.
So I am evil
Because I'm human,
Primeval slime has left its vileness in me.
Yes! This is Iago's creed!
Truly I do believe, just as the credulous
Widow in church believes in God,
That all the evil that I do is destined,
Fate alone directs me.
Man says he's honest, he is a fool and liar
In his face and his heart;
And all he does is falsehood:
Charity, kindness, kissing,
And the lies told by love.
Yes, I believe man is the fool of fortune;
The cradle holds an infant
Who's born to feed the worm.
Then after life has run its course, Death.
And then? And then there's nothing.
And heaven's a foolish tale.

ARRIGO BOITO, libretto to Verdi's opera *Otello*, 1887, trans. Andrew Porter

As I lay asleep in Italy,
There came a voice from over the sea,
And with great power it forth led me
To walk in the visions of Poesy.

I met Murder on the way—
He had a mask like Castlereagh—
Very smooth he looked, yet grim;
Seven bloodhounds followed him:

All were fat; and well they might
Be in admirable plight,

For one by one, and two by two,
He tossed them human hearts to chew,
Which from his wide cloak he drew.

Next came Fraud, and he had on,
Like Lord E——, an ermine gown;
His big tears, for he wept well,
Turned to mill-stones as they fell;

And the little children, who
Round his feet played to and fro,
Thinking every tear a gem,
Had their brains knocked out by them.

Clothed with the bible as with light,
And the shadow of the night,
Like S * * * next, Hypocrisy,
On a crocodile came by.

And many more Destructions played
In this ghastly masquerade,
All disguised, even to the eyes,
Like bishops, lawyers, peers, or spies.

Last came Anarchy; he rode
On a white horse splashed with blood;
He was pale even to the lips,
Like Death in the Apocalypse.

And he wore a kingly crown;
In his hand a sceptre shone;
On his brow this mark I saw—
'I am God, and King, and Law!'

With a pace stately and fast,
Over English land he past,
Trampling to a mire of blood
The adoring multitude.

PERCY BYSSHE SHELLEY, from *The Masque of Anarchy*, 1819

† *In this extract from James Hogg's powerful story of fratricide and diabolical possession, two women discuss Wringhim and his old associate Gil-Martin—the devil himself—who has egged Wringhim on to murder and other crimes.*

'I never in my life saw any human being,' said Mrs Calvert, 'whom I thought so like a fiend. If a demon could inherit flesh and blood, that youth is precisely such a being as I could conceive that demon to be. The depth and the malignity of his eye is hideous. His breath is like the airs from a charnel house, and his flesh seems fading from his bones, as if the worm that never dies were gnawing it away already.'

'He was always repulsive, and every way repulsive,' said the other; 'but he is now indeed altered greatly to the worse. While we were handfasting him, I felt his body to be feeble and emaciated; but yet I know him to be so puffed up with spiritual pride, that I believe he weens every one of his actions justified before God, and instead of having stings of conscience for these, he takes great merit to himself in having effected them. Still my thoughts are less about him than the extraordinary being who accompanies him. He does every thing with so much ease and indifference, so much velocity and effect, that all bespeak him an adept in wickedness. The likeness to my late hapless young master is so striking, that I can hardly believe it to be a chance model; and I think he imitates him in every thing, for some purpose, or some effect on his sinful associate. Do you know that he is so like in every lineament, look, and gesture, that, against the clearest light of reason, I cannot in my mind separate the one from the other, and have a certain indefinable impression on my mind, that they are one and the same being, or that the one was a prototype of the other.'

'If there is an earthly crime,' said Mrs Calvert, 'for the due punishment of which the Almighty may be supposed to subvert the order of nature, it is fratricide. But tell me, dear friend, did you remark to what the subtile and hellish villain was endeavouring to prompt the assassin?'

'No, I could not comprehend it. My senses were altogether so bewildered, that I thought they had combined to deceive me, and I gave them no credit.'

'Then hear me: I am almost certain he was using every persuasion to induce him to make away with his mother; and I likewise conceive that I heard the incendiary give his consent!'

'This is dreadful. Let us speak and think no more about it, till we see the issue. In the meantime, let us do that which is our bounden duty,—go and divulge all that we know relating to this foul murder.'

JAMES HOGG, *Confessions of a Justified Sinner*, 1824

If you still think me mad, you will think so no longer when I describe the wise precautions I took for the concealment of the body. The night waned, and I worked hastily, but in silence. First of all I dismembered the corpse. I cut off the head and the arms and the legs.

I then took up three planks from the flooring of the chamber, and deposited all between the scantlings. I then replaced the boards so cleverly, so cunningly, that no human eye—not even *his*—could have detected any thing wrong. There was nothing to wash out—no stain of any kind—no blood-spot whatever. I had been too wary for that. A tub had caught all—ha! ha!

When I had made an end of these labors, it was four o'clock—still dark as midnight. As the bell sounded the hour, there came a knocking at the street door. I went down to open it with a light heart,—for what had I *now* to fear? There entered three men, who introduced themselves, with perfect suavity, as officers of the police. A shriek had been heard by a neighbour during the night; suspicion of foul play had been aroused; information had been lodged at the police office, and they (the officers) had been deputed to search the premises.

I smiled,—for *what* had I to fear? I bade the gentlemen welcome. The shriek, I said, was my own in a dream. The old man, I mentioned, was absent in the country. I took my visitors all over the house. I bade them search—search *well*. I led them, at length, to *his* chamber. I showed them his treasures, secure, undisturbed. In the enthusiasm of my confidence, I brought chairs into the room, and desired them *here* to rest from their fatigues, while I myself, in the wild audacity of my perfect triumph, placed my own seat upon the very spot beneath which reposed the corpse of the victim.

The officers were satisfied. My *manner* had convinced them. I was singularly at ease. They sat, and while I answered cheerily, they chatted of familiar things. But, ere long, I felt myself getting pale and wished them gone. My head ached, and I fancied a ringing in my ears:

but still they sat and still chatted. The ringing became more distinct:—it continued and became more distinct: I talked more freely to get rid of the feeling: but it continued and gained definiteness—until, at length, I found that the noise was *not* within my ears.

No doubt I now grew *very* pale;—but I talked more fluently, and with a heightened voice. Yet the sound increased—and what could I do? It was *a low, dull, quick sound—much such a sound as a watch makes when enveloped in cotton.* I gasped for breath—and yet the officers heard it not. I talked more quickly—more vehemently; but the noise steadily increased. I arose and argued about trifles, in a high key and with violent gesticulations; but the noise steadily increased. Why *would* they not be gone? I paced the floor to and fro with heavy strides, as if excited to fury by the observations of the men—but the noise steadily increased. Oh God! what *could* I do? I foamed—I raved—I swore! I swung the chair upon which I had been sitting, and grated it upon the boards, but the noise arose over all and continually increased. It grew louder—louder—*louder!* And still the men chatted pleasantly, and smiled. Was it possible they heard not? Almighty God!—no, no! They heard!—they suspected!—they *knew!*—they were making a mockery of my horror!—this I thought, and this I think. But anything was better than this agony! Anything was more tolerable than this derision! I could bear those hypocritical smiles no longer! I felt that I must scream or die! and now—again!—hark! louder! louder! louder! *louder!*

'Villains!' I shrieked, 'dissemble no more! I admit the deed!—tear up the planks! here, here!—it is the beating of his hideous heart!'

EDGAR ALLAN POE, 'The Tell-Tale Heart', 1843

There was really nothing to be said for Mr Karswell. Nobody knew what he did with himself: his servants were a horrible set of people; he had invented a new religion for himself, and practised no one could tell what appalling rites; he was very easily offended, and never forgave anybody: he had a dreadful face (so the lady insisted, her husband somewhat demurring); he never did a kind action, and whatever influence he did exert was mischievous. 'Do the poor man justice, dear,' the husband interrupted. 'You forget the treat he gave the school children.' 'Forget it, indeed! But I'm glad you mentioned it, because it gives an idea of the man. Now, Florence, listen to this.

The first winter he was at Lufford this delightful neighbour of ours wrote to the clergyman of his parish (he's not ours, but we know him very well) and offered to show the school children some magic-lantern slides. He said he had some new kinds, which he thought would interest them. Well, the clergyman was rather surprised, because Mr Karswell had shown himself inclined to be unpleasant to the children —complaining of their trespassing, or something of the sort; but of course he accepted, and the evening was fixed, and our friend went himself to see that everything went right. He said he never had been so thankful for anything as that his own children were all prevented from being there: they were at a children's party at our house, as a matter of fact. Because this Mr Karswell had evidently set out with the intention of frightening these poor village children out of their wits, and I do believe, if he had been allowed to go on, he would actually have done so. He began with some comparatively mild things. Red Riding Hood was one, and even then, Mr Farrer said, the wolf was so dreadful that several of the smaller children had to be taken out: and he said Mr Karswell began the story by producing a noise like a wolf howling in the distance, which was the most gruesome thing he had ever heard. All the slides he showed, Mr Farrer said, were most clever; they were absolutely realistic, and where he had got them or how he worked them he could not imagine. Well, the show went on, and the stories kept on becoming a little more terrifying each time, and the children were mesmerized into complete silence. At last he produced a series which represented a little boy passing through his own park—Lufford, I mean—in the evening. Every child in the room could recognize the place from the pictures. And this poor boy was followed, and at last pursued and overtaken, and either torn in pieces or somehow made away with, by a horrible hopping creature in white, which you saw first dodging about among the trees, and gradually it appeared more and more plainly. Mr Farrer said it gave him one of the worst nightmares he ever remembered, and what it must have meant to the children doesn't bear thinking of. Of course this was too much, and he spoke very sharply indeed to Mr Karswell, and said it couldn't go on. All *he* said was: "Oh, you think it's time to bring our little show to an end and send them home to their beds? *Very* well!" And then, if you please, he switched on another slide, which showed a great mass of snakes, centipedes, and disgusting creatures with wings, and somehow or other he made it seem as if they were climbing out of the picture and getting in amongst the audience;

and this was accompanied by a sort of dry rustling noise which sent the children nearly mad, and of course they stampeded. A good many of them were rather hurt in getting out of the room, and I don't suppose one of them closed an eye that night.'

M. R. JAMES, 'Casting the Runes', 1931

† *The governess, in* The Turn of the Screw, *is not long in her new post before she becomes aware of a malign presence—the ghost of the hateful valet Quint, who, it transpires, has designs on her two young charges.*

I can say now neither what determined nor what guided me, but I went straight along the lobby, holding my candle high, till I came within sight of the tall window that presided over the great turn of the staircase. At this point I precipitately found myself aware of three things. They were practically simultaneous, yet they had flashes of succession. My candle, under a bold flourish, went out, and I perceived, by the uncovered window, that the yielding dusk of earliest morning rendered it unnecessary. Without it, the next instant, I saw that there was someone on the stair. I speak of sequences, but I required no lapse of seconds to stiffen myself for a third encounter with Quint. The apparition had reached the landing half way up and was therefore on the spot nearest the window, where, at sight of me, it stopped short and fixed me exactly as it had fixed me from the tower and from the garden. He knew me as well as I knew him; and so, in the cold, faint twilight, with a glimmer in the high glass and another on the polish of the oak stair below, we faced each other in our common intensity. He was absolutely, on this occasion, a living, detestable, dangerous presence. But that was not the wonder of wonders; I reserve this distinction for quite another circumstance: the circumstance that dread had unmistakably quitted me and that there was nothing in me there that didn't meet and measure him.

I had plenty of anguish after that extraordinary moment, but I had, thank God, no terror. And he knew I had not—I found myself at the end of an instant magnificently aware of this. I felt, in a fierce rigour of confidence, that if I stood my ground a minute I should cease—for the time, at least—to have him to reckon with; and during the minute, accordingly, the thing was as human and hideous as a real interview:

hideous just because it *was* human, as human as to have met alone, in the small hours, in a sleeping house, some enemy, some adventurer, some criminal. It was the dead silence of our long gaze at such close quarters that gave the whole horror, huge as it was, its only note of the unnatural. If I had met a murderer in such a place and at such an hour we still at least would have spoken. Something would have passed, in life, between us; if nothing had passed one of us would have moved.

HENRY JAMES, *The Turn of the Screw*, 1898

† *Dorian Gray has made a diabolical bargain: instead of growing old, he keeps a portrait of himself which does his ageing for him, as well as showing all the marks of his increasing depravity. The final stage in his downward progression comes when he slaughters the portrait painter.*

He went in quietly, locking the door behind him, as was his custom, and dragged the purple hanging from the portrait. A cry of pain and indignation broke from him. He could see no change, save that in the eyes there was a look of cunning, and in the mouth the curved wrinkle of the hypocrite. The thing was still loathsome—more loathsome, if possible, than before—and the scarlet dew that spotted the hand seemed brighter, and more like blood newly spilt. Then he trembled. Had it been merely vanity that had made him do his one good deed? Or the desire for a new sensation, as Lord Henry had hinted, with his mocking laugh? Or that passion to act a part that sometimes makes us do things finer than we are ourselves? Or, perhaps, all these? And why was the red stain larger than it had been? It seemed to have crept like a horrible disease over the wrinkled fingers. There was blood on the painted feet, as though the thing had dripped—blood even on the hand that had not held the knife. Confess? Did it mean that he was to confess? To give himself up, and be put to death? He laughed. He felt that the idea was monstrous. Besides, even if he did confess, who would believe him? There was no trace of the murdered man anywhere. Everything belonging to him had been destroyed. He himself had burned what had been below-stairs. The world would simply say that he was mad. They would shut him up if he persisted in his story. . . . Yet it was his duty to confess, to suffer public shame, and to make public atonement. There was a God who called upon men to tell their sins to earth as well as to heaven. Nothing that he could do would cleanse him till he had told his own sin. His sin? He shrugged his shoulders. The death of Basil Hallward seemed very little to him. He was thinking of Hetty Merton. For it was an unjust mirror, this mirror of his soul that he was looking at. Vanity? Curiosity? Hypocrisy? Had there been nothing more in his renunciation than that? There had been something more. At least he thought so. But who could tell? . . . No. There had been nothing more. Through vanity he had spared her. In hypocrisy he had worn the mask of goodness. For curiosity's sake he had tried the denial of self. He recognised that now.

But this murder—was it to dog him all his life? Was he always to be burdened by his past? Was he really to confess? Never. There was only one bit of evidence left against him. The picture itself—that was evidence. He would destroy it. Why had he kept it so long? Once it had given him pleasure to watch it changing and growing old. Of late he had felt no such pleasure. It had kept him awake at night. When he had been away, he had been filled with terror lest other eyes should look upon it. It had brought melancholy across his passions. Its mere memory had marred many moments of joy. It had been like conscience to him. Yes, it had been conscience. He would destroy it.

He looked round, and saw the knife that had stabbed Basil Hallward. He had cleaned it many times, till there was no stain left upon it. It was bright, and glistened. As it had killed the painter, so it would kill the painter's work, and all that that meant. It would kill the past, and when that was dead he would be free. It would kill this monstrous soul-life, and without its hideous warnings he would be at peace. He seized the thing, and stabbed the picture with it.

OSCAR WILDE, *The Picture of Dorian Gray*, 1890

Mind, I am not trying to excuse or even explain—I am trying to account to myself for—for—Mr Kurtz—for the shade of Mr Kurtz. This initiated wraith from the back of Nowhere honoured me with its amazing confidence before it vanished altogether. This was because it could speak English to me. The original Kurtz had been educated partly in England, and—as he was good enough to say himself—his sympathies were in the right place. His mother was half-English, his father was half-French. All Europe contributed to the making of Kurtz; and by-and-by I learned that, most appropriately, the International

Society for the Suppression of Savage Customs had intrusted him with the making of a report, for its future guidance. And he had written it, too. I've seen it. I've read it. It was eloquent, vibrating with eloquence, but too high-strung, I think. Seventeen pages of close writing he had found time for! But this must have been before his—let us say—nerves, went wrong, and caused him to preside at certain midnight dances ending with unspeakable rites, which—as far as I reluctantly gathered from what I heard at various times—were offered up to him—do you understand?—to Mr Kurtz himself. But it was a beautiful piece of writing. The opening paragraph, however, in the light of later information, strikes me now as ominous. He began with the argument that we whites, from the point of development we had arrived at, 'must necessarily appear to them [savages] in the nature of supernatural beings—we approach them with the might as of a deity,' and so on, and so on. 'By the simple exercise of our will we can exert a power for good practically unbounded,' etc. etc. From that point he soared and took me with him. The peroration was magnificent, though difficult to remember, you know. It gave me the notion of an exotic Immensity ruled by an august Benevolence. It made me tingle with enthusiasm. This was the unbounded power of eloquence—of words—of burning noble words. There were no practical hints to interrupt the magic current of phrases, unless a kind of note at the foot of the last page, scrawled evidently much later, in an unsteady hand, may be regarded as the exposition of a method. It was very simple, and at the end of that moving appeal to every altruistic sentiment it blazed at you, luminous and terrifying, like a flash of lightning in a serene sky: 'Exterminate all the brutes!'

JOSEPH CONRAD, *Heart of Darkness*, 1902

Two doors from one corner, on the left hand going east, the line was broken by the entry of a court; and just at that point, a certain sinister block of building thrust forward its gable on the street. It was two storeys high; showed no window, nothing but a door on the lower storey and a blind forehead of discoloured wall on the upper; and bore in every feature, the marks of prolonged and sordid negligence. The door, which was equipped with neither bell nor knocker, was blistered and distained. Tramps slouched into the recess and struck matches on the panels; children kept shop upon the steps; the schoolboy had tried his knife on the mouldings; and for close on a generation, no one had appeared to drive away these random visitors or to repair their ravages.

Mr Enfield and the lawyer were on the other side of the by-street; but when they came abreast of the entry, the former lifted up his cane and pointed.

'Did you ever remark that door?' he asked; and when his companion had replied in the affirmative, 'It is connected in my mind,' added he, 'with a very odd story.'

'Indeed?' said Mr Utterson, with a slight change of voice, 'and what was that?'

'Well, it was this way,' returned Mr Enfield: 'I was coming home from some place at the end of the world, about three o'clock of a black winter morning, and my way lay through a part of town where there was literally nothing to be seen but lamps. Street after street, and all the folks asleep—street after street, all lighted up as if for a procession and all as empty as a church—till at last I got into that state of mind when a man listens and listens and begins to long for the sight of a policeman. All at once, I saw two figures: one a little man who was stumping along eastward at a good walk, and the other a girl of maybe eight or ten who was running as hard as she was able down a cross street. Well, sir, the two ran into one another naturally enough at the corner; and then came the horrible part of the thing; for the man trampled calmly over the child's body and left her screaming on the ground. It sounds nothing to hear, but it was hellish to see. It wasn't like a man; it was like some damned Juggernaut. I gave a view halloa, took to my heels, collared my gentleman, and brought him back to where there was already quite a group about the screaming child. He was perfectly cool and made no resistance, but gave me one look, so ugly that it brought out the sweat on me like running. The people who had turned out were the girl's own family; and pretty soon, the doctor, for whom she had been sent, put in his appearance. Well, the child was not much the worse, more frightened, according to the Sawbones; and there you might have supposed would be an end to it. But there was one curious circumstance. I had taken a loathing to my gentleman at first sight. So had the child's family, which was only natural. But the doctor's case was what struck me. He was the usual cut and dry apothecary, of no particular age and colour, with a strong Edinburgh accent, and about as emotional as a bagpipe. Well, sir, he was like the rest of us; every time he looked at my prisoner, I saw that Sawbones turn sick and white with the desire to kill him. I knew what was in his mind, just as he knew what was in mine; and killing being out of the question, we did the next best. We told the man we could and would make such a scandal out of this, as should make his name stink from one end of London to the other. If he had any friends or any credit, we undertook that he should lose them. And all the time, as we were pitching it in red hot, we were keeping the women off him as best we could, for they were as wild as harpies. I never saw a circle of such hateful faces; and there was the man in the middle, with a kind of black, sneering coolness—frightened too, I could see that—but carrying it off, sir, really like Satan. "If you choose to make capital out of this accident," said he, "I am naturally helpless. No gentleman but wishes to avoid a scene," says he. "Name your figure." Well, we screwed him up to a hundred pounds for the child's family; he would have clearly liked to stick out; but there was something about the lot of us that meant mischief, and at last he struck.'

ROBERT LOUIS STEVENSON, *The Strange Case of Dr Jekyll and Mr Hyde*, 1886

ON LADY POLTAGRUE, A PUBLIC PERIL

The Devil, having nothing else to do,
Went off to tempt My Lady Poltagrue,
My Lady, tempted by a private whim,
To his extreme annoyance, tempted him.

HILAIRE BELLOC (1870–1953)

† *Isabel Archer finds herself married to a man for whom evil takes the form of emptiness.*

Then the shadows had begun to gather; it was as if Osmond deliberately, almost malignantly, had put the lights out one by one. The dusk at first was vague and thin, and she could still see her way in it. But it steadily deepened, and if now and again it had occasionally lifted there were certain corners of her prospect that were impenetrably black. These shadows were not an emanation from her own mind: she was very sure of that; she had done her best to be just and temperate, to see only the truth. They were a part, they were a kind of creation and consequence, of her husband's very presence. They were not his misdeeds, his turpitudes; she accused him of nothing—that is but of one thing, which was *not* a crime. She knew of no wrong he had done; he was not violent, he was not cruel: she simply believed he hated her. That was all she accused him of, and the miserable part of it was precisely that it was not a crime, for against a crime she might have found redress. He had discovered that she was so different, that she was not what he had believed she would prove to be. He had thought at first he could change her, and she had done her best to be what he would like. But she was, after all, herself—she couldn't help that; and now there was no use pretending, wearing a mask or a dress, for he knew her and had made up his mind. She was not afraid of him; she had no apprehension he would hurt her; for the ill-will he bore her was not of that sort. He would if possible never give her a pretext, never put himself in the wrong. Isabel, scanning the future with dry, fixed eyes, saw that he would have the better of her there. She would give him many pretexts, she would often put herself in the wrong. There were times when she almost pitied him; for if she had not deceived him in intention she understood how completely she must have done so in fact. She had effaced herself when he first knew her; she had made herself small, pretending there was less of her than there really was. It was because she had been under the extraordinary charm that he, on his side, had taken pains to put forth. He was not changed; he had not disguised himself, during the year of his courtship, any more than she. But she had seen only half his nature then, as one saw the disk of the moon when it was partly masked by the shadow of the earth. She saw the full moon now—she saw the whole man. She had kept still, as it were, so that he should have a free field, and yet in spite of this she had mistaken a part for the whole.

HENRY JAMES, *Portrait of a Lady*, 1881

At that time a mighty fiend who lived in darkness suffered greatly. Their happiness, which he heard daily resounding from the hall, grated on his ear: the harp-music, and clear song of a poet relating the creation of man from the earliest times—how God made the world, a shining plain encircled by the sea, and through His power established the sun and moon to light its inhabitants; how He decked the face of the earth with leaves and branches, and besides gave life to all that moves. In this way the fighting-men were happily living, until the fiend from hell began to work them mischief.

The grim demon was called Grendel, a notorious ranger of the borderlands, who inhabited the fastnesses of moors and fens. This unhappy being had long lived in the land of monsters, because God had damned him along with the children of Cain. For the eternal Lord avenged the killing of Abel. He took no delight in that feud, but banished Cain from humanity because of his crime. From Cain were hatched all evil progenies: ogres, hobgoblins, and monsters, not to mention the giants who fought so long against God—for which they suffered due retribution.

Beowulf, late 10th century, trans. David Wright

† *Chesterton was a specialist in paradox, and he turned his police chief Valentin into a murderer and an anti-religious fanatic.*

The borderland of the brain, where all the monsters are made, moved horribly in the Gaelic O'Brien. He felt the chaotic presence of all the horse-men and fish-women that man's unnatural fancy has begotten. A voice older than his first fathers seemed saying in his ear: 'Keep out of the monstrous garden where grows the tree with double fruit. Avoid the evil garden where died the man with two heads.' Yet, while these shameful symbolic shapes passed across the ancient mirror of his Irish soul, his Frenchified intellect was quite alert, and was watching the odd priest as closely and incredulously as all the rest.

Father Brown had turned round at last, and stood against the window with his face in dense shadow; but even in that shadow they could see it was pale as ashes. Nevertheless, he spoke quite sensibly, as if there were no Gaelic souls on earth.

'Gentlemen,' he said, 'you did not find the strange body of Becker in the garden. You did not find any strange body in the garden. In face of Dr Simon's rationalism, I still affirm that Becker was only partly present. Look here!' (pointing to the black bulk of the mysterious corpse) 'you never saw that man in your lives. Did you ever see this man?'

He rapidly rolled away the bald, yellow head of the unknown, and put in its place the white-maned head beside it. And there, complete, unified, unmistakable, lay Julius K. Brayne.

'The murderer,' went on Brown quietly, 'hacked off his enemy's head and flung the sword far over the wall. But he was too clever to fling the sword only. He flung the *head* over the wall also. Then he had only to clap on another head to the corpse, and (as he insisted on a private inquest) you all imagined a totally new man.'

'Clap on another head!' said O'Brien, staring. 'What other head? Heads don't grow on garden bushes, do they?'

'No,' said Father Brown huskily, and looking at his boots; 'there is only one place where they grow. They grow in the basket of the guillotine, beside which the Chief of Police, Aristide Valentin, was standing not an hour before the murder. Oh, my friends, hear me a minute more before you tear me to pieces. Valentin is an honest man, if being mad for an arguable cause is honesty. But did you never see in that cold, grey eye of his that he is mad? He would do anything, *anything*, to break what he calls the superstition of the Cross. He has fought for it and starved for it, and now he has murdered for it. Brayne's crazy millions had hitherto been scattered among so many sects that they did little to alter the balance of things. But Valentin heard a whisper that Brayne, like so many scatter-brained sceptics, was drifting to us; and that was quite a different thing. Brayne would pour supplies into the impoverished and pugnacious Church of France; he would support six Nationalist newspapers like *The Guillotine*. The battle was already balanced on a point, and the fanatic took flame at the risk. He resolved to destroy the millionaire, and he did it as one would expect the greatest of detectives to commit his only crime. He abstracted the severed head of Becker on some criminological excuse, and took it home in his official box. He had that last argument with Brayne, that Lord Galloway did not hear the end of; that failing, he led him out into the sealed garden, talked about swordsmanship, used twigs and a sabre for illustration, and—'

Ivan of the Scar sprang up. 'You lunatic,' he yelled; 'you'll go to my master now, if I take you by—'

'Why, I was going there,' said Brown heavily; 'I must ask him to confess, and all that.'

Driving the unhappy Brown before them like a hostage or sacrifice, they rushed together into the sudden stillness of Valentin's study.

The great detective sat at his desk apparently too occupied to hear their turbulent entrance. They paused a moment, and then something in the look of that upright and elegant back made the doctor run forward suddenly. A touch and a glance showed him that there was a small box of pills at Valentin's elbow, and that Valentin was dead in his chair; and on the blind face of the suicide was more than the pride of Cato.

G. K. CHESTERTON, 'The Secret Garden', 1910

† *A young Englishman travels on business to a castle in Transylvania and soon experiences misgivings as to the amiability of his host.*

The Count himself came forward and took off the cover of a dish, and I fell to at once on an excellent roast chicken. This, with some cheese and a salad and a bottle of old Tokay, of which I had two glasses, was my supper. During the time I was eating it the Count asked me many questions as to my journey, and I told him by degrees all I had experienced.

By this time I had finished my supper, and by my host's desire had drawn up a chair by the fire and begun to smoke a cigar which he offered me, at the same time excusing himself that he did not smoke. I had now an opportunity of observing him, and found him of a very marked physiognomy.

His face was a strong—a very strong—aquiline, with high bridge of the thin nose and peculiarly arched nostrils; with lofty domed forehead, and hair growing scantily round the temples, but profusely elsewhere. His eyebrows were very massive, almost meeting over the nose, and with bushy hair that seemed to curl in its own profusion. The mouth, so far as I could see it under the heavy moustache, was fixed and rather cruel-looking, with peculiarly sharp white teeth; these protruded over the lips, whose remarkable ruddiness showed astonishing vitality in a man of his years. For the rest, his ears were pale and at the tops extremely pointed; the chin was broad and strong, and the cheeks firm though thin. The general effect was one of extraordinary pallor.

Hitherto I had noticed the backs of his hands as they lay on his knees in the firelight, and they had seemed rather white and fine; but seeing them now close to me, I could not but notice that they were rather coarse—broad, with squat fingers. Strange to say, there were hairs in the centre of the palm. The nails were long and fine, and cut to a sharp point. As the Count leaned over me and his hands touched me, I could not repress a shudder. It may have been that his breath was rank, but a horrible feeling of nausea came over me, which, do what I would, I could not conceal. . . . We were both silent for a while; and as I looked towards the window I saw the first dim streak of the coming dawn. There seemed a strange stillness over everything; but as I listened I heard, as if from down below in the valley, the howling of many wolves. The Count's eyes gleamed, and he said:—

'Listen to them—the children of the night. What music they make!' Seeing, I suppose, some expression in my face strange to him, he added:—

'Ah, sir, you dwellers in the city cannot enter into the feelings of the hunter.' Then he rose and said:—

'But you must be tired. Your bedroom is all ready, and to-morrow you shall sleep as late as you will. I have to be away till the afternoon; so sleep well and dream well!' and, with a courteous bow, he opened for me himself the door to the octagonal room, and I entered my bedroom. . . .

I am all in a sea of wonders. I doubt; I fear; I think strange things which I dare not confess to my own soul. God keep me, if only for the sake of those dear to me!

† *Some nights later . . .*

When he left me I went to my room. After a little while, not hearing any sound, I came out and went up the stone stair to where I could look out towards the south. There was some sense of freedom in the vast expanse, inaccessible though it was to me, as compared with the narrow darkness of the courtyard. Looking out on this, I felt that I was indeed in prison, and I seemed to want a breath of fresh air, though it were of the night. I am beginning to feel this nocturnal existence tell on me. It is destroying my nerve. I start at my own shadow, and am full of all sorts of horrible imaginings. God knows that there is ground for any terrible fear in this accursed place! I looked out over the beautiful expanse, bathed in soft yellow moonlight till it was almost as light as day. In the soft light the distant hills became melted, and the shadows in the valleys and gorges of velvety blackness. The mere beauty seemed to cheer me; there was peace and comfort in every breath I drew. As I leaned from the window my eye was caught by something moving a story below me, and somewhat to my left, where I imagined, from the lie of the rooms, that the windows of the Count's own room would look out. The window at which I stood was tall and deep, stone-mullioned, and though weather-worn, was still complete; but it was evidently many a day since the case had been there. I drew back behind the stonework, and looked carefully out.

What I saw was the Count's head coming out from the window. I did not see the face, but I knew the man by the neck and the movement of his back and arms. In any case, I could not mistake the hands which I had had so many opportunities of studying. I was at first interested and somewhat amused, for it is wonderful how small a matter will interest and amuse a man when he is a prisoner. But my very feelings changed to repulsion and terror when I saw the whole man slowly emerge from the window and begin to crawl down the castle wall over that dreadful abyss, *face down*, with his cloak spreading out around him like great wings. At first I could not believe my eyes. I thought it was some trick of the moonlight, some weird effect of shadow; but I kept looking, and it could be no delusion. I saw the fingers and toes grasp the corners of the stones, worn clear of the mortar by the stress of years, and by thus using every projection and inequality move downwards with considerable speed, just as a lizard moves along a wall.

What manner of man is this, or what manner of creature is it in the semblance of man? I feel the dread of this horrible place overpowering me; I am in fear—in awful fear—and there is no escape for me; I am encompassed about with terrors that I dare not think of. . . .

BRAM STOKER, *Dracula*, 1897

So . . . to come to the point, is the Steppenwolf a fiction. When Harry feels himself to be a were-wolf, and chooses to consist of two hostile and opposed beings, he is merely availing himself of a mythological simplification. He is no were-wolf at all, and if we appeared to accept without scrutiny this lie which he invented for himself and believes in, and tried to regard him literally as a two-fold being and a Steppenwolf, and so designated him, it was merely in the hope of being more easily understood with the assistance of a delusion, which we must now endeavour to put in its true light.

The division into wolf and man, flesh and spirit, by means of which Harry tries to make his destiny more comprehensible to himself is a very great simplification. It is a forcing of the truth to suit a plausible, but erroneous, explanation of that contradiction which this man discovers in himself and which appears to himself to be the source of his by no means negligible sufferings. Harry finds in himself a 'human being', that is to say, a world of thoughts and feelings, of culture and tamed or sublimated nature, and besides this he finds within himself also a 'wolf', that is to say, a dark world of instinct, of savagery and cruelty, of unsublimated or raw nature.

HERMANN HESSE, *Steppenwolf*, 1927, trans. Basil Creighton

You are always in danger in the forest, where no people are. Step between the portals of the great pines where the shaggy branches tangle about you, trapping the unwary traveller in nets as if the vegetation itself were in a plot with the wolves who live there, as though the wicked trees go fishing on behalf of their friends—step between the gateposts of the forest with the greatest trepidation and infinite precautions, for if you stray from the path for one instant, the wolves will eat you. They are grey as famine, they are as unkind as plague.

The grave-eyed children of the sparse villages always carry knives with them when they go out to tend the little flocks of goats that provide the homesteads with acrid milk and rank, maggoty cheeses. Their knives are half as big as they are, the blades are sharpened daily.

But the wolves have ways of arriving at your own hearthside. We try and try but sometimes we cannot keep them out. There is no winter's night the cottager does not fear to see a lean, grey, famished snout questing under the door, and there was a woman once bitten in her own kitchen as she was straining the macaroni.

Fear and flee the wolf; for, worst of all, the wolf may be more than he seems. . . .

They say there's an ointment the Devil gives you that turns you into a wolf the minute you rub it on. Or, that he was born feet first and had a wolf for his father and his torso is a man's but his legs and genitals are a wolf's. And he has a wolf's heart.

Seven years is a werewolf's natural span but if you burn his human clothing you condemn him to wolfishness for the rest of his life, so old wives hereabouts think it some protection to throw a hat or an apron at the werewolf, as if clothes made the man. Yet by the eyes, those phosphorescent eyes, you know him in all his shapes; the eyes alone unchanged by metamorphosis.

Before he can become a wolf, the lycanthrope strips stark naked. If you spy a naked man among the pines, you must run as if the Devil were after you.

ANGELA CARTER, *The Company of Wolves*, 1979

† *Bill Sikes after he has murdered Nancy . . .*

He went on doggedly; but as he left the town behind him, and plunged into the solitude and darkness of the road, he felt a dread and awe creeping upon him which shook him to the core. Every object before him, substance or shadow, still or moving, took the semblance of some fearful thing; but these fears were nothing compared to the sense that haunted him of that morning's ghastly figure following at his heels. He could trace its shadow in the gloom, supply the smallest item of the outline, and note how stiff and solemn it seemed to stalk along. He could hear its garments rustling in the leaves, and every breath of wind came laden with that last low cry. If he stopped it did the same. If he ran, it followed—not running too: that would have been a relief: but like a corpse endowed with the mere machinery of life, and borne on one slow melancholy wind that never rose or fell.

At times, he turned, with desperate determination, resolved to beat this phantom off, though it should look him dead; but the hair rose on his head, and his blood stood still, for it had turned with him and was behind him then. He had kept it before him that morning, but it was behind now—always. He leaned his back against a bank, and felt that it stood above him, visibly out against the cold night-sky. He threw himself upon the road—on his back upon the road. At his head it stood, silent, erect, and still—a living grave-stone, with its epitaph in blood.

Let no man talk of murderers escaping justice, and hint that Providence must sleep. There were twenty score of violent deaths in one long minute of that agony of fear.

There was a shed in a field he passed, that offered shelter for the night. Before the door, were three tall poplar trees, which made it very dark within; and the wind moaned through them with a dismal wail. He *could not* walk on, till daylight came again; and here he stretched himself close to the wall—to undergo new torture.

For now, a vision came before him, as constant and more terrible than that from which he had escaped. Those widely staring eyes, so lustreless and so glassy, that he had better borne to see them than think upon them, appeared in the midst of the darkness: light in themselves, but giving light to nothing. There were but two, but they were everywhere. If he shut out the sight, there came the room with every well-known object—some, indeed, that he would have forgotten, if he had gone over its contents from memory—each in its accustomed place. The body was in *its* place, and its eyes were as he saw them when he stole away. He got up, and rushed into the field without. The figure was behind him. He re-entered the shed, and shrunk down once more. The eyes were there, before he had laid himself along.

And here he remained in such terror as none but he can know, trembling in every limb, and the cold sweat starting from every pore, when suddenly there arose upon the night-wind the noise of distant shouting, and the roar of voices mingled in alarm and wonder. Any sound of men in that lonely place, even though it conveyed a real cause of alarm, was something to him. He regained his strength and energy at the prospect of personal danger; and springing to his feet, rushed into the open air.

CHARLES DICKENS, *Oliver Twist*, 1837–8

'Come in! Come in! Is it you, dear child?' the old lady cried eagerly. Little Red Ridinghood wondered how she could know who it was, but she lifted the latch and entered: she could not, however, help being taken aback by the change that a brief illness of two or three days' duration had wrought in the old lady's voice and appearance, in fact, in her whole personality. She had always spoken so softly, but now every word she pronounced seemed to have a rough and furry edge, and each sentence ended in a kind of howl. She must certainly have been very sick. Everything about her had always been dainty and gracious—she had retained her pink-and-white skin, which was set off by her white hair, like silk, and by her cornflower-blue eyes, which smiled perpetually with a kind and cheerful look. The old lady was sitting up in bed, wearing, as she always did on such occasions, a rather elaborate nightdress and an old-fashioned cap. Today, however, though the effect was still that of a Gainsborough portrait, it was of a

Gainsborough portrait gone crazy. Two pointed, furry ears protruded from the mob-cap; her nose, with a sort of black leather substance at the end, round the nostrils, had grown furry too, and her teeth, long yellow fangs where formerly had smiled impeccable dentures, did not seem, set as they were in an expression of welcome, to match the wild and ravenous dark eyes.

'Let me kiss you, dear child,' the old lady howled.

Little Red Ridinghood advanced towards the bed, and in doing so, had to step, she noticed, over a neat pile of bones, picked clean.

'Grandmother,' she explained, 'I've brought you a custard and a pot of butter from Mama, and here is a cloth full of berries that I gathered for you on the way—that's why I'm rather late in getting here. I hope—'

'I like late dinners,' her grandmother interrupted.

'I hope,' Red Ridinghood proceeded, 'that you are better. But you must be, for I see by the bones on the floor,' and she pointed at them, 'that you've been making broth.'

Now that she was near, and looked at her grandmother more attentively, she became bewildered, and, completely forgetting her mother's injunctions, exclaimed:

'Grandmother, what great ears you have!'

'The better to hear you with, my darling.'

'Grandmother, what great eyes you have!'

'The better to see you with, my precious morsel.'

'Grandmother, what great legs you have!' Little Red Ridinghood continued, somewhat unwisely, in her unsolicited litany.

'The better to run after you with, dear child.'

'Grandmother, what great teeth you have!'

'The better to bite you with, my sweet,' the wolf said. 'Your grandmother, whose bones you saw, was only an appetiser—and one more thing,' he continued, with his mouth rather full, 'let your fate teach you not to make personal remarks.' Saying these words, the wolf grasped Little Red Ridinghood firmly in his paws, and began to devour her.

OSBERT SITWELL, 'Little Red Ridinghood', 1959

† *In the following scene from* The Lodger, *the honest boarding-house keeper meets his strange tenant coming in late at night.*

. . . into Bunting's slow and honest mind there suddenly crept the query as to what on earth Mr Sleuth's own business out could be on this bitter night.

'Cold?' the lodger repeated; he was panting a little, and his words came out sharp and quick through his thin lips. 'I can't say that I find it cold, Mr Bunting. When the snow falls, the air always becomes milder.'

'Yes, sir; but to-night there's such a sharp east wind. Why, it freezes the very marrow in one's bones! Still, there's nothing like walking in cold weather to make one warm, as you seem to have found, sir.'

Bunting noticed that Mr Sleuth kept his distance in a rather strange way; he walked at the edge of the pavement, leaving the rest of it, on the wall side, to his landlord.

'I lost my way,' he said abruptly. 'I've been over Primrose Hill to see a friend of mine, a man with whom I studied when I was a lad, and then, coming back, I lost my way.'

Now they had come right up to the little gate which opened on the shabby, paved court in front of the house—that gate which now was never locked.

Mr Sleuth, pushing suddenly forward, began walking up the flagged path, when, with a 'By your leave, sir,' the ex-butler, stepping aside, slipped in front of his lodger, in order to open the front door for him.

As he passed by Mr Sleuth, the back of Bunting's bare left hand brushed lightly against the long Inverness cape the lodger was wearing, and, to Bunting's surprise, the stretch of cloth against which his hand lay for a moment was not only damp, damp maybe from stray flakes of snow which had settled upon it, but wet—wet and gluey.

Bunting thrust his left hand into his pocket; it was with the other that he placed the key in the lock of the door.

The two men passed into the hall together.

The house seemed blackly dark in comparison with the lighted-up road outside, and as he groped forward, closely followed by the lodger, there came over Bunting a sudden, reeling sensation of mortal terror, an instinctive, assailing knowledge of frightful immediate danger.

A stuffless voice—the voice of his first wife, the long-dead girl to whom his mind so seldom reverted nowadays—uttered into his ears the words, 'Take care!'

And then the lodger spoke. His voice was harsh and grating, though not loud.

'I'm afraid, Mr Bunting, that you must have felt something dirty, foul, on my coat? It's too long a story to tell you now, but I brushed up against a dead animal, a creature to whose misery some thoughtful soul had put an end, lying across a bench on Primrose Hill.'

'No, sir, no. I didn't notice nothing. I scarcely touched you, sir.'

It seemed as if a power outside himself compelled Bunting to utter these lying words. 'And now, sir, I'll be saying good night to you,' he said.

Stepping back he pressed with all the strength that was in him against the wall, and let the other pass him.

There was a pause, and then—'Good night,' returned Mr Sleuth, in a hollow voice.

Bunting waited until the lodger had gone upstairs, and then, lighting the gas, he sat down there, in the hall. Mr Sleuth's landlord felt very queer—queer and sick.

He did not draw his left hand out of his pocket till he heard Mr Sleuth shut the bedroom door upstairs. Then he held up his left hand and looked at it curiously; it was flecked, streaked with pale reddish blood.

MRS BELLOC LOWNDES, *The Lodger*, 1932

† *A young surveyor from Cricklewood falls under the spell of a strange girl and learns of a plan she has devised.*

It seemed a solemn occasion. Gravity and an intense seriousness were called for. He said in a steady deliberate way, as if making a vow, 'I love you, Senta.'

'I wish it were enough, saying it. But it isn't enough, Philip. You have to prove your love for me and I have to prove mine for you. I thought about that all the time you were away this morning. I lay here thinking about it, how we each have to do some tremendous thing to prove our love for each other.'

'That's all right,' he said. 'I'll do that. What would you like me to do?'

She was silent. Her crystalline greenish eyes had shifted their gaze from some unknown horizon and returned to meet his. It won't be

Jenny's thing of getting engaged, he thought, that's not Senta's style. And it won't be buying her something. Squeamishly he hoped she wasn't going to ask him to cut a vein and mingle his blood with hers. It would be like her and he would do it but he felt distaste for it.

'I believe life is a great adventure, don't you?' she said. 'We feel the same about these things, so I know you do. Life is terrible and beautiful and tragic but most people make it just ordinary. When you and I make love we have a moment of heightened consciousness, a moment when everything looks clear and brilliant, we have such an intensity of feeling that it's as if we experience everything fresh and new and perfect. Well, it ought to be like that all the time, we can learn the power of making it that way, not by wine or drugs but by living to the limit of our consciousness, by living every day with every fibre of our awareness.'

He nodded. She had been saying something like that on the way back here. The awful thing was he had begun to feel sleepy. He had eaten a heavy lunch and drunk a pint of beer. What he would best have liked would have been to lie down on the bed with her and cuddle her until they fell asleep. Her telling him she loved him had made him very happy and with that knowledge a sleepy desire was returning, the kind of mild lust which can be pleasantly delayed until sleep has come and gone and the body lies warm and easy. He smiled at her and reached for her hand.

She withdrew her hand and held the index finger up at him. 'Some say that to live fully you have to have done four things. Do you know what they are? I'll tell you. Plant a tree, write a poem, make love with your own sex, and kill someone.'

'The first two—well, the first three really—don't seem to have much in common with the last.'

'Please don't laugh, Philip. You laugh too much. There are things that shouldn't be laughed at.'

'I wasn't laughing. I don't suppose I'll ever do any of those things you said, so I hope that won't mean I haven't lived.' He looked at her, taking a deep pleasure in her face, her large clear eyes, the mouth that he could never tire of gazing at. 'When I'm with you I think I'm really living, Senta.'

It was an invitation to love but she ignored it. She said very quietly, with an intense dramatic concentration. 'I shall prove I love you by killing someone for you and you must kill someone for me.'

RUTH RENDELL, *The Bridesmaid*, 1989

† *The Catholic delinquent Pinkie has married a trusting young waitress named Rose to keep her from giving evidence against him. Rose does not understand the baseness of his action.*

'Another thing,' the woman bluffed. 'They can send you to jail. Because you know. You told me so. An accomplice, that's what you are. After the fact.'

'If they took Pinkie, do you think,' she asked with astonishment, 'I'd mind?'

'Gracious,' the woman said, 'I only came here for your sake. I wouldn't have troubled to see you first, only I don't want to let the Innocent suffer'—the aphorism came clicking out like a ticket from a slot machine. 'Why, won't you lift a finger to stop him killing you?'

'He wouldn't do me any harm.'

'You're young. You don't know things like I do.'

'There's things *you* don't know.' She brooded darkly by the bed, while the woman argued on: a God wept in a garden and cried out upon a cross; Molly Carthew went to everlasting fire.

'I know one thing you don't. I know the difference between Right and Wrong. They didn't teach you *that* at school.'

Rose didn't answer; the woman was quite right; the two words meant nothing to her. Their taste was extinguished by stronger foods —Good and Evil. The woman could tell her nothing she didn't know about these—she knew by tests as clear as mathematics that Pinkie was evil—what did it matter in that case whether he was right or wrong?

† *Pinkie is bad all through, like the letters in a stick of rock.*

He thought: there'll be time enough in the years ahead—sixty years —to repent of this. Go to a priest. Say: 'Father, I've committed murder twice. And there was a girl—she killed herself.' Even if death came suddenly, driving home tonight, the smash on the lamp-post— there was still: 'between the stirrup and the ground.' The houses on one side ceased altogether, and the sea came back to them, beating at the undercliff drive, a darkness and deep sound. He wasn't really deceiving himself—he'd learned the other day that when the time was short there were other things than contrition to think about. It didn't matter anyway . . . he wasn't made for peace, he couldn't believe in it. Heaven was a word; Hell was something he could trust. A brain was capable only of what it could conceive, and it couldn't conceive what it had never experienced; his cells were formed of the cement school playground, the dead fire and the dying man in the St Pancras waiting-room, his bed at Billy's and his parents' bed. An awful resentment stirred in him—why shouldn't he have had his chance like all the rest, seen his glimpse of Heaven if it was only a crack between the Brighton walls? . . . He turned as they went down to Rottingdean and took a long look at her as if she might be it—but the brain couldn't conceive—he saw a mouth which wanted the sexual contact, the shape of breasts demanding a child. Oh, she was good all right, he supposed, but she wasn't good enough; he'd got her down.

Above Rottingdean the new villas began: pipe-dream architecture; up on the down the obscure skeleton of a nursing-home, winged like an aeroplane. He said: 'They won't hear us in the country.' The lights petered out along the road to Peacehaven; the chalk of a new cutting flapped like white sheets in the headlight; cars came down on them, blinding them. He said: 'The battery's low.'

She had the sense that he was a thousand miles away—his thoughts had gone on beyond the act she couldn't tell where; he was wise; he was foreseeing, she thought, things she couldn't conceive—eternal punishment, the flames . . . She felt terror, the idea of pain shook her, their purpose drove up in a flurry of rain against the old stained windscreen. This road led nowhere else. It was said to be the worst act of all, the act of despair, the sin without forgiveness; sitting there in the smell of petrol she tried to realize despair, the mortal sin, but she couldn't; it didn't feel like despair. He was going to damn himself, but she was going to show Them that They couldn't damn him without damning her too; there was nothing he could do she wouldn't do; she felt capable of sharing any murder. A light lit his face and left it; a frown, a thought, a child's face; she felt responsibility move in her breasts; she wouldn't let him go into that darkness alone.

GRAHAM GREENE, *Brighton Rock*, 1938

† *The Kray twins, Reginald and Ronnie, and their 'firm' dominated the East London underworld in the 1960s. Laurie Taylor, a professor of sociology, in the company of John McVicar, a reformed criminal, interviews Lennie, a villain who had known the Krays.*

John seemed anxious to outdo Lennie in his appreciation of the Krays' mysterious 'edge'. He joined in eagerly with his analysis. 'Cos you felt, oh my fucking Christ, it's all the way with these, didn't you, Lennie? Out of *nothing*. It could be just out of nothing and yet they'd *kill* ya. And there's very few people would go that far. I mean, there's a lot of gangsters that would go a bit outrageous.'

'Reggie's not so bad. Reggie's not so bad. Reggie? Talk to ya. Not so bad. It depends how much of a doer you are yourself. Ronnie's a different kettle of fish. I tell you the reason why. This is what makes him different from other people. Ronnie, see, wouldn't be fucked about by people. If he thought they was frauds, he'd never say nothing. And if they'd been naughty and had to be cuffed—he wouldn't cuff them like you would a little kid—wouldn't just go "smack". "Behave yourself." Oh no. No cuffing with him. He wouldn't just knock a mug out and leave it at that . . .' What on earth, I wondered, did it mean to say that Ronnie wouldn't 'just' knock a mug out? But there was little chance to climb inside one of Lennie's bulldozing monologues. You had to hang on till the end.

'No, he wouldn't just knock a mug out. Oh he'd just *fuck*ing . . . just completely *fuck*ing . . . like you know, until he'd got his satisfaction, until it had steamed out of him.' Lennie gave a sudden and violent impression of a large ape beating its chest to indicate the savagery of the assault. 'Aaaaargh! Aaaaargh! Aaaaaargh!' His fists rained in on himself. 'See, like he's off his head. Really go over the brink. *Go over the brink* and do more damage than he should do being a gangster.'

Even though it was almost concealed within Lennie's evident enjoyment of Ronnie's unpredictable ferocity, this idea of going over the brink was what I'd been looking for. I wasn't going to get another opportunity. I decided to risk the sensitivities of the L'Escargot customers.

'Why was it more than a gangster should do?' I asked.

'Cos gangsters don't ever act that way. They only do what they got to do and go as far as they got to. You've got to have people respecting you, but never in fear of you. They done what they done because they thought they'd get away with it. But they pushed people to the brink, so people was absolutely in fucking fear of their lives with them. You never felt at ease with them. And when you lose that, you've lost everything. I'll tell you why.'

I could see that John was leaning forward: he wanted Lennie's opinion on the Krays as much as I did.

'Cos you'll never get the gist of nothing. You'll never get the context of nothing. When the people around you have got to watch their Ps and Qs, when you've just got yes-men, you are in danger. You are in *absolute danger*—cos there's no one gonna say to you: "Be careful of so-and-so." And why didn't anyone say it? Why? Rhyme and reason? Why? People are too frightened of you. So the Krays never got their cards marked. They had the West End at their mercy. They could have run the West End. But they never had the fucking brain to manœuvre.'

'Was they stupid then, Lennie?'

'Reggie wasn't stupid.'

'Don't you think so?'

'No.'

'No? But he can't talk can he.'

'Doesn't matter about talking, John. He had the right mind to do it. The right frame to do it. They didn't need to go no further. They was right for it and they was on to it. *But they went a bit too fierce.*'

LAURIE TAYLOR, *In the Underworld*, 1984

† *In* The Mysterious Stranger, *set in an Austrian village in 1590, the speaker is an angel known as Satan (nephew of the more famous one) who turns theological ideas upside down.*

'Strange, indeed, that you should not have suspected that your universe and its contents were only dreams, visions, fiction! Strange, because they are so frankly and hysterically insane—like all dreams: a God who could make good children as easily as bad, yet preferred to make bad ones; who could have made every one of them happy, yet never made a single happy one; who made them prize their bitter life, yet stingily cut it short; who gave his angels eternal happiness unearned, yet required his other children to earn it; who gave his angels painless lives, yet cursed his other children with biting miseries and maladies of mind and body; who mouths justice and invented hell—mouths mercy and invented hell—mouths Golden Rules, and forgiveness multiplied by seventy times seven, and invented hell; who mouths morals to other people and has none himself; who frowns upon crimes, yet commits them all; who created man without invitation, then tries to shuffle the responsibility for man's acts upon man, instead of honorably placing it where it belongs, upon himself; and finally, with altogether divine obtuseness, invites this poor, abused slave to worship him! . . .'

MARK TWAIN, *The Mysterious Stranger*, 1916

II

MASTER CROOKS

IT was not Holmes' nature to take an aimless holiday, and something about his pale, worn face told me that his nerves were at their highest tension. He saw the question in my eyes, and, putting his finger-tips together and his elbows upon his knees, he explained the situation.

'You have probably never heard of Professor Moriarty?' said he.

'Never.'

'Aye, there's the genius and the wonder of the thing!' he cried. 'The man pervades London, and no one has heard of him. That's what puts him on a pinnacle in the records of crime. I tell you, Watson, in all seriousness, that if I could beat that man, if I could free society of him, I should feel that my own career had reached its summit, and I should be prepared to turn to some more placid line in life. Between ourselves, the recent cases in which I have been of assistance to the Royal Family of Scandinavia, and to the French Republic, have left me in such a position that I could continue to live in the quiet fashion which is most congenial to me, and to concentrate my attention upon my chemical researches. But I could not rest, Watson, I could not sit quiet in my chair, if I thought that such a man as Professor Moriarty were walking the streets of London unchallenged.'

'What has he done, then?'

'His career has been an extraordinary one. He is a man of good birth and excellent education, endowed by Nature with a phenomenal mathematical faculty. At the age of twenty-one he wrote a treatise upon the Binomial Theorem, which has had a European vogue. On the strength of it, he won the Mathematical Chair at one of our smaller Universities, and had, to all appearance, a most brilliant career before him. But the man had hereditary tendencies of the most diabolical kind. A criminal strain ran in his blood, which, instead of being modified, was increased and rendered infinitely more dangerous by his extraordinary mental powers. Dark rumours gathered round him in the University town, and eventually he was compelled to resign his Chair and to come down to London, where he set up as an Army coach. So much is known to the world, but what I am telling you now is what I have myself discovered.

'As you are aware, Watson, there is no one who knows the higher criminal world of London so well as I do. For years past I have continually been conscious of some power behind the malefactor, some deep organizing power which for ever stands in the way of the law, and throws its shield over the wrong-doer. Again and again in cases of the most varying sorts—forgery cases, robberies, murders—I have felt the presence of this force, and I have deduced its action in many of those undiscovered crimes in which I have not been personally consulted. For years I have endeavoured to break through the veil which shrouded it, and at last the time came when I seized my thread and followed it, until it led me, after a thousand cunning windings, to ex-Professor Moriarty of mathematical celebrity.

'He is the Napoleon of crime, Watson. He is the organizer of half that is evil and of nearly all that is undetected in this great city. He is a genius, a philosopher, an abstract thinker. He has a brain of the first order. He sits motionless, like a spider in the centre of its web, but that web has a thousand radiations, and he knows well every quiver of each of them. He does little himself. He only plans. But his agents are numerous and splendidly organized. Is there a crime to be done, a paper to be abstracted, we will say, a house to be rifled, a man to be removed—the word is passed to the Professor, the matter is organized and carried out. The agent may be caught. In that case money is found for his bail or his defence. But the central power which uses the agent is never caught—never so much as suspected. This was the organization which I deduced, Watson, and which I devoted my whole energy to exposing and breaking up . . .'

SIR ARTHUR CONAN DOYLE, 'The Final Problem', 1893

MACAVITY: THE MYSTERY CAT

Macavity's a Mystery Cat: he's called the Hidden Paw—
For he's the master criminal who can defy the Law.
He's the bafflement of Scotland Yard, the Flying Squad's despair:
For when they reach the scene of crime—*Macavity's not there*!

Macavity, Macavity, there's no one like Macavity,
He's broken every human law, he breaks the law of gravity.
His powers of levitation would make a fakir stare,
And when you reach the scene of crime—*Macavity's not there*!
You may seek him in the basement, you may look up in the air—
But I tell you once and once again, *Macavity's not there*!

Macavity's a ginger cat, he's very tall and thin;
You would know him if you saw him, for his eyes are sunken in.
His brow is deeply lined with thought, his head is highly domed;
His coat is dusty from neglect, his whiskers are uncombed.
He sways his head from side to side, with movements like a snake;
And when you think he's half asleep, he's always wide awake.

Macavity, Macavity, there's no one like Macavity,
For he's a fiend in feline shape, a monster of depravity.
You may meet him in a by-street, you may see him in the
    square—
But when a crime's discovered, then *Macavity's not there*!

He's outwardly respectable. (They say he cheats at cards.)
And his footprints are not found in any file of Scotland Yard's.
And when the larder's looted, or the jewel-case is rifled,
Or when the milk is missing, or another Peke's been stifled,
Or the greenhouse glass is broken, and the trellis past repair—
Ay, there's the wonder of the thing! *Macavity's not there*!

And when the Foreign Office finds a Treaty's gone astray,
Or the Admiralty lose some plans and drawings by the way.
There may be a scrap of paper in the hall or on the stair—
But it's useless to investigate—*Macavity's not there*!
And when the loss has been disclosed, the Secret Service say:
'It *must* have been Macavity!'—but he's a mile away.
You'll be sure to find him resting, or a-licking of his thumbs,
Or engaged in doing complicated long division sums.

Macavity, Macavity, there's no one like Macavity,
There never was a Cat of such deceitfulness and suavity.
He always has an alibi, and one or two to spare:
At whatever time the deed took place—MACAVITY WASN'T
    THERE!
And they say that all the Cats whose wicked deeds are widely
    known
(I might mention Mungojerrie, I might mention Griddlebone)
Are nothing more than agents for the Cat who all the time
Just controls their operations: the Napoleon of Crime!

T. S. ELIOT, 1939

† *Though he later reformed, Flambeau (in the 'Father Brown' stories) first appears as a master-criminal to rank with the best of them.*

It is many years now since this colossus of crime suddenly ceased keeping the world in a turmoil; and when he ceased, as they said after the death of Roland, there was a great quiet upon the earth. But in his best days (I mean, of course, his worst) Flambeau was a figure as statuesque and international as the Kaiser. Almost every morning the daily paper announced that he had escaped the consequences of one extraordinary crime by committing another. He was a Gascon of gigantic stature and bodily daring; and the wildest tales were told of his outbursts of athletic humour; how he turned the *juge d'instruction* upside down and stood him on his head, 'to clear his mind'; how he ran down the Rue de Rivoli with a policeman under each arm. It is due to him to say that his fantastic physical strength was generally employed in such bloodless though undignified scenes; his real crimes were chiefly those of ingenious and wholesale robbery. But each of his thefts was almost a new sin, and would make a story by itself. It was he who ran the great Tyrolean Dairy Company in London, with no dairies, no cows, no carts, no milk, but with some thousand subscribers. These he served by the simple operation of moving the little milk-cans outside people's doors to the doors of his own customers. It was he who had kept up an unaccountable and close correspondence with a young lady whose whole letter-bag was intercepted, by the extraordinary trick of photographing his messages infinitesimally small upon the slides of a microscope. A sweeping simplicity, however, marked many of his experiments. It is said he once repainted all the numbers in a street in the dead of night merely to divert one traveller into a trap. It is quite certain that he invented a portable pillar-box, which he put up at corners in quiet suburbs on the chance of strangers dropping postal orders into it. Lastly he was known to be a startling acrobat; despite his huge figure, he could leap like a grasshopper and melt into the treetops like a monkey. Hence the great Valentin, when he set out to find Flambeau, was perfectly well aware that his adventures would not end when he had found him.

G. K. CHESTERTON, 'The Blue Cross', 1911

† *Count Fosco is the most colourful villain in Victorian fiction. He masterminds the devilish plot which reveals 'what a woman's patience can endure and what a man's resolution can achieve'. His opponent, Miss Halcombe, who finally defeats him, is fascinated by him on their first meeting.*

What of the Count?

This in two words: He looks like a man who could tame anything. If he had married a tigress, instead of a woman, he would have tamed the tigress. If he had married *me*, I should have made his cigarettes, as his wife does—I should have held my tongue when he looked at me, as she holds hers.

I am almost afraid to confess it, even to these secret pages. The man has interested me, has attracted me, has forced me to like him. In two short days he has made his way straight into my favourable estimation, and how he has worked the miracle is more than I can tell. . . .

How am I to describe him? There are peculiarities in his personal appearance, his habits, and his amusements, which I should blame in the boldest terms, or ridicule in the most merciless manner, if I had seen them in another man. What is it that makes me unable to blame them, or to ridicule them in *him*?

For example, he is immensely fat. Before this time I have always especially disliked corpulent humanity. I have always maintained that the popular notion of connecting excessive grossness of size and excessive good-humour as inseparable allies was equivalent to declaring, either that no people but amiable people ever get fat, or that the accidental addition of so many pounds of flesh has a directly favourable influence over the disposition of the person on whose body they accumulate. I have invariably combated both these absurd assertions by quoting examples of fat people who were as mean, vicious, and cruel as the leanest and the worst of their neighbours. I have asked whether Henry the Eighth was an amiable character? Whether Pope Alexander the Sixth was a good man? Whether Mr Murderer and Mrs Murderess Manning were not both unusually stout people? Whether hired nurses, proverbially as cruel a set of women as are to be found in all England, were not, for the most part, also as fat a set of women as are to be found in all England?—and so on, through dozens of other examples, modern and ancient, native and foreign, high and low. Holding these strong opinions on the subject with might and main as I do at this moment, here, nevertheless, is Count Fosco, as fat as Henry the Eighth himself, established in my favour, at one day's notice, without let or hindrance from his own odious corpulence. Marvellous indeed!

Is it his face that has recommended him?

It may be his face. He is a most remarkable likeness, on a large scale, of the great Napoleon. His features have Napoleon's magnificent regularity—his expression recalls the grandly calm, immovable power of the Great Soldier's face. This striking resemblance certainly impressed me, to begin with; but there is something in him besides the resemblance, which has impressed me more. I think the influence I am now trying to find is in his eyes. They are the most unfathomable grey eyes I ever saw, and they have at times a cold, clear, beautiful, irresistible glitter in them which forces me to look at him, and yet causes me sensations, when I do look, which I would rather not feel. Other parts of his face and head have their strange peculiarities. His complexion, for instance, has a singular sallow-fairness, so much at variance with the dark-brown colour of his hair, that I suspect the hair of being a wig, and his face, closely shaven all over, is smoother and freer from all marks and wrinkles than mine, though (according to Sir Percival's account of him) he is close on sixty years of age. But these are not the prominent personal characteristics which distinguish him, to my mind, from all the other men I have ever seen. The marked peculiarity which singles him out from the rank and file of humanity lies entirely, so far as I can tell at present, in the extraordinary expression and extraordinary power of his eyes.

All the smallest characteristics of this strange man have something strikingly original and perplexingly contradictory in them. Fat as he is and old as he is, his movements are astonishingly light and easy. He is as noiseless in a room as any of us women, and more than that, with all his look of unmistakable mental firmness and power, he is as nervously sensitive as the weakest of us. He starts at chance noises as inveterately as Laura herself. He winced and shuddered yesterday, when Sir Percival beat one of the spaniels, so that I felt ashamed of my own want of tenderness and sensibility by comparison with the Count.

The relation of this last incident reminds me of one of his most curious peculiarities, which I have not yet mentioned—his extraordinary fondness for pet animals.

Some of these he has left on the Continent, but he has brought with him to this house a cockatoo, two canary-birds, and a whole family of white mice. He attends to all the necessities of these strange favourites himself, and he has taught the creatures to be surprisingly fond of him and familiar with him. The cockatoo, a most vicious and treacherous bird towards every one else, absolutely seems to love him. When he lets it out of its cage, it hops on to his knee, and claws its way up his great big body, and rubs its top-knot against his sallow double chin in the most caressing manner imaginable. He has only to set the doors of the canaries' cages open, and to call them, and the pretty little cleverly trained creatures perch fearlessly on his hand, mount his fat outstretched fingers one by one, when he tells them to 'go upstairs,' and sing together as if they would burst their throats with delight when they get to the top finger. His white mice live in a little pagoda of gaily-painted wirework, designed and made by himself. They are almost as tame as the canaries, and they are perpetually let out like the canaries. They crawl all over him, popping in and out of his waistcoat, and sitting in couples, white as snow, on his capacious shoulders. He seems to be even fonder of his mice than of his other pets, smiles at them, and kisses them, and calls them by all sorts of endearing names. If it be possible to suppose an Englishman with any taste for such childish interests and amusements as these, that Englishman would certainly feel rather ashamed of them, and would be anxious to apologise for them, in the company of grown-up people. But the Count, apparently, sees nothing ridiculous in the amazing contrast between his colossal self and his frail little pets. He would blandly kiss his white mice and twitter to his canary-birds amid an assembly of English fox-hunters, and would only pity them as barbarians when they were all laughing their loudest at him.

† *There are two villains in* The Woman in White*—Count Fosco and his weaker associate in intrigue, Sir Percival Glyde.*

Sir Percival was the first to break the silence . . .

'Yes, yes; bully and bluster as much as you like,' he said, sulkily; 'the difficulty about the money is not the only difficulty. You would be for taking strong measures with the women, yourself—if you knew as much as I do.'

'We will come to that second difficulty, all in good time,' rejoined the Count. 'You may confuse yourself, Percival, as much as you please, but you shall not confuse me. Let the question of the money be settled first. Have I convinced your obstinacy? have I shown you that your temper will not let you help yourself?—Or must I go back, and (as you put it in your dear straightforward English) bully and bluster a little more?'

'Pooh! It's easy enough to grumble at *me*. Say what is to be done—that's a little harder.'

'Is it? Bah! This is what is to be done: You give up all direction in the business from to-night; you leave it, for the future, in my hands only. I am talking to a Practical British Man—ha? Well, Practical, will that do for you?'

'What do you propose, if I leave it all to you?'

'Answer me first. Is it to be in my hands or not?'

'Say it is in your hands—what then?'

'A few questions, Percival, to begin with. I must wait a little, yet, to let circumstances guide me; and I must know, in every possible way, what those circumstances are likely to be. There is no time to lose. I have told you already that Miss Halcombe has written to the lawyer to-day, for the second time.'

'How did you find it out? What did she say?'

'If I told you, Percival, we should only come back at the end to where we are now. Enough that I have found out—and the finding has caused that trouble and anxiety which made me so inaccessible to you all through to-day. Now, to refresh my memory about your affairs—it is some time since I talked them over with you. The money has been raised, in the absence of your wife's signature, by means of bills at three months—raised at a cost that makes my poverty-stricken foreign hair stand on end to think of it! When the bills are due, is there really and truly no earthly way of paying them but by the help of your wife?'

'None.'

'What! You have no money at the banker's!'

'A few hundreds, when I want as many thousands.'

'Have you no other security to borrow upon?'

'Not a shred.'

'What have you actually got with your wife, at the present moment?'

'Nothing, but the interest of her twenty thousand pounds—barely enough to pay our daily expenses.'

'What do you expect from your wife?'

'Three thousand a year, when her uncle dies.'

'A fine fortune, Percival. What sort of a man is this uncle? Old?'

'No—neither old nor young.'

'A good-tempered, freely-living man? Married? No—I think my wife told me, not married.'

'Of course not. If he was married, and had a son, Lady Glyde would not be next heir to the property. I'll tell you what he is. He's a maudlin, twaddling, selfish fool, and bores everybody who comes near him about the state of his health.'

'Men of that sort, Percival, live long, and marry malevolently when you least expect it. I don't give you much, my friend, for your chance of the three thousand a year. Is there nothing more that comes to you from your wife?'

'Nothing.'

'Absolutely nothing?'

'Absolutely nothing—except in case of her death.'

'Aha? in the case of her death.'

There was another pause. . . .

WILKIE COLLINS, *The Woman in White*, 1860

† *Raffles is the archetypal 'gentleman burglar' and Bunny is his old school chum and partner-in-crime.*

'Had it in my head for long?' said Raffles, as we strolled through the streets towards dawn, for all the world as though we were returning from a dance. 'No, Bunny, I never thought of it till I saw that upper part empty about a month ago, and bought a few things in the shop to get the lie of the land. That reminds me that I never paid for them; but, by Jove, I will tomorrow, and if that isn't poetic justice, what is? One visit showed me the possibilities of the place, but a second convinced me of its impossibilities without a pal. So I had practically given up the idea, when you came along on the very night and in the very plight for it! But here we are at the Albany, and I hope there's some fire left; for I don't know how you feel, Bunny, but for my part I'm as cold as Keats' owl.'

He could think of Keats on his way from a felony! He could hanker for his fireside like another. Flood-gates were loosened within me, and the plain English of our adventure rushed over me as cold as ice. Raffles was a burglar. I had helped to commit one burglary, therefore I was a burglar too. Yet I could stand and warm myself by his fire and watch him empty his pockets, as though we had done nothing wonderful or wicked!

My blood froze. My heart sickened. My brain whirled. How I had liked this villain! How I had admired him! Now my liking and admiration must turn to loathing disgust. I waited for the change. I longed to feel it in my heart. But—I longed and waited in vain!

I saw he was emptying his pockets; the table sparkled with their hoard. Rings by the dozen, diamonds by the score; bracelets, pendants, aigrettes, necklaces; pearls, rubies, amethysts, sapphires; and diamonds always, diamonds in everything, flashing bayonets of light, dazzling me—blinding me—making me disbelieve because I could no longer forget. Last of all came no gem, indeed, but my own revolver from an inner pocket. And that struck a chord. I suppose I said something—my hand flew out. I can see Raffles now, as he looked at me once more with a high arch over each clear eye. I can see him pick out the cartridges with his quiet cynical smile, before he would give me my pistol back again.

'You mayn't believe it, Bunny,' said he, 'but I never carried a loaded one before. On the whole I think it gives one confidence. Yet it would be very awkward if anything went wrong; one might use it, and that's not the game at all, though I have often thought that the murderer who has just done the trick must have great sensations before things get too hot for him. Don't look so distressed, my dear chap. I've never had those sensations, and I don't suppose I ever shall.'

'But this much you have done before?' said I hoarsely.

'Before? My dear Bunny, you offend me! Did it look like a first attempt? Of course I have done it before.'

'Often?'

'Well—no. Not often enough to destroy the charm, at all events; never, as a matter of fact, unless I'm cursedly hard up. Did you hear about the Thimbleby diamonds? Well, that was the last time—and a poor lot of paste they were. Then there was the little business of the Dormer house-boat at Henley last year. That was mine also—such as it was. I've never brought off a really big *coup* yet; when I do I shall chuck it up.'

Yes, I remember both cases very well. To think that he was their author! It was incredible, outrageous, inconceivable. Then my eyes would fall upon the table, twinkling and glittering in a hundred places, and incredulity was at an end.

'How came you to begin?' I asked, as curiosity overcame mere wonder, and a fascination for his career gradually wove itself into my fascination for the man.

'Ah! that's a long story,' said Raffles. 'It was in the Colonies, when I was out there playing cricket. It's too long a story to tell you now, but I was in much the same fix that you were in to-night, and it was my only way out. I never meant it for anything more; but I'd tasted blood, and it was all over with me. Why should I work when I could steal? Why settle down to some humdrum uncongenial billet, when excitement, romance, danger, and a decent living were all going begging together? Of course, it's very wrong, but we can't all be moralists, and the distribution of wealth is very wrong to begin with. Besides, you're not at it all the time. I'm sick of quoting Gilbert's lines to myself, but they're profoundly true. I only wonder if you'll like the life as much as I do!'

'Like it?' I cried. 'Not I! It's no life for me. Once is enough!'

'You wouldn't give me a hand another time?'

'Don't ask me, Raffles. Don't ask me, for God's sake!'

'Yet you said you would do anything for me! You asked me to name my crime! But I knew at the time that you didn't mean it; you didn't go back on me to-night, and that ought to satisfy me, goodness knows! I suppose I'm ungrateful, and unreasonable, and all that. I ought to let it end at this. But you're the very man for me, Bunny, the—very —man! Just think how we got through to-night. Not a scratch—not a hitch! There's nothing very terrible in it, you see; there never would be, while we worked together.'

He was standing in front of me with a hand on either shoulder; he was smiling as he knew so well how to smile. I turned on my heel, planted my elbows on the chimney-piece, and my burning head between my hands. Next instant a still heartier hand had fallen on my back.

'All right, my boy! You are quite right and I'm worse than wrong. I'll never ask it again. Go, if you want to, and come again about midday for the cash. There was no bargain; but, of course, I'll get you out of your scrape—especially after the way you've stood by me to-night.'

I was round again with my blood on fire.

'I'll do it again,' I said through my teeth.

He shook his head. 'Not you,' he said, smiling quite good-humouredly at my insane enthusiasm.

'I will,' I cried with an oath. 'I'll lend you a hand as often as you like! What does it matter now? I've been in it once. I'll be in it again.

I've gone to the devil anyhow. I can't go back, and wouldn't if I could. Nothing matters another rap! When you want me I'm your man.'

And that is how Raffles and I joined felonious forces on the Ides of March.

E. W. HORNUNG, *Raffles*, 1899

† *Oriental malevolence never stood a chance against the upright Englishness of such characters as Sax Rohmer's Nayland Smith and his friend Dr Petrie; still, by enumerating the attributes of the fearsome Dr Fu-Manchu, the would-be scourge of the west, Nayland Smith leaves us in no doubt about what the two of them were up against.*

The cab moved off with a metallic jerk, and I turned and looked back through the little window in the rear.

'Someone has got into another cab. It is following ours, I think.'

Nayland Smith lay back and laughed unmirthfully.

'Petrie,' he said, 'if I escape alive from this business I shall know that I bear a charmed life.'

I made no reply, as he pulled out the dilapidated pouch and filled his pipe.

'You have asked me to explain matters,' he continued, 'and I will do so to the best of my ability. You no doubt wonder why a servant of the British Government, lately stationed in Burma, suddenly appears in London in the character of a detective. I am here, Petrie —and I bear credentials from the very highest sources—because, quite by accident, I came upon a clue. Following it up, in the ordinary course of routine, I obtained evidence of the existence and malignant activity of a certain man. At the present stage of the case I should not be justified in terming him the emissary of an Eastern Power, but I may say that representations are shortly to be made to that Power's ambassador in London.'

He paused, and glanced back towards the pursuing cab.

'There is little to fear until we arrive home,' he said calmly. 'Afterwards there is much. To continue. This man, whether a fanatic, or a duly appointed agent, is, unquestionably, the most malign and formidable personality existing in the known world to-day. He is a linguist who speaks with almost equal facility in any of the civilised languages, and in most of the barbaric. He is an adept in all the arts and sciences which a great university could teach him. He also is an adept in certain obscure arts and sciences which *no* university of to-day can teach. He has the brains of any three men of genius. Petrie, he is a mental giant.'

'You amaze me!' I said.

'As to his mission among men. Why did M. Jules Furneaux fall dead in a Paris opera-house? Because of heart failure? No! Because his last speech had shown that he held the key to the secret of Tongking. What became of the Grand Duke Stanislaus? Elopement? Suicide? Nothing of the kind. He alone was fully alive to Russia's growing peril. He alone knew the truth about Mongolia. Why was Sir Crichton Davey murdered? Because, had the work he was engaged upon ever seen the light, it would have shown him to be the only living Englishman who understood the importance of the Tibetan frontiers. I say to you solemnly, Petrie, that these are but a few. Is there a man who would arouse the West to a sense of the awakening of the East, who would teach the deaf to hear, the blind to see, that the millions only await their leader? He will die. And this is only one phase of the devilish campaign. The others I can merely surmise.'

'But, Smith, this is almost incredible! What perverted genius controls this awful secret movement?'

'Imagine a person, tall, lean and feline, high-shouldered, with a brow like Shakespeare and a face like Satan, a close-shaven skull, and long, magnetic eyes of the true cat-green. Invest him with all the cruel cunning of an entire Eastern race, accumulated in one giant intellect, with all the resources of science past and present, with all the resources, if you will, of a wealthy government—which, however, already has denied all knowledge of his existence. Imagine that awful being, and you have a mental picture of Dr Fu-Manchu, the yellow peril incarnate in one man.'

SAX ROHMER, *The Mystery of Dr Fu-Manchu*, 1913

'You cannot play for high stakes without taking risks, Mister Bond. I accept the dangers and, so far as I can, I have equipped myself against them. You see, Mister Bond,' the deep voice held a hint of greed, 'I am on the edge of still greater things. The Chapter Two to which I referred holds the promise of prizes which no one but a fool would throw away because he was afraid. I have told you that I can bend the beams on which these rockets fly, Mister Bond. I can make them change course and ignore their radio control. What would you say, Mister Bond, if I could go further? If I could bring them down into the sea near this island and salvage the secrets of their construction. At present American destroyers, far out in the South Atlantic, salvage these missiles when they come to the end of their fuel and parachute down into the sea. Sometimes the parachutes fail to open. Sometimes the self-destruction devices fail to operate. No one on Turks Island would be surprised if every now and then the prototype of a new series broke off its flight and came down near Crab Key. To begin with, at least, it would be put down to mechanical failure. Later, perhaps, they would discover that other radio signals besides theirs were guiding their rockets. A jamming war would start. They would try and locate the origin of the false signals. Directly I found they were looking for me, I would have one last fling. Their rockets would go mad. They would land on Havana, on Kingston. They would turn round and home on Miami. Even without warheads, Mister Bond, five tons of metal arriving at a thousand miles an hour can cause plenty of damage in a crowded town. And then what? There would be panic, a public outcry. The experiments would have to cease. The Turks Island base would have to close down. And how much would Russia pay for that to happen, Mister Bond? And how much for each of the prototypes I captured for them? Shall we say ten million dollars for the whole operation? Twenty million? It would be a priceless victory in the armaments race. I could name my figure. Don't you agree, Mister Bond? And don't you agree that these considerations make your arguments and threats seem rather puny?'

Bond said nothing. There was nothing to say. Suddenly he was back in the quiet room high up above Regent's Park. He could hear the rain slashing softly against the window and M's voice, impatient, sarcastic, saying, 'Oh, some damned business about birds . . . holiday in the sun'll do you good . . . routine inquiry.' And he, Bond, had taken a canoe and a fisherman and a picnic lunch and had gone off—how many days, how many weeks ago?—'to have a look'. Well, he had had his look into Pandora's Box. He had found out the answers, been told the secrets—and now? Now he was going to be politely shown the way to his grave, taking the secrets with him and the waif he had picked up and dragged along with him on his lunatic adventure. The bitterness inside Bond came up into his mouth so that for a moment he thought he was going to retch. He reached for his champagne and emptied the glass. He said harshly, 'All right, Doctor No. Now let's get on with the cabaret. What's the programme—knife, bullet, poison, rope? But make it quick, I've seen enough of you.'

IAN FLEMING, *Dr No*, 1958

Peterson rose and walked over to the window, where he stood motionless staring out into the darkness. For all his assumed flippancy, Hugh realised that the situation was what in military phraseology might be termed critical. There were in the house probably half a dozen men who, like their master, were absolutely unscrupulous. If it suited Peterson's book to kill him, he would not hesitate to do so for a single second. And Hugh realised, when he put it that way in his own mind, that it was no exaggeration, no *façon de parler*, but a plain, unvarnished statement of fact. Peterson would no more think twice of killing a man if he wished to, than the normal human being would of crushing a wasp.

For a moment the thought crossed his mind that he would take no chances by remaining in the house; that he would rush Peterson from behind and escape into the darkness of the garden. But it was only momentary—gone almost before it had come, for Hugh Drummond was not that manner of man—gone even before he noticed that Peterson was standing in such a position that he could see every detail of the room behind him reflected in the glass through which he stared.

A fixed determination to know what lay in that sinister brain replaced his temporary indecision. Events up to date had moved so quickly that he had hardly had time to get his bearings; even now the last twenty-four hours seemed almost a dream. And as he looked at the broad back and massive head of the man at the window, and from him to the girl idly smoking on the sofa, he smiled a little grimly. He had just remembered the thumbscrew of the preceding evening. Assuredly the demobilised officer who found peace dull was getting his money's worth; and Drummond had a shrewd suspicion that the entertainment was only just beginning.

'SAPPER', *Bulldog Drummond*, 1920

His eyes scorched with hate. The vacuous expression was torn away, the hidden personality now out in the open and as mean and savage as any crocodile. He was still Kate's amusing Uncle George in corpulent outline and country-gentleman tweeds, the Uncle George who had written for boys' magazines and taken his wife to matinées, but the face was the one which had had a knife stuck into Joe Nantwich and had urged a bloodthirsty mob to tear me to bits.

His hand snaked out across the desk and came up with a gun. It was a heavy, old-fashioned pistol, cumbersome, but deadly enough, and it was pointing straight at my chest. I resolutely looked at Uncle George's eyes, and not at the black hole in the barrel. I took a step towards him.

Then it came, the instant on which I had gambled my safety.

Uncle George hesitated.

I saw the flicker, the drawing back. For all his sin, for all the horror he had spread into the lives of others, he had never himself committed an act of violence. When he had delivered his threatening warning to me on the telephone on the very morning that I went to stay in his house, he had told me that he hated even to watch violence; and in spite of, or perhaps because of, his vicarious pleasure in the brutalities of primitive nations, I believed him. He was the sort of man, I thought, who liked to contemplate atrocities he could never inflict himself. And now, in spite of the fury he felt against me, he couldn't immediately, face to face, shoot me down.

DICK FRANCIS, *Dead Cert*, 1962

† *John Masefield's novels for children,* The Midnight Folk *and* The Box of Delights, *are full of gusto and full-blooded wickedness. In the following scene, young Kay Harker is shown some nefarious goings-on in a cellar, before being led further underground to where the master-crook Abner Brown is up to no good.*

Kay and the Mouse paused, while within the room a most unpleasant voice broke into song. The singer may have been a little drunk, for he sometimes forgot his words and often forgot his tune, but whenever this happened, the other members of the company cheered and pounded the table. These were the words of the song:

'We fly a banner all of black,
With scarlet Skull and Boneses,
And every merchantman we take
We send to Davey Jones's.

'Chorus gents, please . . .'

And the company broke out into the chorus:

'And every merchantman we take
We send to Davey Jones's.
Sing diddle-diddle-dol.'

The singer went on with his song:

'To fetch the gold out of the hold
We make them shake their shankses.
Then over the side to take a dive
We make them walk the plankses.

'Chorus gents, please . . .'

And the company shouted with drunken cheers and laughter:

'Then over the side to take a dive
We make them walk the plankses.
Sing diddle-diddle-dol.'

They were going on with this disgusting ditty, but the company seemed so overcome by the beauty of the words and the sentiments that they all pushed back their chairs, rose to their feet, and snapped their clay pipes and started to repeat the chorus.

'Quickly, while they sing,' the Mouse whispered.

As they slipped past the open door Kay glanced in. Oh, what a terrible scene was within! There, gathered round a table, lurching, shouting, swaying and clutching at each other to keep their balance, were the Wolves of the Gulf, all Benito's crew, whom the Rat would have described as marine cellarmen. On the table round which they lurched and carolled were the remnants of a ham-bone without any dish, and a big bowl of rum punch. As Kay glanced, one of the ruffians fell forward with his head into the bowl. He splashed the rum over his head and another tried to set fire to him with a candle, but was too unsteady in his aim. All these men wore sea-boots, rough red caps and red aprons. No words can describe the villainy of their faces, all bronzed with tropical suns, purple with drink, scarlet with battle and bloated from evil living.

'Sing diddle-diddle-dol,'

they cried. Then they drew their pistols and fired them at the ceiling, so that the plaster came down with a clatter.

The Mouse plucked Kay on along the corridor. They turned a

corner. There on in front of them, at the passage end, Kay saw the familiar figure of Rat, with a younger marine cellarman. Kay and the Mouse slipped back so as not to be seen. They heard Rat saying:

'Now here we are at the door. Now, nephew, remember what it was I told you. Don't you be afraid of the gent: speak out.'

'I ain't afraid of no gent,' the Rat's nephew answered.

'Well, that's what,' Rat said, and, stooping down, he knocked at a little door.

'What d'you knock for?' the nephew asked.

'To show respect to the great Abner Brown,' the Rat answered.

Kay heard Abner's silky voice say, 'Come in.' Rat and his nephew passed into the room and shut the door behind them.

'Are we in the Rupert's Arms?' Kay asked.

'Yes, this is the Rupert's Arms,' the Mouse said. 'If you will step up here there is a place where you can see right into the room.'

He led Kay up a fallen wooden moulding to a ledge behind the panelling of the old room. There was a crack in the panelling through which Kay could see. There was Abner in a green silk quilted dressing-gown, sitting at a table. Beside him was a rather stout, rosy-faced, but stupid-looking man whom Kay took to be the man Joe. Opposite Joe was the foxy-faced man. Opposite Abner was a lady, whose figure and bearing seemed familiar. She turned her head a moment to light a cigarette at a taper burning beside her and Kay saw that it was, indeed, as he had thought, one who had been his governess: Sylvia Daisy Pouncer, a witch.

'Come in, Rat,' Abner said. 'Who have you got with you?'

'I make so bold as to present my nephew, Master Abner,' Rat said. 'Make a reverence to the gentleman.'

'What's your nephew's name?' Abner asked.

'Oh, he answers to any name,' Rat said; 'Alf or Bert or any name. He ain't earned a name better'n one of those.'

'Now,' Abner said, 'what will you take, Rat?'

'Well, since I've been marine cellarman,' Rat said, 'I can't stand the climate like what I used. I do like a drop of rum. Not because I like it, it's poison, but without it I can't stand the climate.'

'A drop of rum for Rat,' Abner said.

They gave Rat a tot of rum in a thimble. Rat wiped his lips with the back of his paw and said, 'Happy days, gents!' tossed it off and rubbed his chest. 'That's the stuff,' he said—'poison. I can feel it doing me good all the way down.'

'Now, Alf,' the Rat said, when he judged that he would not receive any more rum, 'stand there and tell the gentlemen what you seen last night.'

Alf Rat came forward and seemed much abashed at having to speak in company. Kay thought that he had seldom seen a more hardened young villain; he was pleased to see the brazen face now confused, the eyes downcast, sweat starting from the brow, and the cheeks flushing and turning white by turns.

JOHN MASEFIELD, *The Box of Delights*, 1935

Charlie Yost, the Chicago gunman, called on Horace Appleby one morning in June as he chatted with Basher Evans before going off to the Wellingford races.

Ferdie announced him.

'Charlie's here, guv'nor,' he said, and Horace frowned. He was displeased with this hand across the sea and wished to have nothing more to do with him.

Horace Appleby was the head of the Appleby gang, well known and respected in criminal circles, and Charlie, who for various reasons had felt it wiser to leave Chicago for the time being and transfer his activities to England, had been one of his boys. In his long and prosperous career Horace had always had to depend very much on those who worked for him—Basher Evans, for instance, expert at opening safes, and Ferdie the Fly, who, while definitely not of the intelligentsia, had the invaluable gift of being able to climb up the side of any house you placed before him, using only toes, fingers and personal magnetism. Horace himself played the role of a General in time of war, planning campaigns at the base and leaving his troops to carry them out.

He and his boys were a happy family, and in his dealings with them he strove always to be the kindly father, liking to see them doing well and taking a benevolent pleasure in handing them their cut after each successful coup. But if occasion arose, he could be a stern parent. Charlie Yost had carried a gun with him when on duty, and in the matter of guns Horace's views were rigid. He would not permit them, and of this prejudice of his Charlie had been perfectly well aware. But he had flouted his leader's authority and retribution had been swift.

With a firm hand Horace had held up his latest cut, refusing to give him even a token wage.

So now he frowned. He resented having his privacy invaded by employees whom he had struck off his payroll. He also felt a little nervous. Charlie, informed that he was not to receive any reward for his services, had made no secret of his dissatisfaction, and he was presumably still carrying that gun. A man of his impulsive temperament, taught at his mother's knee to shoot first and argue afterwards, might well take it into his head to open the negotiations by saying it with bullets.

'May as well see him, guv'nor,' said Basher, reading his thoughts. 'He won't start anything, not while I'm here.'

Horace looked at him, and saw what he meant. There was only one adjective to be applied to Llewellyn ('Basher') Evans, and it was one which would have sprung automatically to the lips of any resident of Hollywood—the adjective colossal. Though he was impressively tall, it was not his cubits that filled the beholder with awe so much as his physical development. Wherever a man could bulge with muscle, he bulged. He even bulged in places where one would not have expected him to bulge. The clothes he wore had presumably been constructed by a tailor, but it was hard to believe that he could have been adequately fitted out by anyone less spacious in his methods than Omar the Tent Maker.

The scrutiny convinced Horace that with this colossus beside him he had nothing to fear from the most disgruntled gunman.

'Very well,' he said. 'Bring him in, Ferdie,' and a moment later Charlie entered.

An impression exists in the public mind that there is some system of rules and regulations, rigidly enforced by the men up top, which compels all American gangsters to look like Humphrey Bogart and when speaking to snarl like annoyed cougars. Should one of them fail to meet these requirements, it is supposed, he is placed in the centre of a hollow square of sinister characters with names like Otto the Ox and Beef Stroganoff and formally stripped of his Homburg hat and trench coat.

Actually, however, a considerable latitude is permitted, and the rank and file may indulge their personal tastes without incurring any sort of penalty.

Charlie Yost, to take a case in point, was a pleasant, soft-spoken little man with an inoffensive face rendered additionally inoffensive by large horn-rimmed spectacles. Meeting him on the street you would have set him down as a minor unit in some commercial firm or possibly a clerk in a lawyer's office, never suspecting him of being a man of violence.

Nor, indeed, was he, except when the necessity arose of liquidating some business competitor, and this he did not look on as violence but simply as routine inseparable from commerce. He was rather a sentimental man, who subscribed to homes for unwanted dogs and cats and rarely failed to cry when watching a motion picture with a sad ending.

Horace, fortified by the presence of Basher, greeted him coldly.

'Well, Yost?'

Usually Horace's majesty, so different from anything he had ever encountered in Chicago, overawed Charlie, but such was the magnitude of his grievance that he did not quail before it now. Speaking with equal coldness and out of the left side of his mouth, a thing he never did except when greatly moved, he said:

'I want that money.'

'What money?'

'The money you owe me.'

Horace drew himself to his full height. Even when full, it was not a very high height, but he managed to make the gesture impressive. Napoleon had the same knack.

'I owe you nothing,' he said. 'You knew my rules when you entered my organization. You were told in simple words that I do not permit the carrying of guns. You wilfully disobeyed me and I imposed a salutary fine upon you. There is nothing more to say. Basher, show Mr Yost out.'

'Come along, Charlie,' said Basher, and Charlie gave him a long, thoughtful stare.

Actually, Llewellyn Evans was a mild man, the sobriquet of Basher having been bestowed on him not because he bashed but because he looked so like one who on the slightest provocation would bash. But as there was nothing in his appearance to indicate that he was not a menace to pedestrians and traffic, Charlie, as he had predicted, made no move in the direction of what he had called starting something. He allowed himself to be escorted peacefully to the door. Turning there and speaking quietly but with menace, he said:

'I'll be seeing you.'

And on this significant speech he withdrew.

Basher came back into the room, to find Horace's composure quite restored. These little disturbances never ruffled him for long.

'He's gone,' he said. 'And you'd better be going, too, guv'nor, or you'll be missing your train.'

'You're perfectly right, Basher,' said Horace. 'And that would not do at all. I've a couple of tips on the two-thirty and the three o'clock and am confidently expecting to clean up.'

And so saying he went off to catch the express to Wellingford, where, though he was not aware of it, he would meet Mike Bond, Ada Cootes, Jill Willard, Sergeant Claude Potter of Scotland Yard and others who were to play an important part in his affairs.

So true it is that in this life we never know what may be waiting for us around the next corner.

P. G. WODEHOUSE, *Do Butlers Burgle Banks?*, 1968

III

MINOR CROOKS

VILLON'S STRAIGHT TIP TO ALL CROSS COVES

'Tout aux tavernes et aux filles.'

SUPPOSE you screeve? or go cheap-jack? *write a begging letter*
Or fake the broads? or fig a nag? *cheat at cards; ginger up a horse*
Or thimble-rig? or knap a yack? *play the three thimble trick; steal a watch*
Or pitch a snide? or smash a rag? *pass forged coins; pass forged notes*
Suppose you duff? or nose and lag? *sell contraband goods; grass on a villain*
Or get the straight, and land your pot? *win a bet*
How do you melt the multy swag?
Booze and the blowens cop the lot. *wenches*

Fiddle, or fence, or mace, or mack; *swindle*
Or moskeneer, or flash the drag; *pawn-broke unfairly; rob vehicles*
Dead-lurk a crib, or do a crack; *rob a house during divine service; break in*
Pad with a slang, or chuck a fag; *rob on the highway*
Bonnet, or tout, or mump and gag; *act as decoy; cheat; hoax*
Rattle the tats, or mark the spot; *false dice*
You can not bank a single stag; *shilling*
Booze and the blowens cop the lot.

Suppose you try a different tack,
And on the square you flash your flag? *beg in uniform*
At penny-a-lining make your whack, *journalism*
Or with the mummers mug and gag?
For nix, for nix the dibbs you bag! *money*
At any graft, no matter what,
Your merry goblins soon stravag: *go away*
Booze and the blowens cop the lot.

THE MORAL

It's up the spout and Charley Wag *play truant*
With wipes and tickers and what not.
Until the squeezer nips your scrag,
Booze and the blowens cop the lot.

FRANÇOIS VILLON, *The Testament*, 1461/2, trans. with thieves' slang by William Ernest Henley

. . . in the sixteenth century the science of roguery was patiently studied and thoroughly understood by its professors. The art, as happens so often, lagged far behind the science. When men analyse their handicraft too closely they are wont to forget their skill. Yet signs of improvement were not lacking, and the fact that the pickpocket was throwing the cutpurse into contempt proves that at least one branch of roguery was pursued with lightness of hand and courage of heart. The historians, in brief, separate, by a sharp contrast, the Nip and the Foist. The object of both was the same—a heavily laden purse; but while the Nip was content to use a knife and cut the purse, the Foist drew the pocket into his hand. The artistic superiority of the Foist was evident, and he was not slow to claim it. He called himself always a Gentleman Foist, and so bitterly did he disdain the clumsiness of his brother Nip, that he would not carry a knife in his pocket, wherewith to cut his meat, lest he might be suspected of putting it to any improper use. Here breathes the spirit of true artistry, and it is not surprising that the rhapsodist describes the perfections of the Foist with a thinly veiled enthusiasm.

'An exquisite Foist', says Greene, 'must have three properties that a good surgion should have, and that is an Eagles eie, a Ladies hand, and a Lyons heart: an Eagles eie to spy a purchase, to have a quick insight where the boung* lies, and then a Lyons heart not to feare what the end will bee, and then a Ladies hand to be little and nimble, the better to dive into the pocket.'

CHARLES WHIBLEY, 'Rogues and Vagabonds', in *Shakespeare's England*, 1916

NIGHTINGALE. 'Youth, youth, thou hadst better been starved by thy nurse,
Than live to be hanged for cutting a purse.'

[*As Nightingale sings, Edgworth gets up to Cokes and tickles him in the ear with a straw twice to draw his hand out of his pocket*.

WINWIFE. Will you see sport? look, there's a fellow gathers up to him, mark.

QUARLOUS. Good, i' faith! O, he has lighted on the wrong pocket.

* The boung is the purse, still known as the bung in the flash speech of to-day.

WINWIFE. He has it! 'fore God, he is a brave fellow: pity he should be detected.

NIGHTINGALE. 'But O, you vile nation of cutpurses all,
Relent and repent, and amend and be sound,
And know that you ought not, by honest men's fall,
Advance your own fortunes, to die above ground;
And though you go gay,
In silks, as you may,
It is not the highway to heaven (as they say).
Repent then, repent you, for better, for worse,
And kiss not the gallows for cutting a purse.
Youth, youth, thou hadst better been starved by thy nurse,
Than live to be hanged for cutting a purse.'

ALL. An excellent ballad! an excellent ballad!

EDGWORTH. Friend, let me have the first, let me have the first, I pray you.

[*As Nightingale reaches out the ballad, Edgworth slips the purse into his hand.*

COKES. Pardon me, sir; first come first served; and I'll buy the whole bundle too.

WINWIFE. That conveyance was better than all, did you see't? he has given the purse to the ballad-singer.

QUARLOUS. Has he?

EDGWORTH. Sir, I cry you mercy, I'll not hinder the poor man's profit; pray you, mistake me not.

COKES. Sir, I take you for an honest gentleman, if that be mistaking; I met you to-day afore: ha! humph! O Lord! my purse is gone, my purse, my purse, my purse!

WASPE. Come, do not make a stir, and cry yourself an ass thorough the Fair afore your time.

COKES. Why, hast thou it, Numps? good Numps, how came you by it, I marle?

WASPE. I pray you seek some other gamester to play the fool with; you may lose it time enough, for all your Fair wit.

COKES. By this good hand, glove and all, I have lost it already if thou hast it not; feel else, and Mistress Grace's handkerchief too, out of t'other pocket.

WASPE. Why, 'tis well, very well, exceeding pretty and well.

EDGWORTH. Are you sure you have lost it, sir?

COKES. O Lord! yes; as I am an honest man, I had it but e'en now, at *Youth, youth.*

NIGHTINGALE. I hope you suspect not me, sir?

EDGWORTH. Thee! that were a jest indeed! dost thou think the gentleman is foolish? where hadst thou hands, I pray thee? Away, ass, away! [*Exit Nightingale.*

BEN JONSON, *Bartholomew Fair*, 1614

Ah gentlemen, marchants, yeomen, and farmers, let this to you al, and to every degree els, be a caveat to warn you from lust, that your inordinat desire be not a mean to impoverish your purses, discredit your good names, condemn your soules, but also that your welth got with the sweat of your browes, or left by your parents as a patrimony, shalbe a pray to those cosening cros-biters, some fond men are so far in with these detestable trugs, that they consume what they have upon them, and find nothing but a *neapolitan* favour for their labor. Read the vii. of *Solomons proverbs*, and there at large vew the description of a shameles and impudent curtizan: yet is there another kind of cros-biting which is most pestilent, and thats this. Ther lives about this town certain housholders, yet meere shifters and coseners, who learning some insight in the civil lawe, walke abroad like parators, sumners, and informers, being none at al either in office or credit, and they go spieng about where any marchant, or marchants prentise, citizen, welthy farmer, or other of good credit, ether accompanie with any woman familiarly, or els hath gotten some mayd with child, as mens natures be prone to sin, straight they come over his fallowes thus, they sende for hym to a tavern, and there open the matter unto him, which they have cunningly leaned out, telling him he must be presented to the Arches, and the scitation shalbe peremptorilie served in his parish church. The partie afraid to have his credit crackt with the worshipful of the citie, and the rest of his neighbors, and grieving highly his wife should heare of it, straight takes composition with this cosener for some xx. marke, nay I heard ix. pound cros-bitten at one time, and then the coosening informer or cros-biter promiseth to wipe him out of the court, and discharge him from the matter, when it was neither knowen nor presented: so go they to the woman, and fetch her off if she be married, and though they have this grosse summe, yet oft times they cros-bite her for more: nay thus doe they feare cittizens, prentices and farmers, that they finde but anie way suspicious of the like fault.

ROBERT GREENE, *A Notable Discovery of Cosenage*, 1591/2

MOLL CUTPURSE

The age of Shakespeare produced many admirable artists in crime; yet none of them was more bravely characteristic of the age than was Mary Frith, the famous Moll Cutpurse, a true Elizabethan in courage and flamboyancy of spirit. Everything about her was great—her knowledge, her voice, her heart. She was born four years after the destruction of the Armada, and she died a brief year before the return of Charles II to his rightful throne. Her activities thus covered a long period, and as she was the heroine of a comedy of Middleton, so, says rumour, with her own voice she bade the rebel Fairfax stand and deliver. A woman neither in kind nor manner, she well earned her title of 'Roaring Girl', and she was ready to drink her tobacco or draw her sword with any roysterer in London. 'She has the spirit of four great parishes,' says the dramatist, 'and a voice that will draw all the city.' She cherished also a natural love of skill, and did her best, by discouraging the Nip, to admit the Foist to the fullness of his glory. 'The best signs and marks of a happy industrious hand', she wrote, 'is a long middle finger equally suited with what they call the fool's or first finger.' Later artists called these twain 'the forks'. But it was not long before Moll retired from the eager practice of her craft. She quickly discovered that hers were the gifts of command and government, and thus she made herself the head of a vast gang, which for many years was a terror to Brentford and Shooter's Hill. Not merely did she plan the robberies which her henchmen carried out, but she disposed of their purchases, either to their just owners, if the reward were sufficient, or to certain cunning merchants whom she knew. Thus for many years she ruled the underworld of England with an iron hand, and in the heyday of her youth shared the sovereignty of the realm not unfittingly with the austere, implacable Elizabeth herself.

CHARLES WHIBLEY, 'Rogues and Vagabonds', in *Shakespeare's England*, 1916

† *In* The Roaring Girl *by Middleton and Dekker, Moll Cutpurse is an early feminist and a somewhat heroic character.*

TRAPDOOR. My doxy stays for me in a boozing ken, brave captain.

MOLL. He says his wench stays for him in an ale-house.—[*To Trapdoor, Tearcat*] You are no pure rogues.

TEARCAT. Pure rogues? No, we scorn to be pure rogues; but if you come to our libken, or our stalling-ken, you shall find neither him nor me a queer cuffin.

MOLL. So, sir, no churl of you.

TEARCAT. No, but a ben cove, a brave cove, a gentry cuffin.

LORD NOLAND. Call you this canting?

JACK DAPPER. Zounds, I'll give a schoolmaster half a crown a week and teach me this pedlar's French.

TRAPDOOR. Do but stroll, sir, half a harvest with us, sir, and you shall gabble your bellyful.

MOLL [*to Trapdoor*]. Come you rogue, cant with me.

SIR THOMAS. Well said, Moll.—[*To Trapdoor*] Cant with her, sirrah, and you shall have money—else not a penny.

TRAPDOOR. I'll have a bout if she please.

MOLL. Come on, sirrah.

TRAPDOOR. Ben mort, shall you and I heave a booth, mill a ken, or nip a bung? And then we'll couch a hogshead under the ruffmans, and there you shall wap with me, and I'll niggle with you.

MOLL. Out, you damned impudent rascal! [*Hits and kicks him.*

TRAPDOOR. Cut benar whids, and hold your fambles and your stamps!

LORD NOLAND. Nay, nay, Moll, why art thou angry? What was his gibberish?

MOLL. Marry, this, my lord, says he: 'Ben mort'—good wench—'shall you and I heave a booth, mill a ken, or nip a bung?'—shall you and I rob a house, or cut a purse?

ALL. Very good!

MOLL. 'And then we'll couch a hogshead under the ruffmans,'—and then we'll lie under a hedge.

TRAPDOOR. That was my desire, captain, as 'tis fit a soldier should lie.

MOLL. 'And there you shall wap with me, and I'll niggle with you,'—and that's all.

SIR BEAUTEOUS. Nay, nay, Moll, what's that wap?
JACK DAPPER. Nay, teach me what niggling is; I'd fain be niggling.
MOLL. Wapping and niggling is all one: the rogue my man can tell you.
TRAPDOOR. 'Tis fadoodling, if it please you.
SIR BEAUTEOUS. This is excellent; one fit more, good Moll.

THOMAS MIDDLETON and THOMAS DEKKER, *The Roaring Girl*, ?1611

MOLL'S CONFESSION

Officium Domini contra Mariam ffrithe

This day & place the sayd Mary appeared personally & then & there voluntarily confessed that she had long frequented all or most of the disorderly & licentious places in this Cittie as namely she hath usually in the habit of a man resorted to alehowses Taverns Tobacco shops & also to play howses there to see plaies & pryses & namely being at a playe about 3 quarters of a yeare since at the ffortune in mans apparell & in her bootes & with a sword by her syde, she told the company there present that she thought many of them were of opinion that she was a man, but if any of them would come to her lodging they should finde that she is a woman & some other immodest & lascivious speaches she also used at that time. And also sat there uppon the stage in the publique viewe of all the people there presente in mans apparrell & played uppon her lute & sange a songe. And she further confessed that she hath for this longe time past usually blasphemed & dishonored the name of God by swearing & cursing & by tearing God out of his kingdome yf it were possible, & hath also usually associated her selfe with Ruffinly swaggering & lewd company as namely with cut purses blasphemous drunkardes & others of bad note & of most dissolute behaviour with whom she hath to the great shame of her sexe often tymes (as she sayd) drunke hard & distempered her head with drinke And further confesseth that since she was punished for the misdemeanors afore mentioned in Bridewell she was since upon Christmas day at night taken in Powles Church with her peticoate tucked up about her in the fashion of a man with a mans cloake on her to the great scandall of divers persons who understood the same & to the disgrace of all womanhood And she sayeth & protesteth that she is heartely sory for her foresayd licentious & dissolute lyfe & giveth her earnest promise to carry & behave her selfe ever from hence forwarde honestly soberly & womanly & resteth ready to undergo any censure or punishement for her misdemeanors afore sayd in suche manner & forme as shalbe assigned her by the Lo: Bishop of London her Ordinary. And then she being pressed to declare whether she had not byn dishonest of her body & hath not also drawne other women to lewdnes by her perswasions & by carrying her self lyke a bawde, she absolutly denied that she was chargeable with eyther of these imputacions. And thereuppon his Lordship. thought fit to remand her to Bridewell from whence she nowe came untill he might further examine the truth of the misdemeanors inforced against her without laying as yet any further censure uppon her.

The Consistory of London Correction Book, 1612

That thief, the summoner (the friar went on)
Had pimps ever ready at his beck and call,
Like lures to fetch a hawk; and they'd tell all
The secrets that they came across, or knew;
For their acquaintanceship was nothing new.
They served as his informers; secretly
He won himself a great profit thereby;
The archdeacon didn't always know how much.
For he could summons some illiterate
Without a written warrant, on the threat
Of excommunication and Christ's curse;
And they were glad enough to fill his purse,
And stand him dinners at the alehouses.
And just as Judas kept his Master's purse,
And was a thief, just such a thief was he;
The archdeacon got less than half his fee.
He was, if I'm to give him his just due,
A thief; a pimp; and a summoner too.
Moreover, he had harlots at command,
And so, if Reverend Robert, or Reverend
Hugh, Tom, Dick, or Harry, or whoever
Had one of them, it reached the summoner's ear;
Then, since the girl and he were in collusion,
He'd whip out a faked document to summon
The pair before the chapter court; and so

He'd fleece the man, and let the woman go.
And then he'd say to him, 'Friend, for your sake
I'll see her name is struck from our black list.
Trouble yourself no further about this;
Remember I'm your friend, and at your service.'
To tell of all the fiddles that he knew
Would take a year at least, or maybe two.
And there's no hunting dog on earth that's better
At picking from the herd a wounded deer,
Than he at finding an adulterer,
A concubine, or some sly whoremonger.
And since he got most of his income from it,
He gave his full attention to the matter.

GEOFFREY CHAUCER, 'The Friar's Tale', *c.*1387, trans. David Wright

I rambl'd this whole Night with them, they went from *Chelsea*, being disappointed there as above, to *Kensington*; there they broke into a Brew-house, and Wash-house, and by that means into an Out-Kitchen of a Gentleman's House, where they unhang'd a small Copper, and brought it off, and stole about a Hundred weight of Pewter, and went clear off with that too, and every one going their own by-ways, they found means to get safe to their several Receptacles where they used to dispose of such things.

We lay still the next Day, and shar'd the Effects stolen that Night, of which my Share came to 8*l*. 19*s*. the Copper and Pewter being weigh'd, and cast up, a Person was at hand to take it as Money, at about half Value, and in the Afternoon, *Will* and I came away together: *Will* was mighty full of the Success we had had, and how we might be sure of the like this way every Day. But he observ'd that I did not seem so elevated at the Success of that Night's Ramble as I us'd to be, and also that I did not take any great Notice of the Expectations he was in, of what was to come, yet I had said little to him at that time.

But my Heart was full of the poor Woman's Case at *Kentish* Town, and I resolv'd, if possible to find her out, and give her her Money: With the abhorrence that fill'd my Mind at the Cruelty of that Act, there necessarily follow'd a little Distaste of the thing it self, and now it came into my Head with a double force, that this was the High

Road to the Devil, and that certainly this was not the Life of a Gentleman!

Will and I parted for that time, but next Morning we met again, and *Will* was mighty Brisk and Merry; and now Col. *Jack*, *says he*, we shall be Rich very quickly; well, *says I*, and what shall we do, when we are Rich? do, *says he*, we will buy a Couple of good Horses, and go farther a Field; what do you mean by farther a Field, *said I*? why, *says he*, we will take the Highway like Gentlemen, and then we shall get a great deal of Money indeed; well, *says I*, what then? why then, *says he*, we shall live like Gentlemen.

But *Will*, *says I*, if we get a great deal of Money, shan't we leave this Trade off, and sit down, and be Safe and Quiet?

Ay, says *Will*, when we have got a great Estate we shall be willing to lay it down; but where, *says I*, shall we be before that time comes, if we should drive on this cursed kind of Trade?

Prethee never think of that, *says Will*, if you think of those things, you will never be fit to be a Gentleman; he touch'd me there indeed, for it run much in my Mind still, that I was to be a Gentleman, and it made me Dumb for a while; but I came to my self after a little while, and I said to him, pretty Tartly, Why *Will*, do you call this way of Living the Life of a Gentleman?

Why, *says Will*, why not?

Why, *says I*, was it like a Gentleman for me to take that Two and Twenty Shillings from a poor antient Woman, when she beg'd of me upon her Knees not to take it, and told me it was all she had in the World to buy her Bread for her self and a sick Child which she had at home, do you think I could be so Cruel if you had not stood by, and made me do it? why, I cry'd at doing it, as much as the poor Woman did, tho' I did not let you see me.

You Fool you, *says Will*, you will never be fit for our Business indeed, if you mind such things as those, I shall bring you off of those things quickly; why, if you will be fit for Business, you must learn to fight when they resist, and cut their Throats when they submit; you must learn to stop their Breath, that they may beg and pray no more; what signifies pity? prethee, who will pity us when we come to the *Old-Baily*? I warrant you that whining old Woman that beg'd so heartily for her Two and Twenty Shillings would let you, or I beg upon our Knees, and would not save our Lives by not coming in for an Evidence against us; did you ever see any of them cry when they see Gentlemen go to the Gallows?

Well, *Will, says I*, you had better let us keep to the Business we were in before; there was no such cruel doings in that, and yet we got more Money by it, then I believe we shall get at this.

No, no, says *Will*, you are a Fool, you don't know what fine things we shall do in a little while.

DANIEL DEFOE, *The Life of Colonel Jack*, 1722

† *Jonathan Wild was baptized on 6 May 1683 and was executed before a record crowd at Tyburn in May 1725. During his life he controlled the London underworld, specializing in inducing criminals to rob and then claiming the rewards for informing on them and sending them to the gallows. He was also liberally rewarded for recovering property he had arranged to have stolen. He advertised himself proudly as 'Thief-Taker General of Great Britain and Ireland'. The Great Informer was the subject of a life by Fielding.*

There happened to be in the stage-coach in which Mr Wild traveled from Dover a certain young gentleman who had sold an estate in Kent, and was going to London to receive the money. There was likewise a handsome young woman who had left her parents at Canterbury, and was proceeding to the same city, in order (as she informed her fellow-travelers) to make her fortune. With this girl the young spark was so much enamored that he publicly acquainted her with the purpose of his journey, and offered her a considerable sum in hand and a settlement if she would consent to return with him into the country, where she would be at a safe distance from her relations. Whether she accepted this proposal or no we are not able with any tolerable certainty to deliver: but Wild, the moment he heard of his money, began to cast about in his mind by what means he might become master of it. He entered into a long harangue about the methods of carrying money safely on the road, and said, 'He had at that time two bank-bills of a hundred pounds each sewed in his coat; which,' added he, 'is so safe a way, that it is almost impossible I should be in any danger of being robbed by the most cunning highwayman.'

The young gentleman, who was no descendant of Solomon, or, if he was, did not, any more than some other descendants of wise men, inherit the wisdom of his ancestor, greatly approved Wild's ingenuity, and, thanking him for his information, declared he would follow his example when he returned into the country; by which means he proposed to save the premium commonly taken for the remittance. Wild had then no more to do but to inform himself rightly of the time of the gentleman's journey, which he did with great certainty before they separated.

At his arrival in town he fixed on two whom he regarded as the most resolute of his gang for this enterprise; and, accordingly, having summoned the principal, or most desperate, as he imagined him, of these two (for he never chose to communicate in the presence of more than one), he proposed to him the robbing and murdering this gentleman.

Mr Marybone (for that was the gentleman's name to whom he applied) readily agreed to the robbery, but he hesitated at the murder. He said, as to robbery, he had, on much weighing and considering the matter, very well reconciled his conscience to it; for, though that noble kind of robbery which was executed on the highway was, from the cowardice of mankind, less frequent, yet the baser and meaner species, sometimes called cheating, but more commonly known by the name of robbery within the law, was in a manner universal. He did not therefore pretend to the reputation of being so much honester than other people; but could by no means satisfy himself in the commission of murder, which was a sin of the most heinous nature, and so immediately prosecuted by God's judgment that it never passed undiscovered or unpunished.

Wild, with the utmost disdain in his countenance, answered as follows: 'Art thou he whom I have selected out of my whole gang for this glorious undertaking, and dost thou cant of God's revenge against murder? You have, it seems, reconciled your conscience (a pretty word) to robbery, from its being so common. Is it then the novelty of murder which deters you? Do you imagine that guns, and pistols, and swords, and knives, are the only instruments of death? Look into the world and see the numbers whom broken fortunes and broken hearts bring untimely to the grave. To omit those glorious heroes who, to their immortal honor, have massacred whole nations, what think you of private persecution, treachery, and slander, by which the very souls of men are in a manner torn from their bodies? Is it not more generous, nay, more good-natured, to send a man to his rest, than, after having plundered him of all he hath, or from malice or malevolence deprived him of his character, to punish him with a languishing death, or, what is worse, a languishing life? Murder, therefore, is not so uncommon as you weakly conceive it, though, as you said of robbery, that more noble kind which lies within the paw of the law may be so. But this is the most innocent in him who doth it, and the most eligible to him who is to suffer it. Believe me, lad, the tongue of a viper is less hurtful than that of a slanderer, and the gilded scales of a rattle-snake less dreadful than the purse of the oppressor. Let me therefore hear no more of your scruples; but consent to my proposal without further hesitation, unless, like a woman, you are afraid of blooding your clothes, or, like a fool, are terrified with the apprehensions of being hanged in chains. Take my word for it, you had better be an honest man than half a rogue. Do not think of continuing in my gang without abandoning yourself absolutely to my pleasure; for no man shall ever receive a favor at my hands who sticks at anything, or is guided by any other law than that of my will.'

Wild then ended his speech, which had not the desired effect on Marybone: he agreed to the robbery, but would not undertake the murder, as Wild (who feared that, by Marybone's demanding to search the gentleman's coat, he might hazard suspicion himself) insisted. Marybone was immediately entered by Wild in his black-book, and was presently after impeached and executed as a fellow on whom his leader could not place sufficient dependence; thus falling, as many rogues do, a sacrifice, not to his roguery, but to his conscience.

HENRY FIELDING, *The Life of Jonathan Wild the Great*, 1743

† *It is said that Jonathan Wild met John Gay in a Windsor tavern early in 1729. The poet plied the informer with wine, pretended to be a thief, and so discovered the character of Peachum in* The Beggar's Opera.

Peachum sitting at a table with a large book of accounts before him.

PEACHUM. *Through all the employments of life*
Each neighbour abuses his brother;
Whore and rogue they call husband and wife:
All professions be-rogue one another.
The priest calls the lawyer a cheat,
The lawyer be-knaves the divine;

And the statesman, because he's so great,
Thinks his trade as honest as mine.

A lawyer is an honest employment, so is mine. Like me too he acts in a double capacity, both against rogues and for 'em; for 'tis but fitting that we should protect and encourage cheats, since we live by them. . . .

Enter Filch

FILCH. Sir, Black Moll hath sent word her trial comes on in the afternoon, and she hopes you will order matters so as to bring her off.

PEACHUM. Why, she may plead her belly at worst; to my knowledge she hath taken care of that security. But as the wench is very active and industrious, you may satisfy her that I'll soften the evidence.

FILCH. Tom Gagg, sir, is found guilty.

PEACHUM. A lazy dog! When I took him the time before, I told him what he would come to if he did not mend his hand. This is death without reprieve. I may venture to book him. [*writes*] For Tom Gagg, forty pounds. Let Betty Sly know that I'll save her from transportation, for I can get more by her staying in England.

FILCH. Betty hath brought more goods into our lock to-year than any five of the gang; and in truth, 'tis a pity to lose so good a customer.

PEACHUM. If none of the gang take her off, she may, in the common course of business, live a twelve-month longer. I love to let women scape. A good sportsman always lets the hen partridges fly, because the breed of the game depends upon them. Besides, here the law allows us no reward; there is nothing to be got by the death of women—except our wives.

FILCH. Without dispute, she is a fine woman! 'Twas to her I was obliged for my education, and (to say a bold word) she hath trained up more young fellows to the business than the gaming-table.

PEACHUM. Truly, Filch, thy observation is right. We and the surgeons are more beholden to women than all the professions besides.

FILCH. *'Tis woman that seduces all mankind,*
By her we first were taught the wheedling arts:
Her very eyes can cheat; when most she's kind,
She tricks us of our money with our hearts.
For her, like wolves by night we roam for prey,
And practise ev'ry fraud to bribe her charms;

For suits of love, like law, are won by pay,
And beauty must be fee'd into our arms.

PEACHUM. But make haste to Newgate, boy, and let my friends know what I intend; for I love to make them easy one way or other.

FILCH. When a gentleman is long kept in suspense, penitence may break his spirit ever after. Besides, certainty gives a man a good air upon his trial, and makes him risk another without fear or scruple. But I'll away, for 'tis a pleasure to be the messenger of comfort to friends in affliction. [*Exit*.

PEACHUM. But 'tis now high time to look about me for a decent execution against next Sessions. I hate a lazy rogue, by whom one can get nothing 'till he is hanged. A register of the gang, [*reading*] Crook-fingered Jack. A year and a half in the service; let me see how much the stock owes to his industry; one, two, three, four, five gold watches, and seven silver ones. A mighty clean-handed fellow! Sixteen snuff-boxes, five of them of true gold. Six dozen of handkerchiefs, four silver-hilted swords, half a dozen of shirts, three tye-perriwigs, and a piece of broad cloth. Considering these are only the fruits of his leisure hours, I don't know a prettier fellow, for no man alive hath a more engaging presence of mind upon the road. Wat Dreary, alias Brown Will, an irregular dog, who hath an underhand way of disposing of his goods. I'll try him only for a Sessions or two longer upon his good behaviour. Harry Padington, a poor petty-larceny rascal, without the least genius; that fellow, though he were to live these six months, will never come to the gallows with any credit. Slippery Sam; he goes off the next Sessions, for the villain hath the impudence to have views of following his trade as a tailor, which he calls an honest employment. Mat of the Mint; listed not above a month ago, a promising sturdy fellow, and diligent in his way; somewhat too bold and hasty, and may raise good contributions on the public, if he does not cut himself short by murder. Tom Tipple, a guzzling soaking sot, who is always too drunk to stand himself, or to make others stand. A cart is absolutely necessary for him. Robin of Bagshot, alias Gorgon, alias Bluff Bob, alias Carbuncle, alias Bob Booty.

Enter Mrs Peachum

MRS PEACHUM. What of Bob Booty, husband? I hope nothing bad hath betided him. You know, my dear, he's a favourite customer of mine. 'Twas he made me a present of this ring.

PEACHUM. I have set his name down in the Black-List, that's all, my dear; he spends his life among women, and as soon as his money is gone, one or other of the ladies will hang him for the reward, and there's forty pound lost to us forever.

MRS PEACHUM. You know, my dear, I never meddle in matters of death; I always leave those affairs to you. Women indeed are bitter bad judges in these cases, for they are so partial to the brave that they think every man handsome who is going to the camp or the gallows.

JOHN GAY, *The Beggar's Opera*, 1728

† *Two hundred years later Wild-Peachum reappeared in Brecht's* Threepenny Opera, *and Gay's highwayman Macheath was reborn as Mac the Knife.*

Fair in Soho. The beggars are begging, the thieves are stealing, the whores are whoring. A ballad singer sings a ballad.

See the shark with teeth like razors.
All can read his open face.
And Macheath has got a knife, but
Not in such an obvious place.

See the shark, how red his fins are
As he slashes at his prey.
Mac the Knife wears white kid gloves which
Give the minimum away.

By the Thames's turbid waters
Men abruptly tumble down.
Is it plague or is it cholera?
Or a sign Macheath's in town?

On a beautiful blue Sunday
See a corpse stretched in the Strand.
See a man dodge round the corner . . .
Mackie's friends will understand.

And Schmul Meier, reported missing
Like so many wealthy men:
Mac the Knife acquired his cash box.
God alone knows how or when.

[*Peachum goes walking across the stage from left to right with his wife and daughter.*

Jenny Towler turned up lately
With a knife stuck through her breast
While Macheath walks the Embankment
Nonchalantly unimpressed.

Where is Alfred Gleet the cabman?
Who can get that story clear?
All the world may know the answer
Just Macheath has no idea.

And the ghastly fire in Soho—
Seven children at a go—
In the crowd stands Mac the Knife, but he
Isn't asked and doesn't know.

And the child-bride in her nightie
Whose assailant's still at large
Violated in her slumbers—
Mackie, how much did you charge?

[*Laughter among the whores. A man steps out from their midst and walks quickly away across the square.*

LOW-DIVE JENNY. That was Mac the Knife!

Jonathan Jeremiah Peachum's outfitting shop for beggars.

PEACHUM'S MORNING HYMN

You ramshackle Christian, awake!
Get on with your sinful employment
Show what a good crook you could make.
The Lord will cut short your enjoyment.

Betray your own brother, you rogue
And sell your old woman, you rat.
You think the Lord God's just a joke?
He'll give you His Judgement on that.

PEACHUM [*to the audience*]. Something new is needed. My business is too hard, for my business is arousing human sympathy. There are a few things that stir men's souls, just a few, but the trouble is that after repeated use they lose their effect. Because man has the abominable gift of being able to deaden his feelings at will, so to speak. Suppose, for instance, a man sees another man standing on the corner with a stump for an arm; the first time he may be shocked enough to give him tenpence, but the second time it will only be fivepence, and if he sees him a third time he'll hand him over to the police without batting an eyelash. It's the same with the spiritual approach. [*A large sign saying 'It is more blessed to give than to receive' is lowered from the grid*.] What good are the most beautiful, the most poignant sayings, painted on the most enticing little signs, when they get expended so quickly? The Bible has four or five sayings that stir the heart; once a man has expended them, there's nothing for it but starvation. Take this one, for instance—'Give and it shall be given unto you'—how threadbare it is after hanging here a mere three weeks. Yes, you have to keep on offering something new. So it's back to the good old Bible again, but how long can it go on providing?

[*Knocking*. *Peachum opens*. *Enter a young man by the name of Filch*.

FILCH. Messrs Peachum & Co.?

PEACHUM. Peachum.

FILCH. Are you the proprietor of The Beggar's Friend Ltd.? I've been sent to you. Fine slogans you've got there! Money in the bank, those are. Got a whole library full of them, I suppose? That's what I call really something. What chance has a bloke like me got to think up ideas like that; and how can business progress without education?

PEACHUM. What's your name?

FILCH. It's this way, Mr Peachum, I've been down on my luck since a boy. Mother drank, father gambled. Left to my own resources at an early age, without a mother's tender hand, I sank deeper and deeper into the quicksands of the big city. I've never known a father's care or the blessings of a happy home. So now you see me . . .

PEACHUM. So now I see you . . .

FILCH [*confused*]. . . . bereft of all support, a prey to my baser instincts.

PEACHUM. Like a derelict on the high seas and so on. Now tell me, derelict, which district have you been reciting that fairy story in?

FILCH. What do you mean, Mr Peachum?

PEACHUM. You deliver that speech in public, I take it?

FILCH. Well, it's this way, Mr Peachum, yesterday there was an unpleasant little incident in Highland Street. There I am, standing on the corner quiet and miserable, holding out my hat, no suspicion of anything nasty . . .

PEACHUM [*leafs through a notebook*]. Highland Street. Yes, yes, right. You're the bastard that Honey and Sam caught yesterday. You had the impudence to be molesting passers-by in District 10. We let you off with a thrashing because we had reason to believe you didn't know what's what. But if you show your face again it'll be the chop for you. Got it?

FILCH. Please, Mr Peachum, please. What can I do, Mr Peachum? The gentlemen beat me black and blue and then they gave me your business card. If I took off my coat, you'd think you were looking at a fish on a slab.

PEACHUM. My friend, if you're not flat as a kipper, then my men weren't doing their job properly. Along come these young whipper-snappers who think they've only got to hold out their paw to land a steak. What would you say if someone started fishing the best trout out of your pond?

FILCH. It's like this, Mr Peachum—I haven't got a pond.

PEACHUM. Licences are delivered to professionals only. [*Points in a businesslike way to a map of the city.*] London is divided into fourteen districts. Any man who intends to practise the craft of begging in any one of them needs a licence from Jonathan Jeremiah Peachum & Co. Why, anybody could come along—a prey to his baser instincts.

FILCH. Mr Peachum, only a few shillings stand between me and utter ruin. Something must be done. With two shillings in my pocket I . . .

PEACHUM. One pound.

FILCH. Mr Peachum!

[*Points imploringly at a sign saying 'Do not turn a deaf ear to misery!' Peachum points to the curtain over a showcase, on which is written: 'Give and it shall be given unto you!'*

FILCH. Ten bob.

PEACHUM. Plus fifty per cent of your take, settle up once a week. With outfit seventy per cent.

FILCH. What does the outfit consist of?

PEACHUM. That's for the firm to decide.
FILCH. Which district could I start in?
PEACHUM. Baker Street. Numbers 2 to 104. That comes even cheaper. Only fifty per cent, including the outfit.

BERTOLT BRECHT, *The Threepenny Opera*, 1928, trans Ralph Manheim and John Willett

'Well,' said the Jew, glancing slyly at Oliver, and addressing himself to the Dodger, 'I hope you've been at work this morning, my dears?'

'Hard,' replied the Dodger.

'As Nails,' added Charley Bates.

'Good boys, good boys!' said the Jew. 'What have *you* got, Dodger?'

'A couple of pocket-books,' replied that young gentleman.

'Lined?' inquired the Jew, with eagerness.

'Pretty well,' replied the Dodger, producing two pocket-books; one green, and the other red.

'Not so heavy as they might be,' said the Jew, after looking at the insides carefully; 'but very neat and nicely made. Ingenious workman, ain't he, Oliver?'

'Very, indeed, sir,' said Oliver. At which Mr Charles Bates laughed uproariously; very much to the amazement of Oliver, who saw nothing to laugh at, in anything that had passed.

'And what have you got, my dear?' said Fagan to Charley Bates.

'Wipes,' replied Master Bates; at the same time producing four pocket-handkerchiefs.

'Well,' said the Jew, inspecting them closely; 'they're very good ones, very. You haven't marked them well, though, Charley; so the marks shall be picked out with a needle, and we'll teach Oliver how to do it. Shall us, Oliver, eh? Ha! ha! ha!'

'If you please, sir,' said Oliver.

'You'd like to be able to make pocket-handkerchiefs as easy as Charley Bates, wouldn't you, my dear?' said the Jew.

'Very much, indeed, if you'll teach me, sir,' replied Oliver.

Master Bates saw something so exquisitely ludicrous in this reply, that he burst into another laugh; which laugh, meeting the coffee he was drinking, and carrying it down some wrong channel, very nearly terminated in his premature suffocation.

'He is so jolly green!' said Charley when he recovered, as an apology to the company for his unpolite behaviour.

The Dodger said nothing, but he smoothed Oliver's hair over his eyes, and said he'd know better, by-and-by; upon which the old gentleman, observing Oliver's colour mounting, changed the subject by asking whether there had been much of a crowd at the execution that morning? This made him wonder more and more; for it was plain from the replies of the two boys that they had both been there; and Oliver naturally wondered how they could possibly have found time to be so very industrious.

When the breakfast was cleared away, the merry old gentleman and the two boys played at a very curious and uncommon game, which was performed in this way. The merry old gentleman, placing a snuff-box in one pocket of his trousers, a note-case in the other, and a watch in his waistcoat pocket, with a guard-chain round his neck, and sticking a mock diamond pin in his shirt: buttoned his coat tight round him, and putting his spectacle-case and handkerchief in his pockets, trotted up and down the room with a stick, in imitation of the manner in which old gentlemen walk about the streets any hour in the day. Sometimes he stopped at the fire-place, and sometimes at the door, making believe that he was staring with all his might into shop-windows. At such times, he would look constantly round him, for fear of thieves, and would keep slapping all his pockets in turn, to see that he hadn't lost anything, in such a very funny and natural manner, that Oliver laughed till the tears ran down his face. All this time, the two boys followed him closely about: getting out of his sight, so nimbly, every time he turned round, that it was impossible to follow their motions. At last, the Dodger trod upon his toes, or ran upon his boot accidentally, while Charley Bates stumbled up against him behind; and in that one moment they took from him, with the most extraordinary rapidity, snuff-box, note-case, watch-guard, chain, shirt-pin, pocket-handkerchief, even the spectacle-case. If the old gentleman felt a hand in any one of his pockets, he cried out where it was; and then the game began all over again.

When this game had been played a great many times, a couple of young ladies called to see the young gentlemen; one of whom was named Bet, and the other Nancy. They wore a good deal of hair, not very neatly turned up behind, and were rather untidy about the shoes and stockings. They were not exactly pretty, perhaps; but they had a great deal of colour in their faces, and looked quite stout and hearty.

Being remarkably free and agreeable in their manners, Oliver thought them very nice girls indeed. As there is no doubt they were.

The visitors stopped a long time. Spirits were produced, in consequence of one of the young ladies complaining of a coldness in her inside; and the conversation took a very convivial and improving turn. At length, Charley Bates expressed his opinion that it was time to pad the hoof. This, it occurred to Oliver, must be French for going out; for, directly afterwards, the Dodger, and Charley, and the two young ladies, went away together, having been kindly furnished by the amiable old Jew with money to spend.

'There, my dear,' said Fagin. 'That's a pleasant life, isn't it? They have gone out for the day.'

'Have they done work, sir?' inquired Oliver.

'Yes,' said the Jew; 'that is, unless they should unexpectedly come across any, when they are out; and they won't neglect it, if they do, my dear, depend upon it. Make 'em your models, my dear. Make 'em your models,' tapping the fire-shovel on the hearth to add force to his words; 'do everything they bid you, and take their advice in all matters—especially the Dodger's, my dear. He'll be a great man himself, and will make you one too, if you take pattern by him.—Is my handkerchief hanging out of my pocket, my dear?' said the Jew, stopping short.

'Yes, sir,' said Oliver.

'See if you can take it out, without my feeling it: as you saw them do, when we were at play this morning.'

Oliver held up the bottom of the pocket with one hand, as he had seen the Dodger hold it, and drew the handkerchief lightly out of it with the other.

'Is it gone?' cried the Jew.

'Here it is, sir,' said Oliver, showing it in his hand.

'You're a clever boy, my dear,' said the playful old gentleman, patting Oliver on the head approvingly. 'I never saw a sharper lad. Here's a shilling for you. If you go on, in this way, you'll be the greatest man of the time. And now come here, and I'll show you how to take the marks out of the handkerchiefs.'

Oliver wondered what picking the old gentleman's pocket in play, had to do with his chances of being a great man. But, thinking that the Jew, being so much his senior, must know best, he followed him quietly to the table, and was soon deeply involved in his new study.

CHARLES DICKENS, *Oliver Twist*, 1837–8

† *Laurie Taylor, accompanied by the reformed criminal John McVicar, interviews Phil, a villain, on the subject of robbing banks.*

'I'll tell you something you don't know. There's only 50 people in this country with the ability, facilities and temperament to go out and rob a bank. People who've had the training. Well, there's a lot more, but they're all inside. But I'd say the hard core for that type of crime is 50. You, John, would know 30 of those people and I'd know 20. The rest would be known to each other.'

John was looking a little uncertain. This was his area as well as Phil's.

'Oh no, John—it *is* complicated. Fucking complicated. Oh yeah. Certainly to an everyday person.' He didn't have to look far to find a handy example. 'Take Laurie. If I said to Laurie, "OK, let's rob a bank." Even if he has the ability and even the facilities, what he hasn't got is the training, the expertise.'

John still shook his head unhappily. I wondered why he'd chosen to take issue with his ex-partner over the matter. Surely he'd be only too happy to allow that some special skills had been needed in his long criminal career? Nobody was more likely than him to look down upon the petty thieves he referred to as gas-meter bandits or the undisciplined robbers who were dismissed as cowboys.

'Come on, John. People don't . . . you know, you don't get people at 35 years of age getting together and saying, "Right, we'll rob a bank. Which one shall we do? Right off we go." On television they do. But it doesn't happen.'

When John disagrees, he gets quieter. Eventually he just sits there silently until the person he disagrees with modifies or qualifies his position. It was refreshing to see someone else being wound up by it for a change. Phil tried the shot from another angle.

'Look, John. You know and I know what it's like when you get under pressure—for those three minutes—when the coup is on, when you've got the whole weight of the Metropolitan police and the whole of the world's resources against you. When it's just four of you against the world for those three minutes. A lot of them just fall to bits.'

John nodded. We were back in conversational business. And I realized his objection to Phil's 'training'. It got in the way of the characteristic that he wanted right at the centre of the enterprise. All right, you might have to learn a few simple things to go to work as a robber, but these could be picked up by anyone in a couple of hours; they were as nothing alongside that essential characteristic of 'nerve'. That was what kept the number of armed robbers down to 50. That was what he'd shared with Phil.

'You mean the robbers have got to have *macho*?' (I pronounced it 'matcho' the way they did at the Landsdowne Club.) Up went Phil's eyebrows.

'Not at all.' He pulled himself up from the plump depths of his armchair. 'He's got to be the right guy under pressure. That's all. I used to go to work with a little poofy homosexual weakling who was absolutely superb. I've seen others—big men—who couldn't do it. Their nerve went.'

He reminded John of a bank robbery in Islington. (Unlike con men, robbers don't always go in for 'Lloyds' or 'Barclays': their raids are sufficiently few and far between to be remembered by place. 'Were you on the Wembley job?' 'Oh yes, wasn't he the one that did Hammersmith.') On the Islington raid, this 'little poofy weakling'—Michael—was squeezed into a children's pram, pushed into the bank by one of the gang and then left to leap out at the critical moment to add his share of terror.

But wasn't that macho in a way, I wanted to know? Being tough. Ready for action.

'No, no, no!' John and Phil were back together again. 'Robbers are into risks,' John explained. 'That's their game. They're not into combat for its own sake. That sort of macho is what you find in a gangster. *Risk* and *combat*.' He underlined the terms for me. And started to write the paragraphs. 'That's the distinction between robbers and gangsters, between people like Phil here and Ronnie Kray.'

I persisted. 'I'm sure most people would call it macho though. All that crashing into the bank and firing guns.'

'Yeah, but that's only the couple of minutes you're in the bank,' insisted Phil.

'Well, then, there's all the rushing out, jumping into getaway cars and screaming off through red lights.' I knew my Sweeney, all right.

Phil went measured. Almost pedantic. 'No, no. In many many circumstances you never drive fast away from anywhere. That's almost a rule.'

'But surely you choose people because they're crack drivers?'

'No. You choose drivers because they're people who will sit there nice and cool outside the bank while all those fireworks are happening in there and the police are coming down the road. The most important thing in a driver is that he stays there and never leaves you. Remember Luton, John?'

'What was that?' I could see John half wanted to play old times with Phil, particularly when it would help to make a point against me, but he hesitated.

'That one looked impregnable,' said Phil. John still hesitated.

'Why was it impregnable?' I asked Phil.

'Because . . . because . . . well because it was a big clearing bank for the area, so you not only had tellers and all that, you had people up on the balcony walking around.'

John capitulated. Enthusiastically. '*Yeah*. What about when I pulled that shot-gun out. Just before I pulled it out, I was on the way in. I'm in the doorway. And this geezer was . . .'

'Oh yes. He was coming out.'

'That's right, Phil. He was the gasman, wasn't he? He had a bagful of shillings that he'd been changing. I said, "Oh excuse me a moment." In the doorway. He went: "Oh yes, certainly." And he backed off and I pulled the shot-gun out.'

'But you let him out of the bank. He went off.'

'Did I?' John was laughing now. 'Did I let him out?'

'Yeah. I had to go out and run down the road and bring him back in again. And then I took his money off him.'

'Did you?' John rubbed his hands together at the memory. 'You took that little bag of shillings? All his gas money?' . . .

Phil and John and other robbers like them weren't just working for cash: they were fighting authority. Not in any genuine revolutionary sense—but as a way of asserting themselves against some notional system. They had no alternative but to break the rules: this was how they came to be themselves.

'What did *you* like best about it, John?' I'd pressed the question at him as we were coming to the end of our long session with Phil, the week before.

'Well it wasn't the money, Laurie. Not money. I'll tell you, I used to get a kick . . . especially when I was on the run . . . I used to get a buzz out of being wanted and outwitting them. Being around and surviving—not hiding like an animal in hibernation, but going out on the pavement and making out. I didn't feel superior, but I was playing another game to the one I presented. And most people are not playing another game. What you see is what they are; they're living the same lives as you see. The real criminal isn't: he's play-acting for most people, because his real life, what he really is, is hidden from most people.'

Phil had taken up the thread. 'Ah yes. Like when I was in Marbella with my normal girlfriend and my normal friends. All normal. And none of them knew. Not one. It's like Clark Kent, isn't it? Glasses off and all that.' He laughed nostalgically, and went on.

'Oh yes. Nobody knew, you know. It's like Zorro. He does it, then he totally disappears. Then it's all speculation. People sitting around everywhere. They catch a glimpse and say, "Look! Look! That was a bank robber." And then he's gone. And the bank robber can say to himself, "Yeah that was *me*, but you don't know that." That's why bank robbers all read the papers the next day. They have to make sure it was them. You can guarantee a lot who get arrested still have their Press clippings all folded up at home.'

He was still talking as he led John and myself down the hallway, along the wall-to-wall lime-green carpet. 'D'you know?' he said as he undid the double Chubb to let us out, 'I'm so fucking bored. Miss it all. I went out only last week to see the bank manager about some money I wanted for an investment. There I was, asking him nice and politely. And I suddenly thought: *Fuck me. Two years ago I would have jumped over the counter and helped myself.*'

LAURIE TAYLOR, *In the Underworld*, 1984

THE EPITAPH IN FORM OF A BALLAD

Which Villon made for himself and his comrades, expecting to be hanged along with them.

Men, brother men, that after us yet live,
  Let not your hearts too hard against us be;
For if some pity of us poor men ye give,
  The sooner God shall take of you pity.
  Here are we five or six strung up, you see,
And here the flesh that all too well we fed
Bit by bit eaten and rotten, rent and shred,
  And we the bones grow dust and ash withal;
Let no man laugh at us discomforted,
  But pray to God that he forgive us all.

If we call on you, brothers, to forgive,
  Ye should not hold our prayer in scorn, though we
Were slain by law; ye know that all alive
  Have not wit alway to walk righteously;
  Make therefore intercession heartily
With him that of a virgin's womb was bred,
That his grace be not as a dry well-head
  For us, nor let hell's thunder on us fall;
We are dead, let no man harry or vex us dead,
  But pray to God that he forgive us all.

The rain has washed and laundered us all five,
  And the sun dried and blackened; yea, per die,
Ravens and pies with beaks that rend and rive,
Have dug our eyes out, and plucked off for fee
  Our beards and eyebrows; never are we free,
  Not once, to rest; but here and there still sped,
Drive at its wild will by the wind's change led,
  More pecked of birds than fruits on garden-wall.
Men, for God's love, let no gibe here be said,
  But pray to God that he forgive us all.

Prince Jesus, that of all art lord and head,
Keep us, that hell be not our bitter bed;
  We have nought to do in such a master's hall.
Be not yet therefore our fellowhead,
  But pray to God that he forgive us all.

FRANÇOIS VILLON, *c.*1463, trans. Algernon Charles Swinburne

He leaned across the desk and flicked me across the face backhanded, casually and contemptuously, not meaning to hurt me, and the small smile stayed on his face. Then, when I didn't even move for that, he sat down slowly and leaned an elbow on the desk and cupped his brown chin in his brown hand. The bird-bright eyes stared at me without anything in them but brightness.

'Know who I am, cheapie?'

'Your name's Menendez. The boys call you Mendy. You operate on the Strip.'

'Yeah? How did I get so big?'

'I wouldn't know. You probably started out as a pimp in a Mexican whorehouse.'

He took a gold cigarette case out of his pocket and lit a brown cigarette with a gold lighter. He blew acrid smoke and nodded. He put the gold cigarette case on the desk and caressed it with his fingertips.

'I'm a big bad man, Marlowe. I make lots of dough. I got to make lots of dough to juice the guys I got to juice in order to make lots of dough to juice the guys I got to juice. I got a place in Bel-Air that cost ninety grand and I already spent more than that to fix it up. I got a lovely platinum blonde wife and two kids in private schools back east. My wife's got a hundred and fifty grand in rocks and another seventy-five in furs and clothes. I got a butler, two maids, a cook, a chauffeur, not counting the monkey that walks behind me. Everywhere I go I'm a darling. The best of everything, the best food, the best drinks, the best clothes, the best hotel suites. I got a place in Florida and a sea-going yacht with a crew of five men. I got a Bentley, two Cadillacs, a Chrysler station wagon, and an MG for my boy. Couple of years my girl gets one too. What you got?'

'Not much,' I said. 'This year I have a house to live in—all to myself.'

'No woman?'

'Just me. In addition to that I have what you see here and twelve hundred dollars in the bank and a few thousand in bonds. That answer your question?'

'What's the most you ever made on a single job?'

'Eight-fifty.'

'Jesus, how cheap can a guy get?'

RAYMOND CHANDLER, *The High Window*, 1942

He gave me a most tremendous dip and roll, so that the church jumped over its own weather-cock. Then, he held me by the arms in an upright position on the top of the stone, and went on in these fearful terms:

'You bring me, to-morrow morning early, that file and them wittles. You bring the lot to me, at that old Battery over yonder. You do it, and you never dare to say a word or dare to make a sign concerning your having seen such a person as me, or any person sumever, and you shall be let to live. You fail, or you go from my words in any partickler, no matter how small it is, and your heart and your liver shall be tore out, roasted and ate. Now, I ain't alone, as you may think I am. There's a young man hid with me, in comparison with which young man I am a Angel. That young man hears the words I speak. That young man has a secret way pecooliar to himself, of getting at a boy, and at his heart, and at his liver. It is in wain for a boy to attempt to hide himself from that young man. A boy may lock his door, may be warm in bed, may tuck himself up, may draw the clothes over his head, may think himself comfortable and safe, but that young man will softly creep and creep his way to him and tear him open. I am a keeping that young man from harming of you at the present moment, with great difficulty. I find it wery hard to hold that young man off of your inside. Now, what do you say?'

I said that I would get him the file, and I would get him what broken bits of food I could, and I would come to him at the Battery, early in the morning.

CHARLES DICKENS, *Great Expectations*, 1861

† *In this scene from* The Third Man, *Rollo Martins—or Holly Martin, as he is called in the film—catches up with his old friend Harry Lime and takes a turn with him on the Big Wheel in the Prater Gardens. The setting is post war Vienna, where Harry Lime has made a great deal of money through his involvement in a penicillin racket. The famous lines setting the glories resulting from Renaissance villainy against peaceful Switzerland's one contribution to world culture—the cuckoo clock—(spoken at this point in the film) were written in by Orson Welles.*

Don't picture Harry Lime as a smooth scoundrel. He wasn't that. The picture I have of him on my file is an excellent one: he is caught by a street photographer with his stocky legs apart, big shoulders a little hunched, a belly that has known too much good food for too long, on his face a look of cheerful rascality, a geniality, a recognition that *his* happiness will make the world's day. Now he didn't make the mistake of putting out a hand that might have been rejected, but instead just patted Martins on the elbow and said, 'How are things?'

'We've got to talk, Harry.'

'Of course.'

'Alone.'

'We couldn't be more alone than here.'

He had always known the ropes, and even in the smashed pleasure park he knew them, tipping the woman in charge of the Wheel, so that they might have a car to themselves. He said, 'Lovers used to do this in the old days, but they haven't the money to spare, poor devils, now,' and he looked out of the window of the swaying, rising car at the figures diminishing below with what looked like genuine commiseration.

Very slowly on one side of them the city sank; very slowly on the other the great cross-girders of the Wheel rose into sight. As the horizon slid away the Danube became visible, and the piers of the Kaiser Friedrich Brücke lifted above the houses. 'Well,' Harry said, 'it's good to see you, Rollo.'

'I was at your funeral.'

'That was pretty smart of me, wasn't it?'

'Not so smart for your girl. She was there too—in tears.'

'She's a good little thing,' Harry said. 'I'm very fond of her.'

'I didn't believe the police when they told me about you.'

Harry said, 'I wouldn't have asked you to come if I'd known what was going to happen, but I didn't think the police were on to me.'

'Were you going to cut me in on the spoils?'

'I've never kept you out of anything, old man, yet.' He stood with his back to the door as the car swung upwards, and smiled back at Rollo Martins, who could remember him in just such an attitude in a secluded corner of the school quad, saying, 'I've learned a way to get out at night. It's absolutely safe. You are the only one I'm letting in on it.' For the first time Rollo Martins looked back through the years without admiration, as he thought: He's never grown up. Marlowe's devils wore squibs attached to their tails: evil was like Peter Pan—it carried with it the horrifying and horrible gift of eternal youth.

Martins said, 'Have you ever visited the children's hospital? Have you seen any of your victims?'

Harry took a look at the toy landscape below and came away from the door. 'I never feel quite safe in these things,' he said. He felt the back of the door with his hand, as though he were afraid that it might fly open and launch him into that iron-ribbed space. 'Victims?' he asked. 'Don't be melodramatic, Rollo. Look down there,' he went on, pointing through the window at the people moving like black flies at the base of the Wheel. 'Would you really feel any pity if one of those dots stopped moving—for ever? If I said you can have twenty thousand pounds for every dot that stops, would you really, old man, tell me to keep my money—without hesitation? Or would you calculate how many dots you could afford to spare? Free of income tax, old man. Free of income tax.' He gave his boyish conspiratorial smile. 'It's the only way to save nowadays.'

GRAHAM GREENE, *The Third Man*, 1950

That really good family, the Timsons, was out in force and waiting outside Number 1 Court by the time I had got on the fancy dress, yellowing horse-hair wig, gown become more than a trifle tattered over the years, and bands round the neck that Albert ought to have sent to the laundry after last week's death by dangerous driving. As I looked at the Timson clan assembled, I thought the best thing about them was the amount of work of a criminal nature they had brought into Chambers. They were all dressed for the occasion, the men in dark blazers, suede shoes and grey flannels; the ladies in tight-fitting suits, high heels and elaborately piled hairdos. I had never seen so many ex-clients together at one time.

'Mr Rumpole.'

'Ah, Bernard! You're instructing me.'

Mr Bernard, the solicitor, was a thirtyish, perpetually smiling man in a pinstriped suit. He regarded criminals with something of the naïve fervour with which young girls think of popular entertainers. Had I known the expression at the time, I would have called him a grafters' 'groupie'.

'I'm always your instructing solicitor in a Timson case, Mr Rumpole.' Mr Bernard beamed and Fred Timson, a kindly man and most innocent robber, stepped out of the ranks to do the honours.

'Nothing but the best for the Timsons, best solicitor and best barrister going. You know my wife Vi?'

Young Jim's mother seemed full of confidence. As I took her hand, I remembered I had got Vi off on a handling charge after the Croydon bank raid. Well, there was really no evidence.

'Uncle Cyril.' Fred introduced the plumpish uncle with the small moustache whom I was sure I remembered. What was *his* last outing exactly? Carrying house-breaking instruments by night?

'Uncle Dennis. You remember Den, surely, Mr Rumpole?'

I did. Den's last little matter was an alleged conspiracy to forge log books.

'And Den's Doris.'

Aunty Doris came at me in a blur of henna-ed hair and darkish perfume. What was Doris's last indiscretion? Could it have been receiving a vast quantity of stolen scampi? Acquitted by a majority, at least I was sure of that.

'And yours truly. Frederick Timson. The boy's father.'

Regrettable, but we had a slip-up with Fred's last spot of bother. I was away with flu, George Frobisher took it over and he got three years. He must've only just got out.

'So, Mr Rumpole. You know the whole family.'

A family to breed from, the Timsons. Must almost keep the Old Bailey going single-handed.

'You're going to do your best for our young Jim, I'm sure, Mr Rumpole.'

I didn't find the simple faith of the Timsons that I could secure acquittals in the most unlikely circumstances especially encouraging. But then Jim's mother said something which I was to long remember.

'He's a good boy. He was ever so good to me while Dad was away.'

So that was Jimbo's life. Head of the family at fourteen, when Dad was off on one of his regular visits to Her Majesty.

'It's young Jim's first appearance, like. At the Old Bailey.' Fred couldn't conceal a note of pride. It was Jim boy's Bar Mitzvah, his first Communion.

So we chatted a little about how all the other boys got clean away, which I told them was a bit of luck as none of them would go into the witness box and implicate Jim, and Bernard pointed out that the identification by the butchers was pretty hopeless. Well, what did he expect? Would you have a photographic impression of the young hopeful who struck you a smart blow on the back of the head with a cricket stump? We talked with that curious suppressed excitement there always is before a trial, however disastrous the outcome may be, and I told them the only thing we had to worry about, as if that were not enough, was Jim's confession to the boy in the Remand Centre, a youth who rejoiced in the name of Peanuts Malloy.

'Peanuts Malloy! Little grass.' Fred Timson spoke with a deep contempt.

'Old "Persil" White fitted him up with that one, didn't he?' Uncle

Cyril said as if it were the most natural thing in the world, and only to be expected.

'Chief Detective Inspector White,' Bernard explained.

'Why should the Chief Inspector want to fit up your Jimbo?' It was a question to which I should have known what their answer would be.

'Because he's a Timson, that's why!' said Fred.

'Because he's the apple of our eye, like,' Uncle Den told me, and the boy's mother added:

'Being as he's the baby of the family.'

'Old Persil'd fit up his mother if it'd get him a smile from his Super.' As Fred said this the Chief Inspector himself, grey-haired and avuncular, walked by in plain clothes, with a plain-clothes sergeant.

'Morning, Chief Inspector,' Fred carried on without drawing breath.

'Morning, Fred. Morning, Mrs Timson.' The Chief Inspector greeted the family with casual politeness, after all they were part of his daily work, and Vi sniffed back a 'Good morning, Chief Inspector.'

'Mr Timson. We'll shift our ground. Remove good friends.'

Like Hamlet, after seeing the ghost, I thought it was better to continue our conference in private. So we went and sat round a table in the canteen, and, when we had sorted out who took how many lumps, and which of them could do with a choc roll or a cheese sandwich, the family gave me the lowdown on the chief prosecution witness.

JOHN MORTIMER, 'Rumpole and the Younger Generation', 1978

† *Tom Ripley is Patricia Highsmith's attractive villain. In* Ripley Underground *he gets a letter about an art fraud he is engaged in. This spoils his extremely pleasant existence in France.*

104 Charles Place
N.W.8.

Dear Tom,

The new Derwatt show opens on Tuesday, the 15th, his first in two years. Bernard has nineteen new canvases and other pictures will be lent. Now for the bad news.

There is an American named Thomas Murchison, not a dealer but a collector—retired with plenty of lolly. He bought a Derwatt from us three years ago. He compared it with an earlier Derwatt he has just seen in the States, and now he says his is phoney. It is, of course, as it is one of Bernard's. He wrote to the Buckmaster Gallery (to me) saying he thinks the painting he has is not genuine, because the technique and colours belong to a period of five or six years ago in Derwatt's work. I have the distinct feeling Murchison intends to make a stink here. And what to do about it? You're always good on ideas, Tom.

Can you come over and talk to us? All expenses paid by the Buckmaster Gallery? We need an injection of confidence more than anything. I don't think Bernard has messed up any of the new canvases. But Bernard is in a flap, and we don't want him around even at the opening, especially at the opening.

Please come at once if you can

Best,

Jeff.

P.S. Murchison's letter was courteous, but supposing he's the kind who will insist on looking up Derwatt in Mexico to verify, etc?

The last was a point, Tom thought, because Derwatt didn't exist. The story (invented by Tom) which the Buckmaster Gallery and Derwatt's loyal little band of friends put out, was that Derwatt had gone to a tiny village in Mexico to live, and he saw no one, had no telephone, and forbade the gallery to give his address to anyone. Well, if Murchison went to Mexico, he would have an exhausting search, enough to keep any man busy for a lifetime.

What Tom could see happening was Murchison—who would probably bring his Derwatt painting over—talking to other art dealers and then the press. It could arouse suspicion, and Derwatt might go up in smoke. Would the gang drag him into it? (Tom always thought of the gallery batch, Derwatt's old friends, as 'the gang', though he hated the term every time it came into his head.) And Bernard might mention Tom Ripley, Tom thought, not out of malice but out of his own insane—almost Christlike—honesty.

Tom had kept his name and his reputation clean, amazingly clean, considering all he did. It would be most embarrassing if it were in the French papers that Thomas Ripley of Villeperce-sur-Seine, husband of Heloise Plisson, daughter of Jacques Plisson, millionaire owner of

Pharmaceutiques Plisson, had dreamed up the money-making fraud of Derwatt Ltd, and had for years been deriving a percentage from it, even if it was only ten per cent. . . .

Tom put on a Beatles record to lift his spirits, then walked about the large living-room, hands in his pockets. He loved the house. It was a two-storey squarish grey stone house with four turrets over four round rooms in the upstairs corners, making the house look like a little castle. The garden was vast, and even by American standards the place had cost a fortune. Heloise's father had given the house to them three years ago as a wedding present. In the days before he married, Tom had needed some extra money, the Greenleaf money not being enough for him to enjoy the kind of life he had come to prefer, and Tom had been interested in his cut of the Derwatt affair. Now he regretted that. He had accepted ten per cent, when ten per cent had been very little. Even he had not realized that Derwatt would flourish the way it had.

Tom spent that evening as he did most of his evenings, quietly and alone, but his thoughts were troubled. He played the stereo softly while he ate, and he read Servan-Schreiber in French. There were two words Tom didn't know. He would look them up tonight in his Harrap's beside his bed. He was good at holding words in his memory to look up. . . .

That night, Tom could not fall asleep, so he got out of bed, put on his purple woollen dressing-gown—new and thick, full of military frogs and tassels, a birthday present from Heloise—and went down to the kitchen. He had thought of taking up a bottle of Super Valstar beer, but decided to make some tea. He almost never drank tea, so in a way it was appropriate, as he felt it was a strange night. He tiptoed around the kitchen, so as not to awake Mme Annette. The tea Tom made was dark red. He had put too much in the pot. He carried a tray into the living-room, poured a cup, and walked about, noiseless in felt house-shoes. Why not impersonate Derwatt, he thought. My God, yes! That was the solution, the perfect solution, and the only solution.

PATRICIA HIGHSMITH, *Ripley Underground*, 1970

† *The methods of a burglar, Charles Peace (executed 1879).*

En route to a robbery Peace would carry his burgling kit in a violin case or respectable travelling bag. Often he would arrive in a district, leave the case at the nearest railway station left-luggage office, while he had a last prowl round to ensure the circumstances were favourable for a breaking, collecting the bag again just before he actually went on 'the job'.

Before starting operations he would pull a pair of socks over the women's boots he always wore at 'work'. The socks deadened the sound and preventing any distinguishing footmarks being made. This, combined with the fact that he had tiny feet, several times persuaded the police that the breaking had been done by a child or a woman. He would stow about his pockets various tools he needed and leave his bag hidden nearby. He said later; 'I usually carried an augur, a sharp knife, a jemmy and some screws, and, of course, my revolver.'

He would walk quietly up to the house—he moved as silently and quickly as a cat in the darkness—and, if possible, force the hasp of a downstairs window and climb in. If there was no suitable window downstairs, or a handy upstairs window was already open, he would climb hand over hand up the nearest drainpipe to reach it. Window bars were then a common feature of large houses, but Peace could squeeze himself through these, even if the bars were only six or seven inches apart.

Sometimes when he got into a room he would find the door out of it to the rest of the house, was locked. He would use his augur to bore four holes a few inches apart in one of the panels, split the panel to make a hole large enough to put his hand through and unfasten the door. He would then walk quickly through the house, collecting up anything valuable he could see.

Even in strange houses in the dark he could move as silently as a shadow, picking his way up staircases, carefully testing where to stand to prevent creaking. Rifling a room full of sleeping occupants was done so swiftly and carefully that they did not stir. He would take everything of possible value into one room, with a handy window for a speedy exit if necessary, and carefully sort out the objects that were worth taking away. Silver and gold plate he would crush and flatten until he could hide it under his clothing without leaving a suspicious bulge.

During this sorting out he would screw up the door, so that if the alarm was given he would still have time to pick up his loot and get out of the window before the householders could get into the room. He was always careful to be as neat as he could; householders had very little clearing up to do after Peace had called, unlike some burglars who tear everything apart in a frantic effort to scramble together any valuables.

He was so neat that on occasions when a slight noise aroused a sleeping occupant, a quick look into the room revealed nothing amiss, despite the fact that Peace might well be standing concealed, carefully controlling his breathing to make the minimum of noise. A favourite place to hide during such alarms was under tables covered with drapes, or behind curtains. Once he curled himself around the leg of a single-leg table in such a way that he could not be seen below an overhanging tablecloth, and the sleepy householder stumbled back to bed.

With the loot carefully stowed about his pockets, which included an extra large one specially sewn in his coat, Peace would climb out of the house and steal away into the darkness.

The stealth, deftness and quickness of the man is all the more astonishing when one considers that he would ransack not one house like this in a night, but on occasions half-a-dozen, one after the other.

DAVID WARD, *King of Lags: The Story of Charles Peace*, 1989

THE WORST BURGLAR

The history of crime offers few figures less suited to undetected burglary than Mr Philip McCutcheon.

He was arrested for the twentieth time when, after his latest robbery, he drove his getaway car into two parked vans. During this man's appearance at York Crown Court in 1971, the judge gave a rare display of careers advice from the bench.

Giving our man a conditional discharge, Mr Rodney Percy, the Recorder, said: 'I think you should give burglary up. You have a withered hand, an artificial leg and only one eye. You have been caught in Otley, Leeds, Harrogate, Norwich, Beverley, Hull and York. How can you hope to succeed?

'You are a rotten burglar. You are always being caught.'

STEPHEN PYLE, *Heroic Failures*, 1968

We had been out for one of our evening rambles, Holmes and I, and had returned about six o'clock on a cold, frosty winter's evening. As Holmes turned up the lamp the light fell upon a card on the table. He glanced at it, and then, with an ejaculation of disgust, threw it on the floor. I picked it up and read:

CHARLES AUGUSTUS MILVERTON,
Appledore Towers,
Hampstead.
Agent.

'Who is he?' I asked.

'The worst man in London,' Holmes answered, as he sat down and stretched his legs before the fire. 'Is anything on the back of the card?'

I turned it over.

'Will call at 6:30—C.A.M.,' I read.

'Hum! He's about due. Do you feel a creeping, shrinking sensation, Watson, when you stand before the serpents in the Zoo, and see the slithery, gliding, venomous creatures, with their deadly eyes and wicked, flattened faces? Well, that's how Milverton impresses me. I've had to do with fifty murderers in my career, but the worst of them never gave me the repulsion which I have for this fellow. And yet I can't get out of doing business with him—indeed, he is here at my invitation.'

'But who is he?'

'I'll tell you, Watson. He is the king of all the blackmailers. Heaven help the man, and still more the woman, whose secret and reputation come into the power of Milverton! With a smiling face and a heart of marble, he will squeeze and squeeze until he has drained them dry. The fellow is a genius in his way, and would have made his mark in some more savoury trade. His method is as follows: He allows it to be known that he is prepared to pay very high sums for letters which compromise people of wealth and position. He receives these wares not only from treacherous valets or maids, but frequently from genteel ruffians, who have gained the confidence and affection of trusting women. He deals with no niggard hand. I happen to know that he paid seven hundred pounds to a footman for a note two lines in length, and that the ruin of a noble family was the result. Everything which is in the market goes to Milverton, and there are hundreds in this great city who turn white at his name. No one knows where his grip may fall, for he is far too rich and far too cunning to work from hand to mouth. He will hold a card back for years in order to play it at the moment when the stake is best worth winning. I have said that he is the worst man in London, and I would ask you how could one compare the ruffian, who in hot blood bludgeons his mate, with this man, who methodically and at his leisure tortures the soul and wrings the nerves in order to add to his already swollen money-bags?'

SIR ARTHUR CONAN DOYLE, *The Return of Sherlock Holmes*, 1905

CHARLES AUGUSTUS MILVERTON

see The Return of Sherlock Holmes

Lady Eva Brackwell, the most lovely debutante
  of last
season, will be married (and who dares say that she shan't?)
  to the stern
  and mast-
erly Earl of Dovercourt; a sensitive young plant
  in an urn,
  she fast,

yes, to his pure stiffness in a fortnight will be tied—
  but she
has dispatched imprudent letters, shaming to a bride,
  alas!
  to the
impecunious young squire who adorned her countryside—
  a class
  too free!

Oh, who's purloined those letters but Augustus Milverton?
  and who
's asking seven thousand pounds the lot, cach sprightly one?
  What can
  Holmes do?
Though he looks like Mr Pickwick, he's a fiend—and she's undone!
  A man
  who knew

no compunction for his victims—a genius in his way—
  and he's
much too fond of swollen money-bags; when victims pray—
  smile, face,
  heart, freeze!
She'll be lucky if she falters out the word 'obey'!
  This case,
  Holmes sees,

needs the most oblique approach: impenetrable disguise.
  So he
becomes a gay young workman before Watson's very eyes—
  clay pipe,
  goatee—
walking out with Hampstead housemaids (Watson shows surprise),
  a type,
  you see,

quite above suspicion in the villain's servants' hall.
  Holmes plans
one last throw—a felony—to win or lose it all.
  This quite
  unmans
Watson. 'Think what you are doing!' Anguished, manly call!
  That night
  it pans

out well. With a first-class burgling kit, a nickel plat-
  ed jemm-
y, diamond-tipped glass cutter, and adjustable keys, late,
  with true
  native phlegm
they invade the silent house. The safe! but changeful Fate,
  like you,
  my fem-

inine reader! Holmes has barely time to seize his tools
  when HE
enters. Quick! Behind the curtains! They will both look fools
  if caught—
  but how flee?

Milverton is not a man who plays the game by rules,
his sport
villainy.

Claret-coloured smoking jacket, big red leather chair,
a long
black cigar. Unknowingly he sits before them there
unperturbed.
What's wrong?
It's far past his usual bedtime. Does he gloat on fair
disturbed
belles, a Mong-

olian idiot's grin upon his round blackmailer's face?
The door!
Gentle rustle of a woman's dress. Ah, what disgrace
could bring
her before
this insufferable bounder, seated there so base,
a thing
beyond law?

It's a lady in a mantle, veiled and lithe and tall!
'It is I.'
Handsome, clear-cut face, curved nose, dark eyebrow shading all
the hard
glittering eye.
straight the thin-lipped mouth set in a dangerous and small
smile. Guard
thyself! Fly!

Milverton, however, laughs. 'Ah, you were obstinate.'
'And you
sent the letters to my husband, to my noble mate,
a man
so true
I was never worthy yet to lace his boots! In hate
he ran
quite through

grief's whole bitter gamut till it broke his gallant heart.
He died. . . .'

'Don't imagine you can bully me!' Her thin lips part,
   white hand
   inside,
buried in her bosom. Uncontrolled the wild fears start,
   unplanned,
   to slide

into Milverton's cold, scheming, brilliant, worldly brain,
   so clever.
'You will never wring a woman's innocent heart again,
   you will
   never
ruin lives as you ruined mine, to cause such countless pain,
   to kill,
   or ever

boast of those disasters that it was your trade to bring
   to our
gentle sex. Take that, you hound! Take that, you poisonous thing!'
   Oh, stare!
   Oh, cower!
See the little gleaming pistol emptied in the ting-
   ling air!
   Her hour,

joyfully she takes revenge! 'You've done me.' Still he lies.
   Intent,
she grinds a fashionable heel into the upturned eyes.
   Night air,
   passion spent,
the fair avenger leaves the room to Holmes and Watson, spies
   who share
   secrets meant

for no one but that Justice who must still protect the weak.
   Oh, quick!
open safe and burn the letters, excitement at its peak!
   Escape
   in the nick
of time and run two miles, no breath or even need to speak,
   dim shape
   s night-thick!

Solemn in the morning Baker Streetwards comes Lestrade
with news
of the most unusual murder, masked marauders; seeks their aid.
Holmes says
'I refuse'.
Later, though, in Oxford Street they see a photo of a lad-
y, gaze
and muse . . .

Beauty with a bright tiara on her noble head,
regal,
stately, Court-robed lady, eyebrows strongly marked, well-bred,
nose curve
of eagle.
Could time-honoured titles shoot a fellow mortal dead
or swerve
to the illegal?

GAVIN EWART, 1980

MONK EASTMAN, PURVEYOR OF INIQUITIES

The history of the gangs of New York (revealed in 1928 by Herbert Asbury in a solid volume of four hundred octavo pages) contains all of the confusion and cruelty of the barbarian cosmogonies, and much of their giant-scale ineptitude—cellars of old breweries honeycombed into Negro tenements; a ramshackle New York of three-storey structures; criminal gangs like the Swamp Angels, who rendezvoused in a labyrinth of sewers; criminal gangs like the Daybreak Boys, who recruited precocious murderers of ten and eleven; loners, like the bold and gigantic Plug Uglies, who earned the smirks of passersby with their enormous plug hats, stuffed with wool and worn pulled down over their ears as helmets, and their long shirttails, worn outside the trousers, that flapped in the Bowery breeze (but with a huge bludgeon in one hand and a pistol peeping out of a pocket); criminal gangs like the Dead Rabbits, who entered into battle under the emblem of a dead rabbit impaled on a pike; men like Dandy Johnny Dolan, famous for the oiled forelock he wore curled and plastered against his forehead, for his cane whose handle was carved in the likeness of a monkey, and for the copper device he invented and used on the thumb for gouging out an adversary's eyes; men like Kit Burns, who for twenty-five cents would decapitate a live rat with a single bite; men like Blind Danny Lyons, young and blond and with immense dead eyes, who pimped for three girls, all of whom proudly walked the streets for him; rows of houses showing red lanterns in the windows, like those run by seven sisters from a small New England village, who always turned their Christmas Eve proceeds over to charity; rat pits, where wharf rats were starved and sent against terriers; Chinese gambling dives; women like the repeatedly widowed Red Norah, the vaunted sweetheart of practically the entire Gopher gang; women like Lizzie the Dove, who donned widow's weeds when Danny Lyons was executed for murder, and who was stabbed in the throat by Gentle Maggie during an argument over whose sorrow for the departed blind man was the greater; mob uprisings like the savage week of draft riots in 1863, when a hundred buildings were burned to the ground and the city was nearly taken over; teeming street fights in which a man went down as at sea, trampled to death; a thief and horse poisoner like Yoske Nigger. All these go to weave underworld New York's chaotic history. And its most famous hero is Edward Delaney, alias William Delaney, alias Joseph Marvin, alias Joseph Morris, alias Monk Eastman—boss of twelve hundred men.

These shifts of identity (as distressing as a masquerade, in which one is not quite certain who is who) omit his real name—presuming there is such a thing as a real name. The recorded fact is that he was born in the Williamsburg section of Brooklyn as Edward Osterman, a name later Americanized to Eastman. Oddly enough, this stormy underworld character was Jewish. He was the son of the owner of a kosher restaurant, where men wearing rabbinical beards could safely partake of the bloodless and thrice-cleansed flesh of ritually slaughtered calves. At the age of nineteen, about 1892, his father set him up in business with a bird store. A fascination for animals, an interest in their small decisions and inscrutable innocence, turned into a lifelong hobby. Years afterwards, in a period of opulence, when he scornfully refused the Havana cigars of freckle-faced Tammany sachems or when he paid visits to the best houses of prostitution in that new invention, the automobile (which seemed the bastard offspring of a gondola), he started a second business, a front, that accommodated a hundred cats and more than four hundred pigeons—none of which were for sale to anyone. He loved each one, and often he strolled through his neighbourhood with a happy cat under an arm, while several others trailed eagerly behind.

He was a battered, colossal man. He had a short, bull neck; a barrel chest; long, scrappy arms; a broken nose; a face, although plentifully scarred, less striking than his frame; and legs bowed like a cowboy's or a sailor's. He could usually be found without a shirt or coat, but not without a derby hat several sizes too small perched on his bullet-shaped head. Mankind has conserved his memory. Physically, the conventional moving-picture gunman is a copy of him, not of the pudgy, epicene Capone. It is said of Louis Wolheim that Hollywood employed him because his features suggested those of the lamented Monk Eastman. Eastman used to strut about his underworld kingdom with a great blue pigeon on his shoulder, just like a bull with a cowbird on its rump.

Back in the mid-nineties, public dance halls were a dime a dozen in the city of New York. Eastman was employed in one of them as a bouncer. The story is told that a dance-hall manager once refused to hire him, whereupon Monk demonstrated his capacity for the work by wiping the floor with the pair of giants who stood between him and the job. Single-handed, universally feared, he held the position until 1899. For each troublemaker he quelled, he cut a notch in his brutal bludgeon. One night, his attention drawn to a shining bald pate minding its own business over a bock beer, he laid its bearer out with a blow. 'I needed one more notch to make fifty,' he later explained.

JORGE LUIS BORGES, *A Universal History of Infamy*, 1935, trans. Norman Thomas di Giovanni

REFORMED VILLAINS

Whenever, in a somber mood, I start totting up the many experiences denied me in my lifetime, I think of four above all that I am sure would have been enormously enriching. I never met James Joyce. (A luncheon date in 1934 was cancelled because en route to it he had lost several chapters of *Finnegans Wake* in a cab.) I arrived in China too late to see Peking, and I never danced with that tigress star of Elinor Glyn's *Three Weeks*, Aileen Pringle, the memory of whose voluptuous balcony has haunted me from youth. The fourth deprivation, while nowhere as acute, was professional: I never was a cub reporter assigned to cover police news, and consequently never knew any working criminals. In later years, however, I did encounter two who had retired, if only by their own deposition. The first was Mike O'Dowd, a local real-estate agent in the Pennsylvania boondocks where I reside. Mike was the prototype of the stage Irishman, a fellow of infinite jest and gift of the gab, who at one time had been a celebrated fur thief. His specialty, singular enough to have been immortalized in a study published by the University of Chicago, was the theft of women's fur coats from various New York department stores. He usually entered them just before closing, clad in a capacious ulster or balmacaan, and locked himself straightaway in a pay toilet. After the watchmen had made their rounds, Mike would emerge, select a handsome mink or broadtail from the racks, and saunter out when the store reopened, wearing the booty under his coat. Even more striking, however, was Mike's disposition of the proceeds of his loot. A philosophical anarchist, he contributed all but the merest fraction to persons needier than himself. When the police ultimately caught up with him, they were so baffled by his altruism that they had him adjudged insane, but he beat the rap and ended his days on the steps of our country postoffice, chewing BL Cut Plug and discussing the theories of Kropotkin.

I met my second *gonif*, and an equally eminent one, at the Kentucky Derby in 1952. On the morning of the race, I was strolling along the main street of Louisville with Dr David Maurer, this country's ranking authority on underworld slang and the author of that monumental treatise on the mores and speech of the confidence trickster, *The Big Con*, as well as of countless monographs on the argot of safecrackers, card sharps, junkies, and carnival folk. Through his research in linguistics, Maurer had developed a wide acquaintance among such rapscallions, and I was absorbed in the account of his scholarship when he broke off abruptly. Poised at the traffic light opposite, he whispered, was one of the most expert cannons, or pickpockets, in the business. I expected to meet a furtive character in a gooseneck sweater, the dismal stereotype familiarized by Thomas Burke's *Limehouse Nights* and the novels of Frank L. Packard. Instead, I was introduced to a personable, charming fellow on the order of Jack Donahue, the dancer, who met my gaze unflinchingly as we shook hands and made no move in the direction of my wallet. He chatted genially in an undertone with my companion for several minutes, and after his departure, Maurer provided a few discreet details. Herschel Downs, he said, cloaking him in an obvious pseudonym, had been for some years the head of a whiz mob, or group of pickpockets, a pursuit that earned him a snug annual income in excess of $35,000. Unfortunately, a discarded mistress had planted a gun on his person, resulting in a rap out of all proportion to his misdeeds. He was now engaged in selling vacuum cleaners from door to door and doing so well, it appeared, that he doubted he would ever return to lifting pockets. To me, in that atmosphere of easy money, it was a stunning demonstration of the wisdom of rectitude, of the superiority of good over evil, and for the first time in my life, when I checked out the hotel the next day, I didn't steal a single towel.

S. J. PERELMAN, preface to Inspector Byrnes, *Rogue's Gallery*, 1988

Now it comes on the spring of 1931, after a long hard winter, and times are very tough indeed, what with the stock market going all to pieces, and banks busting right and left, and the law getting very nasty about this and that, and one thing and another, and many citizens of this town are compelled to do the best they can.

There is very little scratch anywhere and along Broadway many citizens are wearing their last year's clothes and have practically nothing to bet on the races or anything else, and it is a condition that will touch anybody's heart.

So I am not surprised to hear rumours that the snatching of certain parties is going on in spots, because while snatching is by no means a high-class business, and is even considered somewhat illegal, it is something to tide over the hard times.

Furthermore, I am not surprised to hear that this snatching is being done by a character by the name of Harry the Horse, who comes from Brooklyn, and who is a character who does not care much what sort of business he is in, and who is mobbed up with other characters from Brooklyn such as Spanish John and Little Isadore, who do not care what sort of business they are in, either.

In fact, Harry the Horse and Spanish John and Little Isadore are very hard characters in every respect, and there is considerable indignation expressed around and about when they move over from Brooklyn into Manhattan and start snatching, because the citizens of Manhattan feel that if there is any snatching done in their territory, they are entitled to do it themselves.

But Harry the Horse and Spanish John and Little Isadore pay no attention whatever to local sentiment and go on the snatch on a pretty fair scale, and by and by I am hearing rumours of some very nice scores. These scores are not extra large scores, to be sure, but they are enough to keep the wolf from the door, and in fact from three different doors, and before long Harry the Horse and Spanish John and Little Isadore are around the race-tracks betting on the horses, because if there is one thing they are all very fond of, it is betting on the horses.

Now many citizens have the wrong idea entirely of the snatching business. Many citizens think that all there is to snatching is to round up the party who is to be snatched and then just snatch him, putting him away somewhere until his family or friends dig up enough scratch to pay whatever price the snatchers are asking. Very few citizens understand that the snatching business must be well organized and very systematic.

In the first place, if you are going to do any snatching, you cannot snatch just anybody. You must know whom you are snatching, because naturally it is no good snatching somebody who does not have any scratch to settle with. And you cannot tell by the way a party looks or how he lives in this town if he has any scratch, because many a party who is around in automobiles, and wearing good clothes, and chucking quite a swell is nothing but the phonus bolonus and does not have any real scratch whatever.

So of course such a party is no good for snatching, and of course guys who are on the snatch cannot go around inquiring into bank accounts, or asking how much this and that party has in a safe-deposit vault, because such questions are apt to make citizens wonder why, and it is very dangerous to get citizens to wondering why about anything. So the only way guys who are on the snatch can find out about parties worth snatching is to make a connection with some guy who can put the finger on the right party.

The finger guy must know the party he fingers has plenty of ready scratch to begin with, and he must also know that this party is such a party as is not apt to make too much disturbance about being snatched, such as telling the gendarmes. The party may be a legitimate party, such as a business guy, but he will have reasons why he does not wish it to get out that he is snatched, and the finger must know these reasons. Maybe the party is not leading the right sort of life, such as running around with blondes when he has an ever-loving wife and seven children in Mamaroneck, but does not care to have his habits known, as is apt to happen if he is snatched, especially if he is snatched when he is with a blonde.

And sometimes the party is such a party as does not care to have matches run up and down the bottom of his feet, which often happens to parties who are snatched and who do not seem to wish to settle their bill promptly, because many parties are very ticklish on the bottom of the feet, especially if the matches are lit. On the other hand maybe the party is not a legitimate guy, such as a party who is running a crap game or a swell speakeasy, or who has some other dodge he does not care to have come out, and who also does not care about having his feet tickled.

Such a party is very good indeed for the snatching business, because he is pretty apt to settle without any argument. And after a party settles one snatching, it will be considered very unethical for anybody else to snatch him again very soon, so he is not likely to make any fuss about the matter. The finger guy gets a commission of twenty-five per cent of the settlement, and one and all are satisfied and much fresh scratch comes into circulation, which is very good for the merchants. And while the party who is snatched may know who snatches him, one thing he never knows is who puts the finger on him, this being considered a trade secret.

DAMON RUNYON, 'The Snatching of Bookie Bob', *More than Somewhat*, 1937

It is a bold thing to say, but nothing will ever persuade me that Society has not a sneaking kindness for a Rogue.

For example, my father never had half the attention shown to him in his own house, which was shown to me in my prison. I have seen High Sheriffs in the great world, whom my father went to see, give him two fingers—the High Sheriff of Barkinghamshire came to see me, and shook hands cordially. Nobody ever wanted my father's autograph—dozens of people asked for mine. Nobody ever put my father's portrait in the frontispiece of a magazine, or described his personal appearance and manners with anxious elaboration, in the large type of a great newspaper—I enjoyed both those honours. Three official individuals politely begged me to be sure and make complaints if my position was not perfectly comfortable. No official individual ever troubled his head whether my father was comfortable or not. When the day of my trial came, the court was thronged by my lovely countrywomen, who stood up panting in the crowd and crushing their beautiful dresses, rather than miss the pleasure of seeing the dear Rogue in the dock. When my father once stood on the lecturer's rostrum, and delivered his excellent discourse, called 'Medical Hints to Maids and Mothers on Tight Lacing and Teething,' the benches were left empty by the ungrateful women of England, who were not in the slightest degree anxious to feast their eyes on the sight of a learned adviser and respectable man. If these facts led to one inevitable conclusion, it is not my fault. We Rogues are the spoilt children of Society. We may not be openly acknowledged as Pets, but we all know, by pleasant experience, that we are treated like them.

WILKIE COLLINS, *A Rogue's Life*, 1879

. . . the typical Hooligan is a boy who, growing up in the area bounded by the Albert Embankment, the Lambeth Road, the Kennington Road, and the streets about the Oval, takes to tea-leafing as a Grimsby lad takes to the sea. If his taste runs to street-fighting there is hope for him, and for the community. He will probably enlist, and, having helped to push the merits of gin and Christianity in the dark places of the earth, die in the skin of a hero. You may see in Lambeth Walk a good many soldiers who have come back from looking over the edge of the world to see the place they were born in, to smell the fried fish and the second-hand shoe-leather, and to pulsate once more to the throb of a piano-organ. On the other hand, if his fingers be lithe and sensitive, if he have a turn for mechanics, he will slip naturally into the picking of pockets and the rifling of other people's houses.

The home of the Hooligan is, as I have implied, within a stone's throw of Lambeth Walk. Law breakers exist in other quarters of London: Drury Lane will furnish forth a small army of pickpockets, Soho breeds parasites, and the basher of toffs flourishes in the Kingsland Road. But in and about Lambeth Walk we have a colony, compact and easily handled, of sturdy young villains, who start with a grievance against society, and are determined to get their own back. That is their own phrase, their own view. Life has little to give them but what they take. Honest work, if it can be obtained, will bring in but a few shillings a week; and what is that compared to the glorious possibility of nicking a red 'un?

Small and compact, the colony is easily organised; and here, as in all turbulent communities, such as an English public school, the leader gains his place by sheer force of personality. The boy who has kicked in a door can crow over the boy who has merely smashed a window. If you have knocked-out your adversary at the little boxing place off the Walk, you will have proved that your friendship is desirable. If it becomes known—and it speedily becomes known to all but the police —that you have drugged a toff and run through his pockets, or, better still, have cracked a crib on your own and planted the stuff, then you are at once surrounded by sycophants. Your position is assured, and you have but to pick and choose those that shall work with you. Your leadership will be recognised, and every morning boys, with both eyes skinned for strolling splits, will seek you out and ask for orders for the day. In time, if you stick to work and escape the cops, you may become possessed of a coffee-house or a sweetstuff shop, and run a profitable business as a fence. Moreover, your juniors, knowing your past experience, will purchase your advice—paying for counsel's opinion—when they seek an entrance to a desirable house in the suburbs, and cannot decide between the fan-light and the kitchen window. So you shall live and die respected by all men in Lambeth Walk.

The average Hooligan is not an ignorant, hulking ruffian, beetle-browed and bullet-headed. He is a product of the Board School, writes a fair hand, and is quick at arithmetic. His type of face approaches nearer the rat than the bulldog; he is nervous, highly-strung, almost neurotic. He is by no means a drunkard; but a very small quantity of liquor causes him to run amuck, when he is not pleasant to meet. Undersized as a rule, he is sinewy, swift, and untiring. For pocket-picking and burglary the featherweight is at an advantage. He has usually done a bit of fighting with the gloves, for in Lambeth boxing is one of the most popular forms of sport. But he is better with the raws, and is very bad to tackle in a street row, where there are no rules to observe. Then he will show you some tricks that will astonish you. No scruples of conscience will make him hesitate to butt you in the stomach with his head, and pitch you backwards by catching you round the calves with his arm. His skill, born of constant practice, in scrapping and hurricane fighting brings him an occasional job in the bashing line. You have an enemy, we will say, whom you wish to mark, but, for one reason and another, you do not wish to appear in the matter. Young Alf will take on the job. Indicate to him your enemy; hand him five shillings (he will ask a sovereign, but will take five shillings), and he will make all the necessary arrangements. One night your enemy will find himself lying dazed on the pavement in a quiet corner, with a confused remembrance of a trip and a crash, and a mad whirl of fists and boots. You need have small fear that the job will be bungled. But it is a matter of complaint among the boys of the Walk, that if they do a bit of bashing for a toff and get caught, the toff seldom has the magnanimity to give them a lift when they come out of gaol.

CLARENCE ROOK, *The Hooligan Nights*, 1901

'She is beautiful,' Tobias Tweeney says, speaking of Miss Deborah Weems. 'I do not think I can live without her. But,' he says, 'Miss Deborah Weems will have no part of me because she is daffy over desperate characters of the underworld such as she sees in the movies at the Model Theatre in Erasmus.

'She wishes to know,' Tobias Tweeney says, 'why I cannot be a big gunman and go around plugging people here and there and talking up to politicians and policemen, and maybe looking picturesque and romantic like Edward G. Robinson or James Cagney or even Georgie Raft. But, of course,' Tobias says, 'I am not the type for such a character. Anyway,' he says, 'Constable Wendell will never permit me to be such a character in Erasmus.

'So Miss Deborah Weems says I have no more nerve than a catfish,' Tobias says, 'and she goes around with a guy by the name of Joe Trivett, who runs the Smoke Shop, and bootlegs ginger extract to the boys in his back room and claims Al Capone once says "Hello" to him, although,' Tobias says, 'personally, I think Joe Trivett is nothing but a great big liar.'

At this, Tobias Tweeney starts crying again, and I feel very sorry for him indeed, because I can see he is a friendly, harmless little fellow, and by no means accustomed to being tossed around by a doll, and a guy who is not accustomed to being tossed around by a doll always finds it most painful the first time.

'Why,' I say, very indignant, 'this Miss Deborah Weems talks great foolishness, because big gunmen always wind up nowadays with the score nine to nought against them, even in the movies. In fact,' I say, 'if they do not wind up this way in the movies, the censors will not permit the movies to be displayed. Why do you not hit this guy

Trivett a punch in the snoot,' I say, 'and tell him to go on about his business?'

'Well,' Tobias says, 'the reason I do not hit him a punch in the snoot is because he has the idea of punching snoots first, and whose snoot does he punch but mine. Furthermore,' Tobias says, 'he makes my snoot bleed with the punch, and he says he will do it again if I keep hanging around Miss Deborah Weems. And,' Tobias says, 'it is mainly because I do not return the punch, being too busy stopping my snoot from bleeding, that Miss Deborah Weems renounces me for ever.

'She says she can never stand for a guy who has no more nerve than me,' Tobias says, 'but,' he says, 'I ask you if I am to blame if my mother is frightened by a rabbit a few weeks before I am born, and marks me for life?

'So I leave town,' Tobias says. 'I take my savings of two hundred dollars out of the Erasmus bank, and I come here, figuring maybe I will meet up with some big gunmen and other desperate characters of the underworld, and get to know them, and then I can go back to Erasmus and make Joe Trivett look sick. By the way,' he says, 'do you know any desperate characters of the underworld?'

DAMON RUNYON, 'Tobias the Terrible', *More than Somewhat*, 1937

THE LEAST SUCCESSFUL DIAMOND ROBBERY

A daring gang of diamond thieves stole a van in 1978 expecting to get away with half a million pounds worth of uncut diamonds. A spokesman for the Limerick police said afterwards that the raid was carried out with military precision, but that 'they obviously had completely the wrong information'.

The gang stole the wrong van and got away with two dusters and a sack full of industrial diamonds, which look like sand and have virtually no value on the stolen goods market. It was the second theft of industrial diamonds that week.

'It seems to be a popular pastime in Ireland at the moment', said the policeman. 'Italian criminals blow themselves up and ours rob the wrong vans.'

THE LEAST SUCCESSFUL BLACKMAILER

Mr Monte Shoemaker shot to the top of this league in 1978. Wishing to photograph a solicitor in a compromising position, Mr Shoemaker hid in a bedroom cupboard.

His girlfriend accomplice led the legal expert into the room and Mr Shoemaker waited a couple of minutes for a suitable indiscretion to be arranged. He then burst out, took a photograph and demanded money.

When developed, the photograph showed not a solicitor disrobed, but a refrigerator in the corner of the room.

STEPHEN PYLE, *Heroic Failures*, 1968

The Appeal Court at Ras Al Katham has confirmed the prison sentences imposed on Bastar el Abbas, his wife Siran and their two sons, Bakae and Jawb.

'They are a family of incorrigible thieves,' Judge Al Ethama said. 'The head of the family, Bastar (92), his wife (83) and their sons (68 and 67 respectively) were caught, with three cousins, as yet unidentified, loading up a donkey-cart with hi-fi equipment and greengroceries at 3.00 am in front of the Plenty For All supermarket in Al Sih.

'Later, the police seized over 5,000 pieces of stolen property from a desert cave near Al Katham where the family has been living for some years. When arrested, the patriarch said: "We have no pensions, what else are we to do? America has all the money." '

He and his wife were fined Dh 500, on account of their age. Their sons were given two years (suspended) each, and the unidentified cousins were sentenced to 10 years each *in absentia*.

Gulf Gazette, 11 December 1990, in CHRISTOPHER LOGUE, *Bumper Book of True Stories*, 1980

In 1725 two highwaymen fell out over the loot from their robberies. Joseph Williams sued John Everitt for £200; the action was not defended and Mr Williams obtained his judgment. Mr Everitt lived in fear of a debtor's prison, and was also exceedingly angry. He reckoned that Mr Williams had kept the greater part of their loot: much more than £200. So he consulted an attorney, William

Wreathock, and that busy but ingenious man instructed Jonathan Collins of counsel to draw up a bill to start an action on the equity side, in the Court of Exchequer, for an account to be taken between the two rogues. Mr Collins must have had a lot of fun in chambers drafting the proceedings.

The statement of facts he drew sets out that 'your orator', John Everitt, is 'skilled in dealing and in buying and selling several sorts of commodities' and that Joseph Williams 'knowing your orator's great care diligence and industry in managing the said dealing' invited him into partnership. They agreed on this and further agreed that they should provide 'all sorts of necessaries at the joint and equal expense of both such as horses, bridles, saddles, assistants and servants'. The bill alleges 'that pursuant to the said agreement your orator and the said Joseph Williams went on and proceeded jointly in the said dealings with good success on Hounslow Heath where they dealt with a gentleman for a gold watch'. Later Mr Williams told Mr Everitt 'that Finchley was a good and convenient place to deal in' and so they 'dealt with several gentlemen for divers watches, rings, swords, canes, hats, cloaks, horses, bridles and other things to the value of £200 and upwards'. Then they met a gentleman at Blackheath 'and after some small discourse . . . they dealt for his horse, bridle, saddle, watch, sword, cane and other things at a very cheap rate'. In pursuit of business they rode to Bagshot, Salisbury and Hampstead, and their profits were over £2,000. Mr Williams took charge of the goods, and Mr Everitt, finding that Mr Williams 'began to shuffle with him' asked for an account, but was refused. The bill ends with a fine formal flourish: Mr Everitt was without remedy at law and 'relievable only in a Court of Equity before Your Honours where just discoveries are made, frauds detected and just accounts stated'.

John Everitt's lawyers confidently expected that the threat of general exposure would bring about a settlement out of court. But Mr Williams kept his nerve and Mr Serjeant Girdler, on his behalf, persuaded the court to refer the bill to the Remembrancer for a report as being 'a scandal and an impertinence'. The action was dismissed. The Remembrancer reported and the court confirmed his report. A week later Mr Everitt's attorneys were brought before the court and fined £50 apiece, and Mr Jonathan Collins of counsel, who had kept discreetly away during the hearings, was ordered to pay the costs himself. I believe this to be the only case when a barrister was ordered to pay up. The final order ends with the words: 'and the court declares the indignity of the court as satisfied by the said fines and the deputy is not to consider the scandal in the taxation'.

Mr Williams was hanged for carrying out further business with travellers two years later, and he probably never got his £200. Mr Everitt's relief was short-lived, for in 1730 he was hanged for a highway robbery in Hampstead. In 1735 William Wreathock, the attorney, was himself condemned to death for a highway robbery, but reprieved, transported for life, returned with a royal pardon and practised again as a solicitor. It took a little while, but he was eventually struck off.

JUDGE STEPHEN TUMIN, *Great Legal Disasters*, 1983

MACHEATH. Gentlemen, well met. My heart hath been with you this hour; but an unexpected affair hath detained me. No ceremony, I beg you.

MATT OF THE MINT. We were just breaking up to go upon duty. Am I to have the honour of taking the air with you, sir, this evening upon the heath? I drink a dram now and then with the stage-coachmen in the way of friendship and intelligence; and I know that about this time there will be passengers upon the Western Road, who are worth speaking with.

MACHEATH. I was to have been of that party—but—

MATT OF THE MINT. But what, sir?

MACHEATH. Is there any man who suspects my courage?

MATT OF THE MINT. We have all been witnesses of it.

MACHEATH. My honour and truth to the gang?

MATT OF THE MINT. I'll be answerable for it.

MACHEATH. In the division of our booty, have I ever shown the least marks of avarice or injustice?

MATT OF THE MINT. By these questions something seems to have ruffled you. Are any of us suspected?

MACHEATH. I have a fixed confidence, gentlemen, in you all, as men of honour, and as such I value and respect you. Peachum is a man that is useful to us.

MATT OF THE MINT. Is he about to play us any foul play? I'll shoot him through the head.

MACHEATH. I beg you, gentlemen, act with conduct and discretion. A pistol is your last resort.

MATT OF THE MINT. He knows nothing of this meeting.

MACHEATH. Business cannot go on without him. He is a man who knows the world, and is a necessary agent to us. We have had a slight difference, and till it is accommodated I shall be obliged to keep out of his way. Any private dispute of mine shall be of no ill consequence to my friends. You must continue to act under his discretion, for the moment we break loose from him, our gang is ruined.

JOHN GAY, *The Beggar's Opera*, 1728

'In my opinion, a poacher's a highly respectable character. What say you, Mr Coates?' turning very gravely to that gentleman.

'Such a question, sir,' replied Coates, bridling up, 'scarcely deserves a serious answer. I make no doubt you will next maintain that a highwayman is a gentleman.'

'Most undoubtedly,' replied Palmer, in the same grave tone, which might have passed for banter, had Jack ever bantered. 'I'll maintain and prove it. I don't see how he can be otherwise. It is as necessary for a man to be a gentleman before he can turn highwayman, as it is for a doctor to have his diploma, or an attorney his certificate. Some of the finest gentlemen of their day, as Captains Lovelace, Hind, Hannum, and Dudley, were eminent on the road, and they set the fashion. Ever since their day a real highwayman would consider himself disgraced, if he did not conduct himself in every way like a gentleman. Of course, there are pretenders in this line, as in everything else. But these are only exceptions, and prove the rule. What are the distinguishing characteristics of a fine gentleman?—perfect knowledge of the world—perfect independence of character—notoriety—command of cash—and inordinate success with the women. You grant all these premises? First, then, it is part of a highwayman's business to be thoroughly acquainted with the world. He is the easiest and pleasantest fellow going. There is Tom King, for example: he is the handsomest man about town, and the best-bred fellow on the road. Then whose inclinations are so uncontrolled as the highwayman's, so long as the mopuses last? who produces so great an effect by so few words?—"STAND AND DELIVER!" is sure to arrest attention. Every one is captivated by an address so *taking*. As to money, he wins a purse of a hundred guineas as easily as you would the same sum from the faro table. And wherein lies the difference? only in the name of the game. Who so little need of a banker as he? all he has to apprehend is a check—all he has to draw is a trigger. As to the women, they dote upon him: not even your red-coat is so successful. Look at a highwayman mounted on his flying steed, with his pistols in his holsters, and his mask upon his face. What can be a more gallant sight? The clatter of his horse's heels is like music to his ear—he is in full quest—he shouts to the fugitive horseman to stay—the other flies all the faster—what chase can be half so exciting as that? Suppose he overtakes his prey, which ten to one he will, how readily his summons to deliver is obeyed! how satisfactory is the appropriation of a lusty purse or corpulent pocket-book!—getting the brush is nothing to it. How tranquilly he departs, takes off his hat to his accommodating acquaintance, wishes him a pleasant journey, and disappears across the heath! England, sir, has reason to be proud of her highwaymen. They are peculiar to her clime, and are as much before the brigand of Italy, the contrabandist of Spain, or the cut-purse of France—as her sailors are before all the rest of the world. The day will never come, I hope, when we shall degenerate into the footpad, and lose our *Night Errantry.*

† *In the same novel, Harrison Ainsworth imagines a conversation between two highwaymen, one of them the famous Dick Turpin.*

'. . . I shall die in a good cause,' said King: 'but

The Tyburn Tree
Has no terrors for me,
Let better men swing—I'm at liberty.

I shall never come to the scragging-post, unless you turn topsman, Dick Turpin. My nativity has been cast, and the stars have declared I am to die by the hand of my best friend—and that's you—eh, Dick?'

'It sounds like it,' replied Turpin; 'but I advise you not to become too intimate with Jack Ketch. He may prove your best friend after all.'

'Why, faith, that's true,' replied King, laughing; 'and if I must ride backwards up Holborn Hill, I'll do the thing in style, and honest Jack Ketch shall never want his dues. A man should always die game. We none of us know how soon our turn may come; but come when it will, *I* shall never flinch from it.

As the highwayman's life is the fullest of zest,
So the highwayman's death is the briefest and best;
He dies not as other men die, by degrees,
But at once! without flinching—and quite at his ease.

as the song you are so fond of says. When I die, it will not be of consumption. And if the surgeon's knife must come near me, it will be after death. There's some comfort in that reflection, at all events.'

'True,' replied Turpin, 'and, with a little alteration, my song would suit you capitally:

There is not a king, should you search the world round,
So blithe as the king's king, TOM KING, to be found.
Dear woman's his empire, each girl is his own,
And he'd have a long reign if he'd let 'em alone.

Ha, ha!'

'Ha, ha!' laughed Tom. 'And now, Dick, to change the subject. You are off, I understand, to Yorkshire to-night. 'Pon my soul, you are a wonderful fellow—an *alibi* personified!—here and everywhere at the same time—no wonder you are called the flying highwayman. To-day in town—to-morrow at York—the day after at Chester. The devil only knows where you will pitch your quarters a week hence. There are rumours of you in all counties at the same moment. This man swears you robbed him at Hounslow; that, on Salisbury Plain; while another avers you monopolise Cheshire and Yorkshire, and that it isn't safe even to hunt without pops in your pocket. I heard some devilish good stories of you at D'Osyndar's t'other day; the fellow who told them to me little thought I was a brother blade.'

'You flatter me,' said Dick, smiling complacently; 'but it's no merit of mine. Black Bess alone enables me to do it, and hers be the credit. Talking of being everywhere at the same time, you shall hear what she once did for me in Cheshire. Meantime, a glass to the best mare in England. You won't refuse that toast, Tom. Ah! if your mistress is only as true to you as my nag to me, you might set at nought the tightest hempen cravat that was ever twisted, and defy your best friend to hurt you. Black Bess! and God bless her!

WILLIAM HARRISON AINSWORTH, *Rookwood*, 1834

He did not come in the dawning. He did not come at noon;
And out o' the tawny sunset, before the rise o' the moon,
When the road was a gipsy's ribbon, looping the purple moor,
A red-coat troop came marching—
        Marching—marching—
King George's men came marching, up to the old inn-door.

They said no word to the landlord. They drank his ale instead.
But they gagged his daughter, and bound her, to the foot of her
    narrow bed.
Two of them knelt at her casement, with muskets at their side!
There was death at every window;
        And hell at one dark window;
For Bess could see, through her casement, the road that *he* would
    ride.

They had tied her up to attention, with many a sniggering jest.
They had bound a musket beside her, with the muzzle beneath her
    breast!
'Now, keep good watch!' and they kissed her.
        She heard the dead man say—
Look for me by moonlight;
        Watch for me by moonlight;
I'll come to thee by moonlight, though hell should bar the way!

She twisted her hands behind her; but all the knots held good!
She writhed her hands till her fingers were wet with sweat or blood!
They stretched and strained in the darkness, and the hours crawled
    by like years,
Till, now, on the stroke of midnight,
        Cold, on the stroke of midnight,
The tip of one finger touched it! The trigger at least was hers!

The tip of one finger touched it. She strove no more for the rest.
Up, she stood up to attention, with the muzzle beneath her breast.
She would not risk their hearing; she would not strive again;
For the road lay bare in the moonlight;
        Blank and bare in the moonlight;
And the blood of her veins, in the moonlight, throbbed to her love's
    refrain.

Tlot-tlot; tlot-tlot! Had they heard it? The horse-hoofs ringing clear;
Tlot-tlot, tlot-tlot, in the distance! Were they deaf that they did not
    hear?
Down the ribbon of moonlight, over the brow of the hill,
The highwayman came riding,
        Riding, riding!
The red-coats looked to their priming! She stood up, straight and still.

    Tlot-tlot, in the frosty silence! *Tlot-tlot*, in the echoing night!
Nearer he came and nearer. Her face was like a light.
Her eyes grew wide for a moment; she drew one last deep breath,
Then her finger moved in the moonlight,
        Her musket shattered the moonlight,
Shattered her breast in the moonlight and warned him—with her
    death.

He turned. He spurred to the west; he did not know who stood
Bowed, with her head o'er the musket, drenched with her own red
    blood!
Not till the dawn he heard it, and his face grew grey to hear
How Bess, the landlord's daughter,
        The landlord's black-eyed daughter,
Had watched for her love in the moonlight, and died in the darkness
    there.

Back, he spurred like a madman, shouting a curse to the sky,
With the white road smoking behind him and his rapier brandished
    high.
Blood-red were his spurs i' the golden noon; wine-red was his
    velvet coat;
When they shot him down on the highway,
        Down like a dog on the highway,
And he lay in his blood on the highway, with the bunch of lace at
    his throat.

And still of a winter's night, they say, when the wind is in the trees,
When the moon is a ghostly galleon tossed upon cloudy seas,
When the road is a ribbon of moonlight over the purple moor,
A highwayman comes riding—
        Riding—riding—
A highwayman comes riding, up to the old inn-door.

Over the cobbles he clatters and clangs in the dark inn-yard.
And he taps with his whip on the shutters, but all is locked and barred.
He whistles a tune to the window, and who should be waiting there
But the landlord's black-eyed daughter,
Bess, the landlord's daughter,
Plaiting a dark red love-knot into her long black hair.

ALFRED NOYES, from *The Highwayman*, 1913

† *Sir Henry Morgan, the Great Buccaneer and Governor of Jamaica lived from 1635 to 1688. In 1671 he 'raped' Panama, and this is the way he treated his men.*

Calmly, he ignored the uproar, the threats of murder and mutiny when his men recalled their hardships and the final outrage of having been searched by the Rio Chagres. 'But Captain *Morgan*,' wrote Esquemeling, 'was deaf unto all these, and many other Complaints of this kind, having designed in his mind to cheat them of as much as he could.' Nor does this charge rest only on Esquemeling's word. Browne, previously a worshipper of his admiral, for the first time began to question that worship and accused him of hiding 'a vast sum.' In spite of having looted Panama, he wrote, 'the sailors had to be content with a pitiful share, or else be clapped in irons.'

Of all Morgan's exploits none can equal this final treachery: it remains both the worst and the most magnificent thing he ever did, showing both the unscrupulousness and the heroism that had made him so mighty a leader of men. He turned his back on the howling, but even he must have shivered to hear it and have wondered whether he would be murdered. Of course, he could not have been alone in this perfidy. He must have had companions to share in the plot, picked men, the most cold-blooded murderers in the army who would have fought beside him to the last, and one can only hope that in their turn he cheated them as well. That he was not safe he realised, and he determined to escape from Chagres as swiftly as he could.

Esquemeling, who suffered with the others, says that Morgan became afraid, that 'finding himself obnoxious to many Obloquies, and Detractions among his people, he began to fear the consequences thereof. And hereupon thinking it unsafe to remain any longer at *Chagres*, he commanded the Ordnance of the said Castle to be carried on board his Ship.' One can scarcely believe that he was able to find men who would obey such an order. The mass of buccaneers, maddened to the point of murder, prodded on by the ever-grumbling French contingent, would never have assisted in carrying off guns that might be turned against themselves, and again we must conclude that Morgan had his personal army, his Praetorian guard, within the army. Then he carried out the threat he had made to Puerto Bello and demolished the castle walls, the batteries and even the houses, leaving not a refuge on the island.

'These Orders being performed, he went secretly on board his own Ship, without giving any notice of his Departure unto his Companions, nor calling any Councel, as he used to do. Thus he set Sayl, and put out to Sea, not bidding any body adieu, being only followed by three or four Vessels of the whole Fleet.'

When after their usual debauch the buccaneers awoke in the morning to discover not only Morgan gone, but the loot with him, their rage become enormous. The French thought only of revenge. They were for following him as speedily as possible and boarding the robber, but when they raced to the harbour they found that not a pinch of gunpowder or a single cannon had been left. Even worse, their admiral had sailed in the provision ships and there was no food on the island. In helpless fury and despair, the abandoned buccaneers must have cursed God and the devil with Morgan his mate, for 'they were destitute of most things necessary thereunto. Yea, they had much ado to find sufficient Victuals and Provisions for their Voyage to *Jamaica*, he having left them totally unprovided of all things.'

Thus, in misery, almost as poor as when they had enthusiastically started on the expedition, the buccaneers came back to Port Royal, while, a man of wealth and power and honours, Morgan was congratulated by the Council 'for the execution of his late Commission . . .'

The wonder remains that nobody ever shot him.

PHILIP LINDSAY, *The Great Buccaneer*, 1950

Standing out to sea again, Kidd met with a Dutch ship, the *Loyal Captain*, commanded by Captain Hoar. Some of the crew were in favour of taking this ship, but Kidd prevented them. There is reason to believe that, so far, Kidd's evil actions had been due to weakness in submitting to the demands of an unruly crew rather than to malice aforethought. On this occasion he was apparently strong enough to resist them. There was a mild sort of mutiny, which he quelled, but bad feeling continued to run through the ship. Matters came to a head about a fortnight later, on 30 October 1697. William Moore, the gunner, was at work on deck, when Kidd chided him with having wished to take the *Loyal Captain*. Moore denied the charge, whereupon the captain called him 'a lousy dog'. 'If I am a lousy dog,' retorted the gunner, 'then you have made me one.' Kidd paced angrily up and down the deck for a moment or two, then picked up an iron-bound bucket and struck Moore so savagely on the head with it that the gunner died the next day.

It may well be that Kidd felt that by this act of murder he had burnt his boats. He would now no longer sail the seas as a guiltless captain; he had definitely sunk into crime, and he might now just as well be hung for a sheep as for a lamb. Be that as it may, his career of definite piracy now begins. On 27 November, when four leagues from Calicut, he sighted a ship. Hoisting French colours, Kidd gave chase. On coming up with his prey, he found her to be the *Maiden*, a ship of 200 tons, bound for Surat with a cargo of two horses, ten or twelve bales of cotton, some quilts, and sugar. The master, a Dutchman named Mitchell, with two other Dutchmen and eight or nine Moors, came aboard the *Adventure Galley* and declared that it was a Moorish ship, producing a French pass. Kidd put the Moors in the longboat, sold the cotton and horses on the coast to the natives for money and gold, and took the ship along with him as a prize.

GRAHAM BOOKS, 'Captain Kidd' in *Famous Trials*, 1963

† *Captain Kidd was executed 23 May 1701.*

They sailed on board the *George* Galley, August the 1st, 1724, from the *Texel* to *Santa Cruz*, having 15000*l* on board, when Gow designed to have seized the Ship as they went out, but could not get a party strong enough to join with him, till he worked up a misunderstanding between the Captain and part of the crew, concerning the provisions of the ship, particularly *Winter, Peterson, and Mc.Cawley*, who came upon the Quarter-Deck, in presence of the Owners, just before they sailed, and made a long complaint against the Captain; who assured them that if there was any wrong done them, it was not by his consent; and that he would enquire into it as soon as they had unmoored the ship.

About eight a clock at night, Captain *Ferneau*, as usual, called them up to prayers in the great Cabin, and then set the watch, and went to sleep, little thinking his end was so near, when *Winter*, *Rawlisson*, and *Melvin*, begun the scene of blood, *Gow* lying snug in his hammock, as if he knew nothing of the matter, till he saw whether the villany would succeed, or not. *Winter* cut the Doctor's throat as he was asleep in his hammock, and then went up to *Melvin* and *Rawlisson*, who in the mean time had seized the Captain and cut his throat also, but not touching the windpipe, *Gow* stept up and shot him with a brace of bullets, and then threw him over-board. *Mc.Cawley* cut *Stephen Algiers* the Clerk's throat, as he lay in the hammock, and *Williams* shot him dead afterwards. *Peterson* cut the throat of *Bonaventure Jelphs*, the Chief Mate; and *Michael Moor*, at the Command of *Williams*, shot him.

After this *Williams* came upon the Quarter-Deck, and saluted *Gow* with Captain *Ferneau*'s sword, first striking it upon one of the guns, and saying, *Welcome Captain* Gow, *welcome to your new Command*. After which, *Gow* told the men, That if any of them durst murmur or cabal together, they must expect to meet the same Fate; and then calling a Council, they agreed to go, *Upon the Account*, as they called it.

They called the ship the *Revenge*, and mounted six more of her guns, she being able to carry four and twenty in all. But instead of going to *Genoa* as intended, they sailed for the coasts of *Spain* and *Portugal*, in hopes of getting a ship laden with wine, to keep up their spirits; but all was alike they met with; and instead of wine, they contented themselves with fish, which they took out of a ship called the *Delight* of *Poole*, *Thomas Wise*, Master, bound from *New-England* to *Cadiz*, out of which they took the men, and what they wanted, and then sunk the Ship, to prevent their being discovered to the *English* Men-of-War who lay in the *Straights*.

On the 18th of *December*, they took the *Snow-Galley*, out of which Crew they kept *Rob*, and discharged the Captain and the rest of the men, after having plundered the Ship of the arms, ammunition, cloth, provisions, sails, anchors, cables, and then let her go.

The History and Lives of All the Most Notorious Pirates and Their Crews, 1735

When I had done breakfasting the squire gave me a note addressed to John Silver, at the sign of the 'Spy-glass,' and told me I should easily find the place by following the line of the docks, and keeping a bright look-out for a little tavern with a large brass telescope for sign. I set off, overjoyed at this opportunity to see some more of the ships and seamen, and picked my way among a great crowd of people and carts and bales, for the dock was now at its busiest, until I found the tavern in question.

It was a bright enough little place of entertainment. The sign was newly painted; the windows had neat red curtains; the floor was cleanly sanded. There was a street on either side, and an open door on both, which made the large, low room pretty clear to see in, in spite of clouds of tobacco smoke.

The customers were mostly seafaring men; and they talked so loudly that I hung at the door, almost afraid to enter.

As I was waiting, a man came out of a side room, and, at a glance, I was sure he must be Long John. His left leg was cut off close by the hip, and under the left shoulder he carried a crutch, which he managed with wonderful dexterity, hopping about upon it like a bird. He was very tall and strong, with a face as big as a ham—plain and pale, but intelligent and smiling. Indeed, he seemed in the most cheerful spirits, whistling as he moved about among the tables, with a merry word or a slap on the shoulder for the more favoured of his guests.

Now, to tell you the truth, from the very first mention of Long John in Squire Trelawney's letter, I had taken a fear in my mind that he might prove to be the very one-legged sailor whom I had watched for so long at the old 'Benbow.' But one look at the man before me was enough. I had seen the captain, and Black Dog, and the blind man Pew, and I thought I knew what a buccaneer was like—a very different creature, according to me, from this clean and pleasant-tempered landlord.

I plucked up courage at once, crossed the threshold, and walked right up to the man where he stood, propped on his crutch, talking to a customer.

'Mr Silver, sir?' I asked, holding out the note.

'Yes, my lad,' said he; 'such is my name, to be sure. And who may you be?' And then as he saw the squire's letter, he seemed to me to give something almost like a start.

'Oh!' said he, quite loud, and offering his hand, 'I see. You are our new cabin-boy; pleased I am to see you.'

And he took my hand in his large firm grasp.

Just then one of the customers at the far side rose suddenly and made for the door. It was close by him, and he was out in the street in a moment. But his hurry had attracted my notice, and I recognised him at a glance. It was the tallow-faced man, wanting two fingers, who had come first to the 'Admiral Benbow.'

'Oh,' I cried, 'stop him! it's Black Dog!'

'I don't care two coppers who he is,' cried Silver. 'But he hasn't paid his score. Harry, run and catch him.'

One of the others who was nearest the door leaped up, and started in pursuit.

'If he were Admiral Hawke he shall pay his score,' cried Silver; and then, relinquishing my hand—'Who did you say he was?' he asked. 'Black what?'

'Dog, sir,' said I. 'Has Mr Trelawney not told you of the buccaneers? He was one of them.'

'So?' cried Silver. 'In my house! Ben, run and help Harry. One of those swabs, was he? Was that you drinking with him, Morgan? Step up here.'

The man whom he called Morgan—an old, grey-haired, mahogany-faced sailor—came forward pretty sheepishly, rolling his quid.

'Now, Morgan,' said Long John, very sternly; 'you never clapped your eyes on that Black—Black Dog before, did you, now?'

'Not I, sir,' said Morgan, with a salute.

'You didn't know his name, did you?'

'No, sir.'

'By the powers, Tom Morgan, it's as good for you!' exclaimed the landlord. 'If you had been mixed up with the like of that, you would never have put another foot in my house, you may lay to that. And what was he saying to you?'

'I don't rightly know, sir,' answered Morgan.

'Do you call that a head on your shoulders, or a blessed dead-eye?' cried Long John. 'Don't rightly know, don't you? Perhaps you don't happen to rightly know who you was speaking to, perhaps? Come, now, what was he jawing—v'yages, cap'ns, ships? Pipe up! What was it?'

'We was a-talkin' of keel-hauling,' answered Morgan.

'Keel-hauling, was you? and a mighty suitable thing, too, and you may lay to that. Get back to your place for a lubber, Tom.'

And then, as Morgan rolled back to his seat, Silver added to me in a confidential whisper, that was very flattering, as I thought:

'He's quite an honest man, Tom Morgan, on'y stupid. And now,' he ran on again aloud, 'let's see—Black Dog? No, I don't know the name, not I. Yet I kind of think I've—yes, I've seen the swab. He used to come here with a blind beggar, he used.'

'That he did, you may be sure,' said I. 'I knew that blind man, too. His name was Pew.'

'It was!' cried Silver, now quite excited. 'Pew! That were his name for certain. Ah, he looked a shark, he did! If we run down this Black Dog, now, there'll be news for Cap'n Trelawney! Ben's a good runner; few seamen run better than Ben. He should run him down, hand over hand, by the powers. He talked o' keel-hauling, did he? *I'll* keel-haul him!'

All the time he was jerking out these phrases he was stumping up and down the tavern on his crutch, slapping tables with his hand, and giving such a show of excitement as would have convinced an Old Bailey judge or a Bow Street runner. My suspicions had been thoroughly reawakened on finding Black Dog at the 'Spy-glass,' and I watched the cook narrowly. But he was too deep, and too ready, and too clever for me, and by the time the two men had come back out of breath, and confessed that they had lost the track in a crowd, and been scolded like thieves, I would have gone bail for the innocence of Long John Silver.

'See here, now, Hawkins,' said he, 'here's a blessed hard thing on a man like me, now, ain't it? There's Cap'n Trelawney—what's he to think? Here I have this confounded son of a Dutchman sitting in my own house, drinking of my own rum! Here you comes and tells me of it plain; and here I let him give us all the slip before my blessed deadlights! Now, Hawkins, you do me justice with the cap'n. You're a lad, you are, but you're as smart as paint. I see that when you first came in. Now, here it is: What could I do, with this old timber I hobble on? When I was an A.B. master mariner I'd have come up alongside of him, hand over hand, and broached him to in a brace of old shakes, I would; but now—'

And then, all of a sudden, he stopped, and his jaw dropped as though he had remembered something.

'The score!' he burst out. 'Three goes o' rum! Why, shiver my timbers, if I hadn't forgotten my score!'

And, falling on a bench, he laughed until the tears ran down his cheeks. I could not help joining; and we laughed together, peal after peal, until the tavern rang again.

'Why, what a precious old sea-calf I am!' he said, at last, wiping his cheeks. 'You and me should get on well, Hawkins, for I'll take my davy I should be rated ship's boy. But, come now, stand by to go about. This won't do. Dooty is dooty, messmates. I'll put on my old cocked hat, and step along of you to Cap'n Trelawney, and report this here affair. For, mind you, it's serious, young Hawkins; and neither you nor me's come out of it with what I should make so bold as to call credit. Nor you neither, says you; not smart—none of the pair of us smart. But dash my buttons! that was a good 'un about my score.'

And he began to laugh again, and that so heartily, that though I did not see the joke as he did, I was again obliged to join him in his mirth.

† *Jim Hawkins sails with Silver on the* Hispaniola *and overhears a plot.*

I ran on deck. The watch was all forward looking out for the island. The man at the helm was watching the luff of the sail, and whistling away gently to himself; and that was the only sound excepting the swish of the sea against the bows and around the sides of the ship.

In I got bodily into the apple barrel, and found there was scarce an apple left; but sitting down there in the dark, what with the sound of the waters and the rocking movement of the ship, I had either fallen asleep, or was on the point of doing so, when a heavy man sat down with rather a clash close by. The barrel shook as he leaned his shoulders against it, and I was just about to jump up when the man began to speak. It was Silver's voice, and, before I had heard a dozen words, I would not have shown myself for all the world, but lay there, trembling and listening, in the extreme of fear and curiosity; for from these dozen words I understood that the lives of all the honest men aboard depended upon me alone. . . .

'Davis was a man, too, by all accounts,' said Silver. 'I never sailed along of him; first with England, then with Flint, that's my story; and now here on my own account, in a manner of speaking. I laid by nine hundred safe, from England, and two thousand after Flint. That ain't bad for a man before the mast—all safe in bank. 'Tain't earning now, it's saving does it, you may lay to that. Where's all England's men now? I dunno. Where's Flint's? Why, most on 'em aboard here, and glad to get the duff—been begging before that, some on 'em. Old

Pew, as had lost his sight, and might have thought shame, spends twelve hundred pound in a year, like a lord in Parliament. Where is he now? Well, he's dead now and under hatches; but for two year before that, shiver my timbers! the man was starving. He begged, and he stole, and he cut throats, and starved at that, by the powers!'

'Well, it ain't much use, after all,' said the young seaman.

' 'Tain't much use for fools, you may lay to it—that, nor nothing,' cried Silver. 'But now, you look here: you're young, you are, but you're as smart as paint. I see that when I set my eyes on you, and I'll talk to you like a man.'

You may imagine how I felt when I heard this abominable old rogue addressing another in the very same words of flattery as he had used to myself. I think, if I had been able, that I would have killed him through the barrel. Meantime, he ran on, little supposing he was overheard.

'Here it is about gentlemen of fortune. They lives rough, and they risk swinging, but they eat and drink like fighting-cocks, and when a cruise is done, why it's hundreds of pounds instead of hundreds of farthings in their pockets.'

ROBERT LOUIS STEVENSON, *Treasure Island*, 1883

The boys vanish in the gloom, and after a pause, but not a long pause, for things go briskly on the island, come the pirates on their track. We hear them before they are seen, and it is always the same dreadful song:

'Avast belay, yo ho, heave to,
A-pirating we go,
And if we're parted by a shot
We're sure to meet below!'

A more villainous-looking lot never hung in a row on Execution dock. Here, a little in advance, ever and again with his head to the ground listening, his great arms bare, pieces of eight in his ears as ornaments, is the handsome Italian Cecco, who cut his name in letters of blood on the back of the governor of the prison at Gao. That gigantic black behind him has had many names since he dropped the one with which dusky mothers still terrify their children on the banks of the

Guidjo-mo. Here is Bill Jukes, every inch of him tattooed, the same Bill Jukes who got six dozen on the *Walrus* from Flint before he would drop the bag of moidores; and Cookson, said to be Black Murphy's brother (but this was never proved); and Gentleman Starkey, once an usher in a public school and still dainty in his ways of killing; and Skylights (Morgan's Skylights); and the Irish bo'sun Smee, an oddly genial man who stabbed, so to speak, without offence, and was the only Nonconformist in Hook's crew; and Noodler, whose hands were fixed on backwards; and Robt. Mullins and Alf Mason and many another ruffian long known and feared on the Spanish Main.

In the midst of them, the blackest and largest jewel in that dark setting, reclined James Hook, or as he wrote himself, Jas. Hook, of whom it is said he was the only man that the Sea-Cook feared. He lay at his ease in a rough chariot drawn and propelled by his men, and instead of a right hand he had the iron hook with which ever and anon he encouraged them to increase their pace. As dogs this terrible man treated and addressed them, and as dogs they obeyed him. In person he was cadaverous and blackavized, and his hair was dressed in long curls, which at a little distance looked like black candles, and gave a singularly threatening expression to his handsome countenance. His eyes were of the blue of the forget-me-not, and of a profound melancholy, save when he was plunging his hook into you, at which time two red spots appeared in them and lit them up horribly. In manner, something of the grand seigneur still clung to him, so that he even ripped you up with an air, and I have been told that he was a *raconteur* of repute. He was never more sinister than when he was most polite, which is probably the truest test of breeding; and the elegance of his diction, even when he was swearing, no less than the distinction of his demeanour, showed him one of a different caste from his crew. A man of indomitable courage, it was said of him that the only thing he shied at was the sight of his own blood, which was thick and of an unusual colour. In dress he somewhat aped the attire associated with the name of Charles II, having heard it said in some earlier period of his career that he bore a strange resemblance to the ill-fated Stuarts; and in his mouth he had a holder of his own contrivance which enabled him to smoke two cigars at once. But undoubtedly the grimmest part of him was his iron claw.

Let us now kill a pirate, to show Hook's method. Skylights will do. As they pass, Skylights lurches clumsily against him, ruffling his lace collar; the hook shoots forth, there is a tearing sound and one screech, then the body is kicked aside, and the pirates pass on. He has not even taken the cigars from his mouth.

Such is the terrible man against whom Peter Pan is pitted. Which will win?

J. M. BARRIE, *Peter and Wendy*, 1911

The mate and crew were bundled into the fo'c'sle (the Fox-hole, the children thought it was called), and confined there, the scuttle being secured with a couple of nails.

The children themselves were shepherded, as related, into the deck-house, where the chairs, and perfectly useless pieces of old rope, and broken tools, and dried-up paint-pots were kept, without taking alarm. But the door was immediately shut on them. They had to wait for hours and hours before anything else happened—nearly all day, in fact: and they got very bored, and rather cross.

The actual number of the men who had effected the capture cannot have been more than eight or nine, most of them 'women' at that, and not armed—at least with any visible weapon. But a second boatload soon followed them from the schooner. These, for form's sake, were armed with muskets. But there was no possible resistance to fear. Two long nails through the scuttle can secure any number of men pretty effectually.

With this second boatload came both the captain and the mate. The former was a clumsy great fellow, with a sad, silly face. He was bulky; yet so ill-proportioned one got no impression of power. He was modestly dressed in a drab shore-going suit: he was newly shaven, and his sparse hair was pomaded so that it lay in a few dark ribbons across his baldish head-top. But all this shore-decency of appearance only accentuated his big splodgy brown hands, stained and scarred and corned with his calling. Moreover, instead of boots he wore a pair of gigantic heel-less slippers in the Moorish manner, which he must have sliced with a knife out of some pair of dead sea-boots. Even his great spreading feet could hardly keep them on, so that he was obliged to walk at the slowest of shuffles, flop-flop along the deck. He stooped, as if always afraid of banging his head on something; and carried the backs of his hands forward, like an orang-outang.

RICHARD HUGHES, *A High Wind in Jamaica*, 1929

A SMUGGLER'S SONG

If you wake at midnight and hear a horse's feet,
Don't go drawing back the blind, or looking in the street,
Them that asks no questions isn't told a lie.
Watch the wall, my darling, while the Gentlemen go by!
    Five and twenty ponies,
    Trotting through the dark—
    Brandy for the Parson,
    'Baccy for the Clerk;
    Laces for a lady; letters for a spy,
And watch the wall, my darling, while the Gentlemen go by!

Running round the woodlump if you chance to find
Little barrels, roped and tarred, all full of brandy-wine;
Don't you shout to come and look, nor take 'em for your play;
Put the brushwood back again,—and they'll be gone next day!

If you see the stableyard setting open wide;
If you see a tired horse lying down inside;
If your mother mends a coat cut about and tore;
If the lining's wet and warm—don't you ask no more!

If you meet King George's men, dressed in blue and red,
You be careful what you say, and mindful what is said.
If they call you 'pretty maid', and chuck you 'neath the chin,
Don't you tell where no one is, nor yet where no one's been!

Knocks and footsteps round the house—whistles after dark—
You've no call for running out till the housedogs bark.
Trusty's here and Pincher's here, and see how dumb they lie—
They don't fret to follow when the Gentlemen go by!

If you do as you've been told, likely there's a chance,
You'll be given a dainty doll, all the way from France,
With a cap of Valenciennes, and a velvet hood—
A present from the Gentlemen, along o' being good!
    Five and twenty ponies,
    Trotting through the dark—

Brandy for the Parson,
'Baccy for the Clerk.
Them that asks no questions isn't told a lie—
Watch the wall, my darling, while the
Gentlemen go by!

RUDYARD KIPLING, 1906

IV

MURDERERS

THE FIRST MURDERER?

AND Adam knew Eve his wife; and she conceived, and bare Cain, and said, I have gotten a man from the Lord.

And she again bare his brother Abel. And Abel was a keeper of sheep, but Cain was a tiller of the ground.

And in process of time it came to pass, that Cain brought of the fruit of the ground an offering unto the Lord.

And Abel, he also brought of the firstlings of his flock and of the fat thereof. And the Lord had respect unto Abel and to his offering:

But unto Cain and to his offering he had not respect. And Cain was very wroth, and his countenance fell.

And the Lord said unto Cain, Why art thou wroth? and why is thy countenance fallen?

If thou doest well, shalt thou not be accepted? and if thou doest not well, sin lieth at the door. And unto thee shall be his desire, and thou shalt rule over him.

And Cain talked with Abel his brother: and it came to pass, when they were in the field, that Cain rose up against Abel his brother, and slew him.

And the Lord said unto Cain, Where is Abel thy brother? And he said, I know not: Am I my brother's keeper?

And he said, What hast thou done? the voice of thy brother's blood crieth unto me from the ground.

And now art thou cursed from the earth, which hath opened her mouth to receive thy brother's blood from thy hand;

When thou tillest the ground, it shall not henceforth yield unto thee her strength; a fugitive and a vagabond shalt thou be in the earth.

And Cain said unto the Lord, My punishment is greater than I can bear.

Behold, thou hast driven me out this day from the face of the earth; and from thy face shall I be hid; and I shall be a fugitive and a vagabond in the earth; and it shall come to pass, that every one that findeth me shall slay me.

And the Lord said unto him, Therefore whosoever slayeth Cain, vengeance shall be taken on him sevenfold. And the Lord set a mark upon Cain, lest any finding him should kill him.

And Cain went out from the presence of the Lord, and dwelt in the land of Nod, on the east of Eden.

Genesis 5

And the Lord discomfited Sisera, and all his chariots, and all his host, with the edge of the sword before Barak; so that Sisera lighted down off his chariot, and fled away on his feet.

But Barak pursued after the chariots, and after the host, unto Harosheth of the Gentiles: and all the host of Sisera fell upon the edge of the sword; and there was not a man left.

Howbeit Sisera fled away on his feet to the tent of Jael the wife of Heber the Kenite: for there was peace between Jabin the king of Hazor and the house of Heber the Kenite.

And Jael went out to meet Sisera, and said unto him, Turn in, my lord, turn in to me; fear not. And when he had turned in unto her into the tent, she covered him with a mantle.

And he said unto her, Give me, I pray thee, a little water to drink; for I am thirsty. And she opened a bottle of milk, and gave him drink, and covered him.

Again he said unto her, Stand in the door of the tent, and it shall be, when any man doth come and enquire of thee, and say, Is there any man here? that thou shalt say, No.

Then Jael Heber's wife took a nail of the tent, and took an hammer in her hand, and went softly unto him, and smote the nail into his temples, and fastened it into the ground: for he was fast asleep and weary. So he died.

And, behold, as Barak pursued Sisera, Jael came out to meet him, and said unto him, Come, and I will shew thee the man whom thou seekest. And when he came into her tent, behold, Sisera lay dead, and the nail was in his temples.

So God subdued on that day Jabin the king of Canaan before the children of Israel.

Judges 4

ODYSSEUS AND THE CYCLOPS

'As for my ship . . . it was wrecked by the Earthshaker Poseidon on the confines of your land. The wind had carried us onto a lee shore.

He drove the ship up to a headland and hurled it on the rocks. But I and my friends here managed to escape with our lives.'

To this the cruel brute made no reply. Instead, he jumped up, and reaching out towards my men, seized a couple and dashed their heads against the floor as though they had been puppies. Their brains ran out on the ground and soaked the earth. Limb by limb he tore them to pieces to make his meal, which he devoured like a mountain lion, never pausing till entrails and flesh, marrow and bones, were all consumed, while we could do nothing but weep and lift up our hands to Zeus in horror at the ghastly sight, paralysed by our sense of utter helplessness. When the Cyclops had filled his great belly with this meal of human flesh, which he washed down with unwatered milk, he stretched himself out for sleep among his flocks inside the cave. . . .

No sooner had the tender Dawn shown her roses in the East, than the Cyclops lit up the fire and milked his splendid ewes, all in their proper order, putting her young to each. This business over and his morning labours done, he once more snatched up a couple of my men and prepared his meal. When he had eaten, he turned his fatted sheep out of the cave, removing the great doorstone without an effort. . . .

Evening came, and with it the Cyclops, shepherding his woolly sheep, every one of which he herded into the broad part of the cave, leaving none out in the walled yard, either because he suspected something or because a god had warned him. He raised the great doorstone, set it in its place, and then sat down to milk his ewes and bleating goats, which he did in an orderly way, giving each mother its young one in due course. When this business was over and his work finished, he once more seized upon two of us and prepared his supper. Then came my chance. With an ivy-wood bowl of my dark wine in my hands, I went up to him and said: 'Here, Cyclops, have some wine to wash down that meal of human flesh, and find out for yourself what kind of vintage was stored away in our ship's hold. I brought it for you by way of an offering in the hope that you would be charitable and help me on my homeward way. But your savagery is more than we can bear. Cruel monster, how can you expect ever to have a visitor again from the world of men, after such deeds as you have done?'

The Cyclops took the wine and drank it up. And the delicious draught gave him such exquisite pleasure that he asked me for another bowlful.

'Be good enough,' he said, 'to let me have some more; and tell me your name, here and now, so that I may make you a gift that you will value. We Cyclopes have wine of our own made from the grapes that our rich soil and timely rains produce. But this vintage of yours is nectar and ambrosia distilled.'

So said the Cyclops, and I handed him another bowlful of the ruddy wine. Three times I filled up for him; and three times the fool drained the bowl to the dregs. At last, when the wine had fuddled his wits, I addressed him with disarming suavity.

'Cyclops,' I said, 'you wish to know the name I bear. I'll tell it to you; and in return I should like to have the gift you promised me. My name is Nobody. That is what I am called by my mother and father and by all my friends.'

The Cyclops answered me with a cruel jest. 'Of all his company I will eat Nobody last, and the rest before him. That shall be your gift.'

He had hardly spoken before he toppled over and fell face upwards on the floor, where he lay with his great neck twisted to one side, conquered, as all men are, by sleep. His drunkenness made him vomit, and a stream of wine mixed with morsels of men's flesh poured from his throat. I went at once and thrust our pole deep under the ashes of the fire to make it hot, and meanwhile gave a word of encouragement to all my men, to make sure that no-one should play the coward and leave me in the lurch. When the fierce glow from the olive stake warned me that it was about to catch alight in the flames, green as it was, I withdrew it from the fire and brought it over to the spot where my men were standing ready. Heaven now inspired them with a reckless courage. Seizing the olive pole, they drove its sharpened end into the Cyclops' eye, while I used my weight from above to twist it home, like a man boring a ship's timber with a drill which his mates below him twirl with a strap they hold at either end, so that it spins continuously. In much the same way we handled our pole with its red-hot point and twisted it in his eye till the blood boiled up round the burning wood. The fiery smoke from the blazing eyeball singed his lids and brow all round, and the very roots of his eye crackled in the heat. I was reminded of the loud hiss that comes from a great axe or adze when a smith plunges it into cold water—to temper it and give strength to the iron. That is how the Cyclops' eye hissed round the olive stake. He gave a dreadful shriek, which echoed round the rocky walls, and we backed away from him in terror, while he pulled the stake from his eye, streaming with blood. Then he hurled it away from him with frenzied hands and raised a great shout for the other Cyclopes who lived in neighbouring caves along the windy heights. These, hearing his screams, came up from every quarter, and gathering outside the cave asked him what ailed him:

'What on earth is wrong with you, Polyphemus? Why must you disturb the peaceful night and spoil our sleep with all this shouting? Is a robber driving off your sheep, or is somebody trying by treachery or violence to kill you?'

Out of the cave came Polyphemus' great voice in reply: 'O my friends, it's Nobody's treachery, no violence, that is doing me to death.'

'Well then,' they answered, in a way that settled the matter, 'if nobody is assaulting you in your solitude, you must be sick. Sickness comes from almighty Zeus and cannot be helped. All you can do is to pray to your father, the Lord Poseidon.'

HOMER, *The Odyssey*, ?8th century BC, trans E. V. Rieu

GHOST. I am thy father's spirit;
Doom'd for a certain term to walk the night,
And for the day confin'd to fast in fires,
Till the foul crimes done in my days of nature
Are burnt and purg'd away. But that I am forbid
To tell the secrets of my prison-house,
I could a tale unfold, whose lightest word
Would harrow up thy soul; freeze thy young blood;
Make thy two eyes, like stars, start from their spheres;
Thy knotted and combined locks to part,
And each particular hair to stand on end,
Like quills upon the fretful porpentine:
But this eternal blazon must not be
To ears of flesh and blood.—List, list, O, list!—
If thou didst ever thy dear father love,—
HAMLET. O God!
GHOST. Revenge his foul and most unnatural murder.
HAMLET. Murder!
GHOST. Murder most foul, as in the best it is;
But this most foul, strange, and unnatural.
HAMLET. Haste me to know 't, that I, with wings as swift
As meditation or the thoughts of love,
May sweep to my revenge.

GHOST. I find thee apt;
And duller shouldst thou be than the fat weed
That roots itself in ease on Lethe wharf,
Wouldst thou not stir in this. Now, Hamlet, hear:
'Tis given out that, sleeping in my orchard,
A serpent stung me; so the whole ear of Denmark
Is by a forged process of my death
Rankly abus'd: but know, thou noble youth,
The serpent that did sting thy father's life
Now wears his crown.

HAMLET. O my prophetic soul!
My uncle!

GHOST. Ay, that incestuous, that adulterate beast,
With witchcraft of his wit, with traitorous gifts,—
O wicked wit and gifts that have the power
So to seduce!—won to his shameful lust
The will of my most seeming-virtuous queen:
O, Hamlet, what a falling-off was there!
From me, whose love was of that dignity,
That it went hand in hand even with the vow
I made to her in marriage; and to decline
Upon a wretch, whose natural gifts were poor
To those of mine!
But virtue, as it never will be moved,
Though lewdness court it in a shape of heaven;
So lust, though to a radiant angel link'd,
Will sate itself in a celestial bed,
And prey on garbage.
But, soft! methinks I scent the morning air;
Brief let me be.—Sleeping within my orchard,
My custom always in the afternoon,
Upon my secure hour thy uncle stole,
With juice of cursed hebenon in a vial,
And in the porches of mine ears did pour
The leperous distilment; whose effect
Holds such an enmity with blood of man,
That, swift as quicksilver, it courses through
The natural gates and alleys of the body;
And, with a sudden vigour, it doth posset
And curd, like eager droppings into milk,

The thin and wholesome blood: so did it mine;
And a most instant tetter bark'd about,
Most lazar-like, with vile and loathsome crust
All my smooth body.
Thus was I, sleeping, by a brother's hand
Of life, of crown, of queen, at once dispatch'd:
Cut off even in the blossoms of my sin,
Unhousel'd, disappointed, unaneled;
No reckoning made, but sent to my account
With all my imperfections on my head:
O, horrible! O, horrible! most horrible!
If thou hast nature in thee, bear it not;
Let not the royal bed of Denmark be
A couch for luxury and damn'd incest.
But, howsoever thou pursuest this act,
Taint not thy mind, nor let thy soul contrive
Against thy mother aught: leave her to heaven,
And to those thorns that in her bosom lodge
To prick and sting her. Fare thee well at once!
The glow-worm shows the matin to be near,
And 'gins to pale his uneffectual fire:
Adieu, adieu, adieu! remember me. [*Exit*.

HAMLET. O all you host of heaven! O earth! what else?
And shall I couple hell?—O, fie!—Hold, hold, my heart,
And you, my sinews, grow not instant old,
But bear me stiffly up.—Remember thee!
Ay, thou poor ghost, while memory holds a seat
In this distracted globe. Remember thee!
Yea, from the table of my memory
I'll wipe away all trivial fond records,
All saws of books, all forms, all pressures past,
That youth and observation copied there;
And thy commandment all alone shall live
Within the book and volume of my brain,
Unmix'd with baser matter: yes, by heaven!—
O most pernicious woman!
O villain, villain, smiling, damned villain!
My tables,—meet it is I set it down,
That one may smile, and smile, and be a villain;
At least I'm sure it may be so in Denmark: [*Writing*.

So, uncle, there you are. Now to my word;
It is, 'Adieu, adieu! remember me':
I have sworn't.

WILLIAM SHAKESPEARE, *Hamlet*, 1603

MACBETH. If we should fail?
LADY MACBETH. We fail:
But screw your courage to the sticking-place,
And we'll not fail. When Duncan is asleep,—
Whereto the rather shall his day's hard journey
Soundly invite him,—his two chamberlains
Will I with wine and wassail so convince,
That memory, the warder of the brain,
Shall be a fume, and the receipt of reason
A limbeck only: when in swinish sleep
Their drenched natures lie as in a death,
What cannot you and I perform upon
Th' unguarded Duncan? what not put upon
His spongy officers, who shall bear the guilt
Of our great quell?
MACBETH. Bring forth men-children only;
For thy undaunted mettle should compose
Nothing but males. Will it not be received,
When we have mark'd with blood those sleepy two
Of his own chamber, and us'd their very daggers,
That they have done't?
LADY MACBETH. Who dares receive it other,
As we shall make our griefs and clamour roar
Upon his death?
MACBETH. I am settled, and bend up
Each corporal agent to this terrible feat.
Away, and mock the time with fairest show:
False face must hide what the false heart doth know. [*Exeunt*.

WILLIAM SHAKESPEARE, *Macbeth*, 1606

DUCHESS. I am Duchess of Malfy still.
BOSOLA. That makes thy sleeps so broken:
Glories, like glow-worms, afar off shine bright;
But, look'd too near, have neither heat nor light.
DUCHESS. Thou art very plain.
BOSOLA. My grade is to flatter the dead, not the living.
I am a tomb-maker.
DUCHESS. And thou comest to make my tomb?
BOSOLA. Yes.
DUCHESS. Let me be a little merry.
Of what stuff wilt thou make it?
BOSOLA. Nay, resolve me first; of what fashion?
DUCHESS. Why, do we grow fantastical in our death-bed?
Do we affect fashion in the grave?
BOSOLA. Most ambitiously. Princes' images on their tombs do not lie as they were wont, seeming to pray up to heaven; but with their hands under their cheeks (as if they died of the tooth-ache): they are not carved with their eyes fixed upon the stars; but, as their minds were wholly bent upon the world, the selfsame way they seem to turn their faces.
DUCHESS. Let me know fully therefore the effect
Of this thy dismal preparation,
This talk, fit for a charnel.
BOSOLA. Now I shall. [*A coffin, cords, and a bell, produced.*
Here is a present from your princely brothers;
And may it arrive welcome, for it brings
Last benefit, last sorrow.
DUCHESS. Let me see it.
I have so much obedience in my blood,
I wish it in their veins to do them good.
BOSOLA. This is your last presence-chamber.
CARIOLA. O my sweet lady!
DUCHESS. Peace, it affrights not me.
BOSOLA. I am the common bellman,
That usually is sent to condemn'd persons
The night before they suffer.
DUCHESS. Even now thou saidst,
Thou wast a tomb-maker.
BOSOLA. 'Twas to bring you
By degrees to mortification. Listen.

Dirge.

Hark, now everything is still;
This screech-owl, and the whistler shrill,
Call upon your dame aloud,
And bid her quickly d'on her shroud.
Much you had of land and rent;
Your length in clay's now competent.
A long war disturb'd your mind;
Here your perfect peace is sign'd.
Of what is 't fools make such vain keeping.
Sin, their conception; their birth, weeping:
Their life, a general mist of error;
Their death, a hideous storm of terror.
Strew your hair with powders sweet,
D'on clean linen, bathe your feet:
And (the foul fiend more to check)
A crucifix let bless your neck.
'Tis now full tide 'tween night and day:
End your groan, and come away.

CARIOLA. Hence, villains, tyrants, murderers: alas!
What will you do with my lady? Call for help.

DUCHESS. To whom; to our next neighbours? They are mad folks.
Farewell, Cariola.
I pray thee look thou givest my little boy
Some syrup for his cold; and let the girl
Say her prayers ere she sleep.—Now what you please;
What death?

BOSOLA. Strangling. Here are your executioners.

DUCHESS. I forgive them.
The apoplexy, catarrh, or cough of the lungs,
Would do as much as they do.

BOSOLA. Doth not death fright you?

DUCHESS. Who would be afraid on 't,
Knowing to meet such excellent company
In the other world?

BOSOLA. Yet methinks,
The manner of your death should much afflict you;
This cord should terrify you.

DUCHESS. Not a whit.
What would it pleasure me to have my throat cut

With diamonds? or to be smother'd
With cassia? or to be shot to death with pearls?
I know, death hath ten thousand several doors
For men to take their exits: and 'tis found
They go on such strange geometrical hinges,
You may open them both ways; any way: (for heaven's sake)
So I were out of your whispering: tell my brothers,
That I perceive, death (now I'm well awake)
Best gift is, they can give or I can take.
I would fain put off my last woman's fault;
I'd not be tedious to you.
Pull, and pull strongly, for your able strength
Must pull down heaven upon me.
Yet stay, heaven gates are not so highly arch'd
As princes' palaces; they that enter there
Must go upon their knees. Come, violent death,
Serve for Mandragora to make me sleep.
Go tell my brothers; when I am laid out,
They then may feed in quiet. [*They strangle her, kneeling.*

JOHN WEBSTER, *The Duchess of Malfy*, ?1614

AFTER THE MURDER

D'AMVILLE. Here's a sweet comedy, begins with *O dolentis*, and concludes with ha, ha, he.

BORACHIO. Ha, ha, he.

D'AMVILLE. O my echo! I could stand reverberating this sweet musical air of joy, till I had perished my sound lungs with violent laughter. Lovely night-raven, thou hast seized a carcase?

BORACHIO. Put him out on 's pain. I lay so fitly underneath the bank from whence he fell, that ere his faltering tongue could utter double O, I knocked out his brains with this fair ruby; and had another stone just of this form and bigness ready, that I laid in the broken skull upon the ground for his pillow, against the which they thought he fell and perished.

D'AMVILLE. Upon this ground I'll build my manor house,
And this shall be chiefest corner-stone.

BORACHIO. This crown'd the most judicious murder, that
The brain of man was e'er delivered of.

D'AMVILLE. Ay, mark the plot. Not any circumstance
That stood within the reach of the design,
Of persons, dispositions, matter, time,
Or place, but by this brain of mine was made
An instrumental help; yet nothing from
The induction to the accomplishment seem'd forced,
Or done o' purpose, but by accident.
[*Here they reckon up the several circumstances.*
BORACHIO. Then darkness did
Protect the execution of the work
Both from prevention and discovery
D'AMVILLE. Here was a murder bravely carried through
The eye of observation, unobserved.
BORACHIO. And those that saw the passage of it, made
The instruments; yet knew not what they did.
D'AMVILLE. That power of rule, philosophers ascribe
To him they call the Supreme of the Stars,
Making their influences governors
Of sublunary creatures, when theirselves
Are senseless of their operations. [*Thunder and lightning.*
What! dost start at thunder? Credit my belief, 'tis a mere effect of nature, an exhalation hot and dry, involved within a watery vapour in the middle region of the air, whose coldness congealing that thick moisture to a cloud, the angry exhalation shut within a prison of contrary quality, strives to be free; and with the violent eruption through the grossness of that cloud, makes this noise we hear.
BORACHIO. 'Tis a fearful noise.
D'AMVILLE. 'Tis a brave noise; and, methinks, graces our accomplished project, as a peal of ordnance does a triumph. It speaks encouragement. Now nature shows thee how it favoured our performance to forbear this noise when we set forth, because it should not terrify my brother's going home, which would have dashed our purpose: to forbear this lightning in our passage, lest it should have warned him of the pitfall. Then propitious nature winked at our proceedings; now, it doth express how that forbearance favoured our success.

CYRIL TOURNEUR, *The Atheist's Tragedy*, 1611

THE TWA BROTHERS

There were twa brethren in the North,
  They went to school thegither;
The one unto the other said,
  'Will you try a warsle, brither?' *wrestle*

They warsled up, they warsled down,
  Till Sir John fell to the ground,
And there was a knife in Sir Willie's pouch
  Gied him a deadly wound.

'Tak' aff, tak' aff my holland sark,
  Rive it frae gare to gare, *tear; gore*
And stap it in my bleeding wound—
  'Twill aiblins bleed nae mair.' *perhaps*

He's pu'it aff his holland sark,
  Rave it frae gare to gare,
And stapt it in his bleeding wound—
  But aye it bled the mair.

'O tak' now aff my green cleiding *clothing*
  And row me saftly in, *wrap*
And carry me up to Chester kirk,
  Whar the grass grows fair and green.

'But what will ye say to your father dear
  When ye gae home at e'en?'—
'I'll say ye're lying at Chester kirk,
  Whar the grass grows fair and green.'—

'Oh no, O no, when he speers for me *asks*
  Saying, "William, whar is John?"
Ye'll say ye left me at Chester school
  Leaving the school alone.'

He's ta'en him up upo' his back,
  And borne him hence away,
And carried him to Chester kirk,
  And laid him in the clay.

But when he sat in his father's chair,
He grew baith pale and wan:
'O what blude's that upon your brow?
And whar is your brither John?'—

'O John's awa' to Chester school,
A scholar he'll return;
He bade me tell his father dear
About him no' to mourn.

'And it is the blude o' my gude grey steed;
He wadna hunt for me.'—
'O thy steed's blude was ne'er so red,
Nor ne'er so dear to me!

'And whaten blude's that upon your dirk?
Dear Willie, tell to me.'—
'It is the blude o' my ae brither
And dule and wae is me!'—

'O what sall I say to your mither?
Dear Willie, tell to me.'—
'I'll saddle my steed and awa' I'll ride,
To dwell in some far countrie.'—

'O when will ye come hame again?
Dear Willie, tell to me!'—
'When the sun and moon dance on yon green:
And that will never be!'

ANON.

† *In 1811, London was shaken by the murders of a linen-draper named Timothy Marr, his wife, 3-month-old son, and 14-year-old apprentice boy. Twelve days later, in the same district, an elderly publican named Williamson, his wife and servant were also done to death in a similar manner. These crimes, for which John Williams was*

convicted, came to be known as 'the Ratcliffe Highway murders' and inspired De Quincey's essay 'On Murder Considered as One of the Fine Arts'.

John Williams, . . . who had been occasionally rated as a seaman on board of various Indiamen, &c., was probably a very accomplished seaman. Pretty generally, in fact, he was a ready and adroit man, fertile in resources under all sudden difficulties, and most flexibly adapting himself to all varieties of social life. Williams was a man of middle stature (five feet seven and a half to five feet eight inches high), slenderly built, rather thin, but wiry, tolerably muscular, and clear of all superfluous flesh. A lady who saw him under examination (I think at the Thames Police Office) assured me that his hair was of the most extraordinary and vivid colour,—viz. bright yellow, something between an orange and a lemon colour. Williams had been in India; chiefly in Bengal and Madras, but he had also been upon the Indus. Now, it is notorious that in the Punjaub horses of a high caste are often painted—crimson, blue, green, purple; and it struck me that Williams might, for some casual purpose of disguise, have taken a hint from this practice of Scinde and Lahore, so that the colour might not have been natural. In other respects his appearance was natural enough, and,—judging by a plaster cast of him which I purchased in London,—I should say mean as regarded his facial structure. One fact, however, was striking, and fell in with the impression of his natural tiger character,—that his face wore at all times a bloodless ghastly pallor. 'You might imagine,' said my informant, 'that in his veins circulated not red life-blood, such as could kindle into the blush of shame, of wrath, of pity—but a green sap that welled from no human heart.' His eyes seemed frozen and glazed, as if their light were all converged upon some victim lurking in the far background. So far his appearance might have repelled; but, on the other hand, the concurrent testimony of many witnesses, and also the silent testimony of facts, showed that the oiliness and snaky insinuation of his demeanour counteracted the repulsiveness of his ghastly face, and amongst inexperienced young women won for him a very favourable reception. In particular, one gentle-mannered girl, whom Williams had undoubtedly designed to murder, gave in evidence that once, when sitting alone with her, he had said, 'Now, Miss R., supposing that I should appear about midnight at your bedside armed with a carving knife, what would you say?' To which the confiding girl had replied, 'Oh, Mr Williams, if it was anybody else, I should be frightened. But, as soon as I heard *your* voice, I should be tranquil.' Poor girl! had this outline sketch of Mr Williams been filled in and realised, she would have seen something in the corpselike face, and heard something in the sinister voice, that would have unsettled her tranquillity for ever. But nothing short of such dreadful experiences could avail to unmask Mr John Williams.

THOMAS DE QUINCEY, 'On Murder Considered as One of the Fine Arts', 1827

THE MURDER OF MARIA MARTEN BY W. CORDER

Come all you thoughtless young men, a warning take by me,
And think upon my unhappy fate to be hanged upon a tree;
My name is William Corder, to you I do declare,
I courted Maria Marten, most beautiful and fair.

I promised I would marry her upon a certain day,
Instead of that, I was resolved to take her life away.
I went into her father's house the 18th day of May,
Saying, my dear Maria, we will fix the wedding day.

If you will meet me at the Red-barn, as sure as I have life,
I will take you to Ipswich town, and there make you my wife;
I then went home and fetched my gun, my pickaxe and my spade,
I went into the Red-barn, and there I dug her grave.

With heart so light, she thought no harm, to meet him she did go;
He murdered her all in the barn, and laid her body low:
After the horrible deed was done, she lay weltering in her gore,
Her bleeding mangled body he buried beneath the Red-barn floor.

Now all things being silent, her spirit could not rest,
She appeared unto her mother, who suckled her at her breast;
For many a long month or more, her mind being sore oppress'd,
Neither night or day she could not take any rest.

Her mother's mind being so disturbed, she dreamt three nights o'er,
Her daughter she lay murdered beneath the Red-barn floor;

She sent the father to the barn, when he the ground did thrust,
And there he found his daughter mingling with the dust.

My trial is hard, I could not stand, most woeful was the sight,
When her jaw-bone was brought to prove, which pierced my heart
quite;
Her aged father standing by, likewise his loving wife,
And in her grief her hair she tore, she scarcely could keep life.

Adieu, adieu, my loving friends, my glass is almost run,
On Monday next will be my last, when I am to be hang'd;
So you, young men, who do pass by, with pity look on me,
For murdering Maria Marten, I was hang'd upon the tree.

ANON.

A STUDENT'S PLEA

The last words in court of the Moscow student Maukoff, who had murdered his wife, were as follows:

'She is dead, she is a martyr, perhaps by now she is a holy being, in paradise; whereas I remain here below to carry, for the rest of my life, the heavy cross of crime and repentance. Why punish me, when I have already punished myself? I can still eat nice little apples and eggs, just as I did before, but they no longer possess their former sweet flavour. Nothing gives me any joy now—why then punish me?'

MAXIM GORKY, *Fragments from My Diary*, 1924

† *Cecil Frances Alexander is well known as the author of such hymns as 'Once in Royal David's City' and 'There is a Green Hill Far Away'; not many people, however, are aware of her one excursion into the field of grisly comedy. 'The Legend of Stumpie's Brae' tells of a frightful old couple in County Donegal who murder a travelling pedlar for the sake of his*

bag of goods. The body proves too large to fit into the man's own sack, so they chop off the legs at the knee.

. . . They shorten'd the corp, and they pack'd
him tight,
Wi' his legs in a pickle hay;
Over the burn, in the sweet moonlight,
They carried him till this brae.

They shovell'd a hole right speedily,
They laid him in on his back—
'A right pair are ye,' quo' the PEDLAR, quo' he,
Sitting bolt upright in the pack.

'Ye think ye've laid me snugly here,
And none shall know my station;
But I'll hant ye far, and I'll hant ye near,
Father and son, wi' terror and fear,
To the nineteenth generation.'

The twa were sittin' the vera next night,
When the dog began to cower,
And they knew, by the pale blue fire light,
That the Evil One had power.

It had stricken nine, just nine o' the clock—
The hour when the man lay dead;
There came to the outer door a knock,
And a heavy, heavy tread.

The old man's head swam round and round,
The woman's blood 'gan freeze,
For it was not like a natural sound,
But like some one stumping o'er the ground
An the banes of his twa bare knees.

And through the door, like a sough of air,
And stump, stump, round the twa,
Wi' his bloody head, and his knee banes bare—
They'd maist ha'e died of awe!

The wife's black locks ere morn grew white,
  They say, as the mountain snaws;
The man was as straight as a staff that night,
  But he stoop'd when the morning rose.

Still year and day, as the clock struck NINE,
  The hour when they did the sin,
The wee bit dog began to whine,
  And the ghaist came clattering in . . .

CECIL FRANCES ALEXANDER, 1896

PORPHYRIA'S LOVER

The rain set early in to-night,
  The sullen wind was soon awake,
It tore the elm-tops down for spite,
  And did its worst to vex the lake:
  I listened with heart fit to break.
When glided in Porphyria; straight
  She shut the cold out and the storm,
And kneeled and made the cheerless grate
  Blaze up, and all the cottage warm;
  Which done, she rose, and from her form
Withdrew the dripping cloak and shawl,
  And laid her soiled gloves by, untied
Her hat and let the damp hair fall,
  And, last, she sat down by my side
  And called me. When no voice replied,
She put my arm about her waist,
  And made her smooth white shoulder bare,
And all her yellow hair displaced,
  And, stooping, made my cheek lie there,
  And spread, o'er all, her yellow hair,
Murmuring how she loved me—she
  Too weak, for all her heart's endeavour,
To set its struggling passion free
  From pride, and vainer ties dissever,
  And give herself to me for ever.

But passion sometimes would prevail,
  Nor could to-night's gay feast restrain
A sudden thought of one so pale
  For love of her, and all in vain:
  So, she was come through wind and rain.
Be sure I looked up at her eyes
  Happy and proud; at last I knew
Porphyria worshipped me; surprise
  Made my heart swell, and still it grew
  While I debated what to do.
That moment she was mine, mine, fair,
  Perfectly pure and good: I found
A thing to do, and all her hair
  In one long yellow string I wound
  Three times her little throat around,
And strangled her. No pain felt she;
  I am quite sure she felt no pain.
As a shut bud that holds a bee,
  I warily oped her lids: again
  Laughed the blue eyes without a stain.
And I untightened next the tress
  About her neck; her cheek once more
Blushed bright beneath my burning kiss:
  I propped her head up as before,
  Only, this time my shoulder bore
Her head, which droops upon it still:
  The smiling rosy little head,
So glad it has its utmost will,
  That all it scorned at once is fled,
  And I, its love, am gained instead!
Porphyria's love: she guessed not how
  Her darling one wish would be heard.
And thus we sit together now,
  And all night long we have not stirred,
  And yet God has not said a word!

ROBERT BROWNING, 1830

So Burke and Hare buy from the tanner the regular sack of bark, and when the coffin carpenter has finished and gone, they prise up the case, hoist out the body and frog-march it to the dark room. Then put the bag of bark, the specific gravity exactly of a wasted body, into the shell, and nail that up for pauper burial. When the town-hearse has passed, they send out one of the women for a tea-chest, for by a mysterious ratio, bag of bark: human body: tea-chest: convenient coffin.

After dark, they sold 'the thing' for £7 10*s*. to Doctor Knox, 10 Surgeon's Square, the noted independent Professor of Anatomy, whose address and reputation for paying the best prices for bodies had been found out somehow by Burke. This Knox, who was ruined as a result of the case, was one of those intelligent eccentrics of whom Scotland has the manufacturing secret. In science he was as remarkable as in appearance, a gnarled little fellow, with 'one blind eye like a grape', with a coffin-shaped forehead; in character, a squirming package of malice, jealousy and pawkiness who did not disdain to eke out his undoubted attainments with all the tricks of an advanced quackery. Knox was as fanatical a self-admirer as Burke; had the murderer met with a like success in his life-cult of himself, his neighbours doubtless would have had to stand the same spectacle of unwearied self-glorification, as Edinburgh Society from that learned Doctor, and complete egotist, Knox. We are indeed in presence, unlike as the social circumstances and the progress of the disease may make them appear, of two phases of the same character, and it is interesting to watch how both Knox and Burke, to make the objective world of their relations to fellow-individuals and society assimilable in the inadjustable centre of their egocentric universe, were obliged to use the same system.

Knox excused to himself all his basenesses, 'because it was a matter of science'. To Burke, his mean swindlings, the agonies of his victims, were only tolerable if he clung to it—'this is a matter of business'. A wavering of the theory even for a second would have brought Burke to his knees, howling for a priest; or sent Knox mad with shame. But till the one stood on the boards of the scaffold, and the other closed a spoilt career 'in the position of showman to a tribe of Ojibbeway Indians in a circus in London', it cannot be found that either wavered in his self-hypnotism for a little instant.

William Bolitho, *Murder for Profit*, 1926

The Reverend Doctor Folliott took his departure about ten o'clock, to walk home to his vicarage. There was no moon; but the night was bright and clear, and afforded him as much light as he needed. He paused a moment by the Roman Camp, to listen to the nightingale; repeated to himself a passage of Sophocles; proceeded through the park gate, and entered the narrow lane that led to the village. He walked on in a very pleasant mood of the state called *reverie*; in which fish and wine, Greek and political economy, the Sleeping Venus he had left behind and poor dear Mrs Folliott, to whose fond arms he was returning, passed as in a *camera obscura* over the tablets of his imagination. Presently the image of Mr Eavesdrop, with a printed sketch of the Reverend Doctor F., presented itself before him, and he began mechanically to flourish his bamboo. The movement was prompted by his good genius, for the uplifted bamboo received the blow of a ponderous cudgel, which was intended for his head. The reverend gentleman recoiled two or three paces, and saw before him a couple of ruffians, who were preparing to renew the attack, but whom, with two swings of his bamboo, he laid with cracked sconces on the earth, where he proceeded to deal with them like corn beneath the flail of the thresher. One of them drew a pistol, which went off in the very act of being struck aside by the bamboo, and lodged a bullet in the brain of the other. There was then only one enemy, who vainly struggled to rise, every effort being attended with a new and more signal prostration. The fellow roared for mercy. 'Mercy, rascal!' cried the divine; 'what mercy were you going to show me, villain? What! I warrant me, you thought it would be an easy matter, and no sin, to rob and murder a parson on his way home from dinner. You said to yourselves, doubtless, "We'll waylay the fat parson (you irreverent knave) as he waddles home (you disparaging ruffian), half-seas-over (you calumnious vagabond)." ' And with every dyslogistic term, which he supposed had been applied to himself, he inflicted a new bruise on his rolling and roaring antagonist. 'Ah, rogue!' he proceeded; 'you can roar now, marauder; you were silent enough when you devoted my brains to dispersion under your cudgel. But seeing that I cannot bind you, and that I intend you not to escape, and that it would be dangerous to let you rise, I will disable you in all your members; I will contund you as Thestylis did strong-smelling herbs,* in the quality whereof you do most gravely partake, as my nose beareth testimony,

* 'Thestylis . . . herbas contundit olentes.' (Virg., *Ecl.* ii. 10, 11.) [P.]

ill weed that you are. I will beat you to a jelly, and I will then roll you into the ditch, to lie till the constable comes for you, thief.'

'Hold! hold! reverend sir,' exclaimed the penitent culprit, 'I am disabled already in every finger, and in every joint. I will roll myself into the ditch, reverend sir.'

'Stir not, rascal,' returned the divine, 'stir not so much as the quietest leaf above you, or my bamboo rebounds on your body like hail in a thunderstorm. Confess speedily, villain; are you simple thief, or would you have manufactured me into a subject, for the benefit of science? Ay, miscreant caitiff, you would have made me a subject for science, would you? You are a schoolmaster abroad, are you? You are marching with a detachment of the march of mind, are you? You are a member of the Steam Intellect Society, are you? You swear by the learned friend, do you?'

'Oh, no! reverend sir,' answered the criminal, 'I am innocent of all these offences, whatever they are, reverend sir. The only friend I had in the world is lying dead beside me, reverend sir.'

The reverend gentleman paused a moment, and leaned on his bamboo. The culprit, bruised as he was, sprang on his legs, and went off in double quick time. The doctor gave him chase, and had nearly brought him within arm's length, when the fellow turned at right angles, and sprang clean over a deep dry ditch. The divine, following with equal ardour, and less dexterity, went down over head and ears into a thicket of nettles. Emerging with much discomposure, he proceeded to the village, and roused the constable; but the constable found, on reaching the scene of action, that the dead man was gone, as well as his living accomplice.

'Oh, the monster!' exclaimed the Reverend Doctor Folliott, 'he has made a subject for science of the only friend he had in the world.' 'Ay, my dear,' he resumed, the next morning at breakfast, 'if my old reading, and my early gymnastics (for as the great Hermann says, before I was demulced by the Muses, I was *ferocis ingenii puer, et ad arma quam ad literas paratior**), had not imbued me indelibly with some of the holy rage of *Frère Jean des Entommeures*, I should be, at this moment, lying on the table of some flinty-hearted anatomist, who would have sliced and disjointed me as unscrupulously as I do these remnants of the capon and chine, wherewith you consoled

* 'A boy of fierce disposition, more inclined to arms than to letters.' (*Hermann's Dedication of Homer's Hymns to His Preceptor Ilgen*) [P.]

yourself yesterday for my absence at dinner. Phew! I have a noble thirst upon me, which I will quench with floods of tea.'

THOMAS LOVE PEACOCK, *Crotchet Castle*, 1831

Nearly a year later, in the month of October 18—, London was startled by a crime of singular ferocity and rendered all the more notable by the high position of the victim. The details were few and startling. A maid servant living alone in a house not far from the river, had gone upstairs to bed about eleven. Although a fog rolled over the city in the small hours, the early part of the night was cloudless, and the lane, which the maid's window overlooked, was brilliantly lit by the full moon. It seems she was romantically given, for she sat down upon her box, which stood immediately under the window, and fell into a dream of musing. Never (she used to say, with streaming tears, when she narrated that experience) never had she felt more at peace with all men or thought more kindly of the world. And as she so sat she became aware of an aged and beautiful gentleman with white hair, drawing near along the lane; and advancing to meet him, another and very small gentleman, to whom at first she paid less attention. When they had come within speech (which was just under the maid's eyes) the older man bowed and accosted the other with a very pretty manner of politeness. It did not seem as if the subject of his address were of great importance; indeed, from his pointing, it sometimes appeared as if he were only inquiring his way; but the moon shone on his face as he spoke, and the girl was pleased to watch it, it seemed to breathe such an innocent and old-world kindness of disposition, yet with something high too, as of a well-founded self-content. Presently her eye wandered to the other, and she was surprised to recognise in him a certain Mr Hyde, who had once visited her master and for whom she had conceived a dislike. He had in his hand a heavy cane, with which he was trifling; but he answered never a word, and seemed to listen with an ill-contained impatience. And then all of a sudden he broke out in a great flame of anger, stamping with his foot, brandishing the cane, and carrying on (as the maid described it) like a madman. The old gentleman took a step back, with the air of one very much surprised and a trifle hurt; and at that Mr Hyde broke out of all bounds and clubbed him to the earth. And next moment, with ape-like fury, he was trampling his victim under foot, and hailing down a storm of blows, under which the bones were audibly shattered and the body jumped upon the roadway. At the horror of these sights and sounds, the maid fainted.

ROBERT LOUIS STEVENSON, *The Strange Case of Dr Jekyll and Mr Hyde*, 1886

† *Raskolnikov, a student, has committed two brutal and senseless murders. Now he faces interrogation by an apparently friendly police officer, Porfiry Petrovich.*

Raskolnikov's whole body quivered, so that Porfiry Petrovich could see it quite plainly.

'You are lying all the time!' he said. 'I don't know what you are aiming at, but you do nothing but lie . . . You weren't talking in that sense a few minutes ago, and I can't be mistaken about that . . . Are you lying?'

'I lying?' rejoined Porfiry, visibly growing a little heated but still preserving the same cheerfully mocking expression and apparently not at all worried by what Mr Raskolnikov might think of him. 'Lying? . . . Well, how was I acting towards you just now (and I an examining magistrate), when I was prompting you, showing you all the ways of defending yourself, supplying all that psychology: "Illness," I said, "delirium, being insulted, melancholia, police officers" and all the rest of it? Eh? he, he, he! There is one thing, however, to be said—all these psychological means of defence, these excuses and evasions, are very insubstantial, and they cut both ways. "Illness, delirium," you say, "fancies, illusions, I don't remember"—that is all very well, but then why is it, old chap, that you see just these illusions in your sick delirium, and not others? There could have been others, couldn't there? He, he, he, he!'

Raskolnikov looked at him proudly and scornfully.

'In one word,' he said loudly and insistently, pushing Porfiry back a little as he stood up, 'in one word, what I want to know is this: Do you admit that I am definitely free from suspicion or *not*? Tell me that, Porfiry Petrovich, tell me definitely and finally, and quickly, at once!'

'Here's a fine fuss! Well, what a fuss you make!' cried Porfiry, with a sly, perfectly cheerful, and unruffled look. 'Why do you want to know, why do you want to know so much, when nobody has even begun to worry you yet? Really you are like a child crying for the fire to play with. And why are you so worried? Why do you thrust yourself upon us? What are your reasons, eh? He, he, he!'

'I tell you again,' shouted Raskolnikov furiously, 'that I cannot any longer endure . . .'

'What? The uncertainty?' interrupted Porfiry.

'Do not taunt me! I will not have it . . . I tell you I won't have it! . . . I can't and I won't! . . . Listen to me!' he shouted, banging the table with his fist again.

'Quietly, quietly! You will be heard! I warn you seriously, look after yourself. I am not joking!' said Porfiry in a whisper, but this time his face had not its former expression of womanish good nature and alarm. On the contrary, now he was *giving orders*, frowning sternly and destroying at one blow, as it were, all mystery and ambiguity. But it was only for a moment. Raskolnikov, perplexed, fell suddenly into a real frenzy; but strangely enough he again obeyed the injunction to speak quietly, although he was in a perfect paroxysm of fury.

'I will not allow myself to be tortured!' As he had before, he suddenly dropped his voice to a whisper, instantly recognizing with anguish and hatred that he felt obliged to submit to the command, and driven to greater fury by the knowledge. 'Arrest me, search me, but be good enough to act in the proper form, and don't play with me! Do not dare . . .'

'Don't worry about the proper form,' interrupted Porfiry, with his former sly smile, apparently even gloating over Raskolnikov. 'I invited you here informally, old man, in a very friendly fashion!'

'I don't want your friendship! I spit upon it! Do you hear? And look: I am taking my cap and going. Well, what will you say now, if you intend to arrest me?'

He seized his cap and went to the door.

'But don't you want to see my little surprise?' chuckled Porfiry, seizing his arm again and stopping him by the door. He seemed to be growing ever more high-spirited and playful, and this made Raskolnikov finally lose control.

'What little surprise? What is this?' he asked, stopping short and looking at Porfiry with terror.

FYODOR DOSTOEVSKY, *Crime and Punishment*, 1866, trans. Jessie Coulson

BAG-SNATCHING IN DUBLIN

Sisley
Walked so nicely
With footsteps so discreet
To see her pass
You'd never guess
She walked upon the street.
Down where the Liffy waters' turgid flood
Churns up to greet the ocean-driven mud,
A bruiser in a fix
Murdered her for 6/6.

STEVIE SMITH (1902–71)

ARTIFICIAL AIM

While they were waiting at a bus stop in Clerimston, Mr and Mrs Daniel Thirsty were threatened by a Mr Robert Clear.

'He demanded that I give him my wife's purse,' said Mr Thirsty. 'Telling him that the purse was in her basket, I bent down, put my hands up her skirt, detached her artificial leg and hit him over the head with it. It was not my intention to do any more than frighten him off but, unhappily for us all, he died.'

Edinburgh Evening News, 18 August 1978 in CHRISTOPHER LOGUE, *Bumper Book of True Stories*, 1980

ASSASSINS

Or who in Moscow, toward the Czar,
With the demurest of footfalls
Over the Kremlin's pavement bright
With serpentine and syenite,
Steps, with five other Generals
That simultaneously take snuff,
For each to have pretext enough
And kerchiefwise unfold his sash
Which, softness' self, is yet the stuff
To hold fast where a steel chain snaps,
And leave the grand white neck no gash?

ROBERT BROWNING, from 'Waring', 1842

A MURDERER IN READING GAOL

He did not wear his scarlet cloak,
  For blood and wine are red,
And blood and wine were on his hands
  When they found him with the dead,
The poor dead woman whom he loved,
  And murdered in her bed.

He walked amongst the Trial Men
  In a suit of shabby grey;
A cricket cap was on his head,
  And his step seemed light and gay;
But I never saw a man who looked
  So wistfully at the day.

I never saw a man who looked
  With such a wistful eye
Upon that little tent of blue
  Which prisoners call the sky,
And at every drifting cloud that went
  With sails of silver by.

I walked, with other souls in pain,
  Within another ring,
And was wondering if the man had done
  A great or little thing,
When a voice behind me whispered low,
  'That fellow's got to swing.'

Dear Christ! the very prison walls
  Suddenly seemed to reel,
And the sky above my head became
  Like a casque of scorching steel;
And, though I was a soul in pain,
  My pain I could not feel.

I only knew what hunted thought
  Quickened his step, and why
He looked upon the garish day
  With such a wistful eye;
The man had killed the thing he loved,
  And so he had to die.

OSCAR WILDE, from *The Ballad of Reading Gaol*, 1898

† *Dr Crippen murdered his wife, 'Belle Elmore', a failed music hall performer, because he wished to live happily with his mistress Ethel Le Neve. The murder he committed was brutal in the extreme. Apart from this crime he appears to have been of a singularly gentle and harmless disposition.*

Across the chasm which separates the ordinary citizen from the criminal, he had taken the fatal and decisive step; but having done so, instead of going off, like so many murderers, to wander in the wilderness as an outlaw, he resumed his ordinary course of life; he kept straight on; only now he walked on the far side of the narrow abyss. If the course of his life were to be marked on a chart one would not see it, as is usual in the case of criminals, turning suddenly at a right angle and continuing in that direction; it would appear as a straight course with one little step aside in the middle of it, and then continuing as before. It is certain that he showed no disturbance, remorse or fright for the horrid deed that he had committed; and I believe that he did not feel any. In some obscure way he justified to himself what he had done without violating his conscience, because, as far as one can judge, his life was now happier than it had been before. But on the assumption that he committed this crime out of love for his mistress, his subsequent conduct was perfectly consistent. He took all the necessary steps, and took them with great skill and coolness, to conceal all traces of the crime. The bones, limbs, and head, as well as certain characteristic organs, had all been removed from the discovered remains, and the evidence was that they had been removed by a hand skilled in dissection. No one knows how they were disposed of; but it must have been a work of days. One theory is that it was done in the bath, and the bones and limbs burned in the kitchen grate, while the head was got rid of during Crippen's subsequent trip to Dieppe—dropped overboard in a handbag. But whatever the method, it must have involved labours physically exhausting, and of a nature horrible to contemplate.

He invented a story to account for his wife's disappearance. With a certain completeness of artistic circumstances he developed her disappearance into her death in far-away California; and he devoted himself to the girl for whose affections he was to pay such a price. It is characteristic of the inconsistency of human prejudice that half the indignation and horror aroused against him was because of the fact that he cut up his wife's remains, and that he wrote hypocritical letters to the music hall ladies about her death in California. How absurd is such an attitude. The crime was in murdering his wife; it was a crime of such magnitude that nothing he could do afterwards could possibly aggravate it, unless it had involved cruelty or betrayal of some one who was alive. On the contrary, granting the crime and granting its enormity, what he did afterwards was technically admirable. It was his business to abolish all trace of it, and that he very nearly succeeded in doing. If he were going to tell a lie about his wife's death in California, he had better do it well than badly; and, in fact, he did it extremely well. If he had murdered his wife in order to be happy with Le Neve, the least he could do was to devote himself to her; and from that moment until the morning he was hanged in Pentonville Prison he had no other thought but of her welfare, no other object but to secure her safety and happiness, no other fear but that any consequence of his action should recoil upon her. . . .

No one will pretend to read in these pages any apology or justification for a proved murder. They are an attempt to trace the threads of motive throughout what is a very remarkable instance of good and bad influences acting on human conduct. Rightly read and understood this is an admonishing, sobering and instructive story. We may consider Crippen a hateful man; but nobody who came in contact with him was able to say so. From those who, whether in business relations or as friends of his wife, had no reason to like or praise him, to the officials of the prison in which he was executed as a condemned murderer, there is but one chorus of testimony to his character as tested by daily intercourse with his fellow-men; even in regard to the very circumstances surrounding his crime, or at any rate following it, there is the same extraordinary feature; the very crime itself brought out in him high human qualities.

There are two sides to the story—the physical, which is sordid, dreadful, and revolting, and the spiritual, which is good and heroic; to the extent that most honest men, finding themselves in the situation in which he ultimately found himself, for whatever reason, and tried by the tests by which he was tried, would be glad to come out of them half so well. Such a story can only be understood by the aid of the imagination; and it should remind us, in the judgments that we pass on our fellow-men, never to forget the dual nature of human character and the mystery in virtue of which acts of great moral obliquity may march with conduct above the ordinary standards—conduct which, if we wish to be just, as we hope for justice to ourselves, should be remembered and recorded no less than the crime.

FILSON YOUNG, introduction to *Harley Harvey Crippen*, 1920

† *Harley Harvey Crippen was executed 23 November 1910.*

THE LEAST SUCCESSFUL ATTEMPT TO MURDER A SPOUSE

Dwarfing all known records for matrimonial homicide, Mr Peter Scott, of Southsea made seven attempts to kill his wife without her once noticing that anything was wrong.

In 1980 he took out an insurance policy on his good lady which would bring him £250,000 in the event of her accidental death. Soon afterwards he placed a lethal dose of mercury in her strawberry flan, but it all rolled out. Not wishing to waste this deadly substance, he next stuffed her mackerel with the entire contents of the bottle. This time she ate it, but with no side-effects whatsoever.

Warming to the task, he then took his better half on holiday to Yugoslavia. Recommending the panoramic views, he invited her to sit on the edge of a cliff. She declined to do so, prompted by what she later described as some 'sixth sense'. The same occurred only weeks later when he urged her to savour the view from Beachy Head.

While his spouse was in bed with chicken-pox he started a fire outside her bedroom door, but some interfering busybody put it out. Undeterred, he started another fire and burnt down the entire flat at Taswell Road, Southsea. The wife of his bosom escaped uninjured.

Another time he asked her to stand in the middle of the road so that he could drive towards her and check if his brakes were working.

At no time did Mrs Scott feel that the magic had gone out of their marriage. Since it appeared nothing short of a small nuclear bomb would have alerted this good woman to her husband's intentions, he eventually gave up and confessed everything to the police. After the case a detective said that Mrs Scott had been 'absolutely shattered' when told of her husband's plot to kill her. 'She had not twigged it at all and was dumbstruck.'

STEPHEN PYLE, *Heroic Failures*, 1968

† *Sweeney Todd was the Demon Barber who—in league with a cook—slit the throats of his clients and made them into pies. This is a 'penny dreadful' version of the climax of the tale.*

One, two, three, four, five, six, seven, eight, nine! Yes, it was nine at last. It strikes by old St Dunstan's Church clock, and in weaker strains the chronometrical machine at the pie shop echoes the sound. What excitement there is now to get at the pies when they shall come! Mrs Lovett lets down the square moveable platform that goes on pullies into the cellar; some machinery which only requires a handle being turned brings up a hundred pies on a tray. These are eagerly seized by parties who have previously paid, and such a smacking of lips ensues as was never known. Down goes the platform for the next hundred and a gentleman says:

'Let me work the handle, Mrs Lovett, if you please. It is too much for you, I am sure.'

'Sir, you are very kind, but I never allow anybody on this side of the counter but my own people, sir. I can turn the handle myself, sir, if you please, with the assistance of this girl. Keep your distance, sir. Nobody wants your help.'

How the waggish young lawyers' clerks laughed as they smacked their lips and sucked in all the golopshious gravy of the pies, which by-the-way appeared to be all delicious veal that time, and Mrs Lovett worked the handle of the machine all the more vigorously that she was a little angered with the officious stranger. What an unusual trouble it seemed to be to wind up those forthcoming hundred pies! How she toiled and how the people waited, but at length there came up the savoury steam and then the tops of the pies were visible.

They came up upon a large tray about six feet square, and at that moment Mrs Lovett ceased turning the handle and let a catch fall that prevented the platform receding again, to the astonishment and terror of everyone away flew all the pies, tray and all, and a man who was lying crouched in an exceedingly flat state under the tray sprang to his feet.

Mrs Lovett shrieked, as well she might, and then she stood trembling and looking as pale as death itself. It was the young cook from the cellar who had adopted this mode of escape.

The throng of persons in the shop looked petrified, and after Mrs

Lovett's shriek there was an awful silence for about a minute and then the young man who officiated as cook spoke.

'Ladies and gentlemen, I fear that what I am going to say will spoil your appetites; but truth is beautiful at all times, and I have to state that Mrs Lovett's pies are made of *human flesh*!'

THOMAS PRESKETT PREST, *The String of Pearls*, 1846/7

† *Many theories and alternative solutions to the murder-mystery at Road Hill House—where a child of the family in residence was found in 1860 with his throat cut—have gone the rounds since Constance Kent was convicted of the crime. Her confession, though, seems to leave no doubt that she was guilty of murdering her infant half-brother. The letter subsequently published by her doctor (and quoted in F. Tennyson Jesse's study of the crime) gives the clearest account of her actions on the dreadful evening.*

A detailed account of the manner in which the crime was committed was . . . furnished to the public by Dr Bucknill, the physician who had examined the prisoner by the desire of the government, in order to form an opinion as to the condition of her mind.

The following letter appeared in the public papers:

Sir,

I am requested by Miss Constance Kent to communicate to you the following details of her crime; which she has confessed to Mr Rodway, her solicitor, and to myself, and which she now desires to be made public.

Constance Kent first gave an account of the circumstances of her crime to Mr Rodway, and she afterwards acknowledged to me the correctness of that account when I recapitulated it to her. The explanation of her motive she gave to me when, with the permission of the Lord Chancellor, I examined her for the purpose of ascertaining whether there were any grounds for supposing that she was labouring under mental disease. Both Mr Rodway and I are convinced of the truthfulness and good faith of what she said to us.

Constance Kent says that the manner in which she committed her crime was as follows: A few days before the murder she obtained possession of a razor from a green case in her father's wardrobe, and secreted it. This was the sole instrument which she used. She also secreted a candle with matches, by placing them in the corner of the closet in the garden, where the murder was committed. On the night of the murder she undressed herself and went to bed, because she expected that her sisters would visit her room. She lay awake watching, until she thought that the household were all asleep, and soon after midnight she left her bedroom and went downstairs and opened the drawing-room door and window shutters. She then went up into the nursery, withdrew the blanket from between the sheet and the counterpane, and placed it on the side of the cot. She then took the child from his bed and carried him downstairs through the drawing-room. She had on her night-dress, and in the drawing-room she put on her goloshes. Having the child in one arm, she raised the drawing-room window with the other hand, went round the house and into the closet, lighted the candle and placed it on the seat of the closet, the child being wrapped in the blanket and still sleeping, and while the child was in this position she inflicted the wound in the throat. She says that she thought the blood would never come, and that the child was not killed, so she thrust the razor into its left side, and put the body, with the blanket round it, into the vault. The light burnt out. The piece of flannel which she had with her was torn from the old flannel garment placed in the waste bag, and which she had taken some time before and sewn it to use in washing herself. She went back to her bedroom, examined her dress, and found only two spots of blood on it. These she washed out in the basin, and threw the water, which was but little discoloured, into the foot-pan in which she had washed her feet overnight. She took another of her night-dresses and got into bed. In the morning her night-dress had become dry where it had been washed. She folded it up and put it into the drawer. Her three night-dresses were examined by Mr Foley, and she believes also by Mr Parsons, the medical attendant of the family. She thought the bloodstains had been effectually washed out, but on holding the dress up to the light a day or two afterwards, she found the stains were still visible. She secreted the dress, moving it from place to place, and she eventually burnt it in her own bedroom, and put the ashes or tinder into the kitchen grate. It was about five or six days after the child's death that she burnt the night-dress. On the Saturday morning, having cleaned the razor, she took an opportunity of replacing it unobserved in the case in the wardrobe. She abstracted her night-dress from the clothes basket when the housemaid went to fetch a glass of water. The stained garment found in the boiler hole had no connection whatever with the deed. As regards the motive of her crime, it seems that, although she entertained at one time a great regard for the present Mrs Kent, yet if any remark was at any time made which in her opinion was disparaging to any member of the first family, she treasured it up, and determined to revenge it. She had no ill-will against the little boy, except as one of the children of her stepmother. She declared that both her father and her stepmother had always been kind to her personally, and the following is a copy of a letter which she addressed to Mr Rodway on this point while in prison before her trial:

DEVIZES, *May 15th*

Sir,

It has been stated that my feelings of revenge were excited in consequence of cruel treatment. This is entirely false, I have received the greatest kindness from both the persons accused of subjecting me to it. I have never had any ill-will towards either of them on account of their behaviour to me, which has been very kind.

I shall feel obliged if you will make use of this statement in order that the public may be undeceived on this point.

I remain, sir,
Yours truly,
CONSTANCE E. KENT

To Mr R. Rodway

She told me that when the nursemaid was accused she had fully made up her mind to confess if the nursemaid had been convicted; and that she had also made up her mind to commit suicide if she herself was convicted. She said that she had felt herself under the influence of the devil before she committed the murder, but that she did not believe, and had not believed, that the devil had more to do with her crime than he had with any other wicked action. She had not said her prayers for a year before the murder, and not afterwards until she came to reside at Brighton. She said that the circumstance which revived religious feelings in her mind was thinking about the Sacrament when confirmed.

An opinion has been expressed that the peculiarities evinced by Constance Kent between the ages of twelve and seventeen may be attributed to the then transition period of her life. Moreover, the fact of her cutting off her hair, dressing herself in her brother's clothes, and then leaving her home with the intention of going abroad, which occurred when she was only thirteen years of age, indicated a peculiarity of disposition, and great determination of character, which foreboded that, for good or evil, her future life would be remarkable.

This peculiar disposition, which led her to such singular and violent resolves of action, seemed also to colour and intensify her thoughts and feelings, and magnify into wrongs that were to be revenged any little family incidents or occurrences which provoked her displeasure.

Although it became my duty to advise her counsel that she evinced no symptom of insanity at the time of my examination, and that, so far as it was possible to ascertain the state of her mind at so remote a period, there was no evidence of it at the time of the murder, I am yet of opinion that, owing to the peculiarities of her constitution, it is probable that under prolonged solitary confinement she would become insane.

The validity of this opinion is of importance now that the sentence of death has been commuted to penal servitude for life; for no one could desire that the punishment of the criminal should be so carried out as to cause danger of a further and greater punishment not contemplated by the law.

I have the honour to remain your very obedient servant,

JOHN CHARLES BUCKNILL, MD

HILMERTON HALL, NEAR RUGBY
August 24th

It will be seen from this detailed confession that Inspector Whicher had been uncannily correct in what he had maintained at the time of the first inquiries about the murder—namely, that the night-dress which was sent to the wash that Saturday, and which the household had imagined was the night-dress she had been wearing the whole of the week, was a clean garment which she had put on after the murder, and the actual gown in which she had done the deed she had succeeded in destroying without it having been found.

F. TENNYSON JESSE, *Murder and its Motives*, 1952

† *In* Lost Man's Lane, *the villain, picturesquely named Obadiah Trohm, is unmasked in the act of trying to add another victim to those he has already incarcerated in a cavern under his lawn. 'Where is Silly Rufus?' asks his accuser, 'and all the rest who have vanished between Deacon Spear's house and the little home of the cripples of the highroad?'*

'Lucetta, you are mad!'

'Mad or sane, my accusation will have its results, Mr Trohm. I believe too deeply in your guilt not to make others do so.'

'Ah,' said he, 'then you have not done so yet? You believe this and that, but you have not told any one what your suspicions are?'

'No,' she calmly returned, though her face blanched to the colorlessness of wax, 'I have not said what I think of you yet.'

Oh, the cunning that crept into his face!

'She has not said. Oh, the little Lucetta, the wise, the careful little Lucetta!'

'But I will,' she cried, meeting his eye with the courage and constancy of a martyr . . .

They were now near the gateway. They had been moving all this time. His hand was on the curb of the old well. His face, so turned that it caught the full glare of the setting sun, leaned toward the girl, exerting a fascinating influence upon her. She took the step he asked, and before we could shriek out 'Beware!' we saw him bend forward with a sudden quick motion and then start upright again, while her form, which but an instant before had stood there in all its frail and inspired beauty, tottered as if the ground were bending under it, and in another moment disappeared from our appalled sight, swallowed in some dreadful cavern that for an instant yawned in the smoothly cut lawn before us, and then vanished again from sight as if it had never been.

A shriek from my whistle mingled with a simultaneous cry of agony from Loreen. We heard Mr Gryce rush from behind us, but we ourselves found it impossible to stir, paralyzed as we were by the sight of the old man's demoniacal delight. He was leaping to and fro over the turf, holding up his fingers in the red sunset glare.

'Six!' he shrieked. 'Six! and room for two more! Oh, it's a merry life I lead! . . .'

We saw, even while we all bounded forward to the rescue of the devoted maiden, that he was one of those maniacs who have perfect control over themselves and pass for very decent sort of men except in the moment of triumph; and, noting his look of sinister delight, perceived that half his pleasures and almost his sole reward for the horrible crimes he had perpetrated, was in the mystery surrounding his victims and the entire immunity from suspicion which up to this time he had enjoyed.

ANNA KATHARINE GREEN, *Lost Man's Lane*, 1898

BORDENMANIA: IMPACT OF LIZZIE BORDEN CASE

No murder case in American history caused more public repercussions than that involving Lizzie Borden, the 32-year-old spinster who was tried and acquitted of killing her father and stepmother with an axe in their home in Fall River, Mass. in 1892. The case was the subject of an endless number of books, magazine articles and newspaper accounts. Edmund Pearson explained the public's fascination with the case may have resulted from its very 'purity.' The murders, and Lizzie's guilt or innocence, were uncomplicated by such sins as ambition, robbery, greed, lust or other usual homicidal motives. Innocent or guilty, Lizzie became an American heroine.

The verse and doggerel on the case varied from the anonymous children's jump rope rhyme:

Lizzie Borden took an ax
And gave her mother forty whacks;
When she saw what she had done,
She gave her father forty-one.

to A. L. Bixby's almost endearing:

There's no evidence of guilt,
  Lizzie Borden,
That should make your spirit wilt,
  Lizzie Borden;
Many do not think that you,
Chopped your father's head in two,
It's so hard a thing to do,
  Lizzie Borden.

The *New York Times* informed its readers that controversy over Lizzie Borden's innocence or guilt was directly responsible for 1,900 divorces. Such was the grip of 'Bordenmania' on the entire nation.

CARL SIFAKIS, *The Encyclopaedia of American Crime*, 1982

Surviving photographs of Lizzie Borden show a face it is difficult to look at as if you knew nothing about her; coming events cast their shadow across her face, or else you see the shadows these events have cast—something terrible, something ominous in this face with its jutting, rectangular jaw and those mad eyes of the New England saints, eyes that belong to a person who does not listen to you . . . fanatic's eyes, you might say, if you knew nothing about her. If you were sorting through a box of old photographs in a junk shop and came across this particular, sepia, faded face above the choked collars of the 1890s, you might murmur when you saw her: 'Oh, what big eyes you have!' as Red Riding Hood said to the wolf, but then you might not even pause to pick her out and look at her more closely, for hers is not, in itself, a striking face.

But as soon as the face has a name, once you recognise her, when you know who she is and what it was she did, the face becomes as if of one possessed, and now it haunts you, you look at it again and again, it secretes mystery.

This woman, with her jaw of a concentration-camp attendant, and such eyes . . .

ANGELA CARTER, *Black Venus*, 1985

† *The Sexton Blake authors, of whom there were many, went in for the utmost staginess and full-blooded villainy. Understatement was quite outside their capacity. One character has 'the eyes of a snake, the head of a vulture and the face of a fiend', an appearance which must have defeated any attempt to lead an ordinary life. However, the more conventional-looking villain in Robert Murray's 'The Four Guests Mystery' is of no less homicidal a disposition.*

Rufus Carter, alias Lucien Droon, suddenly straightened his back; as if throwing a great weight off his shoulders. His face was composed; the fires of defiance and desperation had died in his eyes.

'I give you best, Mr Blake,' he said resignedly. 'By heavens, I never dreamed you would discover the truth. By inviting you here I thought I was taking a step that would absolutely assure the success of my plan.

'You are absolutely correct in your details,' he went on, the others listening with rapt attention. 'I am Rufus Carter. After escaping from Parkmoor I went to America with the stolen money I had hidden. I made a small fortune in speculation on Wall Street, and returned to this country in the name of Lucien Droon.

'Certain people discovered my secret. How, it is not necessary to explain. You know their names. Septimus Trull was my valet in the old days. George Grubb was a client of mine, and Philip Roe a clerk in the office where I worked.'

'And Isabelle Page?' asked Blake.

'An adventuress, who was once known to me,' admitted Carter candidly. 'In less than a year I had been blackmailed of practically every penny I possessed. I was faced with ruin. In a moment of desperation I planned to exterminate the whole gang like a brood of vipers, after placing them under suspicion of causing my own death. My brother was necessary to that plan. It was essential that I should assume his identity in order to claim the insurance money, payable on my own demise.'

Coutts glared incredulously at the man.

'You cold-blooded devil!' he jerked. 'You deliberately killed your own brother because of the close resemblance between the two of you?'

Rufus Carter laughed shortly.

'My brother Marcus was the cold-blooded devil,' he corrected. 'He deserved to die. He was the biggest blackmailer of the lot. I had no compunction in killing him. I played on his sense of greed. I told him that Roe, Grubb, and the others were blackmailing me as well: thus preventing me from paying him what he demanded.

'I hinted that I had a plan that would enable me to turn the tables on them. He readily consented to help me, and without suspecting the truth, came up from Porthcawl prepared to assume my identity for a few hours.

'Like a fool he followed my instructions to the letter, locked himself in my study, and couldn't fail to discover the written message I had left lying on the desk. While he was reading it I thrust the spring-gun through the hole at the back of the elephant's head and killed him like the dog he was.'

Carter's eyes blazed in memory of the mental torture he had suffered.

'I killed Trull, and Philip Roe, in the same way,' he admitted quietly.

'George Grubb I shot from the window of my room, and I was only waiting my chance to dispose of Isabelle Page in the same manner.'

Never had the three detectives listened to such a cool, cold-blooded confession of wholesale, premeditated murder.

'May I smoke,' asked Carter. With his manacled hands he took a cigarette from his waistcoat pocket and placed it between his lips. Mechanically, Coutts gave him a light.

'Why did you leave that written message, hinting that proofs of your murderer's identity would be found in the room?' asked Inspector Rawson.

'To throw a scare into the four of them,' answered the prisoner promptly. 'I guessed that they would attempt to search the room, thinking that I had left evidence of the manner in which they had been blackmailing me. It was successful. It enabled me to use the spring-gun on Roe and Trull.'

'But confound it all,' exploded Coutts, 'how could you be in two places at once? You have just come up from Porthcawl by road. You sent a wire from there. The mud on your boots, that Mr Blake pointed out just now—'

'There is only one answer to that question,' enlightened Sexton Blake. 'Carter has an accomplice, who sent the wire from Porthcawl, and came up by car, bringing those clothes and the muddy boots with him. Carter met him on his arrival, changed, dismissed his accomplice, and came straight here, as if he had just arrived from Porthcawl.'

Rufus Carter nodded.

'Nothing escapes you, Mr Blake,' he said admiringly. 'I had an accomplice—a man I met in prison. He shall remain nameless. It was arranged that he should go to my brother's cottage at Porthcawl, as soon as my brother came to Droon House. He knew exactly what to do. My programme was scheduled almost to the minute; but I had expected to dispose of Isabelle Page several hours earlier. It is your turn, Mr Blake. How did you get on the right track?'

'Fingerprints,' said Blake briefly. 'After that, largely obvious deductions. From fingerprints on your hair-brushes I discovered that the Lucien Droon, who had used the brushes was actually Rufus Carter, an escaped convict. In that fact was the ostensible motive for blackmail.

'Then I was surprised to find that the fingerprints of the Lucien Droon who was dead—were not the same. The whole plot was clear to me from that moment.'

There was a long silence.

Rufus Carter smiled crookedly. There was a slight click as his teeth snapped down on the tiny capsule that was concealed in the end of the cigarette. Blake leapt towards him, grabbed him, and forced it open. But he was too late. The capsule had been swallowed, and the deadly cyanide did its work at once.

The murderer of Droon House had gone to join his victims.

'The case is closed,' said Sexton Blake quietly. 'Perhaps it's better it happened this way.'

ROBERT MURRAY, 'The Four Guests Mystery', 1932

Broadly speaking, the trouble with every villain of a thriller is that he suffers from a fatal excess of ingenuity. When he was a boy, his parents must thoughtlessly have told him that he was clever, and it has absolutely spoiled him for effective work.

The ordinary man, when circumstances compel him to murder a female acquaintance, borrows a revolver and a few cartridges and does the thing in some odd five minutes of the day when he is not at the office or the pictures. He does not bother about art or technique or scientific methods. He just goes and does it.

But the villain cannot understand simplicity. A hundred times he manœuvres the girl into a position where one good dig with a knife or a carefully directed pistol-shot would produce the happiest results, and then, poor ass, he goes and ruins it all by being too clever. It never occurs to him just to point a pistol at the heroine and fire it. If you told him the thing could be done that way, he would suspect you of pulling his leg. The only method he can imagine is to tie her in a chair, erect a tripod, place the revolver on it, tie a string to the trigger, pass the string along the walls till it rests on a hook, attach another string to it, pass this over a hook, tie a brick to the end of the second string and light a candle under it. He has got the thing reasoned out. The candle will burn the second string, the brick will fall, the weight will tighten the first string, thus pulling the trigger, and there you are.

Then somebody comes along and blows the candle out, and all the weary work to do over again.

Still, I suppose it is no use being angry with the poor fellows. They are doing their best according to their lights. It is simply that they are trying to tackle a highly specialized job without the requisite training. What the villain needs is to forget all he thinks he knows and go right back to the beginning and start learning the business from the bottom up. He requires careful schooling. And this is what he ought to be given at once if thrillers are to be purged of heroines.

The keynote of the curriculum of this School for Villains would be the inculcation of simplicity and directness. The pupil would receive at first what one might call a kindergarten education. For the greater part of his opening term he would confine himself to swatting flies. From this he would work up through the animal kingdom in easy stages till eventually he arrived at heroines. By the time he had taken his degree, the Myrtles and Gladyses would be climbing trees and pulling them up after them to avoid the man, for by then he would be really dangerous.

The great difficulty, of course, would be to restrain and hold in check that infernal ingenuity of his. The average villain's natural impulse, if called upon to kill a fly, would be to saw away the supports of the floor, tie a string across the doorway, and then send the fly an anonymous letter urging it to come at once in order to hear of something to its advantage. The idea being that it would hurry to the room, trip over the string, fall on the floor, tumble into the depths, and break its neck.

That, to the villain's mind, is not merely the simplest, it is the only way of killing flies. And the hardest task facing his form-master would be to persuade him that excellent results may be obtained through the medium of a rolled-up *Daily Mail* gripped by the Football Coupon.

The maddening thing is that it is only when dealing with the heroine that he is so beastly clever. With anybody of his own sex he can be as straightforward as a medieval headsman. Give him a baronet and he will stick a knife in his back without a second thought. But the moment he finds himself up against a heroine he seems to go all to pieces, and we get all this stuff of suspending snakes from the chandelier and fooling about with bombs which can only be exploded by means of a gramophone record with an A in alt on it.

I have known a villain to sit the heroine on a keg of gunpowder and expect it to be struck by lightning. You can't run a business that way.

What these men have got to learn is that the best way of disposing of a girl with hair the colour of ripe corn is to hit that hair as hard as possible with a bit of gas-pipe. Buying tarantulas to put in her vanity-bag or little-known Asiatic poisons with which to smear her lipstick do no good whatever and only add to the overhead.

Let them master this fundamental truth, and then we shall see what we shall see.

P. G. WODEHOUSE, *Louder and Funnier*, 1932

BILLY THE KID

The boy of the sewer and the knock on the head rose to become a man of the frontier. He made a horseman of himself, learning to ride straight in the saddle—Wyoming- or Texas-style—and not with his body thrown back, the way they rode in Oregon and California. He never completely matched his legend, but he kept getting closer and closer to it. Something of the New York hoodlum lived on in the cowboy; he transferred to Mexicans the hate that had previously been inspired in him by Negroes, but the last words he ever spoke were (swear) words in Spanish. He learned the art of the cowpuncher's maverick life. He learned another, more difficult art—how to lead men. Both helped to make him a good cattle rustler. From time to time, Old Mexico's guitars and whorehouses pulled on him.

With the haunting lucidity of insomnia, he organized populous orgies that often lasted four days and four nights. In the end, glutted, he settled accounts with bullets. While his trigger finger was unfailing, he was the most feared man (and perhaps the most anonymous and most lonely) of that whole frontier. Pat Garrett, his friend, the sheriff who later killed him, once told him, 'I've had a lot of practice with the rifle shooting buffalo.'

'I've had plenty with the six-shooter,' Billy replied modestly. 'Shooting tin cans and men.'

The details can never be recovered, but it is known that he was credited with up to twenty-one killings—'not counting Mexicans'. For seven desperate years, he practised the extravagance of utter recklessness.

The night of the twenty-fifth of July 1880, Billy the Kid came galloping on his piebald down the main, or only, street of Fort Sumner. The heat was oppressive and the lamps had not been lighted; Sheriff

Garrett, seated on a porch in a rocking chair, drew his revolver and sent a bullet through the Kid's belly. The horse kept on; the rider tumbled into the dust of the road. Garrett got off a second shot. The townspeople (knowing the wounded man was Billy the Kid) locked their window shutters tight. The agony was long and blasphemous. In the morning, the sun by then high overhead, they began drawing near, and they disarmed him. The man was gone. They could see in his face that used-up look of the dead.

He was shaved, sheathed in ready-made clothes, and displayed to awe and ridicule in the window of Fort Sumner's biggest store. Men on horseback and in buckboards gathered for miles and miles around. On the third day, they had to use make-up on him. On the fourth day, he was buried with rejoicing.

JORGE LUIS BORGES, *A Universal History of Infamy*, 1935, trans. Norman Thomas di Giovanni

Al Capone was a mindless, brutal and obscure Brooklyn hood in his teens, but by the age of 26 he had become the most powerful crime boss of his day and could boast that he 'owned' Chicago, that city of gangsters, during the Prohibition years.

At its zenith the Capone mob had probably upward of 1,000 members, most of them experienced gunmen, but this represented only a portion of Capone's overall empire. Capone often proclaimed, 'I own the police,' and it was true. Few estimates would place less than half the police on the mob's payroll in one way or another. Capone's hold on the politicians was probably greater. He had 'in his pocket' aldermen, state's attorneys, mayors, legislators, governors and even congressmen. The Capone organization's domination of Chicago and such suburban areas as Cicero, Ill. was absolute. When Capone wanted a big vote in elections, he got out the vote; when he wanted to control the election returns, his gangsters intimidated and terrorized thousands of voters. The politicians he put in power were expected to act the way the Big Fellow desired. The mayor of Cicero once took an independent action. Capone caught him on the steps of City Hall and beat him to a pulp; a police officer standing nearby had to look elsewhere to avoid seeing the violence.

CARL SIFAKIS, *The Encyclopaedia of American Crime*, 1982

† *Al Capone was finally tried and convicted for tax evasion. Damon Runyon attended the trial.*

Chicago, October 6, 1931

A fragrant whiff of green fields and growing rutabagas and parsnips along with echoes of good old Main Street, crept into the grime-stained Federal Building here today as your Uncle Sam took up the case of Al Capone and gathered a jury in what you might call jigtime.

It is a jury made up mainly of small towners and Michael J. Ahern, chief counsel for Al Capone, frankly admitted dissatisfaction to the Court about it.

He wanted all these persons dismissed but Judge Wilkerson overruled his motion. The jury was sworn in with nine veterans of court room juries among the twelve good men and true, and tomorrow morning at ten o'clock the Government of these United States starts work on Al Capone.

The truly rural atmosphere of the proceedings today was evidenced by horny-handed tillers of the fruitful soil, small town store-keepers, mechanics and clerks, who gazed frankly interested at the burly figure of the moon-faced fellow causing all this excitement and said,

'Why, no: we ain't got no prejudice against Al Capone.'

At least most of them said that in effect, as Judge Wilkerson was expediting the business of getting a jury to try Capone on charges of income tax evasion.

Your Uncle Sam says Al Capone owes him $215,000 on an income of $1,038,000 in six years.

Your Uncle Sam hints that Al Capone derived this tidy income from such illegal didoes as bootlegging, gambling and the like.

'Do you hope the government proves the defendant guilty?' was one question asked a venireman at the request of counsel for the defense.

Apparently none cherished that hope.

'Have you any desire that the defendant be sent to jail?' was another question requested by the defense.

'Well no,' was the general reply.

Al Capone sat up straight in his chair and smoothed his rumpled necktie. He felt better. The G-men—as the boys call 'em—want to put Al Capone in a Federal pokey, or jail, for anywhere from two to thirty-two years, to impress upon him the truth of the adage that honesty is the best policy.

As Al Capone sat there with the scent of the new-mown hay oozing at intervals from the jury box, he was a terrific disappointment to the strictly seeing-Chicago tourist who felt that Al should have been vested at least in some of the panoply of his reputed office as Maharajah of the Hoods. Perhaps a cartridge belt. Some strangers felt this Chicago has been misrepresented to them.

DAMON RUNYON, *Trials and Other Tribulations*, 1946

Mr Bodkin proceeded to open the facts of the second murder. In the autumn of 1913, Smith left Miss Pegler, as he said, 'for a run round' in the antique furniture trade, which she always understood was his business. He always explained the profits which arose from his marriages by saying that he had done very well out of the sale of a work of art: on one occasion it was a Turner; on another, a Chinese image. While he was 'running round' he visited a Nonconformist chapel at Southsea, where he went, as Mr Bodkin said, not to pray, but to 'prey,' on young women of simple faith. His fascinating and predatory gaze fell upon a buxom young nurse named Alice Burnham. She felt his gaze fixed on her all through the service, and he spoke to her outside. She soon fell a victim to the charms of 'George Joseph Smith, Esq., a gentleman of independent means,' and wrote an unaffected letter to her married sister telling her of her happiness. They had 'met at the chapel I attend. George was brought up Wesleyan. . . . I am so happy, Rose dear. My heart and soul thank God continually for joining me to the love of so good a man—a perfect gentleman, very homely. You cannot fail to like him, so genuine, kind. . . . I am the most fortunate and happiest girl in the world.' On November 4th, they were married. Mr Burnham, her father, had been keeping a sum of £104 for his daughter. For this Smith made a formal demand, and, when his father-in-law dared to ask questions about him, he wrote the following astonishing letter.

'Sir,—In answer to your application regarding my parentage, my mother was a Bus-horse, my father a cab-driver, my sister a roughrider over the Arctic Regions. My brothers were all gallant sailors on a steam-roller. This is the only information I can give to those who are not entitled to ask such questions contained in the letter I received on the 24th inst.

'Your despised son-in-law,
'G. SMITH.'

In the end, he obtained through a solicitor payment of his wife's £104. Smith had now learned by experience not to ignore opportunities; if this spouse should also die, he did not wish to be left uncompensated. There had been no need to insure Miss Mundy's life, as she was so well off. But he saw to it that the new 'Mrs Smith's' life was insured for £500, and on December 8th she went alone to a solicitor and made a will leaving everything to the prisoner. The couple then went on a visit to Blackpool. They rejected the first lodgings they visited, because there was no bath, but at Mrs Crossley's, in Regent Road, they found all they wanted. Then almost in the minutest detail the fate of 'Mrs Williams' dogged 'Mrs Smith.' Headaches came, and there were visits to a doctor; this bride wrote home just as her predecessor had done. 'My husband,' she said, 'does all he can for me; in fact, dear, I have the best husband in the world.' In the evening the bride took a walk in the gay, Christmas-lit streets of Blackpool—the last walk she was ever to take on earth. At 8 p.m. on the Friday night, December 12th, she took a bath. While she was taking it, the landlady below saw water coming through the ceiling. A little later the bridegroom knocked at the door; he had been out to buy some eggs for his wife's supper (he had gone out to buy fish when Miss Mundy died). He then went upstairs, and his wife was found dead in her bath; no bruises were found on her body. If he had been hysterical and unnerved by the death of his other bride, he had now become hardened by misfortune. He struck Mrs Crossley as shockingly callous. He wanted to sleep in the room where the dead woman lay; he ordered her a deal coffin and a pauper's funeral; and, when the Crossleys protested, he said, 'When they are dead, they are done with.'

EDWARD MARJORIBANKS, *The Life of Sir Edward Marshall Hall*, 1929

† *George Joseph Smith was executed 13 August 1913.*

MY LAST DUCHESS

Ferrara

That's my last Duchess painted on the wall,
Looking as if she were alive. I call
That piece a wonder, now: Frà Pandolf's hands
Worked busily a day, and there she stands.
Will 't please you sit and look at her? I said
'Frà Pandolf' by design, for never read
Strangers like you that pictured countenance,
The depth and passion of its earnest glance,
But to myself they turned (since none puts by
The curtain I have drawn for you, but I)
And seemed as they would ask me, if they durst,
How such a glance came there; so, not the first
Are you to turn and ask thus. Sir, 't was not
Her husband's presence only, called that spot
Of joy into the Duchess' cheek: perhaps
Frà Pandolf chanced to say 'Her mantle laps
'Over my lady's wrist too much,' or 'Paint
'Must never hope to reproduce the faint
'Half-flush that dies along her throat:' such stuff
Was courtesy, she thought, and cause enough
For calling up that spot of joy. She had
A heart—how shall I say?—too soon made glad,
Too easily impressed; she liked whate'er
She looked on, and her looks went everywhere.
Sir, 't was all one! My favour at her breast,
The dropping of the daylight in the West,
The bough of cherries some officious fool
Broke in the orchard for her, the white mule
She rode with round the terrace—all and each
Would draw from her alike the approving speech,
Or blush, at least. She thanked men,—good! but thanked
Somehow—I know not how—as if she ranked
My gift of a nine-hundred-years-old name
With anybody's gift. Who'd stoop to blame
This sort of trifling? Even had you skill
In speech—(which I have not)—to make your will

Quite clear to such an one, and say, 'Just this
'Or that in you disgusts me; here you miss,
'Or there exceed the mark'—and if she let
Herself be lessoned so, nor plainly set
Her wits to yours, forsooth, and made excuse,
—E'en then would be some stooping; and I choose
Never to stoop. Oh sir, she smiled, no doubt,
Whene'er I passed her; but who passed without
Much the same smile? This grew; I gave commands;
Then all smiles stopped together. There she stands
As if alive. Will 't please you rise? We'll meet
The company below, then. I repeat,
The Count your master's known munificence
Is ample warrant that no just pretence
Of mine for dowry will be disallowed;
Though his fair daughter's self, as I avowed
At starting, is my object. Nay, we'll go
Together down, sir. Notice Neptune, though,
Taming a sea-horse, thought a rarity,
Which Claus of Innsbruck cast in bronze for me!

ROBERT BROWNING, 1842

† *Herbert Rowse Armstrong was a solicitor in Hay, just over the Welsh border. Mr Martin carried on a rival practice as a solicitor in the same small town.*

Armstrong, although he took pains to ingratiate himself with every one, was not at home the martial figure that his military career and gallant adventures might have led one to expect. It was common knowledge that he was, in fact, henpecked. The late Mrs Armstrong was a person of peculiar character. She was both cultivated and clever, played the piano extremely well, and had earned the reputation with every one who had any knowledge of her of being a really good woman. She was, however, notoriously cranky, and extremely severe. She brought up her children with devotion, indeed, but with a strict and sombre austerity, and her husband was ruled with a rod of iron. Until the war broke his boundaries and enlarged his horizon little Armstrong (for he was a very little man, weighing only some 7 stone) had no kind of liberty at home, and, except for certain furtive, amorous adventures of which I have heard, he was obliged to live under the strict conditions imposed by his wife. These conditions were of an unusual severity. No wine or alcohol was admitted to the house. If at the table of some neighbour he was offered wine, his wife would interpose with a negative on his account, except now and then when she had been known to say, 'I think you may have a glass of port, Herbert; it will do your cold good.' If he was smoking as he came along the road, and his wife came in sight, the cigar or pipe had to be hastily put away, and he was only allowed to smoke in one room of his house called 'Mayfield.' On one occasion, at a tennis party, she called to him in the middle of a sett that it was time to go home. 'Six o'clock, Herbert; how can you expect punctuality in the servants if the master is late for his meals?' On another similar occasion, in publicly summoning him to come home, she reminded him that it was his 'bath night.' . . .

On New Year's Day, 1922, the town was dumbfounded to hear that Major Armstrong had been arrested the day before and charged with attempting to murder Mr Martin. This roused the greatest indignation. People went so far as to suggest that it had been engineered by Martin on account of business rivalry. But still more astounding events happened the next day. Strange doctors came to the town; it was known that something was happening up at Cusop Churchyard; and then that Mrs Armstrong's body had been exhumed that very morning and was being examined in a little cottage near the churchyard. Reporters descended apparently from the skies. Sensation after sensation was reported. Gossip upon gossip multiplied, and through five long months, until Armstrong was executed, the town was a centre of sensation and excitement such as is rarely experienced in such a place. . . .

Consider the facts. Only two months before Martin, after repeated invitations, had gone to tea with Armstrong at his house. There was a business difficulty between them, and he thought that Armstrong wished to discuss it, although, as a matter of fact, he never alluded to it. During tea he had handed Martin a buttered scone with the apology, 'Excuse my fingers,' and Martin had eaten that, as well as some currant loaf. He had hardly got home before he was seized with the most violent pains, with vomiting and diarrhœa, which continued throughout the night and reduced him swiftly to a condition of extreme weakness. Dr Hincks was called in, and saw the usual symptoms of a severe bilious attack, and prescribed accordingly. But, as the sickness continued, he was (fortunately) not entirely satisfied, and he had an analysis made, and found in the sample submitted that there was one-thirty-third of a grain of arsenic. This set him thinking and pondering, and one day, riding on horseback over the hills to visit a distant patient, and revolving in his mind the circumstances attending the death of Mrs Armstrong, the key to the whole situation flashed on him. That neuritis of hers, which they had all regarded as merely functional disorder, had not been functional but organic; it was peripheral neuritis—one of the symptoms of arsenical poisoning. He remembered all the other symptoms. Vomiting, the peculiarity known as 'high steppage' gait, discolouration of the skin, &c., &c.—all symptoms of arsenical poisoning. What Martin was suffering from, Mrs Armstrong had died of. And if in a small liquid sample taken from Mr Martin one-thirty-third of a grain of arsenic had been found, what might be found in the body of Mrs Armstrong?

FILSON YOUNG, Introduction to *The Trial of H. R. Armstrong*, 1927

† *Christy Mahon makes a great impression on the inhabitants of a remote Connemara town by boasting, as it turns out falsely, of having slaughtered his father.*

Christy Mahon, a slight young man, comes in very tired and frightened and dirty.

CHRISTY [*in a small voice*]. God save all here!

MEN. God save you kindly!

CHRISTY [*going to the counter*]. I'd trouble you for a glass of porter, woman of the house. [*He puts down coin.*

PEGEEN [*serving him*]. You're one of the tinkers, young fellow, is beyond camped in the glen?

CHRISTY. I am not; but I'm destroyed walking.

MICHAEL [*patronizingly*]. Let you come up then to the fire. You're looking famished with the cold.

CHRISTY. God reward you. [*He takes up his glass and goes a little way across to the left, then stops and looks about him.*] Is it often the polis do be coming into this place, master of the house?

MICHAEL. If you'd come in better hours, you'd have seen 'Licensed for the Sale of Beer and Spirits, to be Consumed on the Premises', written in white letters above the door, and what would the polis want spying on me, and not a decent house within four miles, the way every living Christian is a bona fide, saving one widow alone?

CHRISTY [*with relief*]. It's a safe house, so.

[*He goes over to the fire, sighing and moaning. Then he sits down, putting his glass beside him, and begins gnawing a turnip, too miserable to feel the others staring at him with curiosity.*

MICHAEL [*going after him*]. Is it yourself is fearing the polis? You're wanting, maybe?

CHRISTY. There's many wanting.

MICHAEL. Many, surely, with the broken harvest and the ended wars. [*He picks up some stockings, etc., that are near the fire, and carries them away furtively.*] It should be larceny, I'm thinking?

CHRISTY [*dolefully*]. I had it in my mind it was a different word and a bigger.

PEGEEN. There's a queer lad. Were you never slapped in school, young fellow, that you don't know the name of your deed?

CHRISTY [*bashfully*]. I'm slow at learning, a middling scholar only.

MICHAEL. If you're a dunce itself, you'd have a right to know that larceny's robbing and stealing. Is it for the like of that you're wanting?

CHRISTY [*with a flash of family pride*]. And I the son of a strong farmer [*with a sudden qualm*], God rest his soul, could have bought up the whole of your old house a while since, from the butt of his tail-pocket, and not have missed the weight of it gone.

MICHAEL [*impressed*]. If it's not stealing, it's maybe something big.

CHRISTY [*flattered*]. Aye; it's maybe something big.

JIMMY. He's a wicked-looking young fellow. Maybe he followed after a young woman on a lonesome night.

CHRISTY [*shocked*]. Oh, the saints forbid, mister; I was all times a decent lad.

PHILLY [*turning on Jimmy*]. You're a silly man, Jimmy Farrell. He said his father was a farmer a while since, and there's himself now in a poor state. Maybe the land was grabbed from him, and he did what any decent man would do.

MICHAEL [*to Christy, mysteriously*]. Was it bailiffs?

CHRISTY. The divil a one.

MICHAEL. Agents?

CHRISTY. The divil a one.

MICHAEL. Landlords?

CHRISTY [*peevishly*]. Ah, not at all, I'm saying. You'd see the like of them stories on any little paper of a Munster town. But I'm not calling to mind any person, gentle, simple, judge or jury, did the like of me.

[*They all draw nearer with delighted curiosity*.

PHILLY. Well, that lad's a puzzle-the-world.

JIMMY. He'd beat Dan Davies's circus, or the holy missioners making sermons on the villainy of man. Try him again, Philly.

PHILLY. Did you strike golden guineas out of solder, young fellow, or shilling coins itself?

CHRISTY. I did not, mister, not sixpence nor a farthing coin.

JIMMY. Did you marry three wives maybe? I'm told there's a sprinkling have done that among the holy Luthers of the preaching north.

CHRISTY [*shyly*]. I never married with one, let alone with a couple or three.

PHILLY. Maybe he went fighting for the Boers, the like of the man beyond, was judged to be hanged, quartered, and drawn. Were you off east, young fellow, fighting bloody wars for Kruger and the freedom of the Boers?

CHRISTY. I never left my own parish till Tuesday was a week.

PEGEEN [*coming from counter*]. He's done nothing, so. [*To Christy*.] If you didn't commit murder or a bad, nasty thing; or false coining, or robbery, or butchery, or the like of them, there isn't anything that would be worth your troubling for to run from now. You did nothing at all.

CHRISTY [*his feelings hurt*]. That's an unkindly thing to be saying to a poor orphaned traveller, has a prison behind him, and hanging before, and hell's gap gaping below.

PEGEEN [*with a sign to the men to be quiet*]. You're only saying it. You did nothing at all. A soft lad the like of you wouldn't slit the wind pipe of a screeching sow.

CHRISTY [*offended*]. You're not speaking the truth.

PEGEEN [*in mock rage*]. Not speaking the truth, is it? Would you have me knock the head of you with the butt of the broom?

CHRISTY [*twisting round on her with a sharp cry of horror*]. Don't strike me. I killed my poor father, Tuesday was a week, for doing the like of that.

PEGEEN [*with blank amazement*]. Is it killed your father?

CHRISTY [*subsiding*]. With the help of God I did, surely, and that the Holy Immaculate Mother may intercede for his soul.

PHILLY [*retreating with Jimmy*]. There's a daring fellow.

JIMMY. Oh, glory be to God!

MICHAEL [*with great respect*]. That was a hanging crime, mister honey. You should have had good reason for doing the like of that.

CHRISTY [*in a very reasonable tone*]. He was a dirty man, God forgive him, and he getting old and crusty, the way I couldn't put up with him at all.

JOHN MILLINGTON SYNGE, *The Playboy of the Western World*, 1907

THE VICTIM WINS

Like most old people the countess suffered from sleeplessness. Having undressed, she sat down in a big arm-chair by the window and dismissed her maids. They took away the candles, leaving only the lamp before the icons to light the room. The countess sat there, her skin sallow with age, her flabby lips twitching, her body swaying to and fro. Her dim eyes were completely vacant and looking at her one might have imagined that the dreadful old woman was rocking her body not from choice but owing to some secret galvanic mechanism.

Suddenly an inexplicable change came over the death-like face. The lips ceased to move, the eyes brightened: before the countess stood a strange young man.

'Do not be alarmed, for heaven's sake, do not be alarmed!' he said in a low, clear voice. 'I have no intention of doing you any harm, I have come to beg a favour of you.'

The old woman stared at him in silence, as if she had not heard. Hermann thought she must be deaf and bending down to her ear he repeated what he had just said. The old woman remained silent as before.

'You can ensure the happiness of my whole life,' Hermann went on, 'and at no cost to yourself. I know that you can name three cards in succession . . .'

Hermann stopped. The countess appeared to have grasped what he wanted and to be seeking words to frame her answer.

'It was a joke,' she said at last. 'I swear to you it was a joke.'

'No, madam,' Hermann retorted angrily. 'Remember Tchaplitsky, and how you enabled him to win back his loss.'

The countess was plainly perturbed. Her face expressed profound agitation; but soon she relapsed into her former impassivity.

'Can you not tell me those three winning cards?' Hermann went on.

The countess said nothing. Hermann continued:

'For whom would you keep your secret? For your grandsons? They are rich enough already: they don't appreciate the value of money. Your three cards would not help a spendthrift. A man who does not take care of his inheritance will die a beggar though all the demons of the world were at his command. I am not a spendthrift: I know the value of money. Your three cards would not be wasted on me. Well? . . .'

He paused, feverishly waiting for her reply. She was silent. Hermann fell on his knees.

'If your heart has ever known what it is to love, if you can remember the ecstasies of love, if you have ever smiled tenderly at the cry of your new-born son, if any human feeling has ever stirred in your breast, I appeal to you as wife, beloved one, mother—I implore you by all that is holy in life not to reject my prayer: tell me your secret. Of what use is it to you? Perhaps it is bound up with some terrible sin, with the loss of eternal salvation, with some bargain with the devil . . . Reflect—you are old: you have not much longer to live, and I am ready to take your sin upon my soul. Only tell me your secret. Remember that a man's happiness is in your hands; that not only I, but my children and my children's children will bless your memory and hold it sacred. . . .'

The old woman answered not a word.

Hermann rose to his feet.

'You old hag!' he said, grinding his teeth. 'Then I will make you speak. . . .'

With these words he drew a pistol from his pocket. At the sight of the pistol the countess for the second time showed signs of agitation. Her head shook and she raised a hand as though to protect herself from the shot. . . . Then she fell back . . . and was still.

'Come, an end to this childish nonsense!' said Hermann, seizing her by the arm. 'I ask you for the last time—will you tell me those three cards? Yes or no?'

The countess made no answer. Hermann saw that she was dead....

The whole of that day Hermann was strangely troubled. Repairing to a quiet little tavern to dine, he drank a great deal of wine, contrary to his habit, in the hope of stifling his inner agitation. But the wine only served to excite his imagination. Returning home, he threw himself on his bed without undressing, and fell heavily asleep.

It was night when he woke and the moon was shining into his room. He glanced at the time: it was a quarter to three. Sleep had left him; he sat on the bed and began thinking of the old countess's funeral.

Just then someone in the street looked in at him through the window and immediately walked on. Hermann paid no attention. A moment later he heard the door of his ante-room open. Hermann thought it was his orderly, drunk as usual, returning from some nocturnal excursion, but presently he heard an unfamiliar footstep: someone was softly shuffling along the floor in slippers. The door opened and a woman in white came in. Hermann mistook her for his old nurse and wondered what could have brought her at such an hour. But the woman in white glided across the room and stood before him—and Hermann recognized the countess!

'I have come to you against my will,' she said in a firm voice: 'but I am commanded to grant your request. The three, the seven and the ace will win for you if you play them in succession, provided that you do not stake more than one card in twenty-four hours and never play again as long as you live. I forgive you my death, on condition that you marry my ward, Lizaveta Ivanovna.'

With these words she turned softly, rustled to the door in her slippers, and disappeared. Hermann heard the street-door click and again saw someone peeping in at him through the window.

It was a long time before he could pull himself together and go into the next room. His orderly was asleep on the floor: Hermann had difficulty in waking him. The man was drunk as usual: there was no getting any sense out of him. The street-door was locked. Hermann returned to his room, and, lighting a candle, wrote down all the details of his vision.

ALEXANDER PUSHKIN, *The Queen of Spades*, 1834, trans. Rosemary Edmonds

'Horror ran through the land,' reads a contemporary account; 'Men spoke of it with bated breath, and pale-lipped women shuddered as they read the dreadful details. People afar off smelled blood, and the superstitious said that the skies were of a deeper red that autumn . . .' It was the autumn of 1888, and England, still slightly hung over from the previous year's celebration of Queen Victoria's Golden Jubilee, watched with apprehension as her grandson, Wilhelm II, ascended the throne of Germany.

But it was not the advent of Kaiser Wilhelm that caused men to speak with bated breath or drained the colour from the lips of their womenfolk. It was not the prospect of war, distant in 1888, that caused some to imagine that they could smell blood from afar. The horror which ran through the land and caused cranks to speak of a revisitation of Cain was inspired by a series of murders quite without parallel in the annals of crime. The autumn of 1888 was the period when a mysterious killer was abroad in the streets of London's East End, striking down his women victims without warning, slitting their throats, mutilating their bodies in hideous fashion, and escaping through police cordons to murder again. 'Jack the Ripper' was the name which he gave to himself, and by which he was known to posterity. It is a name which still strikes chill to the heart.

All too soon that autumn the bloodshot sunsets which some interpreted as portents were blotted out by thick, sulphurous fogs of the variety that are known as 'London particulars', and thus a new dimension was added to terror. At the height of the Ripper scare, Russian, Polish and German immigrants arriving in Whitechapel refused to stay there even temporarily, so great was their fear of the unknown killer. And even the local Cockneys would not budge from their hearths after sundown. The landlord of the Star and Garter, near Commercial Road, going broke, put the blame for his troubles squarely on Jack the Ripper. 'People aren't going out at night any more,' he complained to the bankruptcy receiver. 'Since the killings, I hardly get a soul in here of a night.' Even in the quiet, tree-lined squares of Belgravia and South Kensington the curtains were drawn a little tighter than usual, and their masters had difficulty in persuading the servant girls to post a letter after dark.

South of the Thames, in Blackfriars Road, Mrs Mary Burridge, a floor-cloth dealer, was so overcome by reading the *Star*'s lurid account of one of the Ripper murders that she fell dead, a copy of the Late Final clutched in her hand. Perhaps it was this paragraph that had caught her eye: 'A nameless reprobate—half beast, half man—is at large . . . Hideous malice, deadly cunning, insatiable thirst for blood —all these are the marks of the mad homicide. The ghoul-like creature, stalking down his victim like a Pawnee Indian, is simply drunk with blood, and he will have more.'

TOM CULLEN, *Autumn of Terror: Jack the Ripper*, 1965

† *In* The Rising of the Moon *two young brothers, Simon and Keith Innes, assist the redoubtable Mrs Bradley in her investigations, and trace the crimes to a sinister antique dealer named Mrs Cockerton. Not only is this peculiar lady fearfully down on wanton young women, to the extent of cutting them to pieces, but, to protect herself when threatened with discovery, she marries an old rag-and-bone man, on whom suspicion has fallen, and promptly boils up her new husband in a copper boiler.*

'Now to explore the shop and house,' said Keith, advancing towards the back door. I hesitated. I had an overwhelming sense of repugnance at the thought of entering that house, but Keith looked round at me in such immense surprise that I was pricked to shame, and advanced too.

'I thought that's what we *came* for,' he said.

'Yes, it was,' I answered; and, to my own chagrin and his astonishment, my throat was dry, and I could only manage a thick and heavy whisper.

'You don't think he's in there, do you?' asked Keith, catching a little of my unrest. I shook my head. I did not think this for an instant. Not only was it most unlikely that the rag and bone man would haunt a place where he was so close to the police who wanted him so badly, but the idea of his bodily presence was not at the root of my fear.

'And you don't think we'll find one of his victims in there, do you?' Keith went on, but this time with a lightening of his tone. I shook my head again. I did not know what I dreaded. My fear was of the empty house itself, but I could put no name to it. I think the bravest action that ever I performed was to lift the latch of the door.

It had not occurred to either of us that we should be able to march straight into an unoccupied house, and yet I was not much astonished when the door opened and we almost fell in over the threshold.

The next things of which I was aware were that the scullery smelt of cooking, and that the house was not unoccupied. Before I had the chance of remarking to Keith that the copper fire, after all the days that had gone by since I had lighted it at Mrs Cockerton's request, was still burning, and could request his observations on this phenomenon, there was the sound of a door opening, and, coming into the scullery from the kitchen, Mrs Cockerton herself stood before us.

She stood facing us for a full minute without speaking. She wore her usual hat and had her hands on her hips. She wore an apron over a plain black dress, and her feet were astride in an attitude to which we were accustomed. She fixed us with her faded, cornflower eyes.

'Well!' she said. 'I had half a mind to come at you hatchet in hand, Mr Innes, and Mr Keith. What say you to that, sirs?'

Keith laughed and flourished his horse-pistol.

'I have this, Mrs Cockerton,' said he, 'and Sim has the sabre you gave him.' . . .

Keith sniffed the air.

'Cooking, Mrs Cockerton?' he asked. He jerked his head at the copper.

'Not I, Mr Keith. The devil, mayhap,' she replied. 'Ask me no more. I cannot speak of it. Tell me why you have come.'

'Sentimental reasons,' said I. 'We wanted to see the place again.' . . .

'Explore, excavate, disclose,' she said, waving her hand. 'I leave you for half an hour. At the end of that time I must go. My lease of this house is concluded at moonrise to-night.'

'At moonrise? What a funny time,' said Keith.

'I have a morbid and fanciful mind, Mr Keith,' said Mrs Cockerton grandly. 'I give up the keys to-morrow, but at moonrise my tenancy closes.' . . .

She came back once or twice to watch us at work. The redolence of her cooking followed her through the open doorway into the room. Keith looked up at her the second time, and said:

'Not your supper, Mrs Cockerton?'

She smiled. She looked secretive, sly and pleased.

'I keep my meat good,' said she, 'by boiling it up every day. Every day, Mr Keith. Every single day. But what is it? It is goat, Mr Keith. Goat.'

'She *is* more peculiar than she was,' said Keith, when she had gone. . . .

'It's getting very late,' said he, looking out of the window. 'Think we'd better be getting back?' . . .

We had reached the gate, and were about to scramble over when Keith said suddenly:

'She never showed us the copper.'

'She didn't intend to. She was joking when she said it was goat.' He looked obstinate, and said he must see it.

'You don't want to see the copper now,' I objected. . . .

'But I do,' he insisted. 'Nothing would console me if I didn't see the copper. The copper, Sim, is mysterious and improbable. I mean, its contents are. Sim, we *must* see it. It's the only thing worth seeing in the house.'

I could not agree, but he seemed so much set on it that it would have been unkind to have gainsaid him.

'O.K.,' said I. 'Let's go back.'

So we returned to the scullery door. Mrs Cockerton was upstairs. We could hear her singing.

'No time to lose,' said Keith. I made no response to this, but whipped the wooden lid off the copper.

'And now,' said I, laughing, 'to see Bluebeard's eighth wife.'

We peered in. I ceased to laugh. The contents of the copper were indescribable. Even after this considerable lapse of time I cannot bring myself to speak of them in detail.

'And now,' said Keith, with his teeth chattering, 'do you still think we didn't need to look?'

'All I want is to be sick,' I said. Keith *was* sick. His stomach was always far more delicate than mine. He went outside to the drain, and got there just in time. 'But what does it mean?' I demanded, following him out.

'It means we've got to get out of here quick,' he replied.

GLADYS MITCHELL, *The Rising of the Moon*, 1945

THE BALLAD OF THE YORKSHIRE RIPPER

The 'Red Death' had long devastated the country. No pestilence had ever been so fatal, or so hideous. Blood was its Avatar and its seal . . .

Edgar Allan Poe, 'The Masque of the Red Death'

I were just cleaning up streets our kid. Just cleaning up streets.

Peter Sutcliffe to his brother Carl: *Somebody's Husband, Somebody's Son* by Gordon Burn

Voice said 'Lad, get crackin:
ah've med thi bombardier.'
Pete blasted red-light districts,
eight lasses in two year.

E slit em up on waste-ground,
in ginnel, plot an park,
in cemetery an woodyard,
an allus after dark.

Is tools were ball-pein ammers,
acksaws an carvin knives,
an a rusty Phillips screwdriver
oned for ending lives.

Cops dint fuss wi fust three,
paid to out on street,
though e blunted blade on is Stanley
deguttin em like meat.

Nor minded marks on fourth lass,
ripped up in her flat,
wi both ends on a clawhammer,
spilt-splat, split-splat, split-splat.

But Jayne MacDonald were a shopgirl
sellin nobbut shoes.
Pete, e killed er anyway
an now e were front page noos.

They appointed a Special Detective,
George Oldfield e were called.
E looked like a country bumpkin,
puffin, red, alf-bald.

E fixed up a Ripper Freefone,
Leeds 5050,
an asked Joe Soap to ring im up
an 'Tell us what you know.'

An folks, they give im names all right:
cousins, neighbours, mates,
blokes what they didn't tek to—
all were candidates.

But Pete, no e weren't rumbled.
E moved to a slap-up ouse,
pebbledash an wi a garden,
an utch to keep is mouse.

Cos Sonia, though she nittered
an med im giddyup,
were potterin too long in t'attic
to mind that owt were up.

An she went so ard at paintin
an scrubbin on ands an knee
she nivver noticed blood on trews
an t'missin cutlery. . . .

E were a one-man abattoir.
E cleavered girls in alves.
E shishkebab'd their pupils.
E bled em dry like calves.

Their napes as soft as foxglove,
the lovely finch-pink pout,
the feather-fern o t'eyelash—
e turned it all to nowt.

Seventh lass e totted
were in Garrads Timberyard.
E posted corpse in a pinestack
like Satan's visitin card.

Eighth were a badly woman
oo'd just come off o t'ward
o Manchester Royal Infirmary
an went back stiff as board.

E id is next on a wastetip
under a sofa's wings.
E stuffed her mouth wi ossair.
Er guts poked through like springs.

An wee Jo Whitaker, just 19,
an Alifax Buildin clerk,
bled from er smashed-egg foread
till t'gutter ran sump-dark. . . .

Everyweer in Yorkshire
were a creepin fear an thrill.
At Elland Road fans chanted
'Ripper 12 Police Nil.'

Lasses took up karate,
judo an self-defence,
an jeered at lads in porn shops,
an scrawled stuff in pub Gents,

like: 'Ripper's not a psychopath
but every man in pants.
All you blokes would kill like him
given half a chance.

'Listen to your beer-talk—
"hammer", "poke" and "screw",
"bang" and "score" and "lay" us:
that's what the Ripper does too.' . . .

So cops they lobbed im questions
through breakfast, dinner, tea,
till e said: 'All right, you've cracked it.
Ripper, aye, it's me.

'Ah did them thirteen killins.
Them girls live in mi brain,
mindin me o mi evil.
But ah'd do it all again.

'Streets are runnin sewers.
Streets are open sores.
Ah went there wi mi armoury
to wipe away all t'oors.

'Ah were carryin out God's mission.
Ah were followin is commands.
E pumped me like a primus.
Ah were putty in is ands.'

BLAKE MORRISON, 1987

It was a warm, sleepy summer's day in a County Court in Cavan. A youthful counsel of marked efficiency briskly ended the examination of his client by saying in a quiet and even voice. 'And I think you have one, but only one, criminal conviction and that was for murder and was a long time ago.' As the witness said, 'Yes,' the aged judge shot up from his near slumber and said, 'Good God. Were you hanged?'

JAMES COMYN, *Irish at Law*, 1981

The trial for murder of two teenage youths from prominent Chicago families is one of America's outstanding criminal cases.

On 22 May 1924, in a culvert on some waste ground near Chicago, workmen found the naked strangled body of 14-year-old Bobby Franks, son of millionaire businessman Jacob Franks. Near by lay a pair of spectacles.

Jacob Franks had already received a typewritten ransom note for $10,000 from a 'George Johnson', but before he could deal with it his son's body was found. All Johnsons were checked, and the sons of wealthy Chicago families interviewed. Among those who readily offered to help was 18-year-old Richard Loeb, son of the vice-president of Sears, Roebuck Co. He was an able student and proved very talkative.

The police were checking their only real clue—the spectacles found at the scene. These were traced to an oculist whose records showed that they had been sold to a Nathan Leopold. Leopold, who was 19, another son of a wealthy family and a friend of Richard Loeb, was a brilliant student. Shown the spectacles, he said, 'If I were not positive that my glasses were at home, I would say these are mine.' Asked to produce his own spectacles, he was unable to find them.

The other main aim was to find the Underwood machine on which the ransom note had been typed. Questioned about this, Leopold denied that the machine he used was an Underwood. But his fellow-students had borrowed his typewriter, and their typed sheets came from the same machine as the ransom note. Meanwhile Richard Loeb broke down under questioning and made a full confession. He said that he and Leopold had killed Bobby Franks for the excitement of committing a perfect murder that would be incapable of detection.

Leopold and Loeb were tried in Chicago in July 1924 with famous lawyer and humanitarian Clarence Darrow appearing for the defence. He faced fierce public demands for the deaths of the killers. Darrow pleaded mitigation based on reduced responsibility and mental illness. His appeal, however, was only against capital punishment, and he argued the case passionately enough to save the two youths. They were imprisoned for life on the murder charge, and sentenced to 99 years for kidnapping. Richard Loeb was killed in a prison homosexual brawl in 1936, while Nathan Leopold served 33 years and won his freedom in 1958. He married in 1961, and died ten years later.

J. H. H. GAUTE and ROBIN ODELL, *The Murderers' Who's Who*, 1979

† *This is the end of Darrow's speech in mitigation of sentence for Leopold and Loeb.*

The easy thing to do and the popular thing to do is to hang my clients. I know it. Men and women who do not think will applaud. The cruel and thoughtless will approve. It will be easy today; but in Chicago, and reaching over the length and breadth of the land, more and more fathers and mothers, the humane, the kind and the hopeful, who are gaining an understanding and asking questions not only about these poor boys, but about their own—these will join in no acclaim in the death of my clients. They would ask that the shedding of blood be stopped, and that the normal feelings of man resume their sway. And as the days and the months and the years go on, they will ask it more and more.

But, Your Honor, what they shall ask may not count. I know the easy way. I know Your Honor stands between the future and the past. I know the future is with me, and what I stand for here; not merely for the lives of these two unfortunate lads, but for all boys and all girls; and all the young; as far as possible, for all the old. I am pleading for life, understanding, charity, kindness, and the infinite mercy that considers all. I am pleading that we overcome cruelty with kindness and hatred with love. I know the future is on my side. Your Honor stands between the past and the future.

You may hang these boys; you may hang them by the neck until they are dead. But in doing it you will turn your face toward the past. In doing it you are making it harder for every other boy who in ignorance and darkness must grope his way through the mazes which only childhood knows. In doing it you will make it harder for unborn children. You may save them and make it easier for every child that sometime may stand where these boys stand. You will make it easier for every human being with an aspiration and a vision and a hope and a fate. I am pleading for the future; I am pleading for a time when hatred and cruelty will not control the hearts of men, when we can learn by reason and judgment and understanding and faith that all life is worth saving, and that mercy is the highest attribute of man. . . .

If I should succeed in saving these boys' lives and do nothing for the progress of the law, I should feel sad, indeed. If I can succeed, my greatest reward and my greatest hope will be that I have done something for the tens of thousands of other boys, for the countless unfortunates who must tread the same road in blind childhood that these poor boys have trod—that I have done something to help human understanding, to temper justice with mercy, to overcome hate with love.

I was reading last night of the aspiration of the old Persian poet, Omar Khayyám. It appealed to me as the highest that I can vision. I wish it was in my heart, and I wish it was in the hearts of all.

> 'So I be written in the Book of Love,
> I do not care about the Book above;
> Erase my name or write it as you will,
> So I be written in the Book of Love.'

The effect of Darrow's appeal was manifest. As a special correspondent for one paper put it: 'There was scarcely any telling where his voice had finished and where silence had begun. Silence lasted a minute, two minutes. His own eyes, dimmed by years of serving the accused, the oppressed, the weak, were not the only ones that held tears.' Every newspaper in Chicago, and many throughout the nation, printed the long argument in full—a tribute rarely paid to even the greatest of advocates.

FRANCIS X. BUSCH, *Prisoners at the Bar: Notable American Trials*, 1957

† *Ronald True, who had served as an airman in the 1914–18 war and had been seriously injured in a crash, apparently believed that he was being impersonated by a stranger who was forging his cheques. He went about armed with a gun and, in 1922, was sentenced for the murder of a prostitute named Olive Young. He was later found insane and sent to Broadmoor.*

There really was another Ronald True, who, however, spelt his name Ronald Trew; and Mr Trew was a member of Murray's. The two men had never met, but it is tolerably certain that True knew, and had known for some time, that he had a namesake. It may have been this knowledge that started the idea of *doppelgänger* in his mind. Certainly in his excited fits in the London nursing-home, he used to complain of the scandal there would be if a man was going about the streets with a name like his own. To a disordered mind the fact that another person bore the same name would soon suggest a sinister purpose, whence it would be an easy transition to the belief that he was an enemy, carried a deadly weapon, and so forth. True's fraud does not justify us in assuming that the story of the 'other Ronald True' was a criminal device and nothing more. Among the many circumstances that point to its delusional character is the curious fact that True never once alluded to it in [his friend] Armstrong's presence, though he was free enough about it to other people. For some reason he seemed to take pains to conceal it from his favourite male associate, though if he had invented the story simply to 'make evidence', to cover up his misdeeds, this is the very person to whom the story should have been told. Whether in passing the cheque at Murray's True forged the name Trew or used his own name and took advantage of the easy confusion is not clear. The evidence of the club manager is contradictory on the point. The fraud, of course, was soon discovered. Ultimately the club authorities got in touch with Mrs True, who made good the amount. . . .

. . . on [the] fatal night, True did not, as before, stop at the corner of the road, but drove right up to his victim's door. The inference is that on the previous occasions he had merely been reconnoitring and that on his last visit he had ascertained that the opportunity to strike had arrived. A fact elicited at True's trial cleared the whole matter up. Olive Young was in the habit of leaving a light burning in the entrance passage of her flat till she came home, when she used to turn it out; and this light would be visible to anyone who looked down from street level through the fanlight. It is fairly certain that when True drove to the corner of Finborough Road on Thursday, Friday, and Saturday, he ran up to No. 13A, and on each occasion found the light burning in the passage, which meant that his intended victim had not come home yet. But on Sunday night Olive Young arrived home just about eleven o'clock, so that when True peered down from the street a few minutes later he had the satisfaction of observing that the light was out. That was enough. All that remained was to get rid of Armstrong, and then return with all speed to Fulham. There was always the chance, of course, that he might be refused admittance, but that was unlikely. Girls of Olive Young's class cannot afford to make scenes at midnight and appeal to the police on the slightest provocation—particularly when their landlady is not *supposed* to know what their calling is. It is better to take a few risks. And so when Olive found who was knocking at her door, she bowed to her fate. She let him in, and took her chance.

True's demeanour must have been fairly reassuring, for at seven o'clock on Monday morning Olive Young was still peacefully drowsing in her bed, dimly conscious, perhaps, that her companion was up and about at the business of making early morning tea. This, of course, had to be done in the kitchen next door, and then True, rummaging about, found the very thing he wanted in the copper—a stout rolling-pin. He brought in the tea, and Olive sat up sleepily and took her cup. True slipped round the other side of the bed . . .

She gave no trouble. The first blow of the rolling-pin felled her, sending her cup and saucer crashing to the floor, and four more were delivered in swift succession. She was as good as dead, but the murderer was thorough. A towel thrust deep into her gullet, and the girdle of her dressing-gown drawn tightly round her neck, finished the job.

DONALD CARSWELL, *Famous Trials*, 1948

† *In this extract from Eric Ambler's* Journey into Fear *an Englishman named Graham has got himself into a pickle on board an Italian steamer heading for Genoa; the principal villain of the piece is a German agent by the name of Moeller who means to put a permanent stop to Graham's journey.*

They had reached the passport control at the entrance to the Customs shed and José, who had walked on ahead, was waiting as if the seconds were costing him money. She pressed Graham's hand hurriedly. '*Alors, chéri! A tout à l'heure.*'

Graham got his passport and slowly followed them through the Customs shed. . . .

Then he saw Moeller and Banat.

They were standing beside a big American sedan drawn up beyond the taxis. There were two other men on the far side of the car: one was tall and thin and wore a mackintosh and a workman's cap, the other was a very dark, heavy-jowled man with a grey ulster and a soft hat, which he wore without a dent in it. A fifth and younger man sat at the wheel of the car.

His heart thumping, Graham beckoned to the porter, who was making for the taxis, and walked towards them.

Moeller nodded as he came up. 'Good! Your luggage? Ah, yes.' He nodded to the tall man, who came round, took the case from the porter, and put it in the luggage boot at the back.

Graham tipped the porter and got in the car. Moeller followed him and sat beside him. The tall man got in beside the driver. Banat and the man in the ulster sat on the pull-down seats facing Graham and Moeller. Banat's face was expressionless. The man in the ulster avoided Graham's eyes and looked out of the window.

The car started. Almost immediately, Banat took out his pistol and snapped the safety catch.

Graham turned to Moeller. 'Is that necessary?' he demanded. 'I'm not going to escape.'

Moeller shrugged. 'As you please.' He said something to Banat, who grinned, snapped the safety catch again and put the gun back in his pocket.

The car swung into the cobbled road leading to the dock gates.

'Which hotel are we going to?' Graham inquired.

Moeller turned his head slightly. 'I have not yet made up my mind. We can leave that question until later. We shall drive out to Santa Margherita first.'

'But . . .'

'There are no "buts." I am making the arrangements.' He did not bother to turn his head this time.

'What about Kuvetli?'

'He left by the pilot boat early this morning.'

'Then what's happened to him?'

'He is probably writing a report to Colonel Haki. I advise you to forget him.'

Graham was silent. He had asked about Mr Kuvetli with the sole object of concealing the fact that he was badly frightened. He had been in the car less than two minutes, and already the odds against him had lengthened considerably.

The car bumped over the cobbles to the dock gates, and Graham braced himself for the sharp right turn that would take them towards the town and the Santa Margherita road. The next moment he lurched sideways in his seat as the car swerved to the left. Banat whipped out his gun.

Graham slowly regained his position. 'I'm sorry,' he said. 'I thought we turned right for Santa Margherita.'

There was no reply. He sat back in his corner trying to keep his face expressionless. He had assumed quite unwarrantably that it would be through Genoa itself, and on to the Santa Margherita road that he would be taken for his 'ride.' All his hopes had been based on the assumption. He had taken too much for granted.

He glanced at Moeller. The German agent was sitting back with his eyes closed: an old man whose work for the day was done. The rest of the day was Banat's. Graham knew that the small, deep-set eyes were feeling for his, and that the long-suffering mouth was grinning. Banat was going to enjoy his work. The other man was still looking out of the window. He had not uttered a sound.

They reached a fork and turned to the right along a secondary road with a direction sign for Novi-Torimo. They were going north. The road was straight and lined with dusty plane trees. Beyond the trees there were rows of grim-looking houses and a factory or two. Soon, however, the road began to rise and twist, and the houses and factories were left behind. They were getting into the country.

Graham knew that unless some wholly unexpected way of escape presented itself, his chances of surviving the next hour were now practically non-existent. Presently the car would stop. Then he would be taken out and shot as methodically and efficiently as if he had been condemned by a court martial. The blood was thundering in his head, and his breathing was quick and shallow. He tried to breathe slowly and deeply, but the muscles in his chest seemed incapable of making the effort. He went on trying. He knew that if he surrendered himself to fear now, if he let himself go, he would be lost, whatever happened. He must not be frightened.

ERIC AMBLER, *Journey into Fear*, 1940

† *Frederick Henry Seddon was accused of poisoning his lodger, a Miss Barrow, whose money he had obtained. He was cross-examined at the Old Bailey by Rufus Isaacs, the first Marquess of Reading. (He was executed 18 April 1912.)*

Seddon had a very quick and agile mind: at first his clever parries and retorts were very effective. He had an explanation and a reason for everything. But gradually his very cleverness and his inhuman coolness began to disgust the jury. . . . Only towards the end did he break out and lose his composure. When he was asked as to the counting of the gold on the day of Miss Barrow's death, he showed his first sign of anger.

'The prosecution are suggesting that I am dealing with the deceased woman's gold. That I should bring it down from the top of the house to the bottom, into the office in the presence of my assistants, and count it up—is it feasible? . . . I am not a degenerate. That would make it out that I was a greedy, inhuman monster. . . . The suggestion is scandalous.'

Seddon did himself more good by this angry outburst than by all his cool cleverness, but he ruined its effect by adding, with a sarcastic smile, 'I would have all day to count the money.'

He again became very indignant when Mr Attorney came to the statement made by him on his arrest, when he was alleged to have said, 'Are you going to arrest my wife too?' He said the explanation of this was that the officer had first said, 'You will see your wife at the station.' 'That,' he said, 'I swear before God, is the words that took place, and I have been waiting the opportunity to get into this box for to relate the true words that were spoken on this occasion.'

'All the statements,' commented the Attorney-General quietly, 'that you are making are statements before God.'

Little by little, Sir Rufus gained ground, and for all his cleverness the soul of Seddon was laid bare before the Court, if soul it could be called; for its god was gold, and his mean, calculating character, which obviously cared for nothing but Seddon and his worldly possessions, aroused the contempt and loathing of almost everybody in court. Here was a man who would do anything for gain. 'Never,' said an onlooker, 'have I seen a soul stripped so naked as that.'

EDWARD MARJORIBANKS, *The Life of Sir Edward Marshall Hall*, 1929

ANNETTE MYERS, OR, A MURDER IN ST JAMES'S PARK

Another dreadful tale of woe as I will here unfold
Has taken place, and seldom such before was ever told.
Female named Annette Myers—how horrible and true—
On Friday night in St James's Park a soldier there she slew.

Chorus:
Annette Myers in a frenzy went—how awful to impart—
And shot a soldier dead in St James's Park.

A servant girl the female was as we can understand,
Henry Ducker was a soldier and aged twenty-one,
Belonging to the Coldstream Guards, of good character we find;
He loved this maid though jealousy had poisoned his mind.

She and her soldier loving words did to each other talk,
As they were walking arm-in-arm along the Birdcage Walk;
When sudden she the weapon placed unto her lover's head,
And the trigger drew and the soldier slew who on the ground fell
dead.

When she the pistol fired she prepared to go away,
But the officer detained her and thus to her did say:
'Did you the pistol fire?' 'I did' she said 'Indeed
And am quite satisfied' as we may plainly read.

Great consternation it has caused as we can understand,
This soldier one-and twenty was, a sprightly gay young man;
Henry Ducker was his name, of the Coldstream Guards we see.
What dreadful tidings to convey unto his family.

ANON.

EXECUTION OF ALICE HOLT

A dreadful case of murder,
Such as we seldom hear,
Committed was at Stockport,
In the County of Cheshire.
Where a mother, named Mary Bailey,
They did so cruelly slaughter,
By poison administered all in her beer,
By her own daughter.

The daughter insured the life of the mother
For twenty-six pounds at her death,
Then she and the man that she lived with
Determined to take away her breath.
And when Betty Wood represented the mother
She didn't act with propriety,
For the poor mother lost her life,
And they all swindled the Society.

'Now that the old gal's life's insured,'
  Holt to the daughter did say,
'Better in the grave she were immured,
  And the money will make us gay.'
'Now that you have got me in the family way,
  And from me my virtue you've wrung,
You'll never be happy a day
  Till on the gallows I'm hung.'

She laid a plan to murder her,
  As we now see so clear,
To put a quantity of arsenic
  Into her poor mother's beer.
To see her lay in agony,
  Upon that dreadful night,
With a dreadful dose of arsenic,
  Oh, it was a dreadful sight.

She lived but just six hours,
  Then the poor woman did die,
And this base murdering wretch
  The dreadful deed did deny.
On the man Holt she laid the blame,
  Vowed he did her mother slay,
Holt on her did the same,
  Saying she took the mother's life away.

But there's no doubt the base wretch
  Did her poor mother slay,
For which on Chester's scaffold
  Her life did forfeit pay,
So all young women a warning take
  By this poor wretch you see,
A-hanging for the mother's sake
  On Chester's fatal tree.

ANON.

† *In* Double Indemnity, *Hugh, an insurance salesman, and Phyllis Nirdlinger join in a plot to murder her husband for insurance money. At the end they are on a ship at sea—with no way of escape.*

I went to bed right away, and stayed there till early in the afternoon. Then I couldn't stand it any longer, alone there in the stateroom, and went up on deck. I found my chair and sat there looking at the coast of Mexico, where we were going past it. But I had a funny feeling I wasn't going anywhere. I kept thinking about Keyes, and the look he had in his eye that day, and what he meant by what he said. Then, all of a sudden, I found out. I heard a little gasp beside me. Before I even looked I knew who it was. I turned to the next chair. It was Phyllis.

'You.'

'Hello, Phyllis.'

'Your man Keyes—he's quite a matchmaker.'

'Oh yeah. He's romantic.'

I looked her over. Her face was drawn from the last time I had seen her, and there were little puckers around her eyes. She handed me something.

'Did you see it?'

'What is it?'

'The ship's paper.'

'No, I didn't. I guess I'm not interested.'

'It's in there.'

'What's in there?'

'About the wedding. Lola and Nino. It came in by radio a little after noon.'

'Oh, they're married?'

'Yes. It was pretty exciting. Mr Keyes gave her away. They went to San Francisco on their honeymoon. Your company paid Nino a bonus.'

'Oh. It must be out then. About us.'

'Yes. It all came out. It's a good thing we're under different names here. I saw all the passengers reading about it at lunch. It's a sensation.'

'You don't seem worried.'

'I've been thinking about something else.'

She smiled then, the sweetest, saddest smile you ever saw. I thought of the five patients, the three little children, Mrs Nirdlinger, Nirdlinger, and myself. It didn't seem possible that anybody that could be as nice as she was when she wanted to be, could have done those things.

'What were you thinking about?'

'We could be married, Walter.'

'We could be. And then what?'

I don't know how long we sat looking out to sea after that. She started it again. 'There's nothing ahead of us, is there, Walter?'

'No. Nothing.'

'I don't even know where we're going. Do you?'

'No.'

'. . . Walter, the time has come.'

'What do you mean, Phyllis?'

'For me to meet my bridegroom. The only one I ever loved. One night I'll drop off the stern of the ship. Then, little by little I'll feel his icy fingers creeping into my heart.'

'. . . I'll give you away.'

'What?'

'I mean: I'll go with you.'

'It's all that's left, isn't it?'

Keyes was right. I had nothing to thank him for. He just saved the state the expense of getting me.

We walked around the ship. A sailor was swabbing out the gutter outside the rail. He was nervous, and caught me looking at him. 'There's a shark. Following the ship.'

I tried not to look, but couldn't help it. I saw a flash of dirty white down in the green. We walked back to the deck chairs.

'Walter, we'll have to wait. Till the moon comes up.'

'I guess we better have a moon.'

'I want to see that fin. That black fin. Cutting the water in the moonlight.'

The captain knows us. I could tell by his face when he came out of the radio room a little while ago. It will have to be tonight. He's sure to put a guard on us before he puts into Mazatlan.

The bleeding has started again. The internal bleeding, I mean, from the lung where the bullet grazed it. It's not much but I spit blood. I keep thinking about that shark.

I'm writing this in the stateroom. It's about half past nine. She's in her stateroom getting ready. She's made her face chalk white, with black circles under her eyes and red on her lips and cheeks. She's got that red thing on. It's awful-looking. It's just one big square of red silk that she wraps around her, but it's got no armholes, and her hands look like stumps underneath it when she moves them around. She looks like what came aboard the ship to shoot dice for souls in the *Rhyme of the Ancient Mariner*.

I didn't hear the stateroom door open, but she's beside me now while I'm writing. I can feel her.

The moon.

JAMES M. CAIN, *Double Indemnity*, 1945

† *Two men—perfect strangers—get into a conversation on a train, and one puts forward the idea that each should commit a murder on the other's behalf. His fellow-traveller treats the suggestion as a rather unpleasant fantasy, but Bruno is serious. He keeps his part of the bargain.*

Miriam stood on slightly higher ground, not three yards away from him now, and the others slid down the bank towards the water. Bruno inched closer. The lights on the water silhouetted her head and shoulders. Never had he been so close!

'Hey!' Bruno whispered, and saw her turn. 'Say, isn't your name Miriam?'

She faced him, but he knew she could barely see him. 'Yeah. Who're you?'

He came a step nearer. 'Haven't I met you somewhere before?' he asked cynically, smelling the perfume again. She was a warm ugly black spot. He sprang with such concentrated aim, the wrists of his spread hands touched.

'Say what d'you—?'—

His hands captured her throat on the last word, stifling its abortive uplift of surprise. He shook her. His body seemed to harden like rock, and he heard his teeth crack. She made a grating sound in her throat, but he had her too tight for a scream. With a leg behind her, he wrenched her backward, and they fell to the ground together with no sound but of a brush of leaves. He sunk his fingers deeper, enduring the distasteful pressure of her body under his so her writhing would not get them both up. Her throat felt hotter and fatter. Stop, stop,

stop! He willed it! And the head stopped turning. He was sure he had held her long enough, but he did not lessen his grip. Glancing behind him, he saw nothing coming. When he relaxed his fingers, it felt as if he had made deep dents in her throat as in a piece of dough. Then she made a sound like an ordinary cough that terrified him like the rising dead, and he fell on her again, hitched himself on to his knees to do it, pressing her with a force he thought would break his thumbs. All the power in him he poured out through his hands. And if it was not enough? He heard himself whimper. She was still and limp now.

'Miriam?' called the girl's voice.

Bruno sprang up and stumbled straight away towards the centre of the island, then turned left to bring him out near his boat. He found himself scrubbing something off his hands with his pocket handkerchief. Miriam's spit. He threw the handkerchief down and swept it up again, because it was monogrammed. He was thinking! He felt great! It was done!

'Mi-ri-am!' with lazy impatience.

But what if he hadn't finished her, if she were sitting up and talking now? The thought shot him forward and he almost toppled down the bank. A firm breeze met him at the water's edge. He didn't see his boat. He started to take any boat, changed his mind, then a couple of yards farther to the left found it, perched on the little log.

'Hey, she's fainted!'

Bruno shoved off, quickly, but not hurrying.

'Help, somebody!' said the girl's half gasp, half scream.

'Gawd!—Huh-*help*!'

The panic in the voice panicked Bruno. He rowed for several choppy strokes, then abruptly stopped and let the boat glide over the dark water. What was he getting scared about, for Christ's sake? Not a sign of anyone chasing him.

'Hey!'

'F'God's sake, she's *dead*! Call somebody!'

A girl's scream was a long arc in silence and somehow the scream made it final. A beautiful scream, Bruno thought with a queer, serene admiration. He approached the dock easily, behind another boat. Slowly, as slowly as he had ever done anything, he paid the boat-keeper.

PATRICIA HIGHSMITH, *Strangers on a Train*, 1950

THE MURDER ON THE DOWNS

Past a cow and past a cottage,
Past the sties and byres,
Past the equidistant poles
Holding taut the humming wires,

Past the inn and past the garage,
Past the hypodermic steeple
Ever ready to inject
The opium of the people,

In the fresh, the Sussex morning,
Up the Dangerous Corner lane
Bert and Jennifer were walking
Once again.

The spider's usual crochet
Was caught upon the thorns,
The skylark did its stuff,
The cows had horns.

'See,' said Bert, 'my hand is sweating.'
With her lips she touched his palm
As they took the path above the
Valley farm.

Over the downs the wind unveiled
That ancient monument the sun,
And a perfect morning
Had begun.

But summer lightning like an omen
Carried on a silent dance
On his heart's horizon, as he
Gave a glance

At the face beside him, and she turned
Dissolving in his frank blue eyes
All her hope, like aspirin.
On that breeding-place of lies

His forehead, too, she laid her lips.
'Let's find a place to sit,' he said.

MURDERERS

'Past the gorse, down in the bracken
Like a bed.'

Oh the fresh, the laughing morning!
Warmth upon the bramble brake
Like a magnet draws from darkness
A reviving snake:

Just an adder, slowly gliding,
Sleepy curving idleness,
On the Sussex turf now writing
SOS.

Jennifer in sitting, touches
With her hand an agaric,
Like a bulb of rotten rubber
Soft and thick,

Screams, withdraws, and sees its colour
Like a leper's liver,
Leans on Bert so he can feel her
Shiver.

Over there the morning ocean,
Frayed around the edges, sighs,
At the same time gaily twinkles,
Conniving with a million eyes

At Bert whose free hand slowly pulls
A rayon stocking from his coat,
Twists it quickly, twists it neatly,
Round her throat.

'Ah, I knew that this would happen!'
Her last words: and not displeased
Jennifer relaxed, still smiling
While he squeezed.

Under a sky without a cloud
Lay the still unruffled sea,
And in the bracken like a bed
The murderee.

WILLIAM PLOMER, 1960

. . . the whole beach was reverberating in the sun and pressing against me from behind. I took a few steps towards the spring. The Arab didn't move. Even now he was still some distance away. Perhaps because of the shadows on his face, he seemed to be laughing. I waited. The sun was beginning to burn my cheeks and I felt drops of sweat gathering in my eyebrows. It was the same sun as on the day of mother's funeral and again it was my forehead that was hurting me most and all the veins were throbbing at once beneath the skin. And because I couldn't stand this burning feeling any longer, I moved forward. I knew it was stupid and I wouldn't get out of the sun with one step. But I took a step, just one step forward. And this time, without sitting up, the Arab drew his knife and held it out towards me in the sun. The light leapt up off the steel and it was like a long, flashing sword lunging at my forehead. At the same time all the sweat that had gathered in my eyebrows suddenly ran down over my eyelids, covering them with a dense layer of warm moisture. My eyes were blinded by this veil of salty tears. All I could feel were the cymbals the sun was clashing against my forehead and, indistinctly, the dazzling spear still leaping up off the knife in front of me. It was like a red-hot blade gnawing at my eyelashes and gouging out my stinging eyes. That was when everything shook. The sea swept ashore a great breath of fire. The sky seemed to be splitting from end to end and raining down sheets of flame. My whole being went tense and I tightened my grip on the gun. The trigger gave, I felt the underside of the polished butt and it was there, in that sharp but deafening noise, that it all started. I shook off the sweat and the sun. I realized that I'd destroyed the balance of the day and the perfect silence of this beach where I'd been happy. And I fired four more times at a lifeless body and the bullets sank in without leaving a mark. And it was like giving four sharp knocks at the door of unhappiness.

ALBERT CAMUS, *The Outsider*, 1946, trans. Joseph Lavedo

Murder didn't mean much to Raven. It was just a new job. You had to be careful. You had to use your brains. It was not a question of hatred. He had only seen the Minister once: he had been pointed out to Raven as he walked down the new housing estate between the little lit Christmas trees, an old, rather grubby man without any friends, who was said to love humanity.

The cold wind cut his face in the wide continental street. It was a good excuse for turning the collar of his coat well up above his mouth. A hare-lip was a serious handicap in his profession; it had been badly sewn in infancy, so that now the upper lip was twisted and scarred. When you carried about you so easy an identification you couldn't help becoming ruthless in your methods. It had always, from the first, been necessary for Raven to eliminate the evidence.

He carried an attaché case. He looked like any other youngish man going home after his work; his dark overcoat had a clerical air. He moved steadily up the street like hundreds of his kind. A tram went by, lit up in the early dusk: he didn't take it. An economical young man, you might have thought, saving money for his home. Perhaps even now he was on his way to meet his girl.

But Raven had never had a girl. The hare-lip prevented that. He had learnt, when he was very young, how repulsive it was. He turned into one of the tall grey houses and climbed the stairs, a sour bitter screwed-up figure.

Outside the top flat he put down his attaché case and put on gloves. He took a pair of clippers out of his pocket and cut through the telephone wire where it ran out from above the door to the lift shaft. Then he rang the bell.

He hoped to find the Minister alone. This little top-floor flat was the socialist's home; he lived in a poor bare solitary way and Raven had been told that his secretary always left him at half past six; he was very considerate with his employees. But Raven was a minute too early and the Minister half an hour too late. A woman opened the door, an elderly woman with pince-nez and several gold teeth. She had her hat on and her coat was over her arm. She had been on the point of leaving and she was furious at being caught. She didn't allow him to speak, but snapped at him in German: 'The Minister is engaged.'

He wanted to spare her, not because he minded a killing but because his employers might prefer him not to exceed his instructions. He held the letter of introduction out to her silently; as long as she didn't hear his foreign voice or see his hare-lip she was safe. She took the letter primly and held it up close to her pince-nez. Good, he thought, she's short-sighted. 'Stay where you are,' she said, and walked back up the passage. He could hear her disapproving governess voice, then she was back in the passage saying: 'The Minister will see you. Follow me, please.' He couldn't understand the foreign speech, but he knew what she meant from her behaviour.

His eyes, like little concealed cameras, photographed the room instantaneously: the desk, the easy chair, the map on the wall, the door to the bedroom behind, the wide window above the bright cold Christmas street. A little oil-stove was all the heating, and the Minister was using it now to boil a saucepan. A kitchen alarm-clock on the desk marked seven o'clock. A voice said: 'Emma, put another egg in the saucepan.' The Minister came out from the bedroom. He had tried to tidy himself, but he had forgotten the cigarette ash on his trousers. He was old and small and rather dirty. The secretary took an egg out of one of the drawers in the desk: 'And the salt. Don't forget the salt,' the Minister said. He explained in slow English. 'It prevents the shell cracking. Sit down, my friend. Make yourself at home. Emma, you can go.'

Raven sat down and fixed his eyes on the Minister's chest. He thought: I'll give her three minutes by the alarm-clock to get well away: he kept his eyes on the Minister's chest: just there I'll shoot. He let his coat collar fall and saw with bitter rage how the old man turned away from the sight of his hare-lip.

The Minister said: 'It's years since I heard from him. But I've never forgotten him, never. I can show you his photograph in the other room. It's good of him to think of an old friend. So rich and powerful too. You must ask him when you go back if he remembers the time—' A bell began to ring furiously.

Raven thought: the telephone. I cut the wire. It shook his nerve. But it was only the alarm-clock drumming on the desk. The Minister turned it off. 'One egg's boiled,' he said, and stooped for the saucepan. Raven opened his attaché case: in the lid he had fixed his automatic fitted with a silencer. The Minister said: 'I'm sorry the bell made you jump. You see I like my egg just four minutes.'

Feet ran along the passage. The door opened. Raven turned furiously in his seat, his hare-lip flushed and raw. It was the secretary. He thought: my God, what a household. They won't let a man do things tidily. He forgot his lip, he was angry, he had a grievance. She came in flashing her gold teeth, prim and ingratiating. She said: 'I was just going out when I heard the telephone,' then she winced slightly, looked the other way, showed a clumsy delicacy before his deformity which he couldn't help noticing. It condemned her. He snatched the automatic out of the case and shot the Minister twice in the back.

The Minister fell across the oil stove; the saucepan upset and the two eggs broke on the floor. Raven shot the Minister once more in the head, leaning across the desk to make quite certain, driving the bullet hard into the base of the skull, smashing it open like a china doll's. Then he turned on the secretary.

GRAHAM GREENE, *A Gun for Sale*, 1936

INSTRUCTIONS FOR A MURDER

† *Gus and Ben, two professional killers, wait in a room with a dumb waiter*.

GUS. I'm here.

[*Ben frowns and presses his forehead*.

You've missed something out.
BEN. I know. What?
GUS. I haven't taken my gun out, according to you.
BEN. You take your gun out . . .
GUS. After I've closed the door.
BEN. After you've closed the door.
GUS. You've never missed that out before, you know that?
BEN. When he sees you behind him . . .
GUS. Me behind him . . .
BEN. And me in front of him . . .
GUS. And you in front of him . . .
BEN. He'll feel uncertain . . .
GUS. Uneasy.
BEN. He won't know what to do.
GUS. So what will he do?
BEN. He'll look at me and he'll look at you.
GUS. We won't say a word.
BEN. We'll look at him.
GUS. He won't say a word.
BEN. He'll look at us.
GUS. And we'll look at him.
BEN. Nobody says a word.

[*Pause*.

GUS. What do we do if it's a girl?
BEN. We do the same.

GUS. Exactly the same?

BEN. Exactly.

[*Pause*.

GUS. We don't do anything different?

BEN. We do exactly the same.

GUS. Oh. [*He rises, and shivers*.] Excuse me.

[*Gus exits by the door left. Ben remains sitting on the bed, still. The lavatory chain is pulled once off left, but the lavatory does not flush. Silence*.

Gus re-enters and stops inside the door, deep in thought. He looks at Ben, then walks slowly across to his own bed. He is troubled. He stands, thinking. He turns and looks at Ben. He moves a few paces towards him.

[*Slowly in a low, tense voice*.] Why did he send us matches if he knew there was no gas?

[*Silence. Ben stares in front of him. Gus crosses to the left side of Ben, to the foot of his bed, to get to his other ear*.

Ben. Why did he send us matches if he knew there was no gas?

[*Ben looks up*.

Why did he do that?

BEN. Who?

GUS. Who sent us those matches?

BEN. What are you talking about?

[*Gus stares down at him*.

GUS [*thickly*]. Who is it upstairs?

BEN [*nervously*]. What's one thing to do with another?

GUS. Who is it, though?

BEN. What's one thing to do with another? [*He fumbles for his paper on the bed*.

GUS. I asked you a question.

BEN. Enough!

GUS [*with growing agitation*]. I asked you before. Who moved in? I asked you. You said the people who had it before moved out. Well, who moved in?

BEN [*hunched*]. Shut up.

GUS. I told you, didn't I?

BEN [*standing*]. Shut up!

GUS [*feverishly*]. I told you before who owned this place didn't I? I told you.

[*Ben hits him viciously on the shoulder.*

I told you who ran this place, didn't I?

[*Ben hits him again viciously on the shoulder.*

[*Violently*] Well, what's he playing all these games for? That's what I want to know. What's he doing it for?

BEN. What game?

GUS [*passionately, advancing*]. What's he doing it for? We've been through our tests, haven't we? We got right through our tests, years ago, didn't we? We took them together, don't you remember, didn't we? We've proved ourselves before now, haven't we? We've always done our job. What's he doing all this for? What's the idea? What's he playing these games for?

[*The box in the shaft comes down behind them. The noise is this time accompanied by a shrill whistle, as it falls. Gus rushes to the hatch and seizes the note.*

[*Reading*] 'Scampi!' [*He crumples the note, picks up the tube, takes out the whistle, blows and speaks.*] *We've got nothing left! Nothing! Do you understand?*

[*Ben seizes the tube and flings Gus away. He follows Gus and slaps him hard back-handed across the chest.*

BEN. Stop it! You maniac!

GUS. But you heard!

BEN [*savagely*]. That's enough! I'm warning you!

[*Silence. Ben hangs up the tube. He goes to his bed and lies down. He picks up his paper and reads. Silence. The box goes up. They turn quickly, their eyes meet. Ben turns to his paper. Slowly Gus goes back to the right side of his bed, and sits. Silence. The hatch falls back into place. They turn quickly, their eyes meet. Ben turns back to his paper. Silence. Ben throws his paper down.*

Kaw! [*He picks up the paper and looks at it.*] Listen to this! [*Pause*] What about that, eh? [*Pause*] Kaw! [*Pause*] Have you ever heard such a thing?

GUS [*dully*]. Go on!

BEN. It's true.

GUS. Get away.

BEN. It's down here in black and white.
GUS [*very low*]. Is that a fact?
BEN. Can you imagine it?
GUS. It's unbelievable.
BEN. It's enough to make you want to puke, isn't it?
GUS [*almost inaudible*]. Incredible.

[*Ben shakes his head. He puts the paper down and rises. He fixes the revolver in his holster. Gus stands up. He goes towards the door left.*

BEN. Where are you going?
GUS. I'm going to have a glass of water.

[*Gus exits left. Ben brushes the dust off his clothes and off his shoes. The whistle in the speaking tube blows. He goes to it, takes the whistle out and puts the tube to his ear. He listens. He puts it to his mouth.*

BEN. Yes. [*To his ear; he listens. To his mouth.*] Straight away. Right. [*To his ear; he listens. To his mouth.*] Sure we're ready. [*To his ear; he listens. To his mouth.*] Understood. Repeat. He has arrived and will be coming in straight away. The normal method to be employed. Understood. [*To his ear; he listens. To his mouth.*] Sure we're ready [*To his ear; he listens. To his mouth*] Right. [*He hangs up the tube.*] Gus! [*He takes out his comb and combs his hair, adjusts his jacket to diminish the bulge of the revolver. The lavatory flushes off left. Ben goes quickly to the door left.*] Gus!

[*The door right opens sharply. Ben turns, his revolver levelled at the door. Gus stumbles in. He is stripped of his jacket, waistcoat, tie, holster and revolver. He stops, body stooping, his arms at his sides, he raises his head and looks at Ben. A long silence follows and they stare at each other as—*

the Curtain falls

HAROLD PINTER, *The Dumb Waiter*, 1957

V

SEDUCERS AND CADS

NOW the serpent was more subtil than any beast of the field which the Lord God had made. And he said unto the woman, Yea, hath God said, Ye shall not eat of every tree of the garden?

And the woman said unto the serpent, We may eat of the fruit of the trees of the garden:

But of the fruit of the tree which is in the midst of the garden, God hath said, Ye shall not eat of it, neither shall ye touch it, lest ye die.

And the serpent said unto the woman, Ye shall not surely die:

For God doth know that in the day ye eat thereof, then your eyes shall be opened, and ye shall be as gods, knowing good and evil.

And when the woman saw that the tree was good for food, and that it was pleasant to the eyes, and a tree to be desired to make one wise, she took of the fruit thereof, and did eat, and gave also unto her husband with her; and he did eat.

And the eyes of them both were opened, and they knew that they were naked; and they sewed fig leaves together, and made themselves aprons.

And they heard the voice of the Lord God walking in the garden in the cool of the day: and Adam and his wife hid themselves from the presence of the Lord God amongst the trees of the garden.

And the Lord God called unto Adam, and said unto him, Where art thou?

And he said, I heard thy voice in the garden, and I was afraid, because I was naked; and I hid myself.

And he said, Who told thee that thou wast naked? Hast thou eaten of the tree, whereof I commanded thee that thou shouldest not eat?

And the man said, The woman whom thou gavest to be with me, she gave me of the tree, and I did eat.

And the Lord God said unto the woman, What is this that thou hast done? And the woman said, The serpent beguiled me, and I did eat.

Genesis 3

Behold alone
The Woman, opportune to all attempts—
Her husband, for I view far round, not nigh,

Whose higher intellectual more I shun,
And strength, of courage haughty, and of limb
Heroic built, though of terrestrial mould;
Foe not informidable, exempt from wound—
I not; so much hath Hell debased, and pain
Enfeebled me, to what I was in Heaven.
She fair, divinely fair, fit love for Gods,
Not terrible, though terror be in love,
And beauty, not approached by stronger hate,
Hate stronger under show of love well feigned—
The way which to her ruin now I tend.'

So spake the Enemy of Mankind, enclosed
In serpent, inmate bad, and toward Eve
Addressed his way—not with indented wave,
Prone on the ground, as since, but on his rear,
Circular base of rising folds, that towered
Fold above fold, a surging maze; his head
Crested aloft, and carbuncle his eyes;
With burnished neck of verdant gold, erect
Amidst his circling spires, that on the grass
Floated redundant. . . . With track oblique
At first, as one who sought access but feared
To interrupt, sidelong he works his way.
As when a ship, by skilful steersman wrought
Nigh river's mouth, or foreland, where the wind
Veers oft, as oft so steers, and shifts her sail,
So varied he, and of his tortuous train
Curled many a wanton wreath in sight of Eve,
To lure her eye. She, busied, heard the sound
Of rustling leaves, but minded not, as used
To such disport before her through the field
From every beast, more duteous at her call
Than at Circean call the herd disguised.
He, bolder now, uncalled, before her stood,
But as in gaze admiring. Oft he bowed
His turret crest and sleek enamelled neck,
Fawning, and licked the ground whereon she trod.

JOHN MILTON, *Paradise Lost*, 1657

'In due course [Odysseus' crew] came upon Circe's house, which was built of dressed stone and stood in the middle of a clearing in a forest dell. Prowling about the place were mountain wolves and lions, actually the drugged victims of Circe's magic, for they not only refrained from attacking my men, but rose on their hind legs to caress them, with much wagging of their long tails, like dogs fawning on their master, as he comes from table, for the tasty bits they know he always brings. But these were wolves and lions with great claws that were gambolling in this way round my men. Terrified at the sight of the formidable beasts, they shrank away and took refuge in the porch of the fair goddess' castle. From there they could hear Circe within, singing in her beautiful voice as she went to and fro at her great and everlasting loom, on which she was weaving one of those delicate, graceful, and dazzling fabrics that goddesses love to make.

'Polites, one of my captains and the man in my party whom I liked and trusted most, now took the lead. "Friends," he said, "there is someone in the castle working at a loom. The whole place echoes to that lovely voice. It's either a goddess or a woman. Let us waste no more time, but give her a shout."

'So they shouted to attract attention, and the next moment Circe came out, opened the polished doors, and invited them to enter. In their innocence, the whole party except Eurylochus followed her in. But he suspected a trap and stayed outside. Circe ushered the rest into her hall, gave them settles and chairs to sit on, and then prepared them a mixture of cheese, barley-meal, and yellow honey flavoured with Pramnian wine. But into this dish she introduced a powerful drug, to make them lose all memory of their native land. And when they had emptied the bowls in which she had served them, she struck them with her wand, drove them off, and penned them in the pigsties. For now to all appearance they were swine: they had pigs' heads and bristles, and they grunted like pigs; but their minds were as human as they had been before the change. Indeed, they shed tears in their sties. But Circe flung them some mast, acorns, and cornel-berries, and left them to eat this pigs' fodder and wallow in the mud.'

HOMER, *The Odyssey*, ?8th century BC, trans. E. V. Rieu

And it came to pass, after the year was expired, at the time when kings go forth to battle, that David sent Joab, and his servants with him, and all Israel; and they destroyed the children of Ammon, and besieged Rabbah. But David tarried still at Jerusalem.

And it came to pass in an eveningtide, that David arose from off his bed, and walked upon the roof of the king's house: and from the roof he saw a woman washing herself; and the woman was very beautiful to look upon.

And David sent and enquired after the woman. And one said, Is not this Bath-sheba, the daughter of Eliam, the wife of Uriah the Hittite?

And David sent messengers, and took her; and she came in unto him, and he lay with her; for she was purified from her uncleanness: and she returned unto her house.

And the woman conceived, and sent and told David, and said, I am with child.

And David sent to Joab, saying, Send me Uriah the Hittite. And Joab sent Uriah to David.

And when Uriah was come unto him, David demanded of him how Joab did, and how the people did, and how the war prospered.

And David said to Uriah, Go down to thy house, and wash thy feet. And Uriah departed out of the king's house, and there followed him a mess of meat from the king.

But Uriah slept at the door of the king's house with all the servants of his lord, and went not down to his house.

And when they had told David, saying, Uriah went not down unto his house, David said unto Uriah, Camest thou not from thy journey? why then didst thou not go down unto thine house?

And Uriah said unto David, The ark, and Israel, and Judah, abide in tents; and my lord Joab, and the servants of my lord, are encamped in the open fields; shall I then go into mine house, to eat and to drink, and to lie with my wife? as thou livest, and as thy soul liveth, I will not do this thing.

And David said to Uriah, Tarry here to day also, and to morrow I will let thee depart. So Uriah abode in Jerusalem that day, and the morrow.

And when David had called him, he did eat and drink before him; and he made him drunk: and at even he went out to lie on his bed with the servants of his lord, but went not down to his house.

And it came to pass in the morning, that David wrote a letter to Joab, and sent it by the hand of Uriah.

And he wrote in the letter, saying, Set ye Uriah in the forefront of the hottest battle, and retire ye from him, that he may be smitten, and die.

And it came to pass, when Joab observed the city, that he assigned Uriah unto a place where he knew that valiant men were.

And the men of the city went out, and fought with Joab: and there fell some of the people of the servants of David; and Uriah the Hittite died also.

Then Joab sent and told David all the things concerning the war;

And charged the messenger, saying, When thou hast made an end of telling the matters of the war unto the king,

And if so be that the king's wrath arise, and he say unto thee, Wherefore approached ye so nigh unto the city when ye did fight? knew ye not that they would shoot from the wall?

Who smote Abimelech the son of Jerubbesheth? did not a woman cast a piece of a millstone upon him from the wall, that he died in Thebez? why went ye nigh the wall? then say thou, Thy servant Uriah the Hittite is dead also.

So the messenger went, and came and shewed David all that Joab had sent him for.

And the messenger said unto David, Surely the men prevailed against us, and came out unto us into the field, and we were upon them even unto the entering of the gate.

And the shooters shot from off the wall upon thy servants; and some of the king's servants be dead, and thy servant Uriah the Hittite is dead also.

Then David said unto the messenger, Thus shalt thou say unto Joab, Let not this thing displease thee, for the sword devoureth one as well as another: make thy battle more strong against the city, and overthrow it: and encourage thou him.

And when the wife of Uriah heard that Uriah her husband was dead, she mourned for her husband.

And when the mourning was past, David sent and fetched her to his house, and she became his wife, and bare him a son. But the thing that David had done displeased the Lord.

2 Samuel 11

† *Jupiter seduces Leda, disguised as a swan.*

A sudden blow: the great wings beating still
Above the staggering girl, her thighs caressed
By the dark webs, her nape caught in his bill,
He holds her helpless breast upon his breast.

How can those terrified vague fingers push
The feathered glory from her loosening thighs?
And how can body, laid in that white rush,
But feel the strange heart beating where it lies?

A shudder in the loins engenders there
The broken wall, the burning roof and tower
And Agamemnon dead.
Being so caught up,
So mastered by the brute blood of the air,
Did she put on his knowledge with his power
Before the indifferent beak could let her drop?

W. B. YEATS, 'Leda and the Swan', 1923

The shoes upon her legs were laced up high.
She was a peach, a dolly, and a daisy!
Fit for a prince to lay upon his bed
Or some good retainer of his to wed.
Now sir, and again sir! It so fell out
That this Fly Nicholas began one day
To flirt and play about with this young wife,
Her husband having gone off to Osney
(These scholars are so artful, and so sly!)
And on the quiet caught her by the cunt,
And said to her, 'Unless I have my way,
Sweetheart, for love of you I'll surely die.'
He held her by the haunches hard and tight,
'Now let's make love at once,' cried he, 'sweetheart!
Or it's the end of me, so help me God!'
She bucked and shied like a colt being shod,
And quickly wrenched away from him her head,
Saying, 'I'll not kiss you, on my word!

Let go,' she cried, 'now stop it, Nicholas!
I'll scream for help, I'll rouse the neighbourhood!
Take your hands off! It's no way to behave!'
  But Nicholas began to plead; he made
So good a case, offered himself so often,
That in the end her heart began to soften.
She gave her word, and swore by St Thomas,
That when she saw a chance, she would be his.

GEOFFREY CHAUCER, 'The Miller's Tale', *c*.1387, trans. David Wright

† *Lady Anne, the widow of the Prince of Wales, is mourning the death of her father-in-law Henry VI. Richard, Duke of Gloster, afterwards Richard III, stops the funeral cortège.*

GLOSTER. Stay, you that bear the corse, and set it down.
LADY ANNE. What black magician conjures up this fiend,
  To stop devoted charitable deeds?
GLOSTER. Villains, set down the corse; or, by Saint Paul,
  I'll make a corse of him that disobeys!
FIRST GENTLEMAN. My lord, stand back, and let the coffin
    pass.
GLOSTER. Unmanner'd dog! stand thou, when I command:
  Advance thy halberd higher than my breast,
  Or, by Saint Paul, I'll strike thee to my foot,
  And spurn upon thee, beggar, for thy boldness.
LADY ANNE. What, do you tremble? are you all afraid?
  Alas, I blame you not; for you are mortal,
  And mortal eyes cannot endure the devil.—
  Avaunt, thou dreadful minister of hell!
  Thou hadst but power over his mortal body,—
  His soul thou canst not have; therefore, be gone.
GLOSTER. Sweet saint, for charity, be not so curst.
LADY ANNE. Foul devil, for God's sake, hence, and trouble us
    not;
  For thou hast made the happy earth thy hell,
  Fill'd it with cursing cries and deep exclaims.

If thou delight to view thy heinous deeds,
Behold this pattern of thy butcheries.
O, gentlemen, see, see! dead Henry's wounds
Open their congeal'd mouths and bleed afresh!
Blush, blush, thou lump of foul deformity;
For 'tis thy presence that exhales this blood
From cold and empty veins, where no blood dwells;
Thy deed, inhuman and unnatural,
Provokes this deluge most unnatural.—
O God, which this blood mad'st, revenge his death!
O earth, which this blood drink'st, revenge his death!
Either heaven with lightning strike the murderer dead;
Or, earth, gape open wide, and eat him quick,
As thou dost swallow up this good king's blood,
Which his hell-govern'd arm hath butchered!

GLOSTER. Lady, you know no rules of charity,
Which renders good for bad, blessings for curses.

LADY ANNE. Villain, thou know'st no law of God nor man:
No beast so fierce but knows some touch of pity.

GLOSTER. But I know none, and therefore am no beast.

LADY ANNE. O wonderful, when devils tell the truth!

GLOSTER. More wonderful, when angels are so angry.—
Vouchsafe, divine perfection of a woman,
Of these supposed evils, to give me leave,
By circumstance, but to acquit myself.

LADY ANNE. Vouchsafe, defus'd infection of a man,
For these known evils, but to give me leave,
By circumstance, to curse thy cursed self.

GLOSTER. I would they were, that I might die at once;
For now they kill me with a living death.
Those eyes of thine from mine have drawn salt tears,
Sham'd their aspects with store of childish drops:
These eyes, which never shed remorseful tear,
No, when my father York and Edward wept
To hear the piteous moan that Rutland made
When black-fac'd Clifford shook his sword at him;
Nor when thy warlike father, like a child,
Told the sad story of my father's death,
And twenty times made pause to sob and weep,
That all the standers-by had wet their cheeks,

Like trees bedash'd with rain; in that sad time
My manly eyes did scorn an humble tear;
And what these sorrows could not thence exhale,
Thy beauty hath, and made them blind with weeping.
I never sued to friend nor enemy;
My tongue could never learn sweet smoothing words;
But, now thy beauty is propos'd my fee,
My proud heart sues, and prompts my tongue to speak.

[*She looks scornfully at him.*

Teach not thy lips such scorn; for they were made
For kissing, lady, not for such contempt.
If thy revengeful heart cannot forgive,
Lo, here I lend thee this sharp-pointed sword;
Which if thou please to hide in this true breast,
And let the soul forth that adoreth thee,
I lay it naked to the deadly stroke,
And humbly beg the death upon my knee.

[*He lays his breast open; she offers at it with his sword.*

Nay, do not pause; for I did kill King Henry,
But 'twas thy beauty that provoked me.
Nay, now dispatch; 'twas I that stabb'd young Edward,
But 'twas thy heavenly face that set me on.

[*She falls the sword.*

Take up the sword again, or take up me.

LADY ANNE. Arise, dissembler: though I wish thy death,
I will not be thy executioner.

GLOSTER. Then bid me kill myself, and I will do it.

LADY ANNE. I have already.

GLOSTER. That was in thy rage.
Speak it again, and, even with the word,
This hand, which for thy love did kill thy love,
Shall for thy love kill a far truer love;
To both their deaths shalt thou be accessary.

LADY ANNE. I would I knew thy heart.

GLOSTER. 'Tis figur'd in my tongue.

LADY ANNE. I fear me both are false.

GLOSTER. Then never man was true.

LADY ANNE. Well, well, put up your sword.

GLOSTER. Say, then, my peace is made.

LADY ANNE. That shalt thou know hereafter.

GLOSTER. But shall I live in hope?

LADY ANNE. All men, I hope, live so.

GLOSTER. Vouchsafe to wear this ring.

LADY ANNE. To take, is not to give.

GLOSTER. Look, how this ring encompasseth thy finger,
Even so thy breast encloseth my poor heart;
Wear both of them, for both of them are thine.
And if thy poor devoted servant may
But beg one favour at thy gracious hand,
Thou dost confirm his happiness for ever.

LADY ANNE. What is it?

GLOSTER. That it may please you leave these sad designs
To him that hath more cause to be a mourner,
And presently repair to Crosby-place;
Where—after I have solemnly interr'd
At Chertsey monastery this noble king,
And wet his grave with my repentant tears—
I will with all expedient duty see you:
For divers unknown reasons, I beseech you,
Grant me this boon.

LADY ANNE. With all my heart; and much it joys me too
To see you are become so penitent.—
Tressel and Berkeley, go along with me.

GLOSTER. Bid me farewell.

LADY ANNE. 'Tis more than you deserve;
But since you teach me how to flatter you,
Imagine I have said farewell already.

[*Exeunt Lady Anne, Tressel, and Berkeley*.

GLOSTER. Sirs, take up the corse.

GENTLEMEN. Towards Chertsey, noble lord?

GLOSTER. No, to White-Friars; there attend my coming.

[*Exeunt all, except Gloster*.

Was ever woman in this humour woo'd?
Was ever woman in this humour won?
I'll have her;—but I will not keep her long.
What! I, that kill'd her husband and his father,
To take her in her heart's extremest hate;
With curses in her mouth, tears in her eyes,
The bleeding witness of her hatred by;
Having God, her conscience, and these bars against me,

And I no friends to back my suit withal
But the plain devil and dissembling looks,
And yet to win her,—all the world to nothing!

WILLIAM SHAKESPEARE, *Richard III*, 1592/3

† *Iachimo, an Italian gentleman, wagers that he will seduce Posthumus's wife Imogen. He hides in a trunk in Imogen's bedroom and emerges to collect evidence of her alleged seduction.*

Imogen's bedchamber: a trunk in one corner of it.
Enter Imogen in her bed, and a Lady.

IMOGEN. Who's there? my woman Helen?
LADY. Please you, madam.
IMOGEN. What hour is it?
LADY. Almost midnight, madam.
IMOGEN. I have read three hours, then: mine eyes are weak:
Fold down the leaf where I have left: to bed:
Take not away the taper, leave it burning;
And if thou canst awake by four o'clock,
I prithee, call me. Sleep hath seiz'd me wholly.

[*Exit Lady.*

To your protection I commend me, gods!
From fairies, and the tempters of the night,
Guard me, beseech ye!

[*Sleeps. Iachimo comes from the trunk.*

IACHIMO. The crickets sing, and man's o'er-labour'd sense
Repairs itself by rest. Our Tarquin thus
Did softly press the rushes, ere he waken'd
The chastity he wounded.—Cytherea,
How bravely thou becomest thy bed! fresh lily!
And whiter than the sheets! That I might touch!
But kiss; one kiss!—Rubies unparagon'd,
How dearly they do 't!—'Tis her breathing that
Perfumes the chamber thus: the flame o' the taper
Bows towards her; and would under-peep her lids,
To see the enclosed lights, now canopied
Under these windows, white and azure, laced
With blue of heaven's own tinct.—But my design

To note the chamber: I will write all down:—
Such and such pictures;—there the window;—such
The adornment of her bed;—the arras, figures,
Why, such and such;—and the contents o' the story,—
Ah, but some natural notes about her body,
Above ten thousand meaner movables
Would testify, t' enrich mine inventory:—
O sleep, thou ape of death, lie dull upon her!
And be her sense but as a monument,
Thus in a chapel lying!—Come off, come off;—

[*Taking off her bracelet*.

As slippery as the Gordian knot was hard!—
'Tis mine; and this will witness outwardly,
As strongly as the conscience does within,
To the madding of her lord.—On her left breast
A mole cinque-spotted, like the crimson drops
I' the bottom of a cowslip: here's a voucher,
Stronger than ever law could make: this secret
Will force him think I have pick'd the lock, and ta'en
The treasure of her honour. No more. To what end?
Why should I write this down, that's riveted,
Screw'd to my memory?—She hath been reading late
The tale of Tereus: here the leaf's turn'd down
Where Philomel gave up.—I have enough:
To the trunk again, and shut the spring of it.—
Swift, swift, you dragons of the night, that dawning
May bare the raven's eye! I lodge in fear;
Though this a heavenly angel, hell is here.

[*Clock strikes*.

One, two three,—Time, time!

[*Goes into the trunk*. *Scene closes*.

WILLIAM SHAKESPEARE, *Cymbeline*, 1610/11

Not long ago I met a clerk,
And he went craftily to work;
His subtle talk he bade me mark,
And secretly to weigh of it.

Ah dear God, I am forsaken,
Now my maidenhead is taken!

It seems he had a magic skill,
And this is why I think so still:
Because when he declared his will,
I could not say him nay of it.
Ah dear God, etc.

When he and I got under sheet,
I let him have his way complete,
And now my girdle will not meet.
Dear God, what shall I say of it?
Ah dear God, etc.

I shall say to man and page
That I have been on pilgrimage.
If priest again show lustful rage,
I'll not let him make play of it.
Ah dear God, I am forsaken,
Now my maidenhead is taken!

ANON., trans. Brian Stone

SGANARELLE. Ah, my dear Gusman, believe me, you still don't understand what sort of man Don Juan is.

GUSMAN. No, I certainly don't if he has really betrayed us like that. I just can't understand how, after showing so much affection, after being so very importunate, after all his declarations of love, vows, sighs, tears, passionate letters, protestations, and promises repeated over and over again; in short, after such an overwhelming display of passion and going to the lengths of invading the holy precincts of a convent to carry off Dona Elvira—I repeat I just cannot understand how, after all that, he could find it in his heart to go back on his word.

SGANARELLE. I understand well enough, and if you knew our friend as I do you'd understand that he finds it easy enough. I am not saying his feelings for Dona Elvira have changed. I can't be sure yet. As you know, I left before he did, on his instruction, and he has said nothing to me since he arrived here, but I will say this much as a warning—*inter nos*—that in my master, Don Juan, you see the biggest scoundrel that ever cumbered the earth, a madman, a cur, a devil, a Turk, a heretic who believes neither in Heaven, Hell, nor werewolf: he lives like an animal, like a swine of an Epicurean, a veritable Sardanapalus, shutting his ears to every Christian remonstrance, and turning to ridicule everything we believe in. You tell me he has married your mistress—believe me, to satisfy his passion he would have gone further than that, he would have married you as well, ay, and her dog and her cat into the bargain! Marriage means nothing to him. It is his usual method of ensnaring women: he marries 'em left and right, maids or married women, ladies or peasants, shy ones and t'other sort—all come alike to him. If I were to give you the names of all those he has married in one place and another, the list would take till to-night. That surprises you! What I'm saying makes you turn pale, but this is no more than the outline of his character: it would take me much longer to finish the portrait. Let it suffice that the wrath of Heaven is bound to overwhelm him one of these days and that, for my part, I would sooner serve the Devil himself. He's made me witness to so many horrible things that I wish he was—I don't know where! But a nobleman who has given himself over to wickedness is a thing to be dreaded. I am bound to remain with him whether I like it or not: fear serves me for zeal, makes me restrain my feelings and forces me often enough to make a show of approving things that in my heart of hearts I detest. But here he comes—taking a turn in the palace. Let us separate. But just let me say this—I have talked to you frankly and in confidence, and I've opened my mouth pretty freely, but if any word of it were to come to his ears I should declare you had made it all up.

MOLIÈRE, *Don Juan*, 1665, trans. John Wood

LEPORELLO. Little lady, you are not going to like this.
It's a list of the loves of my master.
Though to you it may prove a disaster,
Pay attention, and listen to me.
First Italians, six hundred and forty;
Then the Germans two hundred and thirty;
A hundred in France, only ninety in Turkey;

But, but the Spanish! One thousand and three.
There are chambermaids a-plenty,
Country girls and city gentry,
Baronesses and countesses,
Marchionesses and princesses.
Here you see them:
Every age and every shape and every size,
Every shape and every size.

If she's blonde-haired, his love grows stronger
ev'ry moment he is beside her;
If she's dark-haired, he'll stay longer.
If she's pale-skinned, woe betide her!
In the winter plump and tender,
In the summer oh so slender . . .
If she's buxom, he won't fail her;
Like a mountain he will scale her.
If she's tiny, teeny-tiny,
He'll overwhelm her.
Even widows, shy about their ages,
Still swell numbers here in these pages.
But the highest common factor
Is the girl who's still intacta.
Rich or poor, or wife or whore,
Or on the floor, behind a door,
He'll still perform if hidden by a curtain,
Just as long as she has a skirt on,
You'll be certain what he wants.

LORENZO DA PONTE, libretto to Mozart's *Don Giovanni*, 1787, trans. Amanda and Anthony Holden

Then it occurred to me, 'What an abominable creature am I! and how is this innocent gentleman going to be abused by me! How little does he think, that having divorced a whore, he is throwing himself into the arms of another! that he is going to marry one that had lain with two brothers, and had had three children by her own brother! one that was born in Newgate, whose mother was a whore, and is now a transported thief! one that had lain with thirteen men, and has had a child since he saw me! Poor gentleman!' said I, 'what is he going to do?' After this reproaching myself was over, it followed thus: 'Well, if I must be his wife, if it please God to give me grace, I'll be a true wife to him, and love him suitably to the strange excess of his passion for me; I will make him amends if possible, by what he shall see, for the cheats and abuses I put upon him, which he does not see.'

DANIEL DEFOE, *Moll Flanders*, 1722

† *Mr Horner, a notable seducer, hits on a plan to make all husbands trust him.*

Enter Horner, and Quack following him at a distance.

HORNER [*Aside*]. A quack is as fit for a pimp as a midwife for a bawd. They are still but in their way both helpers of nature. Well, my dear doctor, hast thou done what I desired?

QUACK. I have undone you for ever with the women, and reported you throughout the whole town as bad as an eunuch, with as much trouble as if I had made you one in earnest.

HORNER. But have you told all the midwives you know, the orange wenches at the playhouses, the city husbands, and old fumbling keepers of this end of the town? For they'll be the readiest to report it!

QUACK. I have told all the chamber-maids, waiting-women, tire-women and old women of my acquaintance; nay, and whispered it as a secret to 'em, and to the whisperers of Whitehall. So that you need not doubt 'twill spread, and you will be as odious to the handsome young women as . . .

HORNER. As the smallpox. Well . . .

QUACK. And to the married women of this end of the town as . . .

HORNER. As the great ones; nay, as their own husbands.

QUACK. And to the city dames as Aniseed Robin* of filthy and contemptible memory; and they will frighten their children with your name, especially their females.

HORNER. And cry, 'Horner's coming to carry you away!' I am only afraid 'twill not be believed. You told 'em 'twas by an English-French disaster, and an English-French chirugeon, who has given me at once not only a cure but an antidote for the future against that damned malady, and that worse distemper, love, and all other women's evils?

* Aniseed Robin: a well-known hermaphrodite.

QUACK. Your late journey into France has made it the more credible, and your being here a fortnight before you appeared in public looks as if you apprehended the shame—which I wonder you do not. Well, I have been hired by young gallants to belie 'em t'other way, but you are the first would be thought a man unfit for women.

HORNER. Dear Mr doctor, let vain rogues be contented only to be thought abler men than they are. Generally 'tis all the pleasure they have, but mine lies another way.

QUACK. You take, methinks, a very preposterous way to it, and as ridiculous as if we operators in physic should put forth bills to disparage our medicaments, with hopes to gain customers.

HORNER. Doctor, there are quacks in love, as well as physic, who get but the fewer and worse patients for their boasting. A good name is seldom got by giving it oneself, and women no more than honour are compassed by bragging. Come, come, doctor, the wisest lawyer never discovers the merits of his cause till the trial. The wealthiest man conceals his riches, and the cunning gamester his play. Shy husbands and keepers, like old rooks, are not to be cheated but by a new unpractised trick. False friendship will pass now no more than false dice upon 'em—no, not in the city.

[*Enter Boy*.

BOY. There are two ladies and a gentleman coming up.

HORNER. A pox! Some unbelieving sisters of my former acquaintance who, I am afraid, expect their sense should be satisfied of the falsity of the report. No—this formal fool and women!

[*Enter Sir Jasper Fidget, Lady Fidget, and Mrs Dainty Fidget*.

QUACK. His wife and sister.

SIR JASPER. My coach breaking just now before your door, sir, I look upon as an occasional reprimand to me, sir, for not kissing your hands, sir, since your coming out of France, sir; and so my disaster, sir, has been my good fortune, sir; and this is my wife and sister, sir.

HORNER. What then, sir?

SIR JASPER. My lady and sister, sir.—Wife, this is master Horner.

LADY FIDGET. Master Horner, husband!

SIR JASPER. My lady, my lady Fidget, sir.

HORNER. So, sir.

SIR JASPER. Won't you be acquainted with her, sir? [*Aside*.] So, the report is true, I find, by his coldness or aversion to the sex; but I'll play the wag with him. Pray salute my wife, my lady, sir.

HORNER. I will kiss no man's wife, sir, for him, sir; I have taken my eternal leave, sir, of the sex already, sir.

SIR JASPER [*aside*]. Ha, ha, ha,! I'll plague him yet.—Not know my wife, sir?

HORNER. I do know your wife, sir, she's a woman, sir, and consequently a monster, sir, a greater monster than a husband, sir.

SIR JASPER. A husband! How, sir?

HORNER [*makes horns*]. So, sir. But I make no more cuckolds, sir.

SIR JASPER. Ha, ha, ha! Mercury, Mercury!

LADY FIDGET. Pray, sir Jasper, let us be gone from this rude fellow.

DAINTY. Who, by his breeding, would think he had ever been in France?

LADY FIDGET. Foh! he's but too much a French fellow, such as hate women of quality and virtue for their love to their husbands, sir Jasper. A woman is hated by 'em as much for loving her husband as for loving their money. But pray let's be gone.

HORNER. You do well, madam, for I have nothing that you came for. I have brought over not so much as a bawdy picture, new postures, nor the second part of the *Ecole des Filles*, nor . . .

QUACK [*apart to Horner*]. Hold for shame, sir! What d'ye mean? You'll ruin yourself for ever with the sex . . .

SIR JASPER. Ha, ha, ha! He hates women perfectly, I find.

DAINTY. What pity 'tis he should.

LADY FIDGET. Ay, he's a base rude fellow for't; but affectation makes not a woman more odious to them than virtue.

HORNER. Because your virtue is your greatest affectation, madam.

LADY FIDGET. How, you saucy fellow! Would you wrong my honour?

HORNER. If I could.

LADY FIDGET. How d'y mean, sir?

SIR JASPER. Ha, ha, ha! No, he can't wrong your ladyship's honour; upon my honour! He poor man—hark you in your ear—a mere eunuch.

LADY FIDGET. O filthy French beast! foh, foh! Why do we stay? Let's be gone. I can't endure the sight of him.

SIR JASPER. Stay but till the chairs come. They'll be here presently.

LADY FIDGET. No, no.

SIR JASPER. Nor can I stay longer. 'Tis—let me see—a quarter and a half quarter of a minute past eleven. The Council will be sat, I must away. Business must be preferred always before love and ceremony with the wise, Mr Horner.

HORNER. And the impotent, sir Jasper.

SIR JASPER. Ay, ay, the impotent, Master Horner, ha, ha, ha!

LADY FIDGET. What, leave us with a filthy man alone in his lodgings?

SIR JASPER. He's an innocent man now, you know. Pray stay, I'll hasten the chairs to you.—Mr Horner, your servant; I should be glad to see you at my house. Pray come and dine with me, and play at cards with my wife after dinner—you are fit for women at that game yet, ha, ha! [*Aside.*] 'Tis as much a husband's prudence to provide innocent diversion for a wife as to hinder her unlawful pleasures, and he had better employ her than let her employ herself.—Farewell. [*Exit Sir Jasper.*

WILLIAM WYCHERLEY, *The Country Wife*, ?1675

† *The pursuit of Clarissa Harlowe by the lecherous Lovelace runs to thirty-two volumes, and takes in innumerable ploys, machinations, twists of fortune, threatened assaults, and narrow escapes for the heroine. Clarissa sees herself as greatly sinned against.*

When I reflect upon all that has happened to me, it is apparent, that this generally-supposed *thoughtless* seducer has acted by me upon a regular and preconcerted plan of villainy.

In order to set all his vile plots in motion, nothing was wanting, from the first, but to prevail upon me, either by force or fraud, to throw myself into his power: and when this was effected, nothing less than the intervention of the paternal authority, (which I had not deserved to be exerted in my behalf,) could have saved me from the effect of his deep machinations. Opposition from any other quarter would but too probably have precipitated his barbarous and ungrateful violence . . . never was there, as now I see, a plan of wickedness more steadily and uniformly pursued than *his* has been, against an unhappy creature who merited better of *him*: but the Almighty has thought fit, according to the general course of His providence, to make the fault bring on its own punishment: but surely not in consequence of my father's dreadful imprecation, 'That I might be punished *here*,' . . . 'by the very wretch in whom I had placed my wicked confidence!'

† *Lovelace sums up the whole business as a fuss about nothing.*

Her chamber door has not yet been opened. I must not expect she will breakfast with me. Nor dine with me, I doubt. A little silly soul, what troubles does she make to herself by her over-niceness! All I have done to her would have been looked upon as *frolic* only, a *romping-bout*, and laughed off by nine parts in ten of the sex accordingly. The more she makes of it, the more painful to herself, as well as to me.

SAMUEL RICHARDSON, *Clarissa*, 1748

THE CLARISSA HARLOWE POEM

Down then, thou rogue thou, red three-cornered
varlet,
and hammer not within my breast so fast!
We rakes appreciate a sin so scarlet,
the dear indifferent's trials are not yet past,
she labours under a father's heavy curse
but yet must love me better—or fare worse.

I offered to salute the lovely fair one,
her teasing letters hidden in her stays.
The charming icicle refused. Oh, dare one
not carry her abroad, to Church or plays?
But you was, Lovelace, by her female scorn
then made to doubt she was a woman born,

an angel rather! 'Sir', she cried, 'unhand me!'
when I upraised the covering handkerchief.
It is impossible she should understand me,
or how I glory in her silent grief,
but more when she lets loose her sparkling tears,
prudent and virtuous, though eighteen years—

no more—she has. Yet with her piercing eye-beams
could regulate the *mother* and the *house*;
as the bright sun within a cloudy sky beams
she ruled my bad companions. Yet a mouse
she is, and Lovelace is the cat,
though devil fetch me if I ever sat

so mute before a prouder, haughtier beauty!
Still all I hear is 'Wretch!', 'Dissembler!', 'Vile!',
so conscious of her virtue and her duty,
so over-nice! The condescending smile
I work for always—it eludes me still,
and she falls into fits, indeed she's ill!

The sex, I know, admires a bold encroacher,
at heart the finest ladies love a rake,
and I have always been the devil's poacher
with such fair game. Where then was my mistake?
She loves me, I conceive, but why so prim?
Why calls she so incessantly on Him?

Why loves she so her friend, that pert virago?
Why hates my *morals*—since I may repent?
Scarce from her closet stirs and eyed like Argo
guarding her honour will not once relent?
She throws Miss Bettinson at my 'scheming' head,
with other fair ones long since brought to bed.

I toil and toil, I plot with my expedients.
She's sullen still, and all I have—her hate!
But I will force her to a close obedience
and she shall own a Lovelace for her mate!
I'll be revenged, and she'll come at my call.
Catching such birds is all, and more than all—

she'll learn to come, and end her prudish blushing,
I'll crook my little finger from the bed.
Freedoms are innocent, and the *last*, a rushing
wide torrent from the mountain's awful head—
which once, a puny stream, scarce wet the stone!
And when that day comes, I'll not lie alone.

GAVIN EWART, 1980

ROCHESTER TO THE POST BOY

Son of a whore, God dam you: Can you tell
A Peerless Peer the Readyest way to Hell?
Ive out swilld Baccus, sworn of my own make
Oaths wou'd fright furies and make Pluto quake;
Ive swived more whores more ways than Sodom's walls
Ere knew or the College of Rome's Cardinalls.
Witness Heroick scars, look here (ne'er go)
Sear cloaths and ulcers from the top to toe:
Frighted at my own mischeifes I have fled
And bravely left my life's defender dead;
Broke houses to break chastity and died
That floor with murder which my lust denyed.
Pox on it, why do I speak of these poor things?
I have blasphemed my God and libelld Kings.
The readyest way to Hell, come quick, ne're stirr!
Boy. The readyest way my Lord's by *Rochester*.

JOHN WILMOT, EARL OF ROCHESTER (1647–80)

† *Casanova in London falls in love with La Charpillon. He spends a night with her, but she wraps herself tightly in her night-gown, reducing the great lover to impotent rage. The next day a friend offers him an interesting chair.*

There was also a note from Goudar, saying that he wanted to speak to me and would come at noon. I gave orders that he should be admitted.

This curious individual began by astonishing me; he told me the whole story of what had taken place, the mother having been his informant.

'La Charpillon,' he added, 'has no fever but is covered with bruises. What grieves the old woman most is that she did not get the hundred guineas.'

'She would have had them the next morning,' I said, 'if her daughter had been tractable.'

'Her mother had made her swear that she would not be tractable, and you need not hope to possess her without the mother's consent.'

'Why won't she consent?'

'Because she thinks you will abandon the girl as soon as you have enjoyed her.'

'Possibly, but she would have received many valuable presents and now she is abandoned and has nothing.'

'Have you made up your mind not to have anything more to do with her?'

'Quite.'

'That's your wisest plan and I advise you to keep to it; nevertheless, I want to show you something which will surprise you. I will be back in a moment.'

He returned, followed by a porter who brought up an armchair covered with a cloth. A soon as we were alone, Goudar took off the covering and asked me if I would buy it.

'What should I do with it? It is not a very attractive piece of furniture.'

'Nevertheless, the price of it is a hundred guineas.'

'I would not give three.'

'This armchair has five springs, which come into play all at once as soon as anyone sits down in it. Two springs catch the two arms and hold them tightly, two others separate the legs and the fifth lifts up the seat.'

After this description Goudar sat down quite naturally in the chair and the springs came into play and forced him into the position of a woman in labour.

'Get the fair Charpillon to sit in this chair,' said he, 'and your business is done.'

CASANOVA (1725–98), *Memoirs*, trans. Arthur Machen

† *That tireless seducer the Viscomte de Valmont writes of his exploits to the Marquise de Merteuil.*

You know Madame de Tourvel, her religious devotion, her conjugal love, her austere principles. That is what I am attacking; that is the enemy worthy of me; that is the end I mean to reach:

> 'And if I do not carry off the prize of obtaining her,
> At least I shall have the honour of having attempted it.'

Bad verses may be quoted when they are by a great poet.

You must know that her husband is in Burgundy on account of some big law-suit (I hope to make him lose a still more important one). His inconsolable spouse is compelled to spend here the whole time of her distressing widowhood. A mass every day, a few visits to the poor in the district, morning and evening prayers, solitary walks, pious conversations with my old aunt, and sometimes a dismal rubber of whist, are her only distractions. I am preparing more effectual ones for her. My good angel led me here for her happiness and for my own. Madman that I was! I regretted the twenty-four hours I sacrificed to the demands of convention. How I should be punished were I forced to return to Paris! Luckily, four people are needed for a hand of whist, and since there is no one here but the local *curé* my eternal aunt pressed me to sacrifice a few days to her. You may guess that I consented. You cannot imagine how much she has flattered me since then and above all how edified she is to see me regularly at prayer and at mass. She does not realise who is the divinity I adore.

For the last four days I have given myself up to this powerful passion. You know I always desire keenly and sweep away obstacles; but what you cannot know is how much solitude adds to the ardour of desire. I have but one idea; I think of it by day and dream of it by night. I must have this woman, to save myself from the ridiculous position of being in love with her—for how far may not one be led by a thwarted desire? O delicious possession! I need you for my happiness and still more for my peace of mind. It is fortunate for us that women are so weak in their own defence! Otherwise we should be nothing but their timid slaves.

P. C. DE LACLOS, *Les Liaisons dangereuses*, 1782, trans. Richard Aldington

Lord **** finding he had to do with a mistress of uncommon spirit, thought best to alter the manner of his addresses to her; and approaching her with an air much more humble and submissive than he had hitherto done, 'How I adore,' cried he, 'this noble disinterestedness in you! you will grant nothing but to love alone—be it so: your beauty is, indeed, above all other price. Let your husband reap all the advantages, and let it be yours to have the pleasure, like Heaven, to save from despair the man who cannot live without you.'

Perceiving, or at least imagining he perceived, some abatement in the fierceness of her eyes, on the change of his deportment, he persisted in it—he even threw himself on his knees before her; took hold of her hands, bathed them alternately with tears, then dried them with his kisses: in a word, he omitted nothing that the most passionate love, resolute to accomplish its gratification, could suggest to soften her into compliance.

At another time, how would the vanity of this lady have been elated to see a person of such high consideration in the world thus prostrate at her feet! but at this, the reflection how much she was in his power, and the uncertainty how far he might exert that power, put to silence all the dictates of her pride, and rendered her, in reality, much more in awe of him, than he affected to be of her: she turned her eyes continually towards the door, in hopes of seeing Mr Munden enter; and never had she wished for his presence with the impatience she now did.

The noble lord equally dreaded his return; and finding the replies she made to his pressures somewhat more moderate than they had been on the first opening his suit, flattered himself that a very little compulsion would compleat the work: he therefore resolved to dally no longer; and having ushered in his design with a prelude of some warm kisses and embraces, was about to draw her into another room.

She struggled with all her might; but her efforts that way being in vain, she shrieked, and called aloud for help. This a little shocked him; he let her go: 'What do you mean, Madam?' said he. 'Would you expose yourself and me to the ridicule of my servants?'—'I will expose myself to any thing,' answered she, 'rather than to the ruin and everlasting infamy your lordship is preparing for me!'

ELIZA HAYWOOD, *The History of Miss Betsy Thoughtless*, 1751

† *Squire Thornhill keeps marrying susceptible young women, among them the Vicar of Wakefield's daughter Olivia. In this scene the distraught father finds his outraged child.*

I could hear her remonstrances very distinctly: 'Out, I say; pack out this moment! tramp, thou infamous strumpet, or I'll give thee a mark thou won't be the better for this three months. What! you trumpery, to come and take up an honest house without cross or coin to bless yourself with! Come along, I say!'—'Oh, dear Madam,' cried the stranger, 'pity me—pity a poor abandoned creature, for one night, and death will soon do the rest!' I instantly knew the voice of my poor ruined child Olivia. I flew to her rescue, while the woman was dragging her along by her hair, and I caught the dear forlorn wretch in my arms. 'Welcome, any way welcome, my dearest lost one—my treasure—to your poor old father's bosom! Though the vicious forsake thee, there is yet one in the world that will never forsake thee; though thou hadst ten thousand crimes to answer for, he will forget them all!' —'Oh, my own dear'—for minutes she could say no more—'my own dearest good papa! Could angels be kinder? How do I deserve so much? The villain, I hate him and myself, to be a reproach to so much goodness! You can't forgive me, I know you cannot.'—'Yes, my child, from my heart I do forgive thee: only repent, and we both shall yet be happy. We shall see many pleasant days yet, my Olivia.'—'Ah! never, Sir, never. The rest of my wretched life must be infamy abroad, and shame at home. . . . That villain, Sir,' said she, 'from the first day of our meeting, made me honourable, though private proposals.'

'Villain, indeed!' cried I: 'and yet it in some measure surprises me, how a person of Mr Burchell's good sense and seeming honour could be guilty of such deliberate baseness, and thus step into a family to undo it.'

'My dear papa,' returned my daughter, 'you labour under a strange mistake. Mr Burchell never attempted to deceive me: instead of that, he took every opportunity of privately admonishing me against the artifices of Mr Thornhill, who, I now find, was even worse than he represented him.'—'Mr Thornhill!' interrupted I; 'can it be?'—'Yes, Sir,' returned she, 'it was Mr Thornhill who seduced me; who employed the two ladies, as he called them, but who in fact were abandoned women of the town, without breeding or pity, to decoy us up to London. Their artifices, you may remember, would have certainly succeeded, but for Mr Burchell's letter, who directed those reproaches at them which we all applied to ourselves. How he came to have so much influence as to defeat their intentions still remains a secret to me; but I am convinced he was ever our warmest, sincerest friend.'

'You amaze me, my dear,' cried I; 'but now I find my first suspicions of Mr Thornhill's baseness were too well grounded: but he can triumph in security; for he is rich, and we are poor. But tell me, my child, sure it was no small temptation that could thus obliterate all the impressions of such an education and so virtuous a disposition as thine?'

'Indeed, Sir,' replied she, 'he owes all his triumph to the desire I had of making him, and not myself, happy. I knew that the ceremony of our marriage, which was privately performed by a popish priest, was no way binding, and that I had nothing to trust to but his honour.' —'What!' interrupted I, 'and were you indeed married by a priest in orders?'—'Indeed, Sir, we were,' replied she, 'though we were both sworn to conceal his name.'—'Why, then, my child, come to my arms again; and now you are a thousand times more welcome than before; for you are now his wife to all intents and purposes; nor can all the laws of man, though written upon tables of adamant, lessen the force of that sacred connection.'

'Alas, papa!' replied she, 'you are but little acquainted with his villainies: he has been married already by the same priest to six or eight wives more, whom, like me, he has deceived and abandoned.'

OLIVER GOLDSMITH, *The Vicar of Wakefield*, 1766

She was poor but she was honest,
  Victim of a rich man's game;
First he loved her, then he left her,
  And she lost her maiden name.

Then she hastened up to London,
  For to hide her grief and shame;
There she met another rich man,
  And she lost her name again.

See her riding in her carriage,
  In the Park and all so gay;
All the nibs and nobby persons
  Come to pass the time of day.

See them at the gay theáter
  Sitting in the costly stalls;
With one hand she holds the programme,
  With the other strokes his hand.

See him have her dance in Paris
  In her frilly underclothes;
All those Frenchies there applauding
  When she strikes a striking pose.

See the little country village
  Where her aged parents live;
Though they drink champagne she sends them,
  Still they never can forgive.

In the rich man's arms she flutters
  Like a bird with a broken wing;
First he loved her, then he left her,
  And she hasn't got a ring.

See him in his splendid mansion
  Entertaining with the best,
While the girl as he has ruined
  Entertains a sordid guest.

See him riding in his carriage
  Past the gutter where she stands;
He has made a stylish marriage
  While she wrings her ringless hands.

See him in the House of Commons
  Passing laws to put down crime,
While the victim of his passions
  Slinks away to hide her shame.

See her on the bridge at midnight
  Crying, 'Farewell, faithless love!'
There's a scream, a splash—Good Heavens!
  What is she a-doing of?

Then they dragged her from the river,
  Water from her clothes they wrung;
They all thought that she was drownded,
  But the corpse got up and sung:

'It's the same the whole world over;
  It's the poor as gets the blame,
It's the rich as gets the pleasure—
  Ain't it all a bleeding shame!'

ANON.

THE MAIM'D DEBAUCHEE

As some brave Admiral in former War,
Depriv'd of force, but prest with courage still;
Two Rival-Fleets appearing from afar,
Crawles to the top of an adjacent Hill;

From whence (with thoughts full of concern) he views
The wise and daring Conduct of the fight,
Whilst each bold Action, to his Mind renews,
His present glory, and his past delight;

From his fierce Eyes, flashes of Ire he throws,
As from black Clouds, when Lightning breaks away,
Transported, thinks himself amidst his Foes,
And absent, yet enjoys the Bloody Day;

So when my years of impotence approach,
And I'm by Pox and Wine's unlucky chance,
Forct from the pleasing Billows of debauch,
On the dull Shore of lazy temperance,

My pains at least some respite shall afford,
Whilst I behold the Battails you maintain,
When Fleets of Glasses sail about the Board,
From whose Broad-sides Volleys of Wit shall rain.

Nor let the sight of Honourable Scars,
Which my too forward Valour did procure,
Frighten new listed Souldiers from the Warrs,
Past joys have more than paid what I endure.

Shou'd hopeful Youth (worth being drunk) prove nice,
And from his fair Inviter meanly shrink,
'Twill please the Ghost of my departed Vice,
If at my Councel, he repent and drink.

Or shou'd some cold complexion'd Sot forbid,
With his dull Morals, our Night's brisk Alarmes,
I'll fire his Blood by telling what I did,
When I was strong, and able to bear Armes.

I'll tell of Whores attacqu'd, their Lords at home,
Bawds' Quarters beaten up, and Fortress won,
Windows demolisht, Watches overcome,
And handsome ills by my contrivance done.

Nor shall our Love-fits *Cloris* be forgot,
When each the well-look'd Link-Boy strove t'enjoy
And the best Kiss was the deciding Lot,
Whether the Boy us'd you, or I the Boy.

With Tales like these, I will such thoughts inspire,
As to important mischief shall incline.
I'll make him long some Antient Church to fire,
And fear no lewdness he's call'd to by Wine.

Thus States-man-like, I'll sawcily impose,
And safe from danger Valiantly advise,
Shelter'd in impotence, urge you to blows,
And being good for nothing else, be wise.

JOHN WILMOT, EARL OF ROCHESTER (1647–80)

'Can I relinquish these limbs so white, so soft, so delicate. These swelling breasts, round, full, and elastic! These lips fraught with such inexhaustible sweetness? Can I relinquish these treasures, and leave them to another's enjoyment? No, Antonia; never, never! I swear it by this kiss, and this! and this!'

With every moment the Friar's passion became more ardent, and Antonia's terror more intense. She struggled to disengage herself from his arms: Her exertions were unsuccessful; and finding that Ambrosio's conduct became still freer, She shrieked for assistance with all her strength. The aspect of the Vault, the pale glimmering of the Lamp, the surrounding obscurity, the sight of the Tomb, and the objects of mortality which met her eyes on either side, were ill-calculated to inspire her with those emotions, by which the Friar was agitated. Even his caresses terrified her from their fury, and created no other sentiment than fear. On the contrary, her alarm, her evident disgust, and incessant opposition, seemed only to inflame the Monk's desires, and supply his brutality with additional strength. Antonia's shrieks were unheard: Yet She continued them, nor abandoned her endeavours to escape, till exhausted and out of breath She sank from his arms upon her knees, and once more had recourse to prayers and supplications. This attempt had no better success than the former. On the contrary, taking advantage of her situation, the Ravisher threw himself by her side: He clasped her to his bosom almost lifeless with terror, and faint with struggling. He stifled her cries with kisses, treated her with the rudeness of an unprincipled Barbarian, proceeded from freedom to freedom, and in the violence of his lustful delirium, wounded and bruised her tender limbs. Heedless of her tears, cries and entreaties, He gradually made himself Master of her person, and desisted not from his prey, till He had accomplished his crime and the dishonour of Antonia.

Scarcely had He succeeded in his design, than He shuddered at himself and the means by which it was effected.

M. G. LEWIS, *The Monk*, 1796

On the table lay several costly volumes, which seemed to have been very lately perused by Sir Patrick, as some of them were open, some turned down at particular passages: but as soon as she glanced her eye over their contents, Adeline indignantly threw them down again; and, while her cheek glowed with the blush of offended modesty she threw herself on a sofa, and fell into a long and mournful reverie on the misery which awaited her mother, in consequence of her having madly dared to unite herself for life to a young libertine, who could delight in no other reading but what was offensive to good morals and to delicacy. Nor could she dwell upon this subject without recurring to her former fears for herself; and so lost was she in agonizing reflections, that it was some time before she recollected herself sufficiently to remember that she was guilty of an indecorum, in staying so long in an apartment which contained books that she ought not even to be suspected of having had an opportunity to peruse.

Having once entertained this consciousness, Adeline hastily arose, and had just reached the door when Sir Patrick himself appeared at it. She started back in terror when she beheld him, on observing in his countenance and manner evident marks not only of determined profligacy, but of intoxication. Her suspicions were indeed just. Bold as he was in iniquity, he dared not in a cool and sober moment put his guilty purpose in execution; and he shrunk with temporary horror from an attempt on the honour of the daughter of his wife, though he believed that she would be a willing victim. He had therefore stopped on the road to fortify his courage with wine; and, luckily for Adeline, he had taken more than he was aware of; for when, after a vehement declaration of the ardour of his passion, he dared irreverently to approach her, Adeline, strong in innocence, aware of his intention, and presuming on his situation, disengaged herself from his grasp with ease; and pushing him with violence from her, he fell with such force against the brass edge of one of the sofas, that, stunned and wounded by the fall, he lay bleeding on the ground.

MRS OPIE, *Adeline Mowbray*, 1804

. . . he caught hold of the trembling Rosalina, and dragged her towards him: she screamed with affright, and long did she resist his dark intents; her agonizing sensations gave her fresh strength, and by a sudden effort she disengaged herself, and, opening the door of the dungeon, fled to the farther extremity of the cave: but the prince was resolved to perpetrate the dreadful deed which had long been the subject of his meditations, and he hastily pursued and brought her back.

MARY-ANNE RADCLIFFE, *Manfroné; or, The One-Handed Monk*, 1809

'A glass of wine;—shall I get you one?—You are very ill.'

'No, thank you,' she replied, endeavouring to recover herself. 'There is nothing the matter with me. I am quite well; I am only distressed by some dreadful news which I have just received from Longbourn.'

She bursts into tears as she alluded to it, and for a few minutes could not speak another word. Darcy, in wretched suspense, could only say something indistinctly of his concern, and observe her in compassionate silence. At length she spoke again. 'I have just had a letter from Jane, with such dreadful news. It cannot be concealed from any one. My youngest sister has left all her friends—has eloped;—has thrown herself into the power of—of Mr Wickham. They are gone off together from Brighton. *You* know him too well to doubt the rest. She has no money, no connections, nothing that can tempt him to—she is lost for ever.'

JANE AUSTEN, *Pride and Prejudice*, 1813

She definitely does not wish that I meet her husband, that little old gentleman with the limp whom I glimpsed on the boulevard: she married him for the sake of her son. He is rich and suffers from rheumatism. I did not allow myself a single jibe at him: she respects him as a father—and will deceive him as a husband. What a bizarre thing, the human heart in general, and a woman's heart in particular!

Vera's husband, Semyon Vasilievich G——v, is a distant relation of Princess Ligovskoy. He lives near her: Vera often visits the old princess. I gave her my word that I would get acquainted with the Ligovskoys and court the young princess in order to divert attention from Vera. In this way, my plans have not been upset in the least, and I shall have a merry time. . . .

Merry time! Yes, I have already passed that stage of the soul's life when one seeks only happiness, when the heart feels the need to love someone strongly and passionately. At present, all I wish is to be loved, and that by very few: it even seems to me that I would be content with one permanent attachment, a pitiful habit of the heart!

One thing has always struck me as strange: I never became the slave of the women I loved; on the contrary, I have always gained unconquerable power over their will and heart, with no effort at all. Why is it so? Is it because I never treasured anything too much, while they incessantly feared to let me slip out of their hands? Or is it the magnetic influence of a strong organism? Or did I simply never succeed in encountering a woman with a stubborn will of her own?

I must admit that, indeed, I never cared for women with wills of their own; it is not their department.

MIKHAIL LERMONTOV, *A Hero of Our Time*, 1840, trans. Vladimir and Dmitri Nabokov

BALLAD OF IMMORAL EARNINGS

MACHEATH. There was a time, now very far away
When we set up together, I and she.
I'd got the brain, and she supplied the breast.
I saw her right, and she looked after me—
A way of life then, if not quite the best.
And when a client came I'd slide out of our bed

And treat him nice, and go and have a drink instead
And when he paid up I'd address him: Sir
Come any night you feel you fancy her.
That time's long past, but what would I not give
To see that whorehouse where we used to live?

[*Jenny appears in the door, with Smith behind her.*

JENNY. That was the time, now very far away
He was so sweet and bashed me where it hurt.
And when the cash ran out the feathers really flew
He'd up and say: I'm going to pawn your skirt.
A skirt is nicer, but no skirt will do.
Just like his cheek, he had me fairly stewing
I'd ask him straight to say what he thought he was doing
Then he'd lash out and knock me headlong down the stairs.
I had the bruises off and on for years.

BOTH. That time's long past, but what would I not give
To see that whorehouse where we used to live?

BERTOLT BRECHT, *The Threepenny Opera*, 1928, trans. Ralph Manheim and John Willett

† *James Steerforth befriends and patronizes David Copperfield at school. Later he visits the Peggottys, a fisherman's family, with David, and seduces Little Em'ly, David's childhood sweetheart. She deserts her fiancé Ham Peggotty on the eve of their wedding, but Steerforth soon abandons her to a miserable life until she is found and brought home. The end of Steerforth comes in a storm at sea in which Ham tries to save his life. In this encounter between Rosa Dartle, who is secretly in love with Steerforth, and the ruined Little Em'ly we see the effects of his behaviour.*

'I have come to see,' she said, 'James Steerforth's fancy; the girl who ran away with him, and is the town-talk of the commonest people of her native place; the bold, flaunting, practised companion of persons like James Steerforth. I want to know what such a thing is like.'

There was a rustle, as if the unhappy girl, on whom she heaped these taunts, ran towards the door, and the speaker swiftly interposed herself before it. It was succeeded by a moment's pause.

When Miss Dartle spoke again, it was through her set teeth, and with a stamp upon the ground.

'Stay there!' she said, 'or I'll proclaim you to the house, and the whole street! If you try to evade *me*, I'll stop you, if it's by the hair, and raise the very stones against you!'

A frightened murmur was the only reply that reached my ears. A silence succeeded. I did not know what to do. Much as I desired to put an end to the interview, I felt that I had no right to present myself; that it was for Mr Peggotty alone to see her and recover her. Would he never come? I thought, impatiently.

'So!' said Rosa Dartle, with a contemptuous laugh, 'I see her at last! Why, he was a poor creature to be taken by that delicate mock-modesty, and that hanging head!'

'Oh, for Heaven's sake, spare me!' exclaimed Emily. 'Whoever you are, you know my pitiable story, and for Heaven's sake spare me, if you would be spared yourself!'

'If *I* would be spared!' returned the other fiercely; 'what is there in common between *us*, do you think?'

'Nothing but our sex,' said Emily, with a burst of tears.

'And that,' said Rosa Dartle, 'is so strong a claim, preferred by one so infamous, that if I had any feeling in my breast but scorn and abhorrence of you, it would freeze it up. Our sex! You are an honour to our sex!'

'I have deserved this,' cried Emily, 'but it's dreadful! Dear, dear lady, think what I have suffered, and how I am fallen! Oh, Martha, come back! Oh, home, home!'

Miss Dartle placed herself in a chair within view of the door, and looked downward, as if Emily were crouching on the floor before her. Being now between me and the light, I could see her curled lip, and her cruel eyes intently fixed on one place, with a greedy triumph.

'Listen to what I say!' she said; 'and reserve your false arts for your dupes. Do you hope to move *me* by your tears? No more than you could charm me by your smiles, you purchased slave.'

'Oh, have some mercy on me!' cried Emily. 'Show me some compassion, or I shall die mad!'

'It would be no great penance,' said Rosa Dartle, 'for your crimes. Do you know what you have done? Do you ever think of the home you have laid waste?'

'Oh, is there ever night or day, when I don't think of it?' cried Emily; and now I could just see her, on her knees, with her head thrown back, her pale face looking upward, her hands wildly clasped and held out, and her hair streaming about her. 'Has there ever been a single minute, waking or sleeping, when it hasn't been before me, just as it used to be in the lost days when I turned my back upon it for ever and ever? Oh, home, home! Oh dear, dear uncle, if you ever could have known the agony your love would cause me when I fell away from good, you never would have shown it to me so constant, much as you felt it; but would have been angry to me, at least once in my life, that I might have had some comfort! I have none, none, no comfort upon earth, for all of them were always fond of me!' She dropped on her face, before the imperious figure in the chair, with an imploring effort to clasp the skirt of her dress.

CHARLES DICKENS, *David Copperfield*, 1849–50

† *Tess of the D'Urbervilles confesses to her mother that Alec d'Urberville has taken advantage of her.*

'And yet th'st not got him to marry 'ee!' reiterated her mother. 'Any woman would have done it but you, after that!'

'Perhaps any woman would, except me.'

'It would have been something like a story to come back with, if you had!' continued Mrs Durbeyfield, ready to burst into tears of vexation. 'After all the talk about you and him which has reached us here, who would have expected it to end like this! Why didn't ye think of doing some good for your family instead o' thinking only of yourself? See how I've got to teave and slave, and your poor weak father with his heart clogged like a dripping-pan. I did hope for something to come out o' this! To see what a pretty pair you and he made that day when you drove away together four months ago! See what he has given us—all, as we thought, because we were his kin. But if he's not, it must have been done because of his love for 'ee. And yet you've not got him to marry!'

Get Alec d'Urberville in the mind to marry her. He marry *her*! On matrimony he had never once said a word. And what if he had? How a convulsive snatching at social salvation might have impelled her to answer him she could not say. But her poor foolish mother little knew her present feeling towards this man. Perhaps it was unusual in the circumstances, unlucky, unaccountable; but there it was; and this, as she had said, was what made her detest herself. She had never wholly cared for him, she did not at all care for him now. She had dreaded him, winced before him, succumbed to adroit advantages he took of her helplessness; then, temporarily blinded by his ardent manners, had been stirred to confused surrender awhile: had suddenly despised and disliked him, and had run away. That was all. Hate him she did not quite; but he was dust and ashes to her, and even for her name's sake she scarcely wished to marry him.

'You ought to have been more careful, if you didn't mean to get him to make you his wife!'

'O mother, my mother!' cried the agonized girl, turning passionately upon her parent as if her poor heart would break. 'How could I be expected to know? I was a child when I left this house four months ago. Why didn't you tell me there was danger in men-folk? Why didn't you warn me? Ladies know what to fend hands against, because they read novels that tell them of these tricks; but I never had the chance o' learning in that way, and you did not help me.'

THOMAS HARDY, *Tess of the D'Urbervilles*, 1891

† *Ruby, a servant girl, rejects her honest love in favour of the dubious Sir Felix Carbury.*

'He would marry me out and out immediately, if I'd have him,' continued Ruby . . . 'And he has everything comfortable in the way of furniture, and all that. And they do say he's ever so much money in the bank. But I detest him,' said Ruby, shaking her pretty head, and inclining herself towards her aristocratic lover's shoulder.

This took place in the back parlour, before Mrs Pipkin has ascended from the kitchen prepared to disturb so much romantic bliss with wretched references to the cold outer world. 'Well, now, Sir Felix,' she began, 'if things is square, of course you're welcome to see my niece.'

'And what if they're round, Mrs Pipkin?' said the gallant, careless, sparkling Lothario.

'Well, or round either, so long as they're honest.'

'Ruby and I are both honest;—ain't we, Ruby? I want to take her out to dinner, Mrs Pipkin. She shall be back before late;—before ten; she shall indeed.' Ruby inclined herself still more closely towards his shoulder. 'Come, Ruby, get your hat and change your dress, and we'll be off. I've ever so many things to tell you.'

Ever so many things to tell her! They must be to fix a day for the marriage, and to let her know where they were to live, and to settle what dress she should wear,—and perhaps to give her the money to go and buy it! Ever so many things to tell her! She looked up into Mrs Pipkin's face with imploring eyes. Surely on such an occasion as this an aunt would not expect that her niece should be a prisoner and a slave. 'Have it been put in writing, Sir Felix Carbury?' demanded Mrs Pipkin with cruel gravity. Mrs Hurtle had given it as her decided opinion that Sir Felix would not really mean to marry Ruby Ruggles unless he showed himself willing to do so with all the formality of a written contract.

'Writing be bothered,' said Sir Felix.

'That's all very well, Sir Felix. Writing do bother, very often. But when a gentleman has intentions, a bit of writing shows it plainer nor words. Ruby don't do nowhere to dine unless you puts it into writing.'

'Aunt Pipkin!' exclaimed the wretched Ruby.

'What do you think I'm going to do with her?' asked Sir Felix.

'If you want to make her your wife, put it in writing. And if it be as you don't, just say so, and walk away,—free.'

'I shall go,' said Ruby. 'I'm not going to be kept here a prisoner for any one. I can go when I please. You wait, Felix, and I'll be down in a minute.' The girl, with a nimble spring, ran upstairs, and began to change her dress without giving herself a moment for thought.

'She don't come back no more here, Sir Felix,' said Mrs Pipkin, in her most solemn tones. 'She ain't nothing to me, no more than she was my poor dear husband's sister's child. There ain't no blood between us, and won't be no disgrace. But I'd be loth to see her on the streets.'

'Then why won't you let me bring her back again?'

' 'Cause that'd be the way to send her there. You don't mean to marry her.' To this Sir Felix said nothing. 'You're not thinking of that. It's just a bit of sport,—and then there she is, an old shoe to be chucked away, just a rag to be swept into the dust-bin.

ANTHONY TROLLOPE, *The Way we Live Now*, 1875

† *In Puccini's opera* Tosca *Scarpia, the villainous chief of police, has arrested the opera singer's lover, Mario Cavaradossi. Scarpia offers to save his life if Tosca gives herself to him. The scene takes place with Scarpia dining and Cavaradossi being tortured off stage.*

SCARPIA. And first, a sip of wine. It comes from Spain.
[*Refills the glass and offers it to Tosca.*
A sip to hearten you.
TOSCA [*still staring at Scarpia, she advances towards the table. She sits resolutely facing him, and then asks in a tone of the deepest contempt*]. How much?
SCARPIA [*imperturbable, as she pours his drink*]. How much?
TOSCA. What is your price?
SCARPIA. Yes, they say that I am venal, but it is not
For money that I will sell myself
To beautiful women. I want other recompense
If I am to betray my oath of office.
I have waited for this hour.
Already in the past I burned
With passion for the diva.
But tonight I have beheld you
In a new role I had not seen before.
Those tears of yours were lava
To my senses and that fierce hatred
Which your eyes shot at me, only fanned
The fire in my blood.
Supple as a leopard
You enwrapped your lover. In that instant
I vowed you would be mine!
Mine! Yes, I will have you . . .
[*Rises and stretches out his arms towards Tosca. She has listened motionless to his wanton tirade. Now she leaps up and takes refuge behind the sofa.*
TOSCA [*running towards the window*]. Ah, Ah,
I'll jump out first!
SCARPIA [*coldly*]. I hold your Mario in pawn!
TOSCA. Oh, wretch . . .
Oh, ghastly bargain!

[*It suddenly occurs to her to appeal to the Queen, and she runs towards the door.*

SCARPIA [*ironically*]. I do you no violence. Go. You're free.
But your hope is vain: the Queen would merely
Grant pardon to a corpse.

[*Tosca draws back in fright and, her eyes fixed on Scarpia, drops on the sofa. She then looks away from him with a gesture of supreme contempt.*

How you detest me!

TOSCA. Ah! God!

SCARPIA [*approaching*]. Even so, even so I want you!

TOSCA [*with loathing*]. Don't touch me, devil I hate you, hate you!
Fiend, base villain! [*Flees from him in horror.*

SCARPIA. What does it matter?
Spasms of wrath or spasms of passion . . .

TOSCA. Foul villain!

SCARPIA [*trying to seize her*]. You are mine!

TOSCA. Wretch! [*Retreats behind the table.*

SCARPIA [*pursuing her*]. Mine!

TOSCA. Help! Help!

[*A distant roll of drums draws slowly near and then fades again into the distance.*

SCARPIA. Do you hear?
It is the drum, that leads the way
For the last march of the condemned. Time passes!

[*Tosca listens in terrible dread, and then comes back from the window to lean exhausted on the sofa.*

Are you aware of what dark work is done
Down there? They raise a gallows. By your wish,
Your Mario has but one more hour to live.

[*Coldly leans on a corner of the sofa and stares at Tosca.*

GIUSEPPE GIACOSA and LUIGI ILLICA, libretto to Puccini's *Tosca*, 1900, trans. Edmund Tracey

† *Adam Bede, a carpenter, is in love with a 17-year-old girl, Hetty Sorel, from a local farmer's family. Hetty is seduced by the squire, Captain Donnithorne. Donnithorne deserts her and, at the end of the book, she kills his baby and is sentenced to death. This is Arthur Donnithorne's letter of rejection.*

It was no longer light enough to go to bed without a candle, even in Mrs Poyser's early household, and Hetty carried one with her as she went up at last to her bedroom soon after Adam was gone, and bolted the door behind her.

Now she would read her letter. It must—it must have comfort in it. How was Adam to know the truth? It was always likely he should say what he did say.

She set down the candle, and took out the letter. It had a faint scent of roses, which made her feel as if Arthur were close to her. She put it to her lips, and a rush of remembered sensations for a moment or two swept away all fear. But her heart began to flutter strangely, and her hands to tremble as she broke the seal. She read slowly; it was not easy for her to read a gentleman's handwriting, though Arthur had taken pains to write plainly.

'DEAREST HETTY,—I have spoken truly when I have said that I loved you, and I shall never forget our love. I shall be your true friend as long as life lasts, and I hope to prove this to you in many ways. If I say anything to pain you in this letter, do not believe it is for want of love and tenderness towards you, for there is nothing I would not do for you, if I knew it to be really for your happiness. I cannot bear to think of my little Hetty shedding tears when I am not there to kiss them away; and if I followed only my own inclinations, I should be with her at this moment instead of writing. It is very hard for me to part from her—harder still for me to write words which may seem unkind, though they spring from the truest kindness.

'Dear, dear Hetty, sweet as our love has been to me, sweet as it would be to me for you to love me always, I feel that it would have been better for us both if we had never had that happiness, and that it is my duty to ask you to love me and care for me as little as you can. The fault has all been mine, for though I have been unable to resist the longing to be near you, I have felt all the while that your affection for me might cause you grief. I ought to have resisted my feelings. I should have done so, if I had been a better fellow than I am; but now, since the past cannot be altered, I am bound to save you from any evil that I have power to prevent. And I feel it would be a great evil for you if your affections continued so fixed on me that you could think of no other man who might be able to make you happier by his love than I ever can, and if you continued to look towards something in the future which cannot possibly happen. For, dear Hetty, if I were to do what you one day spoke of, and make you my wife, I should do what you yourself would come to feel was for your misery instead of your welfare. I know you can never be happy except by marrying a man in your own station; and if I were to marry you now, I should only be adding to any wrong I have done, besides offending against my duty in the other relations of life. You know nothing, dear Hetty, of the world in which I must always live, and you would soon begin to dislike me, because there would be so little in which we should be alike.

'And since I cannot marry you, we must part—we must try not to feel like lovers any more. I am miserable while I say this, but nothing else can be. Be angry with me, my sweet one, I deserve it; but do not believe that I shall not always care for you—always be grateful to you—always remember my Hetty; and if any trouble should come that we do not now foresee, trust in me to do everything that lies in my power.

'I have told you where you are to direct a letter to, if you want to write, but I put it down below lest you should have forgotten. Do not write unless there is something I can really do for you; for, dear Hetty, we must try to think of each other as little as we can. Forgive me, and try to forget everything about me, except that I shall be, as long as I live, your affectionate friend,

'ARTHUR DONNITHORNE'

GEORGE ELIOT, *Adam Bede*, 1859

† *Sergeant Troy's sword-play, described below, is a prelude to seduction . . .*

'Now,' said Troy, producing the sword, which, as he raised it into the sunlight, gleamed a sort of greeting, like a living thing, 'first, we have four right and four left cuts; four right and four left thrusts. Infantry cuts and guards are more interesting than ours, to my mind; but they are not so swashing. They have seven cuts and three thrusts. So much as a preliminary. Well, next, our cut one is as if you were sowing your corn—so.' Bathsheba saw a sort of rainbow, upside down in the air, and Troy's arm was still again. 'Cut two, as if you were hedging—so. Three, as if you were reaping—so. Four, as if you were threshing—in that way. Then the same on the left. The thrusts are these: one, two, three, four, right; one, two three, four, left.' He repeated them. 'Have 'em again?' he said. 'One, two—'

She hurriedly interrupted: 'I'd rather not; though I don't mind your twos and fours; but your ones and threes are terrible!'

'Very well. I'll let you off the ones and threes. Next, cuts, points and guards altogether.' Troy duly exhibited them. 'Then there's pursuing practice, in this way.' He gave the movements as before. 'There, those are the stereotyped forms. The infantry have two most diabolical upward cuts, which we are too humane to use. Like this—three, four.'

'How murderous and bloodthirsty!'

'They are rather deathly. Now I'll be more interesting, and let you see some loose play—giving all the cuts and points, infantry and cavalry, quicker than lightning, and as promiscuously—with just enough rule to regulate instinct and yet not to fetter it. You are my antagonist, with this difference from real warfare, that I shall miss you every time by one hair's breadth, or perhaps two. Mind you don't flinch, whatever you do.'

'I'll be sure not to!' she said invincibly.

He pointed to about a yard in front of him.

Bathsheba's adventurous spirit was beginning to find some grains of relish in these highly novel proceedings. She took up her position as directed, facing Troy.

'Now just to learn whether you have pluck enough to let me do what I wish, I'll give you a preliminary test.'

He flourished the sword by way of introduction number two, and the next thing of which she was conscious was that the point and blade of the sword were darting with a gleam towards her left side, just above her hip; then of their reappearance on her right side, emerging as it were from between her ribs, having apparently passed through her body. The third item of consciousness was that of seeing the same sword, perfectly clean and free from blood held vertically in Troy's hand (in the position technically called 'recover swords'). All was as quick as electricity.

'Oh!' she cried out in affright, pressing her hand to her side. 'Have you run me through?—no, you have not! Whatever have you done!'

'I have not touched you,' said Troy, quietly. 'It was mere sleight of hand. The sword passed behind you. Now you are not afraid, are you? Because if you are I can't perform. I give my word that I will not only not hurt you, but not once touch you.'

'I don't think I am afraid. You are quite sure you will not hurt me?'

'Quite sure.'

'Is the sword very sharp?'

'Oh no—only stand as still as a statue.'

THOMAS HARDY, *Far from the Madding Crowd*, 1874

† *If* Lorna Doone *seems stodgy and overblown for present-day tastes, it nevertheless contains a very striking villain. The most pernicious of R. D. Blackmore's marauding band of outlaws, and his narrator John Ridd's principal adversary, is Carver Doone of the black beard and black heart. Lorna, having escaped from the clutches of this terrible person, and thrown in her lot with the Ridds, finds she has not cut off the possibility of unpleasant encounters.*

It was lucky that I came home so soon; for I found the house in a great commotion, and all the women trembling. When I asked what the matter was, Lorna, who seemed the most self-possessed, answered that it was all her fault, for she alone had frightened them. And this in the following manner. She had stolen out to the garden towards dusk, to watch some favourite hyacinths just pushing up, like a baby's teeth, and just attracting the fatal notice of a great house-snail at night-time. Lorna at last had discovered the glutton, and was bearing him off in triumph to the tribunal of the ducks, when she descried two glittering eyes glaring at her steadfastly, from the elder bush beyond the stream. The elder was smoothing its wrinkled leaves, being at least two months behind time; and among them this calm cruel face appeared; and she knew it was the face of Carver Doone.

The maiden, although so used to terror (as she told me once before), lost all presence of mind hereat, and could neither shriek nor fly, but only gaze, as if bewitched. Then Carver Doone, with his deadly smile, gloating upon her horror, lifted his long gun, and pointed full at Lorna's heart. In vain she strove to turn away; fright had stricken her stiff as stone. With the inborn love of life, she tried to cover the vital part wherein the winged death must lodge—for she knew Carver's certain aim—but her hands hung numbed, and heavy: in nothing but her eyes was life.

With no sign of pity in his face, no quiver of relenting, but a well-pleased grin at all the charming palsy of his victim, Carver Doone lowered, inch by inch, the muzzle of his gun. When it pointed to the ground, between her delicate arched insteps, he pulled the trigger, and the bullet flung the mould all over her. It was a refinement of bullying, for which I swore to God that night, upon my knees, in secret, that I would smite down Carver Doone; or else he should smite me down. Base beast! what largest humanity, or what dreams of divinity, could make a man put up with this?

My darling (the loveliest, and most harmless, in the world of maidens) fell away on a bank of grass, and wept at her own cowardice; and trembled, and wondered where I was; and what I would think of this. Good God! What could I think of it? She overrated my slow nature, to admit the question.

While she leaned there, quite unable yet to save herself, Carver came to the brink of the flood, which alone was between them; and then he stroked his jet black beard, and waited for Lorna to begin. Very likely, he thought that she would thank him for his kindness to her. But she was now recovering the power of her nimble limbs; and ready to be off like hope, and wonder at her own cowardice.

'I have spared you this time,' he said, in his deep, calm voice, 'only because it suits my plans; and I never yield to temper. But unless you come back to-morrow, pure, and with all you took away, and teach me to destroy that fool, who has destroyed himself for you, your death is here, your death is here, where it has long been waiting.'

Although his gun was empty, he struck the breech of it with his finger; and then he turned away, not deigning even once to look back again; and Lorna saw his giant figure striding across the meadow-land, as if the Ridds were nobodies, and he the proper owner. Both mother and I were greatly hurt at hearing of this insolence; for we had owned that meadow from the time of the great Alfred; and even when that good king lay in the Isle of Athelney, he had a Ridd along with him.

R. D. BLACKMORE, *Lorna Doone*, 1869

FRENCH LISETTE: A BALLAD OF MAIDA VALE

Who strolls so late, for mugs a bait,
In the mists of Maida Vale,
Sauntering past a stucco gate
Fallen, but hardly frail?

You can safely bet that it's French Lisette,
The Pearl of Portsdown Square,
On the game she has made her name
And rather more than her share.

In a coat of cony with her passport phony
She left her native haunts,
For an English surname exchanging *her* name
And then took up with a ponce.

Now a meaning look conceals the hook
Some innocent fish will swallow,
Chirping 'Hullo, Darling!' like a cheeky starling
She'll turn, and he will follow,

For her eyes are blue and her eyelids too
And her smile's by no means cryptic,
Her perm's as firm as if waved with glue,
She plies an orange lipstick,

And orange-red is her perky head
Under a hat like a tiny pie—
A pie on a tart, it might be said,
Is redundant, but oh, how spry!

From the distant tundra to snuggle under her
Chin a white fox was conveyed,
And with winks and leerings and Woolworth's
   earrings
She's all set up for trade.

Now who comes here replete with beer?
A quinquagenarian clerk
Who in search of Life has left 'the wife'
And 'the kiddies' in Tufnell Park.

Dear sir, beware! for sex is a snare
And all is not true that allures.
Good sir, come off it! She means to profit
By this little weakness of yours:

Too late for alarm! Exotic charm
Has caught in his gills like a gaff,
He goes to his fate with a hypnotized gait,
The slave of her silvery laugh,

And follows her in to her suite of sin,
Her self-contained bower of bliss,
They enter her flat, she takes his hat,
And he hastens to take a kiss.

Ah, if only he knew that concealed from view
Behind a 'folk-weave' curtain
Is her fancy man, called Dublin Dan,
His manner would be less certain,

His bedroom eyes would express surprise,
His attitude less languor,
He would watch his money, not call her 'Honey,'
And be seized with fear or anger.

Of the old technique one need scarcely speak,
But oh, in the quest for Romance
'Tis folly abounding in a strange surrounding
To be divorced from one's pants.

W. M. PLOMER, 1955

'. . . where did you pick her up, Corley?' he asked.

Corley ran his tongue swiftly along his upper lip.

'One night, man,' he said, 'I was going along Dame Street and I spotted a fine tart under Waterhouse's clock and said good night, you know. So we went for a walk round by the canal, and she told me she was a slavey in a house in Baggot Street. I put my arm round her and squeezed her a bit that night. Then next Sunday, man, I met her by appointment. We went out to Donnybrook and I brought her into a field there. She told me she used to go with a dairyman. . . . It was fine, man. Cigarettes every night she'd bring me and paying the tram out and back. And one night she brought me two bloody fine cigars —O, the real cheese, you know, that the old fellow used to smoke. . . . I was afraid, man, she'd get in the family way. But she's up to the dodge.'

'Maybe she thinks you'll marry her,' said Lenehan.

'I told her I was out of a job,' said Corley. 'I told her I was in Pim's. She doesn't know my name. I was too hairy to tell her that. But she thinks I'm a bit of class, you know.'

Lenehan laughed again, noiselessly.

'Of all the good ones ever I heard,' he said, 'that emphatically takes the biscuit.' . . .

As the two young men walked on through the crowd Corley occasionally turned to smile at some of the passing girls, but Lenehan's gaze was fixed on the large faint moon circled with a double halo. He watched earnestly the passing of the grey web of twilight across its face. At length he said:

'Well . . . tell me, Corley, I suppose you'll be able to pull it off all right, eh?'

Corley closed one eye expressively as an answer.

'Is she game for that?' asked Lenehan dubiously. 'You can never know women.'

'She's all right,' said Corley. 'I know the way to get around her, man. She's a bit gone on me.'

'You're what I call a gay Lothario,' said Lenehan. 'And the proper kind of a Lothario, too!'

A shade of mockery relieved the servility of his manner. To save himself he had the habit of leaving his flattery open to the interpretation of raillery. But Corley had not a subtle mind.

'There's nothing to touch a good slavey,' he affirmed. 'Take my tip for it.'

'By one who has tried them all,' said Lenehan.

'First I used to go with girls, you know,' said Corley, unbosoming; 'girls off the South Circular. I used to take them out, man, on the tram somewhere and pay the tram or take them to a band or a play at the theatre, or buy them chocolate and sweets or something that way. I used to spend money on them right enough,' he added, in a convincing tone, as if he was conscious of being disbelieved.

But Lenehan could well believe it; he nodded gravely.

'I know that game,' he said, 'and it's a mug's game.'

'And damn the thing I ever got out of it,' said Corley.

'Ditto here,' said Lenehan.

'Only off of one of them,' said Corley.

He moistened his upper lip by running his tongue along it. The recollection brightened his eyes. He, too, gazed at the pale disk of the moon, now nearly veiled, and seemed to meditate.

'She was . . . a bit of all right,' he said regretfully.

He was silent again. Then he added:

'She's on the turf now. I saw her driving down Earl Street one night with two fellows with her on a car.'

'I suppose that's your doing,' said Lenehan.

'There was others at her before me,' said Corley philosophically.

This time Lenehan was inclined to disbelieve. He shook his head to and fro and smiled.

'You know you can't kid me, Corley,' he said.

'Honest to God!' said Corley. 'Didn't she tell me herself?'

Lenehan made a tragic gesture.

'Base betrayer!' he said.

As they passed along the railings of Trinity College, Lenehan skipped out into the road and peered up at the clock.

'Twenty after,' he said.

'Time enough,' said Corley. 'She'll be there all right. I always let her wait a bit.'

Lenehan laughed quietly.

'Ecod! Corley, you know how to take them,' he said.

'I'm up to all their little tricks,' Corley confessed.

JAMES JOYCE, 'Two Gallants', 1914

Mrs Roberts brought them their beer. Grimes took a long draught and sighed happily.

'This looks like being the first end of term I've seen for two years,' he said dreamily. 'Funny thing, I can always get on all right for about six weeks, and then I land in the soup. I don't believe I was ever meant by Nature to be a schoolmaster. Temperament,' said Grimes, with a far-away look in his eyes—'that's been my trouble, temperament and sex.'

'Is it quite easy to get another job after—after you've been in the soup?' asked Paul.

'Not at first, it isn't, but there are ways. Besides, you see, I'm a public school man. That means everything. There's a blessed equity in the English social system,' said Grimes, 'that ensures the public school man against starvation. One goes through four or five years of perfect hell at an age when life is bound to be hell anyway, and after that the social system never lets one down.

'Not that I stood four or five years of it, mind; I left soon after my sixteenth birthday. But my house-master was a public school man. He knew the system. "Grimes," he said, "I can't keep you in the House after what has happened. I have the other boys to consider. But I don't want to be too hard on you. I want you to start again." So he sat down there and then and wrote me a letter of recommendation to any future employer, a corking good letter, too. I've got it still. It's been very useful at one time or another. That's the public school system all over. They may kick you out, but they never let you down.

'I subscribed a guinea to the War Memorial Fund. I felt I owed it to them. I was really sorry,' said Grimes, 'that that cheque never got through.

'After that I went into business. Uncle of mine had a brush factory at Edmonton. Doing pretty well before the war. That put the lid on the brush trade for me. You're too young to have been in the war, I suppose? Those were days, old boy. We shan't see the like of them again. I don't suppose I was really sober for more than a few hours for the whole of that war. Then I got into the soup again, pretty badly that time. Happened over in France. They said, "Now, Grimes, you've got to behave like a gentleman. We don't want a court-martial in this regiment. We're going to leave you alone for half an hour. There's your revolver. You know what to do. Goodbye, old man," they said quite affectionately.

'Well, I sat there for some time looking at that revolver. I put it up to my head twice, but each time I brought it down again. "Public school men don't end like this," I said to myself. It was a long half-hour, but luckily they had left a decanter of whisky in there with me. They'd all had a few, I think. That's what made them all so solemn. There wasn't much whisky left when they came back, and, what with that and the strain of the situation, I could only laugh when they came in. Silly thing to do, but they looked so surprised, seeing me there alive and drunk.

' "The man's a cad," said the colonel, but even then I couldn't stop laughing, so they put me under arrest and called a court-martial.

'I must say I felt pretty low next day. A major came over from another battalion to try my case. He came to see me first, and bless me if it wasn't a cove I'd known at school!

' "God bless my soul," he said, "if it isn't Grimes of Podger's! What's all this nonsense about a court-martial?" So I told him. "H'm," he said, "pretty bad. Still it's out of the question to shoot an old Harrovian. I'll see what I can do about it." And next day I was sent to Ireland on a pretty cushy job connected with postal service. That saw me out as far as the war was concerned. You can't get into the soup in Ireland, do what you like. I don't know if all this bores you?'

'Not at all,' said Paul. 'I think it's most encouraging.'

'I've been in the soup pretty often since then, but never quite so badly. Someone always turns up and says, "I can't see a public school man down and out. Let me put you on your feet again." I should think,' said Grimes, 'I've been put on my feet more often than any living man.'

Philbrick came across the bar parlour towards them.

'I've been talking to the station-master here,' he said, 'and if either of you ever wants a woman, his sister—'

'Certainly not,' said Paul.

'Oh, all right,' said Philbrick, making off.

'Women are an enigma,' said Grimes, 'as far as Grimes is concerned.'

EVELYN WAUGH, *Decline and Fall*, 1928

NOTHING TO FEAR

All fixed: early arrival at the flat
Lent by a friend, whose note says *Lucky sod*;
Drinks on the tray; the cover-story pat
And quite uncheckable; her husband off
Somewhere with all the kids till six o'clock
(Which ought to be quite long enough);
And all worth while: face really beautiful,
Good legs and hips, and as for breasts—my God.
What about guilt, compunction and such stuff?
I've had my fill of all that cock;
It'll wear off, as usual.

Yes, all fixed. Then why this slight trembling,
Dry mouth, quick pulse-rate, sweaty hands,
As though she were the first? No, not impatience,
Nor fear of failure, thank you, Jack.
Beauty, they tell me, is a dangerous thing,
Whose touch will burn, but I'm asbestos, see?
All worth while—it's a dead coincidence
That sitting here, a bag of glands
Tuned up to concert pitch, I seem to sense
A different style of caller at my back,
As cold as ice, but just as set on me.

KINGSLEY AMIS, 1967

VI

CON MEN

AMONGST us there's a canon regular
Who'd poison a whole city, though it were
Big as Nineveh, Alexandria, Rome,
Troy and three other cities put together.
I don't think you'd be able to set down
His bottomless deceit, his trickeries,
Not if you were to live a thousand years!
There's nobody in the whole world can touch him
At double-dealing; and, when he converses,
He'll talk in such a convoluted jargon
Spoken so craftily, that in no time
He'll make a fool of anyone, unless
He is another devil, like that canon.
He's diddled many people before this,
And will again, so long as he has breath;
Yet folk go miles, on horseback and on foot
To seek him out and make his acquaintance,
Without a notion of his fraudulence.

GEOFFREY CHAUCER, 'The Canon's Assistant's Tale', *c.*1387, trans. David Wright

AUTOLYCUS. My traffic is sheets; when the kite builds, look to lesser linen. My father named me Autolycus; who being, as I am, litter'd under Mercury, was likewise a snapper-up of unconsider'd trifles. With die and drab I purchased this caparison; and my revenue is the silly cheat: gallows and knock are too powerful on the highway; beating and hanging are terrors to me; for the life to come, I sleep out the thought of it.—A prize! a prize!

Enter Clown.

CLOWN. Let me see:—every 'leven wether tods; every tod yields pound and odd shilling: fifteen hundred shorn, what comes the wool to?

AUTOLYCUS [*aside*]. If the springe hold, the cock's mine.

CLOWN. I cannot do 't without counters.—Let me see; what am I to buy for our sheep-shearing feast? Three pound of sugar; five pound of currants; rice—what will this sister of mine do with rice? But my father hath made her mistress of the feast, and she lays it on. She hath made me four-and-twenty nosegays for the shearers,—three-man songmen all, and very good ones; but they are most of them means and bases; but one puritan amongst them, and he sings psalms to hornpipes. I must have saffron, to colour the warden-pies; mace; dates,—none, that's out of my note; nutmegs, seven; a race or two of ginger,—but that I may beg; four pound of prunes, and as many of raisins o' the sun.

AUTOLYCUS. O, that ever I was born! [*Grovelling on the ground.*

CLOWN. I' the name of me,—

AUTOLYCUS. O, help me, help me! pluck but off these rags; and then, death, death!

CLOWN. Alack, poor soul! thou hast need of more rags to lay on thee, rather than have these off.

AUTOLYCUS. O, sir, the loathsomeness of them offend me more than the stripes I have received, which are mighty ones and millions.

CLOWN. Alas, poor man! a million of beating may come to a great master.

AUTOLYCUS. I am robb'd sir, and beaten; my money and apparel ta'en from me, and these detestable things put upon me.

CLOWN. What, by a horseman or a footman?

AUTOLYCUS. A footman, sweet sir, a footman.

CLOWN. Indeed, he should be a footman by the garments he has left with thee: if this be a horseman's coat, it hath seen very hot service. Lend me thy hand, I'll help thee: come, lend me thy hand.

[*Helping him up.*

AUTOLYCUS. O, good sir, tenderly, O!

CLOWN. Alas, poor soul!

AUTOLYCUS. O, good sir, softly, good sir! I fear, sir, my shoulder-blade is out.

CLOWN. How now! canst stand?

AUTOLYCUS. Softly, dear sir [*picks his pocket*]; good sir, softly. You ha' done me a charitable office.

CLOWN. Dost lack any money? I have a little money for thee.

AUTOLYCUS. No, good sweet sir; no, I beseech you, sir: I have a kinsman not past three quarters of a mile hence, unto whom I was going; I shall there have money, or any thing I want: offer me no money, I pray you,—that kills my heart.

CLOWN. What manner of fellow was he that robb'd you?

AUTOLYCUS. A fellow, sir, that I have known to go about with troll-my-dames: I knew him once a servant of the prince: I cannot tell, good sir, for which of his virtues it was, but he was certainly whipp'd out of the court.

CLOWN. His vices, you would say; there's no virtue whipp'd out of the court: they cherish it, to make it stay there; and yet it will no more but abide.

AUTOLYCUS. Vices, I would say, sir. I know this man well: he hath been since an ape-bearer; then a process-server,—a bailiff; then he compass'd a motion of the Prodigal Son, and married a tinker's wife within a mile where my land and living lies; and, having flown over many knavish professions, he settled only in rogue: some call him Autolycus.

CLOWN. Out upon him! prig, for my life, prig: he haunts wakes, fairs, and bear-baitings.

AUTOLYCUS. Very true, sir; he, sir, he; that's the rogue that put me into this apparel.

CLOWN. Not a more cowardly rogue in all Bohemia; if you had but look'd big and spit at him, he'ld have run.

AUTOLYCUS. I must confess to you, sir, I am no fighter; I am false of heart that way; and that he knew, I warrant him.

CLOWN. How do you now?

AUTOLYCUS. Sweet sir, much better than I was; I can stand and walk: I will even take my leave of you, and pace softly towards my kinsman's.

CLOWN. Shall I bring thee on the way?

AUTOLYCUS. No, good-faced sir: no, sweet sir.

CLOWN. Then fare thee well: I must go buy spices for our sheep-shearing.

AUTOLYCUS. Prosper you, sweet sir! [*Exit Clown*.] Your purse is not hot enough to purchase your spice. I'll be with you at your sheep-shearing too: if I make not this cheat bring out another, and the shearers prove sheep, let me be unroll'd, and my name put in the book of virtue. [*Sings*.

Jog on, jog on, the footpath way,
  And merrily hent the stile-a:
A merry heart goes all the day,
  Your sad tires in a mile-a. [*Exit*.

WILLIAM SHAKESPEARE, *The Winter's Tale*, 1609/10

† *Volpone, a rich Venetian nobleman, pretends to be dying, to get gifts from those who hope to be his heirs. Mosca, his confederate, persuades each of them in turn that he is named in the will.*

MOSCA. Most blessed cordial!
This will recover him.
CORBACCIO. Yes, do, do, do.
MOSCA. I think it were not best, sir.
CORBACCIO. What?
MOSCA. To recover him.
CORBACCIO. O, no, no, no; by no means.
MOSCA. Why, sir, this
Will work some strange effect if he but feel it.
CORBACCIO. 'Tis true, therefore forbear, I'll take my venture;
Give me it again.
MOSCA. At no hand; pardon me;
You shall not do yourself that wrong, sir. I
Will so advise you, you shall have it all.
CORBACCIO. How?
MOSCA. All, sir; 'tis your right, your own; no man
Can claim a part; 'tis yours without a rival,
Decreed by destiny.
CORBACCIO. How, how, good Mosca?
MOSCA. I'll tell you, sir. This fit he shall recover.
CORBACCIO. I do conceive you.
MOSCA. And on first advantage
Of his gain'd sense, will I reimportune him
Unto the making of his testament;
And show him this.
CORBACCIO. Good, good.
MOSCA. 'Tis better yet,
If you will hear, sir.
CORBACCIO. Yes, with all my heart.
MOSCA. Now would I counsel you, make home with speed;
There frame a will; whereto you shall inscribe
My master your sole heir.
CORBACCIO. And disinherit
My son?

MOSCA. O sir, the better; for that colour
  Shall make it much more taking.
CORBACCIO. O, but colour?
MOSCA. This will, sir, you shall send it unto me.
  Now, when I come to enforce (as I will do)
  Your cares, your watchings, and your many prayers,
  Your more than many gifts, your this day's present,
  And last produce your will; where (without thought
  Or least regard unto your proper issue,
  A son so brave, and highly meriting)
  The stream of your diverted love hath thrown you
  Upon my master, and made him your heir;
  He cannot be so stupid, or stone-dead,
  But out of conscience, and mere gratitude—
CORBACCIO. He must pronounce me his?
MOSCA. 'Tis true.
CORBACCIO. This plot
  Did I think on before.
MOSCA. I do believe it.
CORBACCIO. Do you not believe it?
MOSCA. Yes, sir.
CORBACCIO. Mine own project.
MOSCA. Which when he hath done, sir—
CORBACCIO. Publish'd me his heir?
MOSCA. And you so certain to survive him—
CORBACCIO. Ay.
MOSCA. Being so lusty a man—
CORBACCIO. 'Tis true.
MOSCA. Yes, sir—
CORBACCIO. I thought on that too. See how he
    should be
  The very organ to express my thoughts!
MOSCA. You have not only done yourself a good—
CORBACCIO. But multiplied it on my son.
MOSCA. 'Tis right, sir.
CORBACCIO. Still my invention.
MOSCA. 'Las, sir, Heaven knows,
  It hath been all my study, all my care
  (I ev'n grow gray withal) how to work things—
CORBACCIO. I do conceive, sweet Mosca.

MOSCA. You are he,
For whom I labour, here.
CORBACCIO. Ay, do, do, do:
I'll straight about it.
MOSCA. Rook go with you, raven.
CORBACCIO. I know thee honest.
MOSCA. You do lie, sir—
CORBACCIO. And—
MOSCA. Your knowledge is no better than your ears, sir.
CORBACCIO. I do not doubt to be a father to thee.
MOSCA. Nor I to gull my brother of his blessing.
CORBACCIO. I may have my youth restored to me; why not?
MOSCA. Your worship is a precious ass—
CORBACCIO. What say'st thou?
MOSCA. I do desire your worship to make haste, sir.
CORBACCIO. 'Tis done, tis done; I go. [*Exit*.
VOLPONE. O, I shall burst;
Let out my sides, let out my sides—
MOSCA. Contain
Your flux of laughter, sir: you know this hope
Is such a bait it covers any hook.
VOLPONE. O, but thy working, and thy placing it!
I cannot hold: good rascal, let me kiss thee:
I never knew thee in so rare a humour.
MOSCA. Alas, sir, I but do as I am taught;
Follow your grave instructions; give them words,
Pour oil into their ears, and send them hence.
VOLPONE. 'Tis true, 'tis true. What a rare punishment
Is avarice to itself!

BEN JOHNSON, *Volpone*, 1605

VILLAINS

Profit and Batten
Had coats lined with satin,
And no wonder either,
For they never owed a stiver;

If folks owed them rent,
They owed at ten per cent.
Sing Batten and Profit
If you've got a hat, doff it.

STEVIE SMITH (1902–71)

† *Casanova has undertaken to discover buried treasure by magic.*

My great operation had to be performed on the following day; otherwise, according to all established rules, I would have had to wait until the next full moon. I had to make the gnomes raise the treasure to the surface of the earth at the very spot on which my incantations would be performed. Of course, I knew well enough that I should not succeed, but I knew likewise that I could easily reconcile Franzia and Capitani to a failure by inventing some excellent reasons for our want of success. In the meantime I had to play my part of a magician, in which I took a real delight. I kept Javotte at work all day, sewing together in the shape of a ring some thirty sheets of paper, on which I painted the most wonderful designs. That ring, which I called *maximus*, had a diameter of three geometric paces. I had manufactured a sort of sceptre, or magic wand, with the branch of olive brought by Franzia from Cesena. Thus prepared, I told Javotte that at twelve o'clock at night, when I came out of the magic ring, she was to be ready for everything. The order did not seem repugnant to her; she longed to give me that proof of her obedience, and, on my side, considering myself as her debtor, I was in a hurry to pay my debt and give her every satisfaction.

The hour having struck, I ordered Franzia and Capitani to stand on the balcony, so as to be ready to come to me if I called for them, and also to prevent anyone in the house seeing my proceedings. I then throw off all profane garments; I clothe myself in the long white robe, the work of a virgin's innocent hands; I allow my long hair to fall loosely, I place the extraordinary crown on my head, the circle *maximus* on my shoulders, and, seizing the sceptre with one hand, the wonderful knife with the other, I go down into the yard. There I spread my circle on the ground, uttering the most barbarous words, and, after going round it three times, I jump into the middle.

Squatting down there, I remain a few minutes motionless, then I rise and fix my eyes upon a heavy, dark cloud coming from the west, whilst from the same quarter the thunder is rumbling loudly. What a sublime genius I should have appeared in the eyes of my two fools if, having a short time before taken notice of the sky in that part of the horizon, I had announced to them that my operation would be attended by that phenomenon!

The cloud spreads with fearful rapidity, and soon the sky seems covered with a funeral pall, on which the most vivid flashes of lightning keep blazing every moment.

Such a storm was a very natural occurrence, and I had no reason to be astonished at it, but somehow fear was beginning to creep into me, and I wished myself in my room. My fright soon increased at sight of the lightning and the sound of the claps of thunder, which succeeded each other with fearful rapidity and seemed to roar over my very head. I then realised what an extraordinary effect fear can have on the mind, for I fancied that, if I was not annihilated by the fires of heaven which were flashing all around me, it was only because they could not enter my magic ring. Thus was I admiring my own deceitful work! That foolish reason prevented me from leaving the circle, in spite of the fear which caused me to shudder. If it had not been for that belief, the result of a cowardly fright, I would not have remained one minute where I was, and my hurried flight would no doubt have opened the eyes of my two dupes, who could not have failed to see that, far from being a magician, I was only a poltroon. The violence of the wind, the claps of thunder, the piercing cold and, above all, fear made me tremble all over like an aspen leaf. My system, which I thought proof against every accident, had vanished; I acknowledged an avenging God, who had waited for this opportunity of punishing me at one blow for all my sins and of annihilating me in order to put an end to my want of faith. The complete immobility which paralysed all my limbs seemed to me a proof of the uselessness of my repentance, and that conviction only increased my consternation.

CASANOVA (1725–98), *Memoirs*, trans. Arthur Machen

† *Dickens is at his most sardonic when he comes to recount the end of Mr Merdle, the crooked financier, in* Little Dorrit, *from the miscreant's off-hand request for the suicide weapon ('"so I am off", added Mr Merdle, getting up. "Could you lend me a penknife?" '), to the eager speculation about his state of health which follows the news of his death: was it overwork that carried him off? Soon the truth of the matter begins to emerge.*

In steady progression, as the day declined, the talk rose in sound and purpose. He had left a letter at the Baths addressed to his physician, and his physician had get the letter, and the letter would be produced at the Inquest on the morrow, and it would fall like a thunderbolt upon the multitude he had deluded. Numbers of men in every profession and trade would be blighted by his insolvency; old people who had been in easy circumstances all their lives would have no place of repentance for their trust in him but the workhouse; legions of women and children would have their whole future desolated by the hand of this mighty scoundrel. Every partaker of his magnificent feasts would be seen to have been a sharer in the plunder of innumerable homes; every servile worshipper of riches who had helped to set him on his pedestal, would have done better to worship the Devil point-blank. So, the talk, lashed louder and higher by confirmation on confirmation, and by edition after edition of the evening papers, swelled into such a roar when night came, as might have brought one to believe that a solitary watcher on the gallery above the Dome of St Paul's would have perceived the night air to be laden with a heavy muttering of the name of Merdle, coupled with every form of execration.

For, by that time it was known that the late Mr Merdle's complaint had been, simply, Forgery and Robbery. He, the uncouth object of such wide-spread adulation, the sitter at great men's feasts, the roc's egg of great ladies' assemblies, the subduer of exclusiveness, the leveller of pride, the patron of patrons, the bargain-driver with a Minister for Lordships of the Circumlocution Office, the recipient of more acknowledgment within some ten or fifteen years, at most, than had been bestowed in England upon all peaceful public benefactors, and upon all the leaders of all the Arts and Sciences, with all their works to testify for them, during two centuries at least—he, the shining wonder, the new constellation to be followed by the wise men bringing gifts, until it stopped over certain carrion at the bottom of a bath and disappeared—was simply the greatest Forger and the greatest Thief that ever cheated the gallows.

CHARLES DICKENS, *Little Dorrit*, 1857

† *Melmotte, in Trollope's* The Way we Live Now, *is another financier whose crimes catch up with him. Faced with an impending trial for forgery, he takes the only way out:*

Melmotte as soon as he reached home got into his own sitting-room without difficulty, and called for more brandy and water. Between eleven and twelve he was left there by his servant with a bottle of brandy, three or four bottles of sodawater, and his cigar-case. Neither of the ladies of the family came to him, nor did he speak of them. Nor was he so drunk then as to give rise to any suspicion in the mind of the servant. He was habitually left there at night, and the servant as usual went to his bed. But at nine o'clock on the following morning the maid-servant found him dead upon the floor. Drunk as he had been,—more drunk as he probably became during the night,—still he was able to deliver himself from the indignities and penalties to which the law might have subjected him by a dose of prussic acid.

ANTHONY TROLLOPE, *The Way we Live Now*, 1875

THE TICHBORNE CLAIMANT

The Tichbornes are genealogically one of the most illustrious families in the country. Horace Round admitted them to his tiny circle of genuine, ancient pedigrees. In the middle of the last century they were rich, having added to their original estates in Hampshire valuable London property of their distant connections the Doughties. There was, however, a paucity of male heirs. Three brothers in turn succeeded to the baronetcy. The third had two sons, Roger and Alfred. Roger was believed to have been lost at sea; Alfred, having succeeded, died in 1866, leaving a posthumous son during whose infancy the estates were being held in trust, when there appeared from Wagga Wagga in Australia a man claiming to be the lost uncle Roger. He arrived in England on Christmas Day 1866. It was not until 10 May 1871 that his case opened. It occupied the courts for 103 sittings until

6 March 1872 and cost the Tichborne family £92,000. The defence plausibly identified the claimant with a Wapping butcher named Orton. The claimant was then committed for perjury and after another enormously protracted trial he was sentenced to seven years on two counts, the terms to run consecutively. He was released on ticket-of-leave in 1884 and lived until 1898 still asserting his claim.

EVELYN WAUGH, in the *Spectator*, 1957

† *This is part of the speech made by Mr Justice Mellor in sentencing the claimant. Kenealy was the barrister for the defence.*

Your entire ignorance of the native tongue of Roger Tichborne coupled with at least the partial acquisition of another language, the tattoo marks which were proved to have existed on the arm of the undoubted Roger Tichborne, and his genuine letters and the letters written by you whether in the character of Roger Tichborne or Arthur Orton, the admission expressly made or implied in your conduct, and all that is known of the history of the life and character of Roger Tichborne and of yourself present an accumulation of proof such as can rarely be given in a court of justice, and which conclusively demonstrates the propriety of the verdict of the jury. No man can look with an unprejudiced mind and a clear observation at the letters of the undoubted Roger Tichborne without coming to the conclusion that they were never written by you, while between the undoubted letters of Arthur Orton and your own there is evidence of identity most complete and convincing. Of what avail would the negative evidence of your identity with Arthur Orton be against the circumstances connected with your visit to Wapping, with your assumption of a false name, and your correspondence and dealings with the family of Arthur Orton, added to the fact that your counsel did not venture to put into the box Arthur Orton's sisters, who from the very first were in your interest, who had received money from you, and had made affidavits in your favour? The inference from your not calling them is irresistible—namely, that they were possessed of knowledge which must have tended strongly to prove your identity with Arthur Orton. That question, important as it is, is only material as affording one of the modes of proof that you are not and cannot be Roger Tichborne.

Whether you originally conceived and planned the entire scheme which you ultimately carried out, I know not. The marvellous growth and development of your knowledge as to the circumstances connected with the history of Roger Tichborne and his military life, leave it uncertain whether your original design was not enlarged by reason of the ease with which you found people so ready to become your dupes, and I fear in some cases your accomplices. However that may be, in the carrying out of your scheme you hesitated at no amount of perjury and fraud which you thought to be necessary to its success. Wicked and nefarious as it was to impose yourself upon society as Roger Charles Tichborne, and to attempt to deprive the lawful heir of his inheritance, that offence sinks almost into insignificance when compared with the still more infamous perjury by which you sought to support your scheme. I refer to your attempt to blast the reputation of Lady Radcliffe. No more foul or deliberate falsehood was ever heard in a court of justice. I can hardly restrain the indignation which I feel at the incredible baseness of your conduct in that respect. Happily, the means of refuting that cowardly calumny were immediately at hand and never was a charge so completely shattered and exposed as was that. It is not, however, because the refutation of the falsehood was singularly easy and complete that the baseness of your conduct is diminished. I believe I am speaking the sentiment of every member of the court when I say that the punishment about to be assigned by the court is wholly inadequate to your offence. The framers of the Act of Parliament that fixes and limits the sentence which the court is authorized to pass upon you, never dreamt of circumstances so aggravated as exist in your case. The sentence of the court which I now pronounce is, that for the perjury alleged in the first count of this indictment upon which you have been convicted, you be kept in penal servitude for the term of seven years; and that for the perjury alleged in the second count of this indictment of which you have also been convicted, you be kept in penal servitude for the further term of seven years, to commence immediately upon the expiration of the term of penal servitude assigned to you in respect of your conviction upon the first count of this indictment, and that is the sentence of the court.

In the silence that followed, the prisoner, as he had now become, said, 'May I be allowed to reply, my lord?' Mellor said, 'Eh?' The Claimant varied his request, 'May I be allowed to say a few words?' Cockburn said sternly, 'No'. The Claimant then shook hands with Kenealy, who said, 'Goodbye, Sir Roger, I am sorry for you', which made a further black mark against Kenealy, and the prisoner was led out of the court while judges and jury exchanged mutual expressions of esteem.

DOUGLAS WOODRUFF, *The Tichborne Claimant: A Victorian Mystery*, 1957

MAD LUCK!

Having concealed himself in a redundant ice-box, Dr R. H. Hales, a 53-year-old criminal psychopath from 'Byeways' (Indiana State's biggest lunatic asylum) escaped and, two days later, presented himself to the Appointments Board of 'Whitehill' (Indiana State's biggest penitentiary) as a potential Senior Medical Advisor.

'Dr Hales gave a brilliant interview,' said Mrs Waram Fulger, the Appointment Board's Chairman. 'We gave him the job at a salary of $35,000 a year.'

Dr Hales remained in his position until his photograph appeared in a local paper.

Daily Mail, 16 July 1975, in CHRISTOPHER LOGUE, *Bumper Book of True Stories*, 1980

An elderly man of remarkably hard features and forbidding aspect, and so low in stature as to be quite a dwarf, though his head and face were large enough for the body of a giant. His black eyes were restless, sly, and cunning; his mouth and chin bristly with the stubble of a coarse hard beard; and his complexion was one of that kind which never looks clean or wholesome. But what added most to the grotesque expression of his face was a ghastly smile, which, appearing to be the mere result of habit, and to have no connection with any mirthful or complacent feeling, constantly revealed the few discoloured fangs that were yet scattered in his mouth, and gave him the aspect of a panting dog. His dress consisted of a large high-crowned hat, a worn dark suit, a pair of capacious shoes, and a dirty white neckerchief sufficiently limp and crumpled to disclose the greater portion of his wiry throat. Such hair as he had was of a grizzled black, cut short and straight upon his temples, and hanging in a frowsy fringe about his ears. His hands, which were of a rough, coarse grain, were very dirty; his finger-nails were crooked, long, and yellow. . . .

Mr Quilp could scarcely be said to be of any particular trade or calling, though his pursuits were diversified and his occupations numerous. He collected the rents of whole colonies of filthy streets and alleys by the water-side, advanced money to the seamen and petty officers of merchant-vessels, had a share in the ventures of divers mates of East-Indiamen, smoked his smuggled cigars under the very nose of the Custom-house, and made appointments on 'Change with men in glazed hats and round jackets pretty well every day.

CHARLES DICKENS, *The Old Curiosity Shop*, 1840–1

One morning about day-break, I found a canoe and crossed over a chute to the main shore—it was only two hundred yards—and paddled about a mile up a crick amongst the cypress woods, to see if I couldn't get some berries. Just as I was passing a place where a kind of a cow-path crossed the crick, here comes a couple of men tearing up the path as tight as they could foot it. I thought I was a goner, for whenever anybody was after anybody I judged it was *me*—or maybe Jim. I was about to dig out from there in a hurry, but they was pretty close to me then, and sung out and begged me to save their lives—said they hadn't been doing nothing, and was being chased for it—said there was men and dogs a-coming. They wanted to jump right in, but I says—

'Don't you do it. I don't hear the dogs and horses yet; you've got time to crowd through the brush and get up the crick a little ways; then you take to the water and wade down to me and get in—that'll throw the dogs off the scent.'

They done it, and soon as they was aboard I lit out for our tow-head, and in about five or ten minutes we heard the dogs and the men away off, shouting. We heard them come along towards the crick, but couldn't see them; they seemed to stop and fool around a while; then, as we got further and further away all the time, we couldn't hardly hear them at all; by the time we had left a mile of woods behind us and struck the river, everything was quiet, and we paddled over to the tow-head and hid in the cotton-woods and was safe.

One of these fellows was about seventy, or upwards, and had a bald head and very gray whiskers. He had an old battered-up slouch hat on, and greasy blue woolen shirt, and ragged old blue jeans britches stuffed into his boot tops, and home-knit galluses—no, he only had one. He had an old long-tailed blue jeans coat with slick brass buttons, flung over his arm, and both of them had big fat ratty-looking carpet-bags.

The other fellow was about thirty and dressed about as ornery. After breakfast we all laid off and talked, and the first thing that come out was that these chaps didn't know one another.

'What got you into trouble?' says the baldhead to t'other chap.

'Well, I'd been selling an article to take the tartar off the teeth—and it does take it off, too, and generly the enamel along with it—but I staid about one night longer than I ought to, and was just in the act of sliding out when I ran across you on the trail this side of town, and you told me they were coming, and begged me to help you to get off. So I told you I was expecting trouble myself and would scatter out *with* you. That's the whole yarn—what's yourn?'

'Well, I'd ben a-runnin' a little temperance revival thar, 'bout a week, and was the pet of the women-folks, big and little, for I was makin' it mighty warm for the rummies, I *tell* you, and takin' as much as five or six dollars a night—ten cents a head, children and niggers free—and business a growin' all the time; when somehow or another a little report got around, last night, that I had a way of puttin' in my time with a private jug, on the sly. A nigger rousted me out this mornin', and told me the people was getherin' on the quiet, with their dogs and horses, and they'd be along pretty soon and give me 'bout half an hour's start, and then run me down, if they could; and if they got me they'd tar and feather me and ride me on a rail, sure. I didn't wait for no breakfast—I warn't hungry.'

'Old man,' says the young one, 'I reckon we might double-team it together; what do you think?'

'I ain't undisposed. What's your line—mainly?'

'Jour printer, by trade; do a little in patent medicines; theatre-actor—tragedy, you know; take a turn at mesmerism and phrenology when there's a chance; teach singing-geography school for a change; sling a lecture, sometimes—oh, I do lots of things—most anything that comes handy, so it ain't work. What's your lay?'

'I've done considerable in the doctoring way in my time. Laying' on o' hands is my best holt—for cancer, and paralysis, and sich things; and I k'n tell a fortune pretty good, when I've got somebody along to find out the facts for me. Preachin's my line, too; and workin' camp-meetin's; and missionaryin' around.'

Nobody never said anything for a while; then the young man hove a sigh and says—

'Alas!'

'What're you alassin' about?' says the baldhead.

'To think I should have lived to be leading such a life, and be degraded down into such company.' And he begun to wipe the corner of his eye with a rag.

'Dern your skin, ain't the company good enough for you?' says the baldhead, pretty pert and uppish.

'Yes, it *is* good enough for me; it's as good as I deserve; for who fetched me so low, when I was so high? *I* did myself. I don't blame *you*, gentlemen—far from it; I don't blame anybody. I deserve it all. Let the cold world do its worst; one thing I know—there's a grave somewhere for me. The world may go on just as it's always done, and take everything from me—loved ones, property, everything—but it can't take that. Some day I'll lie down in it and forget it all, and my poor broken heart will be at rest.' He went on a-wiping.

'Drot your pore broken heart,' says the baldhead; 'what are you heaving your pore broken heart at *us* f'r? *We* hain't done nothing.'

'No, I know you haven't. I ain't blaming you, gentlemen. I brought myself down—yes, I did it myself. It's right I should suffer—perfectly right—I don't make any moan.'

'Brought you down from whar? Whar was you brought down from?'

'Ah, you would not believe me; the world never believes—let it pass—'tis no matter. The secret of my birth—'

'The secret of your birth? Do you mean to say—'

'Gentlemen,' says the young man, very solemn, 'I will reveal it to you, for I feel I may have confidence in you. By rights I am a duke!'

Jim's eyes bugged out when he heard that; and I reckon mine did, too. Then the baldhead says: 'No! you can't mean it?'

'Yes. My great-grandfather, eldest son of the Duke of Bridgewater, fled to this country about the end of the last century, to breathe the pure air of freedom; married here, and died, leaving a son, his own father dying about the same time. The second son of the late duke seized the title and estates—the infant real duke was ignored. I am the lineal descendant of that infant—I am the rightful Duke of Bridgewater; and here am I, forlorn, torn from my high estate, hunted of men, despised by the cold world, ragged, worn, heart-broken, and degraded to the companionship of felons on a raft!'

Jim pitied him ever so much, and so did I. We tried to comfort him, but he said it warn't much use, he couldn't be much comforted; said if we was a mind to acknowledge him, that would do him more good than most anything else; so we said we would, if he would tell us how. He said we ought to bow, when we spoke to him, and say 'Your Grace,' or 'My Lord,' or 'Your Lordship'—and he wouldn't mind if it we called him plain 'Bridgewater,' which he said was a title, anyway, and not a name; and one of us ought to wait on him at dinner, and do any little thing for him he wanted done.

Well, that was all easy, so we done it. All through dinner Jim stood around and waited on him, and says, 'Will yo' Grace have some o' dis, or some o' dat?' and so on, and a body could see it was mighty pleasing to him.

But the old man got pretty silent, by-and-by—didn't have much to say, and didn't look pretty comfortable over all that petting that was going on around that duke. He seemed to have something on his mind. So, along in the afternoon, he says:

'Looky here, Bilgewater,' he says, 'I'm nation sorry for you, but you ain't the only person that's had troubles like that.'

'No?'

'No, you ain't. You ain't the only person that's ben snaked down wrongfully out'n a high place.'

'Alas!'

'No, you ain't the only person that's had a secret of his birth.' And by jing, *he* begins to cry.

'Hold! What do you mean?'

'Bilgewater, kin I trust you?' says the old man, still sort of sobbing.

'To the bitter death!' He took the old man by the hand and squeezed it, and says, 'The secret of your being: speak!'

'Bilgewater, I am the late Dauphin!'

You bet you Jim and me stared, this time. Then the duke says:

'You are what?'

'Yes, my friend, it is too true—your eyes is lookin' at this very moment on the pore disappeared Dauphin, Looy the Seventeen, son of Looy the Sixteen and Marry Antonette.'

'You! At your age! No! You mean you're the late Charlemagne; you must be six or seven hundred years old, at the very least.'

'Trouble has done it, Bilgewater, trouble has done it; trouble has brung these gray hairs and this premature balditude. Yes, gentlemen, you see before you, in blue jeans and misery, the wanderin', exiled, trampled-on and sufferin' rightful King of France.'

MARK TWAIN, *Huckleberry Finn*, 1885

Probably the most efficient method ever devised by confidence men to 'blow the mark off,' i.e., to get rid of a victim after fleecing him is the use of a 'cackle-bladder.' The victim is lured into a supposedly sure thing such as betting on what he is assured to be a fixed horse race. He is steered to a phony betting parlor where everyone is an actor playing a role, from the supposed tellers to the bettors winning and losing fortunes. Naturally, the horse he bets on loses, but before the mark can remonstrate another supposed loser, who is actually in on the scheme, turns on the con man playing the role of the chief conspirator. He screams he has been ruined, pulls a gun and shoots the con man dead. There seems no doubt the man is dead as blood literally gushes from his mouth. Everyone starts to scatter, and so does the bilked victim. Not only has he lost his money, but even worse, he's now involved in a homicide. Sometimes the supposed murderer will flee with the mark, even conning the sucker into leaving the city with him. Eventually, of course, the mark decides he is better off to part company with a man who has committed murder and who could now drag him into prison as an accessory.

This type of scam is made convincing through the use of a cackle-bladder, a tiny bag of chicken blood concealed in the mouth and bitten open at the appropriate moment. The gimmick was also used in the last century at fixed running races and boxing matches as well, where the 'sure thing' runner or boxer the sucker had bet on seemed to drop dead. Since gambling on such races or fights was illegal and all the bettors were therefore liable to imprisonment, everyone, including the gullible victims, fled when the faking runner or boxer dropped.

While the cackle-bladder is only used on rare occasions in contemporary confidence games, it remains a favorite with insurance accident fakers, who use the dramatic spurt of blood to convince witnesses that they have really been injured.

CARL SIFAKIS, *The Encyclopaedia of American Crime*, 1982

Mr Horatio Bottomley, the editor of *John Bull*, was a national figure who had talked himself out of trouble time and time again. In 1922 he was charged with fraudulently converting to his own use the funds of a club he had started in connection with the Government's Victory Loan. His case was hopeless, but he addressed the jury with spirit. 'You have got to find that I had the intention to steal the money of poor devils, such as ex-soldiers, who subscribed to the club. You have got to find that Horatio Bottomley, editor of *John Bull*, Member of Parliament, the man who wrote and spoke throughout the war with the sole object of inspiring the troops and keeping up the morale of the country, who went out to the front to do his best to cheer the lads —you have got to find that the man intended to steal their money. God forbid! God forbid.'

He was convicted and sentenced to seven years' imprisonment, the judge commenting on his 'callous effrontery'.

BOTTOMLEY. I was under the impression that it is put to an accused person, 'Have you anything to say before sentence is passed?'

JUDGE. It is not customary in the case of a misdemeanour like fraudulent conversion.

BOTTOMLEY. Had it been so, My Lord, I would have had something rather offensive to say about your summing-up.

JUDGE STEPHEN TUMIN, *Great Legal Disasters*, 1983

Semi-private inducement
Said Mr RothSchild, hell knows which Roth-schild
1861, '64 or there sometime, 'Very few people
'will understand this. Those who do will be occupied
'getting profits. The general public will probably not
'see it's against their interest.'
Seventeen years on the case; here
Gents, is/are the confession.
'Can we take this into court?
'Will any jury convict on this evidence?
1694 anno domini, on through the ages of usury
On, right on, into hair-cloth, right on into rotten building,
Right on into London houses, ground rents, foetid brick work,
Will any jury convict 'um? The Foundation of Regius Professors
Was made to spread lies and teach Whiggery, will any
JURY convict 'um?
The Macmillan Commission about two hundred and forty years
LATE
with great difficulty got back to Paterson's:
The bank makes it *ex nihil*,
Denied by five thousand professors, will any
Jury convict 'um? This case, and with it

the first part, draws to a conclusion,
of the first phase of this opus, Mr Marx, Karl, did not
foresee this conclusion, you have seen a good deal of
the evidence, not knowing it evidence, si monumentum
look about you, look, if you can, at St Peters
Look at the Manchester slums, look at Brazilian coffee
or Chilean nitrates. This case is the first case
Si requieres monumentum?
This case is not the last case or the whole case, we ask a
REVISION, we ask for enlightenment in a case
moving concurrent, but this case is the first case:
Bank creates it ex nihil. Creates it to meet a need,
Hic est hyper-usura. Mr Jefferson met it:
No man hath natural right to exercise profession
of lender, save him who hath it to lend.
Replevin, estopple, what wangle which wangle, VanBuren met it.
Before that was tea dumped into harbour, before that was a
great deal still in the school books, placed there
NOT as evidence. Placed there to distract idle minds,
Murder, starvation and bloodshed, seventy four red revolutions
Ten empires fell on this grease spot.
'I rule the Earth' said Antonius 'but LAW rules the sea'
meaning, we take it, lex Rhodi, the Law Maritime
of sea lawyers.
usura and sea insurance
wherefrom no State was erected greater than Athens.

EZRA POUND (1885–1972), *from* Canto XLVI

LORD BARRENSTOCK

Lord Barrenstock and Epicene,
What's it to me that you have been
In your pursuit of interdicted joys
Seducer of a hundred little boys?

Your sins are red about your head
And many people wish you dead.

You trod the widow in the mire
Wronged the son, deceived the sire.

CON MEN

You put a fence about the land
And made the people's cattle graze on sand.

Ratted from many a pool and forced amalgamation
And dealt in shares which never had a stock exchange
quotation.

Non flocci facio, I do not care
For wrongs you made the other fellow bear:
'Tis not for these unsocial acts not these
I wet my pen. I would not have you tease,
With a repentance smug and overdue
For all the things you still desire to do,
The ears of an outraged divinity:
But oh your tie is crooked and I see
Too plain you had an éclair for your tea.

It is this nonchalance about your person—
That is the root of my profound aversion.

You are too fat. In spite of stays
Your shape is painful to the polished gaze;
Your uncombed hair grows thin and daily thinner,
In fact you're far too ugly to be such a sinner.

Lord Barrenstock and Epicene, consider all that you
have done
Lord Epicene and Barrenstock, yet not two Lords but
one,
I think you are an object not of fear but pity
Be good, my Lord, since you can not be pretty.

STEVIE SMITH (1902–71)

† *The Northern Irish author—or authoress, as she preferred it—Amanda McKittrick Ros achieved fame as the world's worst novelist and attracted a cult following in the early part of the twentieth century. In her third and last novel* Helen Huddleson *(published thirty years after her death in 1939), she manages to get in an attack on one of her two* bêtes noires, *lawyers (the other profession which she detested equally was that of literary critic).*

They now stood in the hall. It ran directly from front to rear where a glass door opened into a well-appointed conservatory banked with bloom, scenting the house with a delicious perfume whither art would stand gulled. The walls were of polished mahogany, the doors on every side of the same wood panelled with mirrors, the handles and finger-plates of solid silver beautifully polished.

Above each door right in the centre were heads representing so many human characters, fashioned from the commonest coarsest timber which grew in a hungry uncared-for tract of land not far distant.

Each head differed slightly in shape, just as lawyers' heads do, each face seemed ugly to Helen and dissimilarly featured as that common gang to which such usually belong. Most prominent of all was the bull-dog expression that leered from their dog-shaped visages, plus that brand of tyranny always lurking round where an honest modesty should exhibit itself.

So naturally carved were they as to impress one with the fact that they were so many eavesdroppers peering above the doors of their respective rooms to try and catch some tidings from the lips of any visitors who perchance entered this quaint reserved area. There was a strong impression that something radically righteous instilled one to abhor this cabal of rustic heads—viewed from any standpoint.

'Do these heads represent people whom you know?' queried Helen, looking towards his lips for a reply from which the words slowly slid.

'Surely, surely. I knew them all some years ago when Helen Huddleson and I were in the heyday of our happiness. They represent liars, in other words lawyers, for they are all liars. I've found them so, without as much as *one solitary exception*. The most abominable trait in the human character is lying, be that character prince or pauper, lord or layman, clergyman or cowboy, viscount or vagrant.'

Helen was silent as he went on.

'Yes, yes, give me poverty, starvation, trial or torture in all their horrible aspects, but a liar I can't tolerate, consequently I detest lawyers, for as I have said they are all liars, liars—Ah, God, yes.'

'If so,' Helen asked, 'why have you their heads arranged around these pretty walls? They spoil the effect of an apartment where refinement reigns.'

She waited to hear his reply with a certain amount of sang-froid. Smiling benignly on her, he resumed.

'You have surely dissected my theory to perfection. My chief and only reason for having these heads here is to draw comment. Never a soul enters this hall in my presence but halts to enquire about these vulgar looking vipers with a past.'

So saying they entered the study.

'I well know,' he continued, 'the effect here is lowered limitlessly because of these rustic rascalities.'

The study was a beautiful room to the left, its walls studded with bookshelves filled with all manner of literature, Agra Raymond's works claiming more space and rank than any other individual's writings.

'Do you admire Agra Raymond's works?' he interrogated.

'I love them,' replied Helen Potter, clapping her hands eagerly.

He took a volume from a shelf.

'Have you read "Barney Bloater, KC" by this eminent author?'

'No,' Helen Potter admitted.

'She writes chiefly about lawyers,' said Maurice Munro, 'whipping them severely with the lash of truth, never ceasing to scourge them with the force of its thong.'

AMANDA MCKITTRICK ROS, *Helen Huddleson*, 1969

GREEK MYTHOLOGY

Charged with a $42 million social security fraud, 153 Australian Greeks, plus their wives, their children and their lawyers assembled in a Sydney court only to be informed that the team of prosecutors had asked for a further year's adjournment because the police had been unable to sort out which of the accused was which.

Prior to the adjournment being granted, Mr Clive Evatt QC rose to his feet and admitted that he could not pronounce his client's name. Several women shouted the client's name out, one of them adding, 'He committed suicide six months ago!'

During the pandemonium that followed this announcement, Mr

Walter George and Miss Erika Clooney, both solicitors, found they had been briefed to defend the same man and, harangued by a group of the accused, began to fight each other for the papers.

Leaping into the well of the court, another man, who identified himself as 'Achilles X', floored Mr George and held Miss Clooney's hand aloft, shouting, 'This is the one for me!'

When things had calmed down, Miss Clooney said she had never seen the man before although she 'had known him well for over a year'.

'I would have done my best to get the trial under way,' said Judge Griffin. 'However, among the accused we found a Mrs Chong Wah Wong-Diamantopoulos who admitted that her husband was among the crowd but was unable to identify him at short notice.'

Age, 13 June 1978, in CHRISTOPHER LOGUE, *Bumper Book of True Stories*, 1980.

[*Jacinta Condor flying first class*.]

JACINTA. Flight to England that little grey island in the clouds where governments don't fall overnight and children don't sell themselves in the street and my money is safe. I'll buy a raincoat, I'll meet Jake Todd, I'll stay at the Savoy by a stream they call a river with its Bloody Tower and dead queens, a river is too wide to bridge. The unfinished bridge across the canyon where the road ends in the air, waiting for dollars. The office blocks Father started, imagining glass, leather, green screens, the city rising high into the sky, but the towers stopped short, cement, wires, the city spreading wider instead with a blur of shacks, miners coming down from the mountains as the mines close. The International Tin Council, what a scandal, thank God I wasn't in tin, the price of copper ruined by the frozen exchange rate, the two rates, and the government will not let us mining companies exchange enough dollars at the better rate, they insist we help the country in this crisis, I do not want to help, I want to be rich, I close my mines and sell my copper on the London Metal Exchange. It is all because of the debt that will never be paid because we have to borrow more and more to pay the interest on the money that came from oil when OPEC had too much money and your western banks wanted to lend it to us because who else would pay such high interest, needing it so badly? Father got his hands on enough of it but what happened, massive inflation, lucky he'd put the money somewhere safe, the Swiss mountains so white from the air like our mountains but the people rich with cattle and clocks and secrets, the American plains yellow with wheat, the green English fields where lords still live in grey stone, all with such safe banks and good bonds and exciting gambles, so as soon as any dollars or pounds come, don't let them go into our mines or our coffee or look for a sea of oil under the jungle, no get it out quickly to the western banks (a little money in cocaine, that's different). Peru leads the way resisting the IMF, refusing to pay the interest, but I don't want to make things difficult for the banks, I prefer to support them, why should my money stay in Peru and suffer? The official closing price yesterday for grade A copper was 878–8.5, three months 900.5–1, final kerb close 901–2. Why bother to send aid so many miles, put it straight into my Eurobonds.

[*Meanwhile the London metal exchange starts quietly trading copper. When Jacinta finishes speaking the trading reaches its noisy climax.*

ZAC. There's some enterprising guys around and here's an example.
You know how if you want to get a job in the States you have to give a urine sample?
(this is to show you're not on drugs.)
There's a company now for a fifty dollar fee
They'll provide you with a guaranteed pure, donated by a churchgoer, bottle of pee.
(They also plan to market it dehydrated in a packet and you just add water.)
And Aids is making advertisers perplexed
Because it's no longer too good to have your product associated with sex.
But it's a greater marketing opportunity.
Like the guys opening up blood banks where you pay to store your own blood in case of an accident and so be guaranteed immunity.
(It's also a great time to buy into rubber.)
Anyone who can buy oranges for ten and sell at eleven in a souk or bazaar
Has the same human nature and can go equally far.

The so-called third-world doesn't want our charity or aid.
All they need is the chance to sit down in front of some green screens and trade.
(They don't have the money, sure, but just so long as they have freedom from communism so they can do it when they do have the money.)
Pictures of starving babies are misleading and patronizing.
Because there's plenty of rich people in those countries, it's just the masses that's poor, and Jacinta Condor flew into London and was quite enterprising.
It was the day before Jake Todd was found dead
And the deal was really coming to a head.
Jake was helping us find punters because anyone with too much money and Jake would know them.
You'd just say, Jake, who's in town, what have you got, and he'd bring them in and show them.

CARYL CHURCHILL, *Serious Money*, 1987

VII

HYPOCRITES

THEY that have power to hurt and will do none,
That do not do the thing they most do show,
Who, moving others, are themselves as stone,
Unmov'd, cold, and to temptation slow;
They rightly do inherit heaven's graces,
And husband nature's riches from expense;
They are the lords and owners of their faces,
Others but stewards of their excellence.
The summer's flower is to the summer sweet,
Though to itself it only live and die;
But if that flower with base infection meet,
The basest weed outbraves his dignity:
For sweetest things turn sourest by their deeds;
Lilies that fester smell far worse than weeds.

WILLIAM SHAKESPEARE, Sonnet 94, pub. 1609

SUSANNA AND THE ELDERS

Once, while they were watching for an opportune day, she went in as before with only two maids, and wished to bathe in the garden, for it was very hot. And no one was there except the two elders, who had hid themselves and were watching her. She said to her maids, 'Bring me oil and ointments, and shut the garden doors so that I may bathe.' They did as she said, shut the garden doors, and went out by the side doors to bring what they had been commanded; and they did not see the elders, because they were hidden.

When the maids had gone out, the two elders rose and ran to her, and said: 'Look, the garden doors are shut, no one sees us, and we are in love with you; so give your consent, and lie with us. If you refuse, we will testify against you that a young man was with you, and this was why you sent your maids away.'

Susanna sighed deeply, and said, 'I am hemmed in on every side. For if I do this thing, it is death for me; and if I do not, I shall not escape your hands. I choose not to do it and to fall into your hands, rather than to sin in the sight of the Lord.'

Then Susanna cried out with a loud voice, and the two elders shouted against her. And one of them ran and opened the garden doors. When the household servants heard the shouting in the garden, they rushed in at the side door to see what had happened to her. And when the elders told their tale, the servants were greatly ashamed, for nothing like this had ever been said about Susanna.

The next day, when the people gathered at the house of her husband Joakim, the two elders came, full of their wicked plot to have Susanna put to death. They said before the people, 'Send for Susanna, the daughter of Hilkiah, who is the wife of Joakim.' So they sent for her. And she came, with her parents, her children, and all her kindred.

Now Susanna was a woman of great refinement, and beautiful in appearance. As she was veiled, the wicked men ordered her to be unveiled, that they might feast upon her beauty. But her family and friends and all who saw her wept.

Then the two elders stood up in the midst of the people, and laid their hands upon her head. And she, weeping, looked up toward heaven, for her heart trusted in the Lord. The elders said, 'As we were walking in the garden alone, this woman came in with two maids, shut the garden doors, and dismissed the maids. Then a young man who had been hidden, came to her and lay with her. We were in a corner of the garden, and when we saw this wickedness we ran to them. We saw them embracing, but we could not hold the man, for he was too strong for us, and he opened the doors and dashed out. So we seized this woman and asked her who the young man was, but she would not tell us. These things we testify!'

The assembly believed them, because they were elders of the people and judges; and they condemned her to death.

Then Susanna cried out with a loud voice, and said, 'O eternal God, who dost discern what is secret, who art aware of all things before they come to be, thou knowest that these men have borne false witness against me. And now I am to die! Yet I have done none of the things that they have wickedly invented against me!'

The Lord heard her cry. And as she was being led away to be put to death, God aroused the holy spirit of a young lad named Daniel; and he cried with a loud voice, 'I am innocent of the blood of this woman.'

All the people turned to him, and said, 'What is this that you have said?' Taking his stand in the midst of them, he said, 'Are you such fools, you sons of Israel? Have you condemned a daughter of Israel without examination and without learning the facts? Return to the place of judgment. For these men have borne false witness against her.'

Then all the people returned in haste. And the elders said to him, 'Come, sit among us and inform us, for God has given you that right.' And Daniel said to them, 'Separate them far from each other, and I will examine them.'

When they were separated from each other, he summoned one of them and said to him, 'You old relic of wicked days, your sins have now come home, which you have committed in the past, pronouncing unjust judgments, condemning the innocent and letting the guilty go free, though the Lord said, "Do not put to death an innocent and righteous person." Now then, if you really saw her, tell me this: Under what tree did you see them being intimate with each other?' He answered, 'Under a mastic tree.' And Daniel said, 'Very well! You have lied against your own head, for the angel of God has received the sentence from God and will immediately cut you in two.'

Then he put him aside, and commanded them to bring the other. And he said to him, 'You offspring of Canaan and not of Judah, beauty has deceived you and lust has perverted your heart. This is how you both have been dealing with the daughters of Israel, and they were intimate with you through fear; but a daughter of Judah would not endure your wickedness. Now then, tell me: Under what tree did you catch them being intimate with each other?' He answered, 'Under an evergreen oak.' And Daniel said to him, 'Very well! You also have lied against your own head, for the angel of God is waiting with his sword to saw you in two, that he may destroy you both.'

Then all the assembly shouted loudly and blessed God, who saves whose who hope in him. And they rose against the two elders, for out of their own mouths Daniel had convicted them of bearing false witness; and they did to them as they had wickedly planned to do to their neighbour; acting in accordance with the law of Moses, they put them to death. Thus innocent blood was saved that day.

And Hilkiah and his wife praised God for their daughter Susanna, and so did Joakim her husband and all her kindred, because nothing shameful was found in her. And from that day onward Daniel had a great reputation among the people.

Daniel 13

† *Angelo tries to bargain with Isabella: her brother's life in exchange for her virginity.*

ISABELLA. . . . most pernicious purpose!—Seeming, seeming!—
I will proclaim thee, Angelo; look for 't:
Sign me a present pardon for my brother,
Or with an outstretch'd throat I'll tell the world
Aloud what man thou art.

ANGELO. Who will believe thee, Isabel?
My unsoil'd name, th' austereness of my life,
My vouch against you, and my place i' the state,
Will so your accusation overweigh,
That you shall stifle in your own report,
And smell of calumny. I have begun;
And now I give my sensual race the rein:
Fit thy consent to my sharp appetite;
Lay by all nicety and prolixious blushes,
That banish what they sue for; redeem thy brother
By yielding up thy body to my will;
Or else he must not only die the death,
But thy unkindness shall his death draw out
To lingering sufferance. Answer me to-morrow,
Or, by the affection that now guides me most,
I'll prove a tyrant to him. As for you,
Say what you can, my false o'erweighs your true.

WILLIAM SHAKESPEARE, *Measure for Measure*, 1604

† *Tartuffe, by pretending to be painfully and rigorously devout has gained complete control over Orgon, whose wife he tries to seduce. When Orgon's son Damis tells his father about this unchristian behaviour Tartuffe defends himself with hypocritical skill.*

ORGON. Oh Heavens! Can what they say be true?

TARTUFFE. Yes, brother, I am a guilty wretch, a miserable sinner steeped in iniquity, the greatest villain that ever existed; not a moment of my life but is sullied with some foul deed: it's a succession of wickedness and corruption. I see now that Heaven is taking this opportunity of chastising me for my sins. Whatever crime

I may be charged with, far be it from me to take pride in denying it! Believe what they tell you. Set no bounds to your resentment! Hound me like a felon from your doors! Whatever shame is heaped upon me I shall have deserved much more.

ORGON [*to his son*]. Ah! Miscreant! How dare you seek to tarnish his unspotted virtue with this false accusation?

DAMIS. What! Can a pretence of meekness from this hypocrite make you deny . . .

ORGON. Silence! You accused plague!

TARTUFFE. Ah, let him speak. You do wrong to accuse him. You would do better to believe what he tells you. Why should you take such a favourable view of me? After all, do you know what I am capable of? Why should you trust appearances? Do you think well of me because of what I seem to be? No, no, you are letting yourself be deceived by outward show. I am, alas, no better than they think; everyone takes me for a good man but the truth is I'm good for nothing. [*Speaking to Damis*] Yes, my son, speak freely, call me deceitful, infamous, abandoned, thief, murderer, load me with names yet more detestable, I'll not deny them. I've deserved them all, and on my knees I'll suffer the ignominy, in expiation of my shameful life.

ORGON [*to Tartuffe*]. Brother, this is too much. [*To his son*] Doesn't your heart relent, you dog!

DAMIS. What! Can what he says so far prevail with you that . . .

ORGON [*raising up Tartuffe*]. Silence you scoundrel! [*To Tartuffe*] Rise brother—I beg you. [*To his son*] You scoundrel!

DAMIS. He may—

ORGON. Silence!

DAMIS. This is beyond bearing! What! I'm to . . .

ORGON. Say another word and I'll break every bone in your body!

TARTUFFE. In God's name, brother, calm yourself. I would rather suffer any punishment than he should receive the slightest scratch on my account.

ORGON [*to his son*]. Ungrateful wretch!

TARTUFFE. Leave him in peace! If need be, I'll ask your pardon for him on my knees . . .

ORGON [*to Tartuffe*]. Alas! What are you thinking of? [*To his son*] See how good he is to you, you dog!

DAMIS. Then . . .

ORGON. Enough!

DAMIS. What! Can't I . . .

ORGON. Enough, I say! I know too well why you attack him. You hate him. Every one of you, wife, children, servants, all are in full cry against him. You use every impudent means to drive this devout and holy person from my house: but the more you strive to banish him the more determined I am not to let him go. I'll hasten his marriage with my daughter and confound the pride of the whole family.

MOLIÈRE, *Tartuffe*, 1664, trans. John Wood

† *In the 'Prologue to the Satires' Pope addresses Dr Arbuthnot on the follies of their times and contemporaries.*

Let Sporus tremble—*A*. What? that thing of silk,
Sporus, that mere white curd of ass's milk?
Satire or sense, alas! can Sporus feel,
Who breaks a butterfly upon a wheel?
P. Yet let me flap this bug with gilded wings,
This painted child of dirt, that stinks and stings;
Whose buzz the witty and the fair annoys,
Yet wit ne'er tastes, and beauty ne'er enjoys:
So well-bred spaniels civilly delight
In mumbling of the game they dare not bite.
Eternal smiles his emptiness betray,
As shallow streams run dimpling all the way.
Whether in florid impotence he speaks,
And, as the prompter breathes, the puppet squeaks;
Or at the ear of Eve, familiar toad!
Half froth, half venom, spits himself abroad,
In puns, or politics, or tales, or lies,
Or spite, or smut, or rhymes, or blasphemies.
His wit all see-saw, between that and this,
Now high, now low, now master up, now miss,
And he himself one vile antithesis.
Amphibious thing! that acting either part,
The trifling head, or the corrupted heart;
Fop at the toilet, flatterer at the board,
Now trips a lady, and now struts a lord.
Eve's tempter thus the Rabbins have express'd,

A cherub's face, a reptile all the rest.
Beauty that shocks you, parts that none will trust,
Wit that can creep, and pride that licks the dust.

ALEXANDER POPE, from 'Prologue to the Satires', 1734

† *Sir Oliver tests the character of his hypocritical nephew Joseph Surface by appearing as 'Mr Stanley'.*

Re-enter Joseph Surface.

JOSEPH SURFACE. Sir, I beg you ten thousand pardons for keeping you a moment waiting.—Mr Stanley, I presume.

SIR OLIVER. At your service.

JOSEPH SURFACE. Sir, I beg you will do me the honour to sit down —I entreat you, sir.

SIR OLIVER. Dear sir—there's no occasion.—[*Aside*.] Too civil by half!

JOSEPH SURFACE. I have not the pleasure of knowing you, Mr Stanley; but I am extremely happy to see you look so well. You were nearly related to my mother, I think, Mr Stanley?

SIR OLIVER. I was, sir; so nearly that my present poverty, I fear, may do discredit to her wealthy children, else I should not have presumed to trouble you.

JOSEPH SURFACE. Dear sir, there needs no apology;—he that is in distress, though a stranger, has a right to claim kindred with the wealthy. I am sure I wish I was one of that class, and had it in my power to offer you even a small relief.

SIR OLIVER. If your uncle, Sir Oliver, were here, I should have a friend.

JOSEPH SURFACE. I wish he was, sir, with all my heart: you should not want an advocate with him, believe me, sir.

SIR OLIVER. I should not need one—my distresses would recommend me. But I imagined his bounty would enable you to become the agent of his charity.

JOSEPH SURFACE. My dear sir, you were strangely misinformed. Sir Oliver is a worthy man, a very worthy man; but avarice, Mr Stanley, is the vice of age. I will tell you, my good sir, in confidence, what he has done for me has been a mere nothing; though people, I know, have thought otherwise, and, for my part, I never chose to contradict the report.

SIR OLIVER. What! has he never transmitted you bullion—rupees—pagodas?

JOSEPH SURFACE. Oh, dear sir, nothing of the kind! No, no; a few presents now and then—china, shawls, congou tea, avadavats, and Indian crackers—little more, believe me.

SIR OLIVER. Here's gratitude for twelve thousand pounds!—Avadavats and Indian crackers! [*Aside*.

JOSEPH SURFACE. Then, my dear sir, you have heard, I doubt not, of the extravagance of my brother: there are very few would credit what I have done for that unfortunate young man.

SIR OLIVER. Not I, for one! [*Aside*.

JOSEPH SURFACE. The sums I have lent him! Indeed I have been exceedingly to blame; it was an amiable weakness; however, I don't pretend to defend it—and now I feel it doubly culpable, since it has deprived me of the pleasure of serving you, Mr Stanley, as my heart dictates.

SIR OLIVER [*aside*]. Dissembler!—[*Aloud*.] Then, sir, you can't assist me?

JOSEPH SURFACE. At present, it grieves me to say, I cannot; but, whenever I have the ability, you may depend upon hearing from me.

SIR OLIVER. I am extremely sorry—

JOSEPH SURFACE. Not more than I, believe me; to pity, without the power to relieve, is still more painful than to ask and be denied.

SIR OLIVER. Kind sir, your most obedient humble servant.

JOSEPH SURFACE. You leave me deeply affected, Mr Stanley.—William, be ready to open the door. [*Calls to Servant*.

SIR OLIVER. Oh, dear sir, no ceremony.

JOSEPH SURFACE. Your very obedient.

SIR OLIVER. Your most obsequious.

JOSEPH SURFACE. You may depend upon hearing from me, whenever I can be of service.

SIR OLIVER. Sweet sir, you are too good!

JOSEPH SURFACE. In the meantime I wish you health and spirits.

SIR OLIVER. Your ever grateful and perpetual humble servant.

JOSEPH SURFACE. Sir, yours as sincerely.

SIR OLIVER [*aside*]. Now I am satisfied. [*Exit*.

JOSEPH SURFACE. This is one bad effect of a good character; it invites application from the unfortunate, and there needs no small degree of address to gain the reputation of benevolence without incurring the expense. The silver ore of pure charity is an expensive article in the catalogue of a man's good qualities; whereas the sentimental French plate I use instead of it makes just as good a show, and pays no tax.

RICHARD BRINSLEY SHERIDAN, *The School for Scandal*, 1777

BYRON ON SOUTHEY

He had written praises of a regicide;
He had written praises of all kings whatever;
He had written for republics far and wide,
And then against them bitterer than ever;
For pantisocracy he once had cried
Aloud—a scheme less moral than 'twas clever;
Then grew a hearty anti-Jacobin—
Had turn'd his coat—and would have turn'd his skin.

He had sung against all battles, and again
In their high praise and glory: he had call'd
Reviewing 'the ungentle craft,' and then
Become as base a critic as e'er crawl'd—
Fed, paid and pamper'd by the very men
By whom his muse and morals had been maul'd:
He had written much blank verse, and blanker prose,
And more of both than anybody knows.

LORD BYRON, from *The Vision of Judgement*, 1822

ON SIR JOSHUA REYNOLDS

Can there be anything more mean,
More malice in disguise,
Than praise a man for doing what
That man does most despise?
Reynolds lectures exactly so
When he praises Michael Angelo.

ON HAYLEY

To forgive enemies H—— does pretend,
Who never in his life forgave a friend,
And when he could not act upon my wife
Hired a villain to bereave my life.

Thy friendship oft has made my heart to ache:
Do be my enemy—for friendship's sake.

WILLIAM BLAKE (1787–1827)

But, seeing a light in the little round office, and immediately feeling myself attracted towards Uriah Heep, who had a sort of fascination for me, I went in there instead. I found Uriah reading a great fat book, with such demonstrative attention, that his lank fore-finger followed up every line as he read, and made clammy tracks along the page (or so I fully believed) like a snail.

'You are working late to-night, Uriah,' says I.

'Yes, Master Copperfield,' says Uriah.

As I was getting on the stool opposite, to talk to him more conveniently, I observed that he had not such a thing as a smile about him, and that he could only widen his mouth and make two hard creases down his cheeks, one on each side, to stand for one.

'I am not doing office-work, Master Copperfield,' said Uriah.

'What work, then?' I asked.

'I am improving my legal knowledge, Master Copperfield,' said Uriah. 'I am going through Tidd's Practice. Oh, what a writer Mr Tidd is, Master Copperfield!'

My stool was such a tower of observation, that as I watched him reading on again, after this rapturous exclamation, and following up the lines with his fore-finger, I observed that his nostrils, which were thin and pointed, with sharp dints in them, had a singular and most uncomfortable way of expanding and contracting themselves; that they seemed to twinkle instead of his eyes, which hardly ever twinkled at all.

'I suppose you are quite a great lawyer?' I said, after looking at him for some time.

'Me, Master Copperfield?' said Uriah. 'Oh, no! I'm a very umble person.'

It was no fancy of mine about his hands, I observed; for he frequently ground the palms against each other as if to squeeze them dry and warm, besides often wiping them, in a stealthy way, on his pocket-handkerchief.

'I am well aware that I am the umblest person going,' said Uriah Heep, modestly; 'let the other be where he may. My mother is likewise a very umble person. We live in a numble abode, Master Copperfield, but have much to be thankful for. My father's former calling was umble. He was a sexton.'

'What is he now?' I asked.

'He is a partaker of glory at present, Master Copperfield,' said Uriah Heep. 'But we have much to be thankful for.'

CHARLES DICKENS, *David Copperfield*, 1849–50

It has been remarked that Mr Pecksniff was a moral man. So he was. Perhaps there never was a more moral man than Mr Pecksniff: especially in his conversation and correspondence. It was once said of him by a homely admirer, that he had a Fortunatus's purse of good sentiments in his inside. In this particular he was like the girl in the fairy tale, except that if they were not actual diamonds which fell from his lips, they were the very brightest paste, and shone prodigiously. He was a most exemplary man: fuller of virtuous precept than a copy-book. Some people likened him to a direction-post, which is always telling the way to a place, and never goes there: but these were his enemies; the shadows cast by his brightness; that was all. His very throat was moral. You saw a good deal of it. You looked over a very low fence of white cravat (whereof no man had ever beheld the tie, for he fastened it behind), and there it lay, a valley between two jutting heights of collar, serene and whiskerless before you. It seemed to say, on the part of Mr Pecksniff, 'There is no deception, ladies and gentlemen, all is peace, a holy calm pervades me.' So did his hair, just grizzled with an iron-grey, which was all brushed off his forehead, and stood bolt upright, or slightly drooped in kindred action with his heavy eyelids. So did his person, which was sleek though free from corpulency. So did his manner, which was soft and oily. In a word, even his plain black suit, and state of widower, and dangling double eye-glass, all tended to the same purpose, and cried aloud, 'Behold the moral Pecksniff!'

CHARLES DICKENS, *Martin Chuzzlewit*, 1843–4

SOLILOQUY OF THE SPANISH CLOISTER

Gr-r-r—there go, my heart's abhorrence!
  Water your damned flower-pots, do!
If hate killed men, Brother Lawrence,
  God's blood, would not mine kill you!
What? your myrtle-bush wants trimming?
  Oh, that rose has prior claims—
Needs its leaden vase filled brimming?
  Hell dry you up with its flames!

At the meal we sit together;
  Salve tibi! I must hear
Wise talk of the kind of weather,
  Sort of season, time of year:
Not a plenteous cork-crop: scarcely
  Dare we hope oak-galls, I doubt;
What's the Latin name for 'parsley'?
  What's the Greek name for Swine's Snout?

Whew! We'll have our platter burnished,
  Laid with care on our own shelf!
With a fire-new spoon we're furnished,
  And a goblet for ourself,
Rinsed like something sacrificial
  Ere 'tis fit to touch our chaps—
Marked with L. for our initial!
  (He-he! There his lily snaps!)

Saint, forsooth! While brown Dolores
  Squats outside the Convent bank
With Sanchicha, telling stories,
  Steeping tresses in the tank,
Blue-black, lustrous, thick like horsehairs,
  —Can't I see his dead eye glow,

Bright as 'twere a Barbary corsair's?
  (That is, if he'd let it show!)

When he finishes refection,
  Knife and fork he never lays
Cross-wise, to my recollection,
  As do I, in Jesu's praise.
I, the Trinity illustrate,
  Drinking watered orange-pulp—
In three sips the Arian frustrate;
  While he drains his at one gulp!

Oh, those melons! If he's able
  We're to have a feast; so nice!
One goes to the Abbot's table,
  All of us get each a slice.
How go on your flowers? None double?
  Not one fruit-sort can you spy?
Strange!—And I, too, at such trouble,
  Keep them close-nipped on the sly!

There's a great text in Galatians,
  Once you trip on it, entails
Twenty-nine distinct damnations,
  One sure, if another fails;
If I trip him just a-dying,
  Sure of heaven as sure can be,
Spin him round and send him flying
  Off to hell, a Manichee?

Or, my scrofulous French novel
  On grey paper with blunt type!
Simply glance at it, you grovel
  Hand and foot in Belial's gripe;
If I double down its pages
  At the woeful sixteenth print,
When he gathers his greengages,
  Ope a sieve and slip it in't?

Or, there's Satan!—one might venture
  Pledge one's soul to him, yet leave

Such a flaw in the indenture
As he'd miss till, past retrieve,
Blasted lay that rose-acacia
We're so proud of! *Hy, Zy, Hine*. . . .
'St, there's Vespers! *Plena gratia*
Ave, Virgo! Gr-r-r—you swine!

ROBERT BROWNING, 1842

† *Trollope's comically obsequious and unpleasant clergyman Mr Slope is a hypocrite and self-seeker.*

He is possessed of more than average abilities, and is of good courage. Though he can stoop to fawn, and stoop low indeed, if need be, he has still within him the power to assume the tyrant; and with the power he has certainly the wish. His acquirements are not of the highest order, but such as they are they are completely under control, and he knows the use of them. He is gifted with a certain kind of pulpit eloquence, not likely indeed to be persuasive with men, but powerful with the softer sex. In his sermons he deals greatly in denunciations, excites the minds of his weaker hearers with a not unpleasant terror, and leaves an impression on their minds that all mankind are in a perilous state, and all womankind too, except those who attend regularly to the evening lectures in Baker Street. His looks and tones are extremely severe, so much so that one cannot but fancy that he regards the greater part of the world as being infinitely too bad for his care. As he walks through the streets, his very face denotes his horror of the world's wickedness; and there is always an anathema lurking in the corner of his eye. . . .

Mr Slope is tall, and not ill made. His feet and hands are large, as has ever been the case with all his family, but he has a broad chest and wide shoulders to carry off these excrescences, and on the whole his figure is good. His countenance, however, is not specially prepossessing. His hair is lank, and of a dull pale reddish hue. It is always formed into three straight lumpy masses, each brushed with admirable precision, and cemented with much grease; two of them adhere closely to the sides of his face, and the other lies at right angles above them. He wears no whiskers, and is always punctiliously shaven. His face is nearly of the same colour as his hair, though perhaps a little redder: it is not unlike beef—beef, however, one would say, of a bad quality.

HYPOCRITES

His forehead is capacious and high, but square and heavy, and unpleasantly shining. His mouth is large, though his lips are thin and bloodless; and his big, prominent, pale brown eyes inspire anything but confidence. His nose, however, is his redeeming feature: it is pronounced straight and well-formed; though I myself should have liked it better did it not possess a somewhat spongy, porous appearance, as though it had been cleverly formed out of a red coloured cork.

I never could endure to shake hands with Mr Slope. A cold, clammy perspiration always exudes from him, the small drops are ever to be seen standing on his brow, and his friendly grasp is unpleasant.

ANTHONY TROLLOPE, *Barchester Towers*, 1857

BASE DETAILS

If I were fierce, and bald, and short of breath,
I'd live with scarlet Majors at the Base,
And speed glum heroes up the line to death.
You'd see me with my puffy petulant face,
Guzzling and gulping in the best hotel,
Reading the Roll of Honour. 'Poor young chap,'
I'd say—'I used to know his father well;
Yes, we've lost heavily in this last scrap.'
And when the war is done and youth stone dead,
I'd toddle safely home and die—in bed.

SIEGFRIED SASSOON (1886–1967)

BALLADE D'UNE GRANDE DAME

Heaven shall forgive you Bridge at dawn,
The clothes you wear—or do not wear—
And Ladies' Leap-frog on the lawn
And dyes and drugs, and *petits verres*.
Your vicious things shall melt in air . . .
. . . But for the Virtuous Things you do,
The Righteous Work, the Public Care,
It shall not be forgiven you.

Because you could not even yawn
When your Committees would prepare
To have the teeth of paupers drawn,
Or strip the slums of Human Hair;
Because a Doctor Otto Maehr
Spoke of 'a segregated few'—
And you sat smiling in your chair—
It shall not be forgiven you.

Though your sins cried to—Father Vaughan,
These desperate you could not spare
Who steal, with nothing left to pawn;
You caged a man up like a bear
For ever in a jailor's care
Because his sins were more than *two* . . .
. . . I know a house in Hoxton where
It shall not be forgiven you.

ENVOI

Princess, you trapped a guileless Mayor
To meet some people that you knew . . .
When the Last Trumpet rends the air
It shall not be forgiven you.

G. K. CHESTERTON, 1914

Rasputin, in his early manhood, appears to have become known as a horse-thief; and this period of his life seems to have been the least discreditable. He never became a priest; nor was he ever a monk, though he spent some time in a monastery and, having a good memory, learned by heart many passages of scripture. He was a libertine who tried to cover his licentious orgies with pietistic cant and religious mysticism. He professed to set great store by confession and claimed that its value was all the greater if there was much to confess. Though only half-educated, he possessed a low cunning and was able to persuade not a few of those who met him to regard him as a *staretz*, that is a holy man. Undoubtedly, he possessed remarkable hypnotic powers, which he exploited in Court circles.

The Czarina had longed for a son, and at last in the year 1904 one was born to her. He was an only son, and on him his parents' hopes were centred, but he suffered from haemophilia, an hereditary disease which is passed to male members of a family through the female line. Thanks to his hypnotic powers, Rasputin, who had been introduced to the Royal Family in 1905, proved himself able to arrest the bleeding when the Court physicians had failed.

Sir Bernard Pares recounted to me the following incident of which he had knowledge. The Imperial family, with the Czarevitch, were on one occasion travelling from their palace at Tsarskoe Selo by train. As the boy stood at the window looking at the passing scene, the slight vibration caused his nose to bleed. The Court physician, who always travelled with him, did his best to stop the bleeding. He failed and the train put back to the palace. Notwithstanding all he could do, the bleeding continued. Then, in her desperation, the poor distracted mother sent for Rasputin. He came, looked at the child, made over him the sign of the cross, and the bleeding stopped.

It is easy to see what immense power was thus placed in the hands of an unscrupulous man over a superstitious mother. It was by playing on the feelings of parents anxious for their son and for the future of their dynasty that Rasputin achieved his position. The Czarina, a devoted mother, fearing for the life of her son and reproaching herself as the transmitter of his disease, took refuge in occultism; and Rasputin took advantage of her credulity.

EARL JOWITT, *Some Were Spies*, 1954

'But wait a bit,' the Oysters cried,
'Before we have our chat;
For some of us are out of breath,
And all of us are fat!'
'No hurry!' said the Carpenter.
They thanked him much for that.

'A loaf of bread,' the Walrus said,
'Is what we chiefly need:
Pepper and vinegar besides,
Are very good indeed—
Now, if you're ready, Oysters dear,
We can begin to feed.'

'But not on us!' the Oysters cried,
  Turning a little blue.
'After such kindness, that would be
  A dismal thing to do!'
'The night is fine,' the Walrus said.
  'Do you admire the view?

'It was so kind of you to come!
  And you are very nice!'
The Carpenter said nothing but
  'Cut us another slice.
I wish you were not quite so deaf—
  I've had to ask you twice!'

'It seems a shame,' the Walrus said,
  'To play them such a trick.
After we've brought them out so far,
  And made them trot so quick!'
The Carpenter said nothing but
  'The butter's spread too thick!'

'I weep for you,' the Walrus said:
  'I deeply sympathize.'
With sobs and tears he sorted out
  Those of the largest size,
Holding his pocket-handkerchief
  Before his streaming eyes.

'O Oysters,' said the Carpenter,
  'You've had a pleasant run!
Shall we be trotting home again?'
  But answer came there none—
And this was scarcely odd, because
  They'd eaten every one.

LEWIS CARROLL, from 'The Walrus and the Carpenter', 1872

VIII

TRAITORS AND SPIES

THEN one of the twelve, called Judas Iscariot, went unto the chief priests,

And said unto them, What will ye give me, and I will deliver him unto you? And they convenanted with him for thirty pieces of silver.

And from that time he sought opportunity to betray him.

Now the first day of the feast of unleavened bread the disciples came to Jesus, saying unto him, Where wilt thou that we prepare for thee to eat the passover?

And he said, Go into the city to such a man, and say unto him, The Master saith, My time is at hand; I will keep the passover at thy house with my disciples.

And the disciples did as Jesus had appointed them; and they made ready the passover.

Now when the even was come, he sat down with the twelve.

And as they did eat, he said, Verily I say unto you, that one of you shall betray me.

And they were exceeding sorrowful, and began every one of them to say unto him, Lord, is it I?

And he answered and said, He that dippeth his hand with me in the dish, the same shall betray me.

The Son of man goeth as it is written of him: but woe unto that man by whom the Son of man is betrayed! it had been good for that man if he had not been born.

Then Judas, which betrayed him, answered and said, Master, is it I? He said unto him, Thou hast said . . .

Then cometh he to his disciples, and saith unto them, Sleep on now, and take your rest: behold the hour is at hand, and the Son of man is betrayed into the hands of sinners.

Rise, let us be going: behold, he is at hand that doth betray me.

And while he yet spake, lo, Judas, one of the twelve, came, and with him a great multitude with swords and staves, from the chief priests and elders of the people.

Now he that betrayed him gave them a sign, saying, Whomsoever I shall kiss, that same is he: hold him fast.

And forthwith he came to Jesus, and said, Hail, master; and kissed him.

And Jesus said unto him, Friend, wherefore art thou come? Then came they, and laid hands on Jesus, and took him.

Matthew 26

Sir Mordred, traitor false and vile,
King Arthur's sister's son
(And Arthur's too, as all believe,
And that is why he won
The stewardship), was to the land
A wily, treacherous lord:
He wished to wed his father's wife,
Which many men abhorred.

Great were the gifts and feasts he gave
With lavish pomp and show
And people said his rule brought joy,
Arthur's but grief and woe.
So good allegiance turned to bad:
The hearts of Englishmen
Deserted Arthur and their vows
Were made to Mordred then.

Sir Mordred had false letters written,
Which he made heralds bring,
Saying that Arthur had been killed:
They must choose another king.
The people spoke their minds and said
Arthur loved only war,
And since he'd lost his life in battle,
He had deserved no more.

Then Mordred summoned parliament:
Great was the gathering,
And there they all with full consent
Crowned Sir Mordred king.
At Canterbury for two whole weeks
The revels never ceased,
And then he went to Winchester
To hold the wedding feast.

In summer when the sun shone bright
His father's wife he'd wed,
And her he'd hold in warm embrace
And bring as bride to bed.
Dismayed, she begged a fortnight's leave
To buy of London's best
In clothes, that she and her cortège
Might be the better dressed.

The Queen was white as lily-flower:
With knights of her own kin
She hurried to London to the Tower
And shut herself within.
Mordred rode after, pale with rage:
His archers shot off showers
Of arrows, but to win those walls
Was much beyond his powers.

The Archbishop of Canterbury
Rode there with cross on high:
'By Christ crucified, think again!'
Was the holy man's loud cry.
'You cannot wed your father's wife!
You must be mad in mind!
And come the King across the sea,
You'll pay for it, you'll find!'

'A foolish priest!' then Mordred said,
'Do you think to thwart my will?
By Him who suffered pain for us,
Your words will work you ill.
I'll have you dragged by wild horses
And hanged upon a hill!'
The Archbishop fled, leaving him
His mad plan to fulfil.

He cursed him then with book and bell
At Canterbury in Kent.
As soon as Mordred heard of that,
For the Archbishop he sent.

But he had fled, leaving his treasure—
No time for argument!
While Mordred seized his gold and silver,
To the wilderness he went.

Thus the Archbishop fled the world
And its joys for evermore.
He had a chapel built between
Two copses high and hoar,
And as a hermit in the woods
Black cowl and habit wore.
He often lay awake and wept
For England's sorrows sore.

ANON., *Le Morte Arthur*, *c*.1350, trans. Brian Stone

. . . when the people had ratified the election, [Camillus] marched with his forces into the territories of the Faliscans, and laid siege to Falerii, a well-fortified city, and plentifully stored with all necessaries of war. And although he perceived it would be no small work to take it, and no little time would be required for it, yet he was willing to exercise the citizens and keep them abroad, that they might have no leisure, idling at home, to follow the tribunes in factions and seditions; a very common remedy, indeed, with the Romans, who thus carried off, like good physicians, the ill humours of their commonwealth. The Falerians, trusting in the strength of their city, which was well fortified on all sides, made so little account of the siege, that all, with the exception of those that guarded the walls, as in times of peace, walked about the streets in their common dress, the boys went to school, and were led by their master to play and exercise about the town walls; for the Falerians, like the Greeks, used to have a single teacher for many pupils, wishing their children to live and be brought up from the beginning in each other's company.

This schoolmaster, designing to betray the Falerians by their children, led them out every day under the town wall, at first but a little way, and, when they had exercised, brought them home again. Afterwards by degrees he drew them farther and farther, till by practice he had made them bold and fearless, as if no danger was about them; and at last, having got them all together, he brought them to the outposts of the Romans, and delivered them up, demanding to be led to Camillus. Where being come, and standing in the middle, he said that he was the master and teacher of these children, but preferring his favour before all other obligations, he was come to deliver up his charge to him, and, in that, the whole city. When Camillus had heard him out, he was astounded at the treachery of the act, and, turning to the standers-by, observed that 'war, indeed, is of necessity attended with much injustice and violence! Certain laws, however, all good men observe even in war itself, nor is victory so great an object as to induce us to incur for its sake obligations for base and impious acts. A great general should rely on his own virtue, and not on other men's vices.' Which said, he commanded the officers to tear off the man's clothes, and bind his hands behind him, and give the boys rods and scourges, to punish the traitor and drive him back to the city. By this time the Falerians had discovered the treachery of the schoolmaster, and the city, as was likely, was full of lamentations and cries for their calamity, men and women of worth running in distraction about the walls and gates; when, behold, the boys came whipping their master on naked and bound, calling Camillus their preserver and god and father. Insomuch that it struck not only into the parents, but the rest of the citizens that saw what was done, such admiration and love of Camillus's justice, that, immediately meeting in assembly, they sent ambassadors to him, to resign whatever they had to his disposal. Camillus sent them to Rome, where, being brought into the senate, they spoke to this purpose: that the Romans, preferring justice before victory, had taught them rather to embrace submission than liberty; they did not so much confess themselves to be inferior in strength as they must acknowledge them to be superior in virtue. The senate remitted the whole matter to Camillus, to judge and order as he thought fit; who, taking a sum of money of the Falerians, and, making a peace with the whole nation of the Faliscans, returned home.

PLUTARCH (*c.*46–*c.*127), *Lives*, trans. John Dryden, revised by Arthur Hugh Clough

MESSALINA

She came to me shyly one evening, peeped up at my face without saying anything, and at last asked, plainly embarrassed, and after one or two false starts: 'Do you love me, dearest husband?'

I assured her that I loved her beyond anyone else in the world.

'And what did you tell me, the other day, were the Three Main Pillars of the Temple of Love?'

'I said that the Temple of True Love was pillared on kindness, frankness and understanding. Or rather I quoted the philosopher Mnasalcus as having said so.'

'Then will you show me the greatest kindness and understanding that your love for me is capable of showing? *My* love will have to provide only the frankness. I'll come straight to the point. If it's not too hard for you, would you—could you possibly—allow me to sleep in a bedroom apart from you for a little while? It isn't that I don't love you every bit as much as you love me, but now that we have had two children in less than two years of marriage, oughtn't we to wait a little before we risk having a third? It is a very disagreeable thing to be pregnant: I have morning-sickness and heartburn and my digestion goes wrong, and I don't feel I could go through that again just yet. And, to be honest, quite apart from this dread, I somehow feel less passionately towards you than I did. I swear that I love you as much as ever, but now it's rather as my dearest friend and as the father of my children than as my lover. Having children uses up a lot of woman's emotions, I suppose. I'm not hiding anything from you. You do believe me, don't you?'

'I believe you, and I love you.'

She stroked my face. 'And I'm not like any ordinary woman, am I, whose business is merely to have children and children and children until she wears out? I am your wife—the Emperor's wife—and I help him in his Imperial work, and that should take precedence over everything, shouldn't it? Pregnancy interferes with work terribly.'

I said rather ruefully: 'Of course, my dearest, if you really feel like that, I am not the sort of husband to insist on forcing anything on you. But is it really necessary for us to sleep apart? Couldn't we at least occupy the same bed, for company's sake?'

'O Claudius,' she said, nearly crying, 'it has been difficult enough for me to make up my mind to ask you about this, because I love you so much and don't want to hurt you in the least. Don't make it more difficult. And now that I have frankly told you how I feel, wouldn't it be dreadfully difficult for you if you had violently passionate feelings for me while we were sleeping together and I could not honestly return them? If I repulsed you, that would be as destructive of our love as if I yielded against my will; and I am sure you would feel very remorseful afterwards if anything happened to destroy my love for you. No, can't you see now how much better it would be for us to sleep apart until I feel about you again as I used to do? Suppose, just to distance myself from temptation, I were to move across to my suite in the New Palace? It's more convenient for my work to be over there. I can get up in the morning and go straight to my papers. This lying-in has put me greatly behindhand with my Citizens' Roll.'

I pleaded: 'How long do you think you will want to be away?'

'We'll see how it works out,' she said, kissing the back of my neck tenderly. 'Oh, how relieved I am that you aren't angry. How long? Oh, I don't know. Does it matter so much? After all, sex is not essential to love if there is any other strong bond between lovers such as common idealistic pursuit of Beauty or Perfection. I do agree with Plato about that. He thought sex positively an obstruction to love.'

'He was talking of homosexual love,' I reminded her, trying not to sound depressed.

'Well, my dear,' she said lightly, 'I do a man's work, the same as you, and so it comes to much the same thing, doesn't it? And as for a common idealism, we have to be very idealistic indeed to get through all this drudgery in the name of attempted political perfection, don't we? Well, is that really settled? Will you really be a dear, dear Claudius, and not insist on my sharing your bed—in a literal sense, I mean? In all other senses I am still your devoted little Messalina, and do remember that it has been very, very painful for me to ask you this.'

I told her that I respected and loved her all the more for her frankness, and of course she must have her way. But that naturally I would be impatient for the time when she felt again for me as she once had done.

'Oh, please don't be impatient,' she cried. 'It makes it so difficult for me. If you were impatient I would feel that I was being unkind to you, and would probably pretend feelings that I didn't have. I may be an exception, but somehow sex doesn't mean much to me. I suspect, though, that many women get bored with it—without ceasing to love their husbands or to want their husbands to love them. But I'll always continue to be suspicious of other women. If you were to have affairs with other women I think I would go mad with jealousy. It isn't that I mind the thought of your sleeping with someone other than me; it's the fear that you might come to love her better than me, not merely regarding her as a pleasant sexual convenience, and then want to divorce me. I mean, if you were to sleep with a pretty housemaid occasionally, or some nice clean woman too low in rank for me to be jealous of, I should be very glad, really delighted, to think that you were having a nice time with her; and if you and I ever slept together afterwards we wouldn't consider it as anything that had come between us. We'd merely think of it as a measure that you had taken for the sake of your health—like a purge or an emetic. I wouldn't expect you even to tell me the woman's name, in fact I'd prefer you not to, so long as you first promised not to have doings with anyone about whom I would have a right to feel jealous. Wasn't that how Livia is said to have felt about Augustus?'

'Yes, in a way. But she never really loved him. She told me so. That made it easier for her to be attentive to him. She used to pick out young women from the slave-market and bring them secretly into his bedroom at night. Syrians, mostly, I believe.'

'Well, you're not asking me to do *that*, are you? I'm human, after all.'

This was how Messalina played, very cleverly and very cruelly, on my blind love for her. She moved over to the New Palace that very evening. And for a long time I said nothing further, hoping that she would come back to me. But she said nothing, only indicating by her tender behaviour that a very fine understanding existed between us. As a great concession she did sometimes consent to sleep with me. It was seven years before I heard so much as a whisper of what went on in her suite at the New Palace when the old cuckold-husband was away at his work or safely snoring in his bed at the Old Palace.

ROBERT GRAVES, *Claudius the God*, 1934

SIR WALTER RALEIGH ON TRIAL FOR TREASON 1603

SIR WALTER RALEIGH. If My Lord Cobham be a Traitor, what is that to me?

SIR EDWARD COKE, ATTORNEY-GENERAL. All that he did was by thy instigation, thou viper; for I 'thou' thee, thou traitor.

RALEIGH. It becometh not a man of quality and virtue to call me so: but I take comfort in it, it is all you can do.

COKE. Have I angered you?

RALEIGH. I am in no case to be angry.

LORD CHIEF-JUSTICE POPHAM. Sir Walter Raleigh, Mr Attorney

speaketh out of the zeal of his duty, for the service of the King, and you for your life; be valiant on both sides.

COKE. Thou art the most vile and execrable traitor that ever lived.

RALEIGH. You speak indiscreetly, barbarously and uncivilly.

COKE. I want words sufficient to express thy viperous treasons.

RALEIGH. I think you want words indeed, for you have spoken one thing half a dozen times.

COKE. Thou art an odious fellow, thy name is hateful to all the realm of England for thy pride.

RALEIGH. It will go near to prove a measuring cast between you and me, Mr Attorney.

JUDGE STEPHEN TUMIN, *Great Legal Disasters*, 1983

† *Titus Oates won notoriety for inventing a 'popish plot' against Charles II, supposedly Jesuit inspired and due to erupt at the end of the 1670s. On his word alone, many suspected conspirators were tried and executed. Here is Macaulay's description of the man known as 'one of the greatest perjurers in history'.*

. . . his short neck, his legs uneven, the vulgar said, as those of a badger, his forehead low as that of a baboon, his purple cheeks, and his monstrous length of chin, had been familiar to all who frequented the courts of law. He had then been the idol of the nation. Wherever he had appeared men had uncovered their heads to him. The lives and estates of the magnates of the realm had been at his mercy. Times had now changed; and many who had formerly regarded him as the deliverer of his country, shuddered at the sight of those hideous features on which villainy seemed to be written by the hand of God.

THOMAS BABINGTON, LORD MACAULAY, *The History of England*, 1849–61

† *And the summing up:*

He had loosed on England to prey on society the worst criminals of the underworld, so that in the King's Presence Chamber, in the lobbies of Westminster, in the fashionable coffee-houses, rakehell footmen, confidence tricksters, forgers, and murderers had mingled familiarly with the highest in the land.

To great men like the Five Lords, as to humble men like Stratford and Medburne, his bare word had brought death, imprisonment, or ruin. But for him, Lord Stafford would not have lost his head on Tower Hill, nor would Archbishop Plunket have endured the anguish of the quartering-block at Tyburn. Through his agency, hundreds of loyal Englishmen had been driven into exile, thousands of families had lost their livelihood, numberless innocents had succumbed to the filth and fetters of a jail. His voice, that peculiar, affected voice, uplifted in accusation had instituted a period of terror unparalleled in the history of a great and ancient people.

JANE LANE and ANDREW DAKINS, *Titus Oates*, 1949

THE 'GOLDEN VANITY'

A ship I have got in the North Country
And she goes by the name of the *Golden Vanity*,
O I fear she'll be taken by a Spanish Ga-la-lee,
    As she sails by the Low-lands low.

To the Captain then upspake the little Cabin-boy,
He said, 'What is my fee, if the galley I destroy?
The Spanish Ga-la-lee, if no more it shall annoy,
    As you sail by the Low-lands low.'

'Of silver and of gold I will give to you a store;
And my pretty little daughter that dwelleth on the shore,
Of treasure and of fee as well, I'll give to thee galore,
    As we sail by the Low-lands low.'

Then they row'd him up tight in a black bull's skin,
And he held all in his hand an augur sharp and thin,
And he swam until he came to the Spanish Gal-a-lin,
    As she lay by the Low-lands low.

He bored with his augur, he bored once and twice,
And some were playing cards, and some were playing
        dice,
When the water flowèd in it dazzled their eyes,
    And she sank by the Low-lands low.

So the Cabin-boy did swim all to the larboard side,
Saying 'Captain! take me in, I am drifting with the tide',

'I will shoot you ! I will kill you!' the cruel Captain cried,
'You may sink by the Low-lands low.'

Then the Cabin-boy did swim all to the starboard side,
Saying, 'Messmates, take me in, I am drifting with the tide',
Then they laid him on the deck, and he closed his eyes
and died,
As they sailed by the Low-lands low.

They sew'd his body tight in an old cow's hide,
And they cast the gallant cabin-boy out over the ship side,
And left him without more ado to drift with the tide,
And to sink by the Low-lands low.

ANON.

† *Benedict Arnold (1741–1801), an American major-general during the War of Independence, planned to betray an important post to the British. The plot was discovered, but Arnold escaped and became a brigadier in the British army. He died in London. Here he moves towards treason.*

. . . the years of political infighting, even as the British held out the olive branch of reconciliation, had turned Arnold against many of the original revolutionaries. As the economy deteriorated and the revolutionaries became more radical, Arnold moved ever closer to sympathizing with conservative Americans who were swelling the ranks of Loyalists. Added to his natural affinity for men of industry and thrift who feared they would lose everything if radical revolutionaries were permitted to continue on their ruinous course, Arnold was flattered more and more by Loyalists and disaffected revolutionaries around him. . . . By early 1779, there were reportedly fifty thousand Loyalists under arms or offering their services to the British—more than double the force Washington had at his disposal. Arnold would have his revenge by leading American Tories in a decisive civil war that would return America to peace with England. By 1778, British peace commissioners were offering to rectify all the American grievances of 1776, ignoring only the demand for independence.

More and more, conservative men that Arnold had come to respect were urging return of the colonies to their *status quo ante bellum*, before the age of tumults had begun in 1763, as the British now said they were willing to do. Persecuted and disenchanted by his old compatriots in revolutionary politics, Arnold opened up a secret correspondence with British military leaders inside New York City.

WILLARD STERNE RANDALL, *Benedict Arnold*, 1990

† *The villain Chauvelin has contrived a disagreeable predicament for Marguerite Blakeney while he waits for her husband, the Scarlet Pimpernel, to fall into his clutches.*

'Before that handkerchief is removed from your pretty mouth, fair lady,' whispered Chauvelin close to her ear, 'I think it right to give you one small word of warning. What has procured me the honour of being followed across the Channel by so charming a companion, I cannot, of course, conceive, but, if I mistake not, the purpose of this flattering attention is not one that would commend itself to my vanity, and I think that I am right in surmising, moreover, that the first sound which your pretty lips would utter, as soon as the cruel gag is removed, would be one that would perhaps prove a warning to the cunning fox, which I have been at such pains to track to his lair.'

He paused a moment, while the steel-like grasp seemed to tighten round her wrist; then he resumed in the same hurried whisper:

'Inside that hut, if again I am not mistaken, your brother, Armand St Just, waits with that traitor de Tournay, and two other men unknown to you, for the arrival of the mysterious rescuer, whose identity has for so long puzzled our Committee of Public Safety—the audacious Scarlet Pimpernel. No doubt if you scream, if there is a scuffle here, if shots are fired, it is more than likely that the same long legs that brought this scarlet enigma here, will as quickly take him to some place of safety. The purpose, then, for which I have travelled all these miles will remain unaccomplished. On the other hand, it only rests with yourself that your brother—Armand—shall be free to go off with you tonight if you like, to England, or any other place of safety.'

Marguerite could not utter a sound, as the handkerchief was wound very tightly around her mouth, but Chauvelin was peering through the darkness very closely into her face; no doubt, too, her hand gave a responsive appeal to his last suggestion, for presently he continued:

'What I want you to do to ensure Armand's safety is a very simple thing, dear lady.'

'What is it?' Marguerite's hand seemed to convey to his in response.

'To remain—on this spot, without uttering a sound, until I give you leave to speak. Ah! but I think you will obey,' he added, with that funny dry chuckle of his, as Marguerite's whole figure seemed to stiffen, in defiance of this order; 'for let me tell you that if you scream, nay! if you utter one sound, or attempt to move from here, my men—there are thirty of them about—will seize St Just, de Tournay, and their two friends, and shoot them here—by my orders—before your eyes.'

Marguerite had listened to her implacable enemy's speech with ever-increasing terror. Numbed with physical pain, she yet had sufficient mental vitality in her to realize the full horror of this terrible 'either–or' he was . . . putting before her . . .

Oh! that fiend in human shape, next to her, knew human—female—nature well. He had played upon her feelings as a skilful musician plays upon an instrument. He had gauged her very thoughts to a nicety.

She could not give that signal—for she was weak, and she was a woman. How could she deliberately order Armand to be shot before her eyes, to have his dear blood upon her head, he dying perhaps with a curse on her upon his lips. And little Suzanne's father, too! he, an old man! and the others!—oh! it was all too, too horrible.

Wait! wait! wait! how long? The early morning hours sped on, and yet it was not dawn: the sea continued its incessant mournful murmur, the autumnal breeze sighed gently in the night: the lonely beach was silent, even as the grave.

Suddenly from somewhere, not very far away, a cheerful strong voice was heard singing 'God Save the King!'

BARONESS ORCZY, *The Scarlet Pimpernel*, 1905

† *Trebitsch Lincoln was an extraordinary character. Born the son of a Jewish merchant in Hungary on 4 April 1879 he became a juvenile criminal and, during the course of his bizarre career, a missionary in Montreal, an Anglican curate in Kent, the Liberal Member of Parliament for Darlington, a member of the German military government in 1920, an adviser to the warlords in China, and a Buddhist abbot in Shanghai. This is an account of his brief and unsuccessful career as a double agent in the 1914–18 war.*

Trebitsch embarked on a series of moves which, while they failed in their immediate aim, were to win him international notoriety and to become encrusted in fanciful legend—much of it invented by Trebitsch himself. In this, the most fateful turn in his tortuous life, Trebitsch in effect launched himself into a new career. The former journalist, ex-missionary, unfrocked (if not actually defrocked) curate, failed politician, and bankrupt businessman sought to establish himself in the profession in which he was to become world-famous—that of international spy.

Trebitsch himself, as well as other writers, later claimed that his involvement in espionage long antedated the First World War. Not a shred of convincing evidence has ever been adduced in support of such statements. . . . If we sift out the truth from Trebitsch's later exercises in myth-making, it emerges that . . . Trebitsch called on his former employers at the War Office and asked to be introduced to an intelligence officer. He was eventually granted an interview with Captain P. W. Kenny of MO5 (the Security Service later known as MI5), to whom he volunteered for work as a double agent. Trebitsch suggested that he be permitted to travel to the (neutral) Netherlands and enlist in the service of the German espionage network there. Once the Germans trusted him, Trebitsch argued, he would be able to feed them with snippets of information about British fleet movements. Eventually he hoped by this means to lure the entire German battle fleet out into positions in the North Sea which would be communicated by Trebitsch to the British. As a result the Royal Navy would be able to lie in wait for the Germans, ambush and destroy them. The consequent complete British mastery of the seas around Germany would bring about a swift British victory—to this satisfying dénouement the most important contribution would have been made by Trebitsch!

The scheme was a childish and ridiculous figment of Trebitsch's overwrought and self-dramatising imagination. Probably he anticipated that, in the aftermath of such a heroic feat of deceptive warfare, the small matter of his irregular finances would be somehow smoothed out by the authorities. Even if the plan did not produce total victory over the Central Powers, it might bring Trebitsch a personal triumph over his creditors. At the least it might afford him an escape route from Britain, where the police seemed likely to knock on the door of the Torrington Square boarding-house at any moment with the request that Mr Lincoln accompany them to the station to assist in certain enquiries. . . .

On 18 December 1914 Trebitsch arrived in Rotterdam travelling on a legally issued British passport. . . . In Rotterdam Trebitsch obtained an interview with the German Consul-General, Gneist, to whom he offered his services as a double agent in the German interest. Gneist hardly appears to have taken Trebitsch any more seriously than Kenny. Trebitsch succeeded, however, in making enough of an impression on Gneist (who was actively involved in the German intelligence apparatus) for the consul to give him some harmless information to take back to England. It was not, after all, every day that a former British MP turned up to volunteer for the German espionage service. As a native of Hungary it would not have seemed improbable that he should wish to render some assistance to the ally of his homeland at this critical moment in its history. . . . Gneist risked little in giving Trebitsch the opportunity to prove himself by means of a trial run back to England.

Before leaving Holland Trebitsch prepared a lengthy memorandum for his German spymasters. Written in longhand on the notepaper of the 'Grand Café-Restaurant "Riche" ' in Rotterdam ('Speciale Restaurant voor fijne Vischsoorten'—even on this undercover mission Trebitsch had not forsaken his taste for the good things in life), the document affords damning proof of Trebitsch's treason against his adopted country. But it also sheds a revealing light on the egotism and amateurishness of the freelance spy.

† *This document ends:*

11. Should the sum which I take with me for expenses be spent I shall cable to one of the addresses which I have taken with me as follows: '*Book me saloon passage New York Dutch mailboat next week*.

Carr.' And I ask that in that case a further sum be sent to me by cheque drawn on London with the following accompanying letter: '*I. T. T. Lincoln Esq., National Liberal Club, London S.W. Dear Sir, Mr H. Tillman of Bucarest* [This was another former business associate of Trebitsch.] *has requested us to forward you Frs.—which we are doing enclosed by draft on London in English equivalent. Kindly acknowledge receipt. Yours truly. (Signature).*' . . .

On 28 January 1915 he was summoned by telegram to the Admiralty and told to take along his passport. Margaret Trebitsch later recollected that he seemed uneasy before he went there, although, with his characteristically self-deluding optimism, he speculated that perhaps he might be sent away on a mission.

The ensuing interview with Captain Hall marked a turning-point in Trebitsch's life—one on which he was to ruminate for years afterwards with thoughts of revenge. Hall was one of the few among Trebitsch's interlocutors who seems to have succeeded in dominating his generally irrepressible personality. The prematurely bald, perpetually blinking, no-nonsense naval officer informed Trebitsch that his services were not required by the British Government in any capacity and that it was not proposed to pay him anything for the supposed codes he had obtained in Rotterdam. . . .

The interview was a terrible shock to Trebitsch. His dreams of being dispatched abroad on an official mission gave way to fear of imminent arrest for fraud. . . . He told his wife that he would have to leave the country immediately, and he set about making plans for his escape. . . . At five o'clock on the morning of 30 January 1915, Trebitsch got up, said goodbye to his wife and sons, and crept out of the boarding-house.

For most of the rest of his life Trebitsch was a man on the run. He behaved like a hunted fugitive even when the police of several countries had stopped looking for him. Indeed he seemed almost to invite their attentions, relishing the role of international outlaw. The restless wanderlust which [was] a prime characteristic of the respectable phase of his life was now heightened as he moved into the shadowy realm of illegality. Moreover, although he was to be re-united with his wife and sons for brief periods, his abandonment of his family in their mean lodgings in Torrington Square essentially marked the end of his married life. Trebitsch was a wanted man, but in a sense he was also now, for the first time, a free man. He had no responsibilities to employers, parishioners, constituents, shareholders or creditors. Unconstrained by legality, whether canonical, commercial or criminal, and with little concern for the fate of his still devoted and faithful wife, Trebitsch could now allow his natural selfishness to flower into a bloated and grotesque bloom.

BERNARD WASSERSTEIN, *The Secret Lives of Trebitsch Lincoln*, 1988

† *The diplomat Mr Vladimir is instructing one of his clandestine employees, the anarchist Mr Verloc, in the most effective way of making a stir with a bomb. The outcome of this speech is a botched attempt to blow up the Greenwich observatory, and with it the death of Mr Verloc's brother-in-law, an innocent and dim-witted cat's-paw.*

A bomb outrage to have any influence on public opinion now must go beyond the intention of vengeance or terrorism. It must be purely destructive. It must be that, and only that, beyond the faintest suspicion of any other object. You anarchists should make it clear that you are perfectly determined to make a clean sweep of the whole social creation. But how to get that appallingly absurd notion into the heads of the middle classes so that there should be no mistake? That's the question. By directing your blows at something outside the ordinary passions of humanity is the answer. Of course, there is art. A bomb in the National Gallery would make some noise. But it would not be serious enough. Art has never been their fetish. It's like breaking a few back windows in a man's house; whereas, if you want to make him really sit up, you must try at least to raise the roof. There would be some screaming of course, but from whom? Artists—art critics and such like—people of no account. Nobody minds what they say. But there is learning—science. Any imbecile that has got an income believes in that. He does not know why, but he believes it matters somehow. It is the sacrosanct fetish. All the damned professors are radicals at heart. Let them know that their great panjandrum has got to go, too, to make room for the Future of the Proletariat. A howl from all these intellectual idiots is bound to help forward the labours of the Milan Conference. They will be writing to the papers. Their indignation would be above suspicion, no material interests being openly at stake, and it will alarm every selfishness of the class which should be impressed. They believe that in some mysterious way science is at the source of their material prosperity. They do. And the absurd ferocity of such a demonstration will affect them more profoundly than the mangling of a whole street—or theatre—full of their own kind. To that last they can always say: 'Oh! it's mere class hate.' But what is one to say to an act of destructive ferocity so absurd as to be incomprehensible, inexplicable, almost unthinkable; in fact, mad? Madness alone is truly terrifying, inasmuch as you cannot placate it either by threats, persuasion, or bribes. Moreover, I am a civilized man. I would never dream of directing you to organize a mere butchery, even if I expected the best results from it. But I wouldn't expect from a butchery the result I want. Murder is always with us. It is almost an institution. The demonstration must be against learning—science. But not every science will do. The attack must have all the shocking senselessness of gratuitous blasphemy. Since bombs are your means of expression, it would be really telling if one could throw a bomb into pure mathematics. But that is impossible. I have been trying to educate you; I have expounded to you the higher philosophy of your usefulness, and suggested to you some serviceable arguments. The practical application of my teaching interests *you* mostly. But from the moment I have undertaken to interview you I have also given some attention to the practical aspect of the question. What do you think of having a go at astronomy?'

JOSEPH CONRAD, *The Secret Agent*, 1907

† *A policeman named Syme manages to ingratiate himself with a band of anarchists . . .*

'Don't you see we've checkmated each other?' cried Syme. 'I can't tell the police you are an anarchist. You can't tell the anarchists I'm a policeman. I can only watch you, knowing what you are; you can only watch me, knowing what I am. In short, it's a lonely, intellectual duel, my head against yours. I'm a policeman deprived of the help of the police. You, my poor fellow, are an anarchist deprived of the help of that law and organisation which is so essential to anarchy. The one solitary difference is in your favour. You are not surrounded by inquisitive policemen; I am surrounded by inquisitive anarchists. I cannot betray you, but I might betray myself. Come, come! wait and see me betray myself. I shall do it so nicely.' . . .

'Comrades,' cried Gregory, in a voice like that of a martyr who in an ecstacy of pain has passed beyond pain, 'it is nothing to me whether you detest me as a tyrant or detest me as a slave. If you will not take my command, accept my degradation. I kneel to you. I throw myself at your feet. I implore you. Do not elect this man.'

'Comrade Gregory,' said the chairman after a painful pause, 'this is really not quite dignified.'

For the first time in the proceedings there was for a few seconds a real silence. Then Gregory fell back in his seat, a pale wreck of a man, and the chairman repeated, like a piece of clock-work suddenly started again—

'The question is that Comrade Syme be elected to the post of Thursday on the General Council.'

The roar rose like the sea, the hands rose like a forest, and three minutes afterwards Mr Gabriel Syme, of the Secret Police Service, was elected to the post of Thursday on the General Council of the Anarchists of Europe.

Everyone in the room seemed to feel the tug waiting on the river, the sword-stick and the revolver, waiting on the table. The instant the election was ended and irrevocable, and Syme, had received the paper proving his election, they all sprang to their feet, and the fiery groups moved and mixed in the room. Syme found himself, somehow or other, face to face with Gregory, who still regarded him with a stare of stunned hatred. They were silent for many minutes.

'You are a devil!' said Gregory at last.

'And you are a gentleman,' said Syme with gravity.

G. K. CHESTERTON, *The Man who was Thursday*, 1908

† *In Irish life and letters, a particular repugnance attaches to the word 'informer'—and in Gypo Nolan, Liam O'Flaherty has created the archetypal weakling and unsavoury character who does not scruple to sell the life of a fellow republican. The novel is set during the Black-and-Tan war.*

At twenty-five minutes past eight Gypo left the police-station by a door in the rear of the building. In his pocket he carried twenty pounds in Treasury notes, the reward for information concerning Francis Joseph McPhillip.

He walked quickly along a narrow passage into a dark lane. The lane was empty. So it appeared at first. But as Gypo stood hidden in the doorway of an old empty house, piercing the darkness with wild eyes, he heard a footstep. The footstep made him start. It was the first human footstep he had heard, the first sound of his fellow human beings, since he had become an informer and . . . and an outcast. . . .

No. 44 was the centre of interest. The horror that had come to it had aroused the whole street. It had aroused the whole quarter. Three streets away, bar attendants stood gaping behind their counters, while some man, with an excited red face and a big mouth, recounted the manner of Frank McPhillip's death, with oaths and frenzied gesticulations. Everywhere, in the streets, in the public-houses, in the tenement kitchens, where old red-nosed men craned forward their shrivelled necks to hear the dreadful news, one word was whispered with fear and hatred.

It was the word 'Informer.'

Gypo heard that word as he reached the junction of Titt Street and Bryan Road—a long wide road, lined with little shops, the sidewalks strewn with papers, little heaps of dirt in the gutters, two tramcar lines rusted by the drizzling rain, groups of loafers at every lamp-post, at the public-house doors and on the Canal Bridge, where the road disappeared abruptly over the horizon, as if it had fallen over a precipice into space. He was passing Ryan's public-house that stood at the corner, half in Titt Street, half in Bryan Road. The word came to him through the open door of the public bar. He had slowed down his pace on reaching the neighbourhood, and when he heard the word uttered, he brought his left leg up to the right and instead of thrusting it forward for another pace, he dropped it heavily but noiselessly to the wet pavement of red and white glazed brick diamonds, with which the front of the public-house was decorated.

LIAM O'FLAHERTY, *The Informer*, 1925

THE TRAITOR WHO SHOPPED THE BRIDGE SCHOOL

The pair followed him into the private side, upstairs, and into the sick-room. There were three beds in it; upon one sat Beaumont-Greene. His complexion turned a sickly drab when he saw Lovell and Scaife. He even glanced at the window with a hunted expression. The window was three stories from the ground, and heavily barred ever since a boy in delirium had tried to jump from it.

'Your night-things will be brought to you,' said Warde.

He went out slowly. The boys heard the key turn in the massive lock. They were prisoners. Scaife walked up to Beaumont-Greene.

'You told Warde about the bridge?'

'Ye-es; I had to. Scaife, don't look at me like that. Lovell'—his voice broke into a terrified scream—'don't let him hit me. I couldn't help it—I swear I—'

'You cur!' said Scaife. 'I wouldn't touch you with a forty-foot pole.'

HORACE ANNESLEY VACHELL, *The Hill*, 1906

† *Richard Hannay learns of an international plot against Britain and her allies from a stranger whom he later finds stabbed in his flat. Hannay, after a long pursuit by the police and foreign agents, traces the spies to a seaside villa where they are waiting for a yacht to take them to Germany. They protest their innocence, pretend to be ordinary holiday-makers, and invite him to a round of bridge.*

Then something awoke me.

The old man laid down his hand to light a cigar. He didn't pick it up at once, but sat back for a moment in his chair, with his fingers tapping on his knees.

It was the movement I remembered when I had stood before him in the moorland farm, with the pistols of his servants behind me.

A little thing, lasting only a second, and the odds were a thousand to one that I might have had my eyes on my cards at the time and missed it. But I didn't, and, in a flash, the air seemed to clear. Some shadow lifted from my brain, and I was looking at the three men with full and absolute recognition.

The clock on the mantelpiece struck ten o'clock.

The three faces seemed to change before my eyes and reveal their secrets. The young one was the murderer. Now I saw cruelty and ruthlessness, where before I had only seen good-humour. His knife, I made certain, had skewered Scudder to the floor. His kind had put the bullet in Karolides.

The plump man's features seemed to dislimn, and form again, as I looked at them. He hadn't a face, only a hundred masks that he could assume when he pleased. That chap must have been a superb actor. Perhaps he had been Lord Alloa of the night before; perhaps not; it didn't matter. I wondered if he was the fellow who had first tracked Scudder, and left his card on him. Scudder had said he lisped, and I could imagine how the adoption of a lisp might add terror.

But the old man was the pick of the lot. He was sheer brain, icy, cool, calculating, as ruthless as a steam hammer. Now that my eyes were opened I wondered where I had seen the benevolence. His jaw was like chilled steel, and his eyes had the inhuman luminosity of a bird's. I went on playing, and every second a greater hate welled up in my heart. It almost choked me, and I couldn't answer when my partner spoke. Only a little longer could I endure their company.

'Whew! Bob! Look at the time,' said the old man. 'You'd better think about catching your train. Bob's got to go to town to-night,' he added, turning to me. The voice rang now as false as hell.

I looked at the clock, and it was nearly half-past ten.

'I am afraid he must put off his journey,' I said.

'Oh, damn,' said the young man, 'I thought you had dropped that rot. I've simply got to go. You can have my address, and I'll give any security you like.'

'No,' I said, 'you must stay.'

At that I think they must have realized that the game was desperate. Their only chance had been to convince me that I was playing the fool, and that had failed. But the old man spoke again.

'I'll go bail for my nephew. That ought to content you, Mr Hannay.' Was it fancy, or did I detect some halt in the smoothness of that voice?

There must have been, for as I glanced at him, his eyelids fell in that hawk-like hood which fear had stamped on my memory.

I blew my whistle.

JOHN BUCHAN, *The Thirty-Nine Steps*, 1915

† *Somerset Maugham's Ashenden ('the British Agent') is obliged in the course of his work to associate with some peculiar characters, including the one known as 'the Hairless Mexican' (General Manuel Carmona). In the following extract, it becomes clear that the Mexican has overreached himself.*

The Hairless Mexican ate with huge mouthfuls, enjoying himself vastly; his eyes shone and he was loquacious. The woman he had danced with had in that short time told him all about herself and he repeated now to Ashenden what she had said. He stuffed huge pieces of bread into his mouth. He ordered another bottle of wine.

'Wine?' he cried scornfully. 'Wine is not a drink, only champagne; it does not even quench your thirst. Well, *amigo*, are you feeling better?'

'I'm bound to say I am,' smiled Ashenden.

'Practice, that is all you want, practice.'

He stretched out his hand to pat Ashenden on the arm.

'What's that?' cried Ashenden with a start. 'What's that stain on your cuff?'

The Hairless Mexican gave his sleeve a glance.

'That? Nothing. It's only blood. I had a little accident and cut myself.'

Ashenden went silent. His eyes sought the clock that hung over the door.

'Are you anxious about your train? Let me have one more dance and then I'll accompany you to the station.'

The Mexican got up and with his sublime self-assurance seized in his arms the woman who sat nearest to him and danced away with her. Ashenden watched him moodily. He was a monstrous, terrible figure with that blond wig and his hairless face, but he moved with a matchless grace; his feet were small and seemed to hold the ground like the pads of a cat or a tiger; his rhythm was wonderful and you could not but see that the bedizened creature he danced with was intoxicated by his gestures. There was music in his toes and in the long arms that held her so firmly, and there was music in those long legs that seemed to move strangely from the hips. Sinister and grotesque though he was, there was in him now a feline elegance, even something of beauty, and you felt a secret, shameful fascination. To Ashenden he suggested one of those sculptures of the pre-Aztec hewers of stone, in which there is barbarism and vitality, something terrible and cruel, and yet withal a brooding and significant loveliness. All the same he would gladly have left him to finish the night by himself in that sordid dance-hall, but he knew that he must have a business conversation with him. He did not look forward to it without misgiving. He had been instructed to give Manuel Carmona certain sums in return for certain documents. Well, the documents were not forthcoming; and as for the rest—Ashenden knew nothing about that; it was no business of his. The Hairless Mexican waved gaily as he passed him.

'I will come the moment the music stops. Pay the bill and then I shall be ready.'

Ashenden wished he could have seen into his mind. He could not even make a guess at its workings. Then the Mexican, with his scented handkerchief wiping the sweat from his brow, came back.

'Have you had a good time, General?' Ashenden asked him.

'I always have a good time. Poor white trash, but what do I care? I like to feel the body of a woman in my arms and see her eyes grow languid and her lips part as her desire for me melts the marrow in her bones like butter in the sun. Poor white trash, but women.'

They sallied forth. The Mexican proposed that they should walk and in that quarter, at that hour, there would have been little chance of finding a cab; but the sky was starry. It was a summer night and the air was still. The silence walked beside them like the ghost of a dead man. When they neared the station the houses seemed on a sudden to take on a greyer, more rigid line, and you felt that the dawn was at hand. A little shiver trembled through the night. It was a moment of apprehension and the soul for an instant was anxious; it was as though, inherited down the years in their countless millions, it felt a witless fear that perhaps another day would not break. But they entered the station and the night once more enwrapped them. One or two porters lolled about like stage-hands after the curtain has rung down and the scene is struck. Two soldiers in dim uniforms stood motionless.

The waiting-room was empty, but Ashenden and the Hairless Mexican went to sit in the most retired part of it.

'I still have an hour before my train goes. I'll just see what this cable's about.'

He took it out of his pocket and from the despatch-case got his code. He was not then using a very elaborate one. It was in two parts, one contained in a slim book and the other, given him on a sheet of paper and destroyed by him before he left allied territory, committed to memory. Ashenden put on his spectacles and set to work. The Hairless Mexican sat in a corner of the seat, rolling himself cigarettes and smoking; he sat there placidly, taking no notice of what Ashenden did, and enjoyed his well-earned repose. Ashenden deciphered the groups of numbers one by one and as he got it out jotted down each word on a piece of paper. His method was to abstract his mind from the sense till he had finished, since he had discovered that if you took notice of the words as they came along you often jumped to a conclusion and sometimes were led into error. So he translated quite mechanically, without paying attention to the words as he wrote them one after the other. When at last he had done he read the complete message. It ran as follows:

Constantine Andreadi has been detained by illness at Piraeus. He will be unable to sail. Return Geneva and await instructions.

At first Ashenden could not understand. He read it again. He shook from head to foot. Then, for once robbed of his self-possession, he blurted out, in a hoarse, agitated and furious whisper:

'You bloody fool, you've killed the wrong man.'

W. Somerset Maugham, *Ashenden*, 1928

† *In this wartime novel a strange man named Harrison approaches the heroine, Stella, suggests to her that her lover Robert is acting the traitor, and offers her a means of saving him.*

'. . . The thing could just turn on the stuff on him I send up. As to that, if you follow me, I do use my judgment. I *could* use my judgment a bit more . . . I am, for instance, holding quite a bit of stuff on him that I haven't turned in yet. It ought to go in—I can't quite make my mind up. Perhaps you could help me to?'

She looked at him and began to laugh.

'I *could* leave things over,' he went on, with the air of one intensely pursuing an inner argument, 'for quite a time. In that case who knows what might not have happened—this whole show might be over; he might for some reason think better of it and drop this little game of his of his own accord; he might just somehow be lucky. There's no saying. Anyhow, it's a hope—if he *could* be kept out of trouble a bit longer. And when I say that rather depends on me, what I feel is, it rather depends on you.'

'Yes, I quite see.'

He said with relief: 'You do?'

'Perfectly. I'm to form a disagreeable association in order that a man be left free to go on selling his country.'

'That's putting it a bit crudely,' Harrison said, downcast. . . .

All that time, all the same, the current had been against his face. The war-warmed impulse of people to be *a* people had been derisory; he had hated the bloodstream of the crowds, the curious animal psychic oneness, the human lava-flow. Even the leaden unenthusiasm, by its being so common, so deeply shared, had provoked him—and as for the impatiences, the hopes, the reiteration of unanswerable questions and the spurts of rumour, he must have been measuring them with a calculating eye. The half-sentence of the announcer's voice coming out of a window at News hour, the flopping rippling headlines of Late Night Final at the newsvendor's corner—what nerve, what nerve in reverse, had they struck on in him? Knowing what he knew, doing what he did. Idly, more idly than all the others doing the same thing, in the streets with her he had thieved the headline out of the corner of his eye, without a break in their talk, with a hiatus in his long pitching step so slight as to be registered by her only through their being arm-in-arm in the falling evening. She now saw his smile as the smile of one who has the laugh.

ELIZABETH BOWEN, *The Heat of the Day*, 1949

LORD HAW-HAW

The idea of a traitor first became real to the British of our time when they heard the voice of William Joyce on the radio during the war. The conception of treachery first became real to them when he was brought to trial as a radio traitor. For he was something new in the history of the world. Never before have people known the voice of one they had never seen as well as if he had been a husband or a brother or a close friend; and had they foreseen such a miracle they could not have imagined that this familiar unknown would speak to them only to prophesy their death and ruin. A great many people had experienced that hideous novelty, for it was easy to chance on Joyce's wavelength when one was tuning-in on the English stations, and there was a rasping yet rich quality about his voice which made it difficult not to go on listening, and he was nearly convincing in his assurance. It seemed as if one had better hearken and take warning when he suggested that the destiny of the people he had left in England was death, and the destiny of his new masters in Germany life and conquest, and that, therefore, his listeners had better change sides and submit; and he had the advantage that the news in the papers confirmed what he said. He was not only alarming, he was ugly. He opened a vista into a mean life. He always spoke as if he were better fed and better clothed than we were, and so, we now know, he was. He went farther than that mockery of his own people's plight. He sinned that sin which travesties legitimate hatred because it is felt for kindred, as incest is the travesty of legitimate love. When the U boats were sinking so many of our ships that to open the newspapers was to see the faces of drowned sailors, he rolled the figures of our lost tonnage on his tongue. When we were facing the hazard of D-day, he rejoiced in the thought of the English dead which would soon lie under the West Wall.

So all the curious went off to the Central Criminal Court on 17 September 1945 when he came up for trial. The Old Bailey was as it had not been before the war and is not now. Because of the blitz it stood in a beautiful desert of charred stone. Churches stood blackened but apparently intact; birds, however, flew through the empty sockets of the windows and long grass grew around their altars. A red-brick Georgian mansion, hidden for a century by sordid warehouses, looked at the dome of St Paul's, now astonishingly great, across acres where willow-herb, its last purple flowers passing into silver clouds of seed dust, and yellow ragwort grew from the ground plan of a city drawn in rubble. The grey stone of the Old Bailey itself had been gashed by a bomb. Its solidity had been sliced as if it were a cake, and the walls of the slice were crude new red brick. Inside the building, because there was not yet the labour to take down the heavy blackout, the halls and passages and stairs were in perpetual dusk. The court-room —Court No. 1 where all the most famous criminal trials of modern times have taken place—was lit by electric light, for the shattered glass dome had not yet been rebuilt. Bare boards filled it in, giving an odd-come-short look to what had been a fine room in its austere way.

The strong light was merciless to William Joyce, whose appearance was a shock to all of us who knew him only over the air. His voice had suggested a large and flashy handsomeness, but he was a tiny little creature and not handsome at all. His hair was mouse-coloured and sparse, particularly above his ears, and his pinched and misshapen nose was joined to his face at an odd angle. His eyes were hard and shiny, and above them his thick eyebrows were pale and irregular. His neck was long, his shoulders narrow and sloping, his arms very short and thick. His body looked flimsy and coarse. There was nothing individual about him except a deep scar running across his right cheek from his ear to the corner of his mouth. But this did not create the savage and marred distinction that it might suggest, for it gave a mincing immobility to his small mouth. He was dressed with a dandyish preciosity, which gave no impression of well-being, only of nervousness. He was like an ugly version of Scott Fitzgerald, but more nervous. He moved with a jerky formality, and when he bowed to the judge his bow seemed sincerely respectful but entirely inappropriate to the occasion, and it was difficult to think of any occasion to which it would have been appropriate.

REBECCA WEST, *The Meaning of Treason*, 1949, rev. ed. 1965

† *A local grandee is unmasked as a German spy.*

'I wouldn't be here, in this condition, telling you all this,' I said to him, 'if the whole case wasn't in the bag, with all the essential evidence already in the hands of the police. I only came—and stayed on—because I like to round off my own jobs myself. Vanity, if you like. Probably that's my weakness. Yours is pride, Tarlington. You see yourself as a rightly privileged person, quite different from the common crowd, and you're ready to pay a big price to keep your privileges. You hate democracy, and all it means. There's something fundamentally stiff-necked, arrogant, dominating and conceited about you that just can't take it. When Hess flew over here, he was looking for people like you. It isn't that you're pro-German, unpatriotic in the ordinary sense. In the last war, which seemed to you a straightforward nationalistic affair, I've no doubt you did a good job. But this war, which is quite different, was too much for you. I heard you speak the other night. You only said what a lot of people of your kind keep on saying—telling the people to keep in their old place, to fight and work and suffer to maintain something they no longer believe in—and, if you ask me, every word of this stuff is worth another gun or whip to Hitler and his gang. But you're a bit more intelligent and a bit more unscrupulous than most of your kind, and so you realized that to keep all you wanted to keep, it meant that the people mustn't win and that Fascism mustn't lose. So they persuaded you that a Nazi victory only meant that you'd have the sort of England you've always wanted, with yourself and a few others securely on top, and the common people kept in their place for ever. And you went down the old steep way . . . the well-known toboggan run . . . insane pride . . . lies . . . treachery . . . murder. . . . And you've lost, Tarlington, you've lost . . . and if you don't want . . . to be remembered . . . as an English Quisling . . . there's only one way . . . one way . . . out . . .'

I couldn't have added another word, for the whole room was throbbing, between bright dazzling light and blackness, just like my shoulder, but luckily it wasn't necessary. I saw without surprise, like a man in a confused dream, that the door had opened, and that the massive figure of the Superintendent filled the door-way. And I knew, even then, that it only needed that.

'All right, Superintendent,' I heard the colonel say. 'Just a minute.' And he went into the other room.

There was a shot before anybody had a chance to move.

Apparently I was heard to say: 'Well, there wasn't any other way of doing it.' But I don't remember. I was out.

J. B. PRIESTLEY, *Blackout in Gretley*, 1942

How much harm did Burgess and Maclean do to their country? This can never be known. Every secret they learned during their official lives was certainly transmitted to the Soviet Union. Burgess must have learned much that was useful to his masters when he was running about London in the company of the odd-come-shorts who, like himself, mixed with unsuspecting heroes to form the army which was dropped on Europe to help the resistance forces. It is painful to think how much more he must have learned when he was personal assistant to Hector McNeil. The Official Secrets Act must often have been fractured by his hand. As for Maclean, he was secretary of the Combined Policy Committee on Atomic Development, which gave him no scientific information but much knowledge of a general kind, particularly relating to security and supply. He is said to have had a grave influence on the course followed by the Korean War. . . . On the other hand, we may draw comfort from the certainty that the bulk of the official papers which came into the hands of Burgess and Maclean could have been of interest to neither man nor beast.

But the damage done by these two on the hither side of the law has to be considered. Maclean served for some time under Lord Inverchapel, the eccentric diplomat whose presence as British Ambassador at Moscow, Peking, and Washington made many an astonished traveller marvel at the Foreign Office system of promotion. His habit of having the bagpipes played by kilted pipers round the dining-room at the British Embassy at Washington caused many persons to calculate, often with fury, whether Stirling lies north of that city, since this Highland rite cannot properly be performed south of Stirling. This problem of etiquette has probably never been raised before or since; and it was typical of Lord Inverchapel's fantastic oddity. Not least among his disadvantages was a steady passion for the Soviet Union. This he did not conceal from the Foreign Office, giving a pro-Soviet lecture to the experts employed during the war in the Far Eastern section which none of them has ever forgotten. While it would be most unlikely that Lord Inverchapel ever committed an act of treachery, he certainly extended the hand of friendship to all who shared his passion, which sometimes caused him to commit official acts not treacherous but inconvenient. A German who had formed part of the extensive Soviet spy-ring in the Pacific area, and who had no connexion whatsoever with Great Britain, was not so many years ago expelled from France, and made his way to England. To the surprise of the immigration authorities he produced a British passport, which he had been given by Lord Inverchapel when he was in China; and in Great Britain, a country towards which he had always professed the greatest hostility, this undesirable alien lived until his death. There is no limit to what Maclean must have been able to do with such a chief.

Burgess must have had many achievements to his credit on the hither side of the law. He had two permanent lines of activity: he had close relations, before, during, and after the war, with various French Communists who had infiltrated their own Civil Service and the Paris radio, and relations at least as close with certain Communist Germans of good family who were working in concert with the left-wing and a certain peer and peeress friendly to the Nazis. There was also much finding of jobs for the right people. . . .

But perhaps the worst offence of the two men was the spreading and degrading cloud of doubt their flight engendered. Burgess and Maclean were employed together with a number of other men, they were acquainted with many through their clubs and through their ordinary social ties. Let us suppose that the ordinary Londoner was acquainted with three of their associates. A.B., C.D., and E.F. He knew that A.B. was a homosexual, that C.D. joined the Communist party at Cambridge but left it long ago, and that E.F. was a decent soul, who knew Maclean and Burgess because he was at the same school or for some other neutral reason. Inevitably this scandal darkened and fused the Londoner's knowledge of these three men. Inevitably he suspected all these three men of Communism, of which none was guilty, and of homosexuality, which was practised by only one. Inevitably he smeared the organization to which Burgess and Maclean belonged, the society which they frequented, with a bigger and blacker smear than they deserved. This is a natural consequence of Communist activity. Once a secret society establishes itself within an open society there is no end to the hideous mistrust that it must cause. But there was not the slightest hope that this situation had not been made even uglier than it was bound to be. Burgess and Maclean would be under an obligation to lay a trail of bogus evidence behind them which would divert suspicion from the Communists who had really been their *aides*; and these Communists, and all others of their faith, had had to join in the game of misleading the authorities. It followed that suspicion often fell on people who were innocent.

REBECCA WEST, *The Meaning of Treason*, 1949, rev. ed. 1965

† *Alger Hiss, who was employed in the US State Department during the New Deal, was accused by Whittaker Chambers, admittedly an ex-communist and a most unreliable witness, of having been a communist also and of having handed over State Department papers to him. Hiss was tried and re-tried for perjury in 1949, in a New York District Court, and finally sentenced to five years imprisonment. This is Alistair Cooke on the characters of the two men.*

There was little to add in the Second Trial to the overwhelming impression of the First that wherever Hiss had been, and whatever he had done, he had left an enviable reputation for 'integrity, loyalty, veracity.' Most of the character witnesses came again and several new ones though the defense decided not to call the two Supreme Court justices. . . .

Mr Murphy's tack was to sail head on into Hiss's reputation through the character witnesses; he went at them with a boisterous indifference to their own good name that perceptibly shook some and infuriated others. Dr Stanley Hornbeck, for instance, said he could 'see no good reason for bringing in' the name of a man who had gossiped, possibly as far away as 1939, that Hiss was a fellow traveler. But Mr Murphy was immune to such scruples and made him say it. It was William C. Bullitt, former Ambassador to Paris and Moscow, who also—Dr Hornbeck admitted in suppressed anger—had called Hiss a Communist eight years later. Even Mr Marbury, Hiss's lawyer, was forced by the new Murphy truculence into repeating a rumor picked up from Robert Patterson, when Secretary of War,—a rumor they had both dismissed as 'ridiculous.' Mr Cross put in evidence a document excluded from the First Trial which demonstrated that one month after the Nazi-Soviet Pact, Hiss was urging American aid to the Allies over the objection of Dr Philip Jessup. (In summation, Mr Murphy ridiculed this stand. Once Chambers had broken with the party, Mr Murphy explained, 'Hiss because the hottest thing in Washington . . . [he] *had* then to take the opposite position.') Mr Murphy put up to Hiss his attitude to the lie-detector test the House Committee had proposed; and while Hiss agreed he had not insisted on it, it was the House Committee, he said, that had dropped the idea. Without any discoverable nuance, Mr Murphy got clearly into the record two facts against the mention of which Mr Stryker had reeled in protest: the suicides of Hiss's father and sister. Hiss calmly thought they were both due to financial trouble; and Mr Murphy took him at his word. From John Foster Dulles came another guarded denial of Hiss's story of his resignation from the Carnegie Endowment and a politic rephrasing of what in the First Trial had amounted to a character reference. This time Mr Dulles said precisely that Hiss's reputation was 'very high . . . up to that date [his election to the endowment] you mention.' Dr Philip Jessup appeared in person this time. Without expression, and without yielding any helpful reservations, he stood by his view of Hiss's reputation. Mr Murphy tried to hint at Dr Jessup's dark affinity for various liberal causes, but Mr Cross promptly deflated this attack by having Dr Jessup list some old colleagues on one suspect organization—the Institute of Pacific Relations: they were such unlikely subversives as Newton Baker, Henry Luce, and the president of General Electric.

As the accuser, and the cause of all Hiss's present misery, Chambers was necessarily exposed in both Trials to a massive attack on his character and by inference his credibility in this incredible story. Mr Murphy took up the canny attitude, the Second time, of conceding at the start the trickeries of Chambers's party life and indulgently allowing the perjuries that the defense last time had hailed as strikes of purest gold. Mr Murphy was even conscientious enough to put in evidence Chambers's 'blasphemous' play, which had got him into trouble at Columbia; and so there should be no doubt about its impieties, Mr Murphy read it aloud. Outside the courtroom it might have been identified as an ironic passage from Anatole France's *Procurator of Judea* but the defense had shouted it was an atheistic horror. This time, Mr Murphy implied, he was only too willing to take the same view. This almost sacerdotal partnership between Mr Murphy and the accuser lent to Chambers the calm of a man who has gone through purgatory and who now, like the emerging Dante, sees the clear vault of heaven above with the wonder of a child and the purity of a saint. It was a very useful protection against the cross-examination. For Chambers now had a stagger-proof stance, which implied that while he was a Communist there was no honor in him, but since he had become a God-fearing man his memory was as human as anybody else's. Accordingly he could feint and tumble with Mr Cross in a spirit of good clean fun and stay cheerful as a pixie when he was confronted for many hours on end with his old disreputable life, his life in the underground, his discrepancies of testimony. For two days the blithe responses came back at the dogged Mr Cross: 'that is correct,' 'that is also correct,' 'I don't recall,' 'it may well have been,' 'it may well be you're right.' Mr Cross showed him a letter to a Columbia teacher to prove that Chambers had been a year out all along in his recollection of when he became a Communist (it was 1925 not 1924). He appeared almost grateful to Mr Cross for setting him right. He was then challenged to deny Wadleigh's memory of the shadowy Colonel Bykov as a one-armed man. Chambers found this interesting but unimpressive; he remembered two arms. Mr Cross dared him to say that Wadleigh had not been reproved for turning over useless documents. Chambers granted that he had. And had not Colonel Bykov then said: 'We want something hot'? Chambers pursed his lips, implying that Wadleigh had a right to his colorful memoirs. 'Very prettily phrased,' he commented, and looked at the ceiling as steadily as Sydney Carton. Before he left the stand, Mr Murphy wanted to be quite clear what was his defense to the libel suit. That was very simple. 'It's true,' said Chambers.

ALISTAIR COOKE, *A Generation on Trial*, 1950

A friend called on Cyril Connolly and reported that Maclean had asked him: 'What would you do if I told you I was a Communist agent?'

Maclean added: 'Well, I am. Go on, report me.' But the next day the incident seemed 'preposterous'.

In April 1951, according to Connolly, Maclean knocked down a friend who was siding against Alger Hiss, the American State Department official who was unmasked as a Soviet agent. Muttered Maclean: 'I am the English Hiss.'

The Great Spy Scandal, 1955

The trial of H. A. R. Philby was held at MI5 headquarters in Leconfield House, Curzon Street, Mayfair, in November 1952. Philby would have been perfectly within his rights to refuse to attend; MI5 had no legal powers to compel him to do so. But he had decided that his best hope of remaining in touch with his old service was to cooperate, to show that he was as anxious as anyone to get to the bottom of the Burgess–Maclean business. The officer detailed to conduct what MI5 chose to call 'a judicial inquiry' was Helenus Milmo, later a King's Counsel and a judge, who had worked for MI5 during the war as an interrogator. His bluff, forceful manner had won him the nickname 'Buster'. His approach to Philby was to attempt to bully him into a confession.

From the beginning it was apparent that this was not going to work. Milmo needed rapid-fire questions and rapid-fire answers to corner his quarry. Philby fell back on his intermittent stammer to slow the cross-examination to a pace to suit him. In 1968 *The Sunday Times* spoke with an MI5 officer who was present at the inquiry and he gave this hypothetical example of the type of exchange that drove Milmo to fury. Milmo: 'Was it a fine day?' Philby: 'Yes.' Milmo (pouncing): 'How do you know?' Philby: 'Well . . . there wwwas a temperature of about ffffifty-eight degrees, I suppose. And there wwwas a ssssslight wind from the sssouth. It sssseems to me that constitutes a ffffffine day.'

As we wrote in 1968, 'Not only can a bad stammer be highly destructive of the rhythm and tension of an essentially verbal performance like a cross-examination, it also engenders, however irrationally, a certain sympathy, or at least involuntary queasiness, in even the most hostile listeners.' We decided that Philby had triumphed easily over Milmo and we quoted one of the lawyers present as saying: 'It began to look like the stupidest man in the world cross-examining the cleverest.'

In retrospect, that was a harsh conclusion. For one thing, a former MI5 officer I spoke with in 1984 made the point that although the inquiry failed to produce sufficient evidence to justify a legal action against Philby, 'there was not a single officer who sat through the proceedings who came away not totally convinced of Philby's guilt.' And then, in Moscow, Philby himself complained that accounts of the mock trial made it appear that he had got off lightly.

'It was not like you made out,' he said. 'In the introduction to your book, le Carré argues that the trial was a farce because of the way it was conducted. What does he say. Here it is: "A good interrogator never specifies the charges, never reveals the extent of his knowledge, does not give the suspect the comfort and security of being accompanied by his colleagues, nor the fillip of an examination before an appreciative audience." Well, I was not accompanied by a single one of my colleagues who supported me. The audience was distinctly hostile. Don't forget that Milmo had a highly successful wartime career behind him and he had a very able junior, an MI5 officer, assisting him. Both were notably unfriendly. I don't know who gave you your information, but I've always assumed the course of the interrogation was recorded in some other room, so what I'm telling you can be checked out.

'You have to understand the rarity of the case. For eleven years I had been right inside the service, mostly on the counter-espionage side. I had studied the files in minute detail. I knew all about the procedures. How could Milmo have specified charges which I had not long before anticipated? How could he have revealed knowledge not already in my possession? He did, in fact, slip me one or two surprises, but nothing to signify.

'Now whether the MI5 authorities were right or wrong to confront me with Milmo is a question verging on the moot. They must have known I was exceptionally well armed for the test. The unknown factor was my nerve. They probably hoped that I would break under Milmo's thundering, or at least that it would soften me up for a subsequent probing by the dangerous Skardon [William Skardon, the wartime MI5 interrogator who later broke Fuchs]. Happily my nerve held, as I suspected it might. But if it had broken, the authorities would have been vindicated.'

PHILIP KNIGHTLEY, *Philby*, 1988

† *Coral Browne, while on tour in* Hamlet *in Moscow in 1958, met Guy Burgess, who had defected to Russia. Alan Bennett wrote a play on the subject.*

CORAL. When I came into the flats I noticed a boy sitting on the stairs playing chess.

BURGESS. Police. When I first came I used to be shadowed by rather grand policemen. That was when I was a celebrity. Nowadays they just send the trainees. I wish I could lead them a dance. But I can't think of a dance to lead them.

Mind you, they're more conscientious than their English counterparts. All that last week before we left we were tailed. Maclean lived in Sussex so on the Friday evening we went to Waterloo, dutifully followed by these two men in raincoats. They saw us as far as the barrier and then went home. On the very civilized principle, I suppose, that nothing happens at the weekend. It was the only reason we got away. [*Pause*.] Waterloo the same, is it?

CORAL. Yes. [*Pause*.] What do you miss most?

BURGESS. Apart from the Reform Club, the streets of London, and occasionally the English countryside, the only thing I truly miss is gossip. The comrades, though splendid in every other respect, don't gossip in quite the way we do or about quite the same subjects.

CORAL. Pardon me for saying so, dear, but the comrades seem to me a sad disappointment in every department. There's no gossip, their clothes are terrible and they can't make false teeth. What else is there?

BURGESS [*gently*]. The system. Only, being English, you wouldn't be interested in that. [*Pause*.] My trouble is, I lack what the English call character. By which they mean the power to refrain. Appetite.

The English never like that, do they? Unconcealed appetite. For success. Women. Money. Justice. Appetite makes them uncomfortable. What do people say about me in England?

CORAL. They don't much any more.

[*She gets up and starts tidying the room. Folding clothes, washing dishes. Burgess watches.*

I thought of you as a bit like Oscar Wilde. [*Burgess laughs.*

BURGESS. No, no. Though he was a performer. And I was a performer. Both vain. But I never pretended. If I wore a mask it was to be exactly what I seemed. And I made no bones about politics. My analyses of situations, the précis I had to submit at the Foreign Office, were always Marxist. Openly so. Impeccably so. Nobody minded. 'It's only Guy.' 'Dear old Guy.' Quite safe. If you don't wish to conform in one thing, you should conform in all the others. And in all the important things I did conform. 'How can he be a spy? He goes to my tailor.' The average Englishman, you see, is not interested in ideas. You can say what you like about political theory and no one will listen. You could shove a slice of the Communist Manifesto in the Queen's Speech and no one would turn a hair. Least of all, I suspect, HMQ. Am I boring you?

CORAL. It doesn't matter.

ALAN BENNETT, *An Englishman Abroad*, 1988

IX

TYRANTS

FOR what was left of Rome, Antony, owed its final annihilation to yourself. In your home everything had a price: and a truly sordid series of deals it was. Laws you passed, laws you caused to be put through in your interests, had never even been formally proposed. You admitted this yourself. You were an augur, yet you never took the auspices. You were a consul, yet you blocked the legal right of other officials to exercise the veto. Your armed escort was shocking. You are a drink-sodden, sex-ridden wreck. Never a day passes in that ill-reputed house of yours without orgies of the most repulsive kind. . . . Antony is not attending the Senate today. Why? He is giving a birthday-party on his estate. . . . What a disgusting, intolerable sensualist the man is, as well as a vicious, unsavoury crook!

CICERO, *Cicero against Antony*, 44–43 BC, trans. Michael Grant

. . . the most conspicuous and numerous instances and demonstrations of [Verres'] criminality come from his governorship in Sicily. For three long years he so thoroughly despoiled and pillaged the province that its restoration to its previous state is out of the question. A succession of honest governors, over a period of many years, could scarcely achieve even a partial rehabilitation. While Verres was governor the Sicilians enjoyed the benefit neither of their own laws, nor of the Roman Senate's decrees, nor even of the rights to which everyone in the world is entitled. All the property that anyone in Sicily still has for his own today is merely what happened to escape the attention of this avaricious lecher, or survived his glutted appetites. . . .

When I turn to his adulteries and similar outrages, considerations of decency deter me from giving details of these loathsome manifestations of his lusts. Besides, I do not want, by describing them, to worsen the calamities of the people who have not been permitted to save their children and their wives from Verres' sexual passions. It is, however, incontestable that he himself did not take the slightest precaution to prevent these abominations from becoming universally known. On the contrary, I believe that every man alive who has heard the name of Verres would be able to recount the atrocities which he has committed. I am more likely, therefore, to be criticized for omitting many of his evil deeds than to be suspected of inventing non-existent ones.

CICERO, *Cicero against Verres*, 70 BC, trans. Michael Grant

Caligula deprived the noblest men at Rome of their ancient family emblems—Torquatus lost his golden collar, Cincinnatus his lock of hair, and Gnaeus Pompey the famous surname 'Great'. He invited King Ptolemy to visit Rome, welcomed him with appropriate honours, and then suddenly ordered his execution—as mentioned above—because at Ptolemy's entrance into the amphitheatre during a gladiatorial show the fine purple cloak which he wore had attracted universal admiration. Any good-looking man with a fine head of hair whom Caligula ran across—he himself was bald—had the back of his scalp brutally shaved. One Aesius Proculus, a leading-centurion's son, was so well-built and handsome that people nicknamed him 'Giant Cupid'. Without warning, Caligula ordered Aesius to be dragged from his seat in the amphitheatre into the arena, and matched first with a Thracian net-fighter, then with a man-at-arms. Through Aesius won both combats, he was thereupon dressed in rags, led fettered through the streets to be jeered at by women, and finally executed; the truth being that however low anyone's fortune or condition might be, Caligula always found some cause for envy. Thus he sent a stronger man than the then Sacred King of Nemi to challenge him, after many years of office—because this king, or priest of Diana, was by tradition a fugitive slave who had killed his predecessor with a sword. A chariot-fighter called Parius drew such tremendous applause for freeing his slave in celebration of a victory at the Games that Caligula indignantly rushed from the amphitheatre. In so doing he tripped over the fringe of his robe and pitched down the steps, at the bottom of which he complained that the most powerful race in the world seemed to take greater notice of a gladiator's trifling gesture than of all their deified emperors, or even the one still among them.

He had not the slightest regard for chastity, either his own or others', and was accused of homosexual relations, both active and passive, with Marcus Lepidus, also with Mnester the actor, and various foreign hostages; moreover, a young man of consular family, Valerius Catullus, revealed publicly that he had enjoyed the

Emperor, and that they quite wore one another out in the process. Besides incest with his sisters, and a notorious passion for the prostitute Pyrallis, he made advances to almost every well-known married woman in Rome; after inviting a selection of them to dinner with their husbands he would slowly and carefully examine each in turn while they passed his couch, as a purchaser might assess the value of a slave, and even stretch out his hand and lift up the chin of any woman who kept her eyes modestly cast down. Then, whenever he felt so inclined, he would send for whoever pleased him best, and leave the banquet in her company. A little later he would return, showing obvious signs of what he had been about, and openly discuss his bed-fellow in detail, dwelling on her good and bad physical points and criticizing her sexual performance. To some of these unfortunates he issued, and publicly registered, divorces in the name of their absent husbands.

Caligula had dared commit fearful crimes, and contemplated even worse ones: such as murdering the most distinguished of the senators and knights, and then moving the seat of government first to Antium, and afterwards to Alexandria. If, at this point, my readers become incredulous, let me record that two books were found among his papers entitled *The Dagger* and *The Sword*, each of them containing the names and addresses of men whom he had planned to kill. A huge chest filled with poisons also came to light. It is said that when Claudius later threw this into the sea, quantities of dead fish, cast up by the tide, littered the neighbouring beaches.

Physical characteristics of Caligula:

Height: tall.
Complexion: pallid.
Body: hairy and badly built.
Neck: thin.
Legs: spindling.
Eyes: sunken.
Temples: hollow.
Forehead: broad and forbidding.
Scalp: almost hairless, especially on the poll.

Because of his baldness and hairiness he announced that it was a capital offence for anyone either to look down on him as he passed or to mention goats in any context. He worked hard to make his naturally uncouth face even more repulsive, by practising fearful grimaces in front of a mirror. Caligula was, in fact, sick both physically and mentally. As a boy, he suffered from epilepsy; and although his resistance to the disease gradually strengthened, there were times when he could hardly walk, stand, think, or hold up his head, owing to sudden fits. He was well aware that he had mental trouble, and sometimes proposed taking a leave of absence from Rome to clear his brain; Caesonia is reputed to have given him an aphrodisiac which drove him mad. Insomnia was his worst torment. Three hours a night of fitful sleep were all that he ever got, and even then terrifying visions would haunt him—once, for instance, he dreamed that he had a conversation with the Mediterranean Sea. He tired of lying awake the greater part of the night, and would alternately sit up in bed and wander through the long corridors, invoking the day which seemed as if it would never break.

SUETONIUS (AD *c*.69–*c*.140), *The Twelve Caesars*, trans. Robert Graves

Physical characteristics of Nero:

Height: average.
Body: pustular and malodorous.
Hair: light blond.
Features: pretty, rather than handsome.
Eyes: dullish blue.
Neck: squat.
Belly: protuberant.
Legs: spindling.

His health was amazingly good: for all his extravagant indulgence he had only three illnesses in fourteen years, and none of them serious enough to stop him from drinking wine or breaking any other regular habit. He did not take the least trouble to dress as an Emperor should, but always had his hair set in rows of curls and, when he visited Greece, let it grow long and hang down his back. He often gave audiences in an unbelted silk dressing-gown, slippers, and a scarf.

As a boy Nero read most of the usual school subjects except philosophy which, Agrippina warned him, was no proper study for a future ruler. His tutor Seneca hid the works of the early rhetoricians from him, intending to be admired himself as long as possible. So Nero turned his hand to poetry, and would dash off verses without any effort. It is often claimed that he published other people's work as his own; but notebooks and loose pages have come into my possession, which contain some of Nero's best-known poems in his own handwriting, and have clearly been neither copied nor dictated. Many erasures and cancellations, as well as words substituted above the lines prove that he was thinking things out for himself. Nero also took more than an amateur's interest in painting and sculpture.

Just before the end Nero took a public oath that if he managed to keep his throne he would celebrate the victory with a music festival, performing successively on water-organ, flute, and bagpipes; and when the last day came would dance the role of Turnus in Virgil's *Aeneid*. He was supposed to have killed the actor Paris because he considered him a serious professional rival.

SUETONIUS (AD *c*.69–*c*.140), *The Twelve Caesars*, trans. Robert Graves

CHAUCER ON NERO

Just for the fun of it, he burned down Rome;
Killed all the senators another day,
Only to hear how they would weep and scream;
He killed his brother; with his sister lay;
Dealt with his mother most unspeakably,
And had her womb slit open, to see where
He'd been conceived—alas, alas that he
Should show so little feeling for his mother! . . .

In youth the emperor had a tutor who
Taught him booklearning, manners, courtesy;
He in his time was held to be the flower
Of moral wisdom, if the books don't lie;
And while this tutor held authority,
Nero was made so docile and so clever,
Long was it before vice and tyranny
Dared show themselves in him. This Seneca,

The man I'm talking of—for the good reason
That Nero stood in awe of him—for he'd
Always chastise him, but with tact, for sin,
Never with a blow, but only with a word:
'Sir,' he would say, 'an emperor should indeed
Be virtuous and an enemy of despotism'
—Just for this saying, Nero made him bleed
To death in a bath, with both his arms cut open. . . .

TYRANTS

Now the time came when Fortune would no longer
Cosset this Nero's overbearing pride;
For although he was strong, yet she was stronger.
She reasoned thus: 'By God! I must be mad
To set a man so crammed with every vice
High in the world, and call him emperor!
By God! I'll topple him out of his seat,
And he will fall when he expects it least.'

The people rose against him one dark night
Rebelling at his crimes; upon which he
Hastened alone out of his palace gate
And went where he expected help to be,
And hammered at the door; the more he cried,
The faster all the doors were shut and barred.
Then he realized how he'd been self-deceived;
Not daring to call out, he went away.

The people muttered, crying everywhere,
And he with his own ears heard what they cried.
'Where's that damned tyrant, Nero? Is he here?'
Almost he went out of his wits for fear,
Most pitifully to his gods he prayed
For succour, but it wasn't any good.
For fear of this he thought he would have died,
And ran into a garden, there to hide.

GEOFFREY CHAUCER, 'The Monk's Tale', *c.*1387, trans. David Wright

EPITAPH ON A TYRANT

Perfection, of a kind, was what he was after,
And the poetry he invented was easy to understand;
He knew human folly like the back of his hand,
And was greatly interested in armies and fleets;
When he laughed, respectable senators burst with
laughter,
And when he cried the little children died in the streets.

W. H. AUDEN, 1966

POPE ALEXANDER VI

When Rodrigo Borgia was 62, after 35 years as Cardinal and Vice-Chancellor, his character, habits, principles or lack of them, uses of power, methods of enrichment, mistresses and seven children were well enough known to his colleagues in the College and Curia to evoke from young Giovanni de' Medici at his first conclave the comment on Borgia's elevation to the Papacy, 'Flee, we are in the hands of a wolf.' To the wider circle of the princes of Italy and the rulers of Spain, Borgia's native land, and by repute abroad, the fact that, though cultivated and even charming, he was thoroughly cynical and utterly amoral was no secret and no surprise, although his reputation for depravity was not yet what it would become. His frame of mind was heartily temporal: to celebrate the final expulsion of the Moors from Spain, in 1492, the year of his election, he staged not a Te Deum of thanksgiving but a bullfight in the Piazza of St Peter's with five bulls killed.

BARBARA TUCHMAN, *The March of Folly*, 1988

POISONERS POISONED: CAESAR BORGIA AND POPE ALEXANDER

When the price of their elevation was duly paid, and the places left vacant by them had been sold, the pope made his selection of those who were to be poisoned. The number was fixed at three—one of earlier creation, Cardinal Casanova, and two of the new set, Melchior Copis, and Adriano Castellense, the latter of whom took the name of Adriano di Corneto, from the town where he was born; he had amassed an immense fortune in the offices of clerk of the chamber, treasurer-general, and secretary of apostolic letters.

When this course of action was fully agreed upon by Caesar and the pope, they issued invitations to a supper-party to be given at a villa not far from the Vatican belonging to Cardinal di Corneto. In the morning of the day appointed for this festival, which was the second of August, they sent their own servants and their *maitre d'hotel* to make all necessary preparations, and Caesar himself handed to the pope's butler two bottles of wine, with which was mixed a quantity of that white powder resembling sugar, the deadly properties of which he had so often put to the test. He directed him not to serve it until he should tell him to do so, and then only to such of the guests as he should indicate. The butler therefore placed it on a buffet by itself, and cautioned the servants not to touch it, as it was reserved for the pope.

Toward evening Alexander left the Vatican on foot, leaning on Caesar's arm, and walked in the direction of the villa, accompanied by Cardinal Caraffa. It was very hot and the ascent was somewhat sharp, so that the pope when he reached the terrace stopped to take breath. At that moment, as he put his hand to his breast, he found that he had left in his bedroom a chain which he was accustomed to wear around his neck, and to which was attached a gold locket containing a consecrated wafer. He had adopted the habit of wearing it because an astrologer had predicted that, so long as he carried a consecrated wafer about with him neither steel nor poison could harm him. He at once ordered Cardinal Caraffa to hurry back to the Vatican to fetch the talisman, describing to him minutely just the spot where he left it. As the walk had made him very thirsty, he turned to a servant and asked him for something to drink; and Caesar, whose thirst was equally great, ordered him to bring two glasses.

By a strange chance it happened that the butler had returned to the Vatican to fetch some superb fish, which were presented to the pope that very day, and which he forgot to bring with him. The servant therefore applied to the under-butler, saying to him that his Holiness and the Duke of Romagna were very thirsty and desired something to quench their thirst. The under-butler, seeing two bottles of wine standing apart, and remembering that he had heard some one say that they were for the pope, took one of them, and from it filled two glasses, which the servant carried to them upon a salver. They both drank without a suspicion that it was the wine which they had themselves prepared to poison their guests.

The two sick men were carried side by side to the Vatican, where they parted, each to go to his own apartments; from that moment they never saw each other more.

As soon as he was put to bed, the pope was seized with a violent fever which refused to yield, either to emetics or to blood-letting, and it was deemed best to administer the last sacraments of the Church almost immediately. But his vigorous constitution, which seemed to have set the natural effect of advancing years at defiance, struggled against death for a whole week. He died at last without once mentioning the name of Caesar or Lucrezia, although they were the two centres around which all his affections and all his crimes revolved. He was seventy-two years old, and his pontificate had lasted eleven years.

It may be that Caesar drank less of the deadly compound than his father, it may be that the vigor of his youth overpowered the vigor of the poison, it may be, as some claimed, that, when he was taken to his room he swallowed an antidote which was known to none but himself; at all events he did not for an instant lose his perception of the terrible position in which he was placed. He sent at once for his faithful Michelotto with those of his men in whom he placed the most confidence, and distributed them through the various rooms preceding his own; he ordered the leader not to leave the foot of his bed for an instant, and to sleep upon a blanket with his hand on his sword hilt.

The treatment employed in Caesar's case was the same as in his father's, emetics and blood-letting, with the addition of a strange kind of bath which he asked for himself, having heard it said that King Ladislas of Naples was once cured thereby under similar circumstances.

Four upright posts were firmly attached to the floor of his room; every day a bull was brought in and thrown over on his back, and his legs made fast to the posts. Then an incision a foot and a half long was made in his belly, through which the intestines were taken out, and Caesar crawled into the still living receptacle, and bathed himself in the animal's blood. When the bull was dead he crawled out again and was rolled in blankets soaked in boiling water, and the profuse perspiration thus induced almost always relieved him.

ALEXANDER DUMAS, *Celebrated Crimes*, 1839–41, trans. I. C. Burnham

'This beautiful face touches across the centuries, it is so subtle and yielding, yet innocent. Her name is Lucrezia Borgia.'

'Yes, I know. I knew her brother once—but only for a short time.'

STEVIE SMITH (1902–71), 'Some are More Human than Others'.

TYRANTS

The hand that signed the paper felled a city;
Five sovereign fingers taxed the breath,
Doubled the globe of dead and halved a country;
These five kings did a king to death.

The mighty hand leads to a sloping shoulder,
The finger joints are cramped with chalk;
A goose's quill has put an end to murder
That put an end to talk.

The hand that signed the treaty bred a fever,
And famine grew, and locusts came;
Great is the hand that holds dominion over
Man by a scribbled name.

The five kings count the dead but do not soften
The crusted wound nor stroke the brow;
A hand rules pity as a hand rules heaven;
Hands have no tears to flow.

DYLAN THOMAS (1914–53)

JUDGE JEFFREYS

His enemies could not deny that he possessed some of the qualities of a great judge. His legal knowledge, indeed, was merely such as he had picked up in practice of no very high kind. But he had one of those happily constituted intellects which, across labyrinths of sophistry, and through masses of immaterial facts, go straight to the true point. Of his intellect, however, he seldom had the full use. Even in civil causes his malevolent and despotic temper perpetually disordered his judgment. To enter his court was to enter the den of a wild beast, which none could tame, and which was as likely to be roused to rage by caresses as by attacks. He frequently poured forth on plaintiffs and defendants, barristers and attorneys, witnesses and jurymen, torrents of frantic abuse, intermixed with oaths and curses. His looks and tones had inspired terror when he was merely a young advocate struggling into practice. Now that he was at the head of the most formidable tribunal in the realm, there were few indeed who did not tremble before him. Even when he was sober, his violence was sufficiently frightful. But in general his reason was overclouded and his evil passions stimulated by the fumes of intoxication. His evenings were ordinarily given to revelry. People who saw him only over his bottle would have supposed him to be a man gross indeed, sottish, and addicted to low company and low merriment, but social and goodhumoured. He was constantly surrounded on such occasions by buffoons selected, for the most part, from among the vilest pettifoggers who practised before him. These men bantered and abused each other for his entertainment. He joined in their ribald talk, sang catches with them, and, when his head grew hot, hugged and kissed them in an ecstasy of drunken fondness. But, though wine at first seemed to soften his heart, the effect a few hours later was very different. He often came to the judgment seat, having kept the court waiting long, and yet having but half slept off his debauch, his cheeks on fire, his eyes staring like those of a maniac. When he was in this state, his boon companions of the preceding night, if they were wise, kept out of his way: for the recollection of the familiarity to which he had admitted them inflamed his malignity; and he was sure to take every opportunity of overwhelming them with execration and invective. Not the least odious of his many odious peculiarities was the pleasure which he took in publicly browbeating and mortifying those whom, in his fits of maudlin tenderness, he had encouraged to presume on his favour.

The services which the government had expected from him were performed, not merely without flinching, but eagerly and triumphantly. His first exploit was the judicial murder of Algernon Sidney. What followed was in perfect harmony with this beginning. Respectable Tories lamented the disgrace which the barbarity and indecency of so great a functionary brought upon the administration of justice. But the excesses which filled such men with horror were titles to the esteem of James. Jeffreys, therefore, after the death of Charles, obtained a seat in the cabinet and a peerage. This last honour was a signal mark of royal approbation. For, since the judicial system of the realm had been remodelled in the thirteenth century, no Chief Justice had been a Lord of Parliament.

THOMAS BABINGTON, LORD MACAULAY, *The History of England*, 1849–61

A HANGING JUDGE

My Lord Hermiston occupied the bench in the red robes of criminal jurisdiction, his face framed in the white wig. Honest all through, he did not affect the virtue of impartiality; this was no case for refinement; there was a man to be hanged, he would have said, and he was hanging him. Nor was it possible to see his lordship, and acquit him of gusto in the task. It was plain he gloried in the exercise of his trained faculties, in the clear sight which pierced at once into the joint of fact, in the rude, unvarnished gibes with which he demolished every figment of defence. He took his case and jested, unbending in that solemn place with some of the freedom of the tavern; and the rag of man with the flannel round his neck was hunted gallowsward with jeers.

Duncan had a mistress, scarce less forlorn and greatly older than himself, who came up, whimpering and curtseying, to add the weight of her betrayal. My lord gave her the oath in his most roaring voice, and added an intolerant warning.

'Mind what ye say now, Janet,' said he. 'I have an e'e upon ye, I'm ill to jest with.'

Presently, after she was tremblingly embarked on her story, 'And what made ye do this, ye auld runt?' the Court interposed. 'Do ye mean to tell me ye was the panel's mistress?'

'If you please, ma loard,' whined the female.

'Godsake! ye made a bonny couple,' observed his lordship; and there was something so formidable and ferocious in his scorn that not even the galleries thought to laugh.

The summing up contained some jewels.

'These two peetiable creatures seem to have made up thegither, it's not for us to explain why.'—'The panel, who (whatever else he may be) appears to be equally ill set-out in mind and boady.'—'Neither the panel nor yet the old wife appears to have had so much common sense as even to tell a lie when it was necessary.' And in the course of sentencing, my lord had this *obiter dictum*: 'I have been the means, under God, of hanging a great number, but never just such a disjaskit rascal as yourself.' The words were strong in themselves; the light and heat and detonation of their delivery, and the savage pleasure of the speaker in his task, made them tingle in the ears.

ROBERT LOUIS STEVENSON, *Weir of Hermiston*, 1896

† *Rumpole defends a parson charged with stealing shirts from a department store, before Judge Bullingham.*

I tried to instil a suitable sense of the solemnity of the occasion in my clerical customer by telling him that God, with that wonderful talent for practical joking which has shown itself throughout recorded history, had dealt us His Honour Judge Bullingham.

'Is he very dreadful?' Mr Skinner asked almost hopefully.

'Why he was ever made a judge is one of the unsolved mysteries of the universe.' I was determined not to sound reassuring. 'I can only suppose that his unreasoning prejudice against all black persons, defence lawyers and probation officers, comes from some deep psychological cause. Perhaps his mother, if such a person can be imagined, was once assaulted by a black probation officer who was on his way to give evidence for the defence.'

'I wonder how he feels about parsons.' My client seemed not at all put out.

'God knows. I rather doubt if he's ever met one. The Bull's leisure taste runs to strong drink and all-in wrestling. Come along, we might as well enter the *corrida*.'

A couple of hours later, His Honour Judge Bullingham, with his thick neck and complexion of a beetroot past its first youth, was calmly exploring his inner ear with his little finger and tolerantly allowing me to cross-examine a large gentleman named Pratt, resident flatfoot at the Oxford Street Bazaar.

'Mr Pratt? How long have you been a detective in this particular store?'

'Ten years, sir.'

'And before that?'

'I was with the Metropolitan Police.'

'Why did you leave?'

'Pay and conditions, sir, were hardly satisfactory.'

'Oh, really? You found it more profitable to keep your beady eyes on the ladies' lingerie counter than do battle in the streets with serious crime?'

'Are you suggesting that this isn't a serious crime, Mr Rumpole?' The learned judge, who pots villains with all the subtlety of his namesake animal charging a gate, growled this question at me with his face going a darker purple than ever, and his jowls trembling.

'For many people, my Lord,' I turned to the jury and gave them the message, 'six shirts might be a mere triviality. For the Reverend Mordred Skinner, they represent the possibility of total ruin, disgrace and disaster. In this case my client's whole life hangs in the balance.' I turned a flattering gaze on the twelve honest citizens who had been chosen to pronounce on the sanctity or otherwise of the Reverend Mordred. 'That is why we must cling to our most cherished institution, trial by jury. It is not the value of the property stolen, it is the priceless matter of a man's good reputation.'

'Mister Rumpole,' the Bull lifted his head as if for the charge. 'You should know your business by now. This is not the time for making speeches, you will have an opportunity at the end of the case.'

'And as your Honour will have an opportunity *after* me to make a speech, I thought it as well to make clear who the judges of *fact* in this matter are.' I continued to look at the jury with an expression of flattering devotion.

'Yes. Very well. Let's get on with it.' The Bull retreated momentarily. I rubbed in the victory.

'Certainly. That is what I was attempting to do.' I turned to the witness. 'Mr Pratt. When you were in the gents' haberdashery . . .'

'Yes, sir?'

'You didn't see my client remove the shirts from the counter and make off with them?'

'No, sir.'

'If he had, no doubt he would have told us about it,' Bullingham could not resist growling. I gave him a little bow.

'Your Honour is always so quick to notice points in favour of the defence.' I went back to work on the store detective. 'So why did you follow my client?'

'The Supervisor noticed a pile of shirts missing. She said there was a Reverend been turning them over, your Honour.'

This tit-bit delighted the Bull, he snatched at it greedily. 'He might not have told us that, if you hadn't asked the wrong question, Mr Rumpole.'

'No question is wrong, if it reveals the truth,' I informed the jury, and then turned back to Pratt. I had an idea, an uncomfortable feeling that I might just have guessed the truth of this peculiar case. 'So you don't know if he was carrying the basket when he left the shirt department?'

'No.'

'Was he carrying it when you first spotted him, on the moving staircase?'

'I only saw his head and shoulders . . .'

The pieces were fitting together. I would have to face my client with my growing notion of defence as soon as possible. 'So you first saw him with the basket in the Hall of Food?'

'That's right, sir.'

At which point Bullingham stirred dangerously and raised the curtain of his top lip on some large yellowing teeth. He was about to make a joke. 'Are you suggesting, Mr Rumpole, that a basket full of shirts mysteriously materialized in your client's hand in the Tinned Meat Department?'

At which the jury laughed obsequiously. Rumpole silenced them in a voice of enormous gravity.

'Might I remind your Honour of what he said. This is a serious case.'

'As you cross-examined, Mr Rumpole, I was beginning to wonder.' Bullingham was still grinning.

'The art of cross-examination, your Honour, is a little like walking a tight-rope.'

'Oh is it?'

'One gets on so much better if one isn't continually interrupted.'

At which Bullingham relapsed into a sullen silence and I got on with the work in hand.

JOHN MORTIMER, 'Rumpole and the Man of God', 1979

Mr Justice Graves. What a contradiction in terms! Mr 'Injustice' Graves, Mr 'Penal' Graves, Mr 'Prejudice' Graves, Mr 'Get into Bed with the Prosecution' Graves—all these titles might be appropriate. But Mr 'Justice' Graves, so far as I'm concerned, can produce nothing but a hollow laugh. From all this you may deduce that the old darling is not my favourite member of the Judiciary. Now he has been promoted, on some sort of puckish whim of the Lord Chancellor's from Old Bailey Judge to a scarlet and ermine Justice of the Queen's Bench, his power to do harm has been considerably increased. Those who have followed my legal career will remember the awesome spectacle of the mad Judge Bullingham, with lowered head and bloodshot eyes, charging into the ring in the hope of impaling Rumpole upon a horn.

But now we have lost him, I actually miss the old Bull. There was a sort of excitement in the *corridas* we lived through together and I often emerged with a couple of ears and a tail. A session before Judge Graves has all the excitement and colour of a Wesleyan funeral on a wet day in Wigan. His pale Lordship presides sitting bolt upright as though he had a poker up his backside, his voice is dirge-like and his eyes close in pain if he is treated with anything less than an obsequious grovel.

JOHN MORTIMER, 'Rumpole at Sea', 1990

SIMILE FOR TWO POLITICAL CHARACTERS OF 1819

As from an ancestral oak
  Two empty ravens sound their clarion,
Yell by yell, and croak by croak,
When they scent the noonday smoke
  Of fresh human carrion:—

As two gibbering night-birds flit
  From their bowers of deadly yew
Through the night to frighten it,
When the moon is in a fit,
  And the stars are none, or few:—

As a shark and dog-fish wait
  Under an Atlantic isle,
For the negro-ship, whose freight
Is the theme of their debate,
  Wrinkling their red gills the while—

Are ye, two vultures sick for battle,
  Two scorpions under one wet stone,
Two bloodless wolves whose dry throats rattle,
Two crows perched on the murrained cattle,
  Two vipers tangled into one.

PERCY BYSSHE SHELLEY, 1819

HITLER

I have the gift of reducing all problems to their simplest foundations.

Why babble about brutality and be indignant about tortures? The masses want that. They need something that will give them a thrill of horror.

The day of individual happiness has passed.

Don't waste your time over 'intellectual' meetings and groups drawn together by mutual interests. Anything you may achieve with such folk to-day by means of reasonable explanation may be erased tomorrow by an opposite explanation. But what you tell the people in the mass, in a receptive state of fanatic devotion, will remain words received under an hypnotic influence, ineradicable, and impervious to every reasonable explanation.

A new age of magic interpretation of the world is coming, of interpretation in terms of the will and not of the intelligence. There is no such thing as truth, either in the moral or in the scientific sense.

I am restoring to force its original dignity, that of the source of all greatness and the creatrix of order.

ADOLF HITLER, quoted in W. H. Auden, *A Certain World*, 1971

THE DEATH OF MUSSOLINI

The end came on April 25, 1945. The Germans had signed a secret armistice with the Allies, behind his back, and were giving themselves up to the Allies as prisoners of war. He tried to negotiate his own armistice through the Archbishop of Milan but soon realized he had no power . . . He made up his mind to go directly to Switzerland, without wasting time in more futile and bloody heroics, carrying all his money and all his most useful documents, those he would employ to frighten Allied statesmen and to defend himself if he were tried as a war criminal. He was found and arrested by partisans on the road going north along the shore of Lake Como, hiding in a German truck, dressed in the heavy coat of a German petty officer and a German helmet. Claretta Petacci was arrested with him.

They were both shot against the ornate gate of a pompous villa, the next morning. The woman had tried to shield his body and was mown down with him. The money and documents disappeared for ever. The bodies were taken to Milan and hung . . . feet high, from a petrol station roof, alongside those of all the other Fascist chiefs caught and killed on the same road, on their way to Switzerland. Thirteen years before he had told Emil Ludwig: 'Everybody dies the death that corresponds to his character.' He had deluded the people, that was his crime. But his fatal error was that he had not known that the people were also deluding him. They led him to the catastrophe which was the only way they knew to get rid of him.

LUIGI BARZINI, *The Italians*, 1964

SENATOR McCARTHY

The most interesting talk I recall having in that barren week of my trial was with former senator Harry P. Cain, whom Rauh had brought up from his semi-retirement in Florida to testify as my 'expert witness on Communism.' He had read my plays and did not believe I had been 'under the discipline of the Communist Party.' Normally in such trials it was the government alone that produced 'expert testimony,' usually from ex-Communist officials, to prove that the defendant showed all the necessary hoof-marks of the Communist Lucifer. This routine, incidentally, was an all but exact duplication of the use of clergy as experts on witchcraft in the Salem of 1692; one of them, Reverend Hale of Beverly, is a character in *The Crucible*. Hale in my play, like his original in history, defected from the prosecution's side on realizing that he had been had by the 'afflicted girls' and, filled with remorse, tried unsuccessfully to save the people his earlier 'expertise' had helped condemn to hang. Harry Cain's story, I now learned, was amazingly similar.

A much decorated marine who had fought in the Korean War, Cain was one of a very few Red-hunters to have turned against the whole business, in his case with a vengeance. He had ridden the anti-Communist tide out of his native state of Washington when, with no trace of any political background, he was picked up by the Republicans and run for the Senate. His sole campaign theme was the Communist menace, about which he had such powerful feelings that he would demand Chaplin's deportation for having asked 'the self-admitted

Communist Picasso' to help organize French protests against American repression.

Joe McCarthy came out to help him, and even then, in the full flood of his fervor, Cain noticed something disconcerting about Joe's paranoid vindictiveness. One night they were both on the platform in an American Legion hall when 'some guy got up in the back and began heckling McCarthy. The boys threw him out in the street, but you couldn't help noticing how really mad McCarthy was at the guy—I mean he was mad *personally*, he was damn near shaken. It was weird.

'Anyway, some years passed, and we were playing poker with the wives one evening, and suddenly Joe looks at me and says, "What'd you do about that guy?"

'I didn't know who he was talking about. "That guy in the Legion hall that night who was bugging me."

'It took me a minute to recall, it had been so long ago. I couldn't believe he'd even remember it, but it still really bothered him that somebody way, way back there in Tacoma hadn't gone along with him. And I said something like, "I don't know, I guess they just tossed him out of the hall. Why?"

' "*Why!* For Chrissake, the son of a bitch was heckling me!"—and he was mad as hell all over again.'

ARTHUR MILLER, *Time Bends*, 1987

† *The nineteenth-century Irish novelist William Carleton was one who made his villains as villainous as possible; and he did not hesitate to lumber his 'Irish agent' (Valentine M'Clutchy) with as many defects as he could muster.*

'Well now,' said M'Loughlin, rising up, whilst his honest features were lit with indignation, 'this joke or this impudence on your part has gone far enough—listen to me. What did I or my family do, I ask my own conscience in the name of God—what sin did we commit—whom did we oppress—whom did we rob—whom did we persecute—that a scoundrel like you, the bastard spawn of an unprincipled profligate, remarkable only for drunkenness, debauchery, and blasphemy; what, I say, did I and my family do, that you, his son, who were, and are to this day, the low, mean, willing scourge of every oppressor, the agent of their crimes—the instrument of their villanies—you who undermined the honest man—who sold and betrayed the poor man—who deceived and misled the widow and her orphans, and rose upon their ruin—who have robbed your employers as well as those you were employed against—a double traitor—steeped in treachery, and perjured a thousand times to the core of your black and deceitful heart—what crime, I say again, did I or mine commit—that we, whose name and blood have been without a stain for a thousand years, should suffer the insult that you have now offered us? Eh, look me in the face now if you can, and answer me if you are able?'

M'Loughlin, as he concluded, calmly folded his arms, and looked at his companion resolutely, but sternly. The other, to do him justice, did certainly raise his head, and fix his evil eye upon him for a moment, but only for a moment—it dropped after a single glance; in truth, he quailed before M'Loughlin; his upper lip, as usual quivered—his brow lowered, and looked black as midnight, whilst all the rest of his face became the colour of ashes. In fact, that white smile, which is known to be the very emblem of cowardice and revenge, sat upon his countenance, stamping on it at once the character of the spectre and the demon—a being to be both feared and hated.

WILLIAM CARLETON, *Valentine M'Clutchy, the Irish Agent*, 1846

† *Victorian fiction produced a crop of tyrannical schoolmasters. Of those who practised mental cruelty and physical deprivation to the top of their bent, Mr Brocklehurst of Lowood School is a prime example.*

. . . Mr Brocklehurst, standing on the hearth, with his hands behind his back, majestically surveyed the whole school. Suddenly his eye gave a blink, as if it had met something that either dazzled or shocked its pupil; turning, he said in more rapid accents than he had hitherto used:—

'Miss Temple, Miss Temple, what—*what* is that girl with curled hair? Red hair, ma'am, curled—curled all over?' And extending his cane he pointed to the awful object, his hand shaking as he did so.

'It is Julia Severn,' replied Miss Temple, very quietly.

'Julia Severn, ma'am! And why has she, or any other, curled hair? Why, in defiance of every precept and principle of this house, does she conform to the world so openly—here, in an evangelical, charitable establishment—as to wear her hair one mass of curls?'

'Julia's hair curls naturally,' returned Miss Temple, still more quietly.

'Naturally! Yes, but we are not to conform to nature. I wish these girls to be the children of Grace; and why that abundance? I have again and again intimated that I desire the hair to be arranged closely, modestly, plainly. Miss Temple, that girl's hair must be cut off entirely; I will send a barber to-morrow; and I see others who have far too much of the excrescence—that tall girl, tell her to turn round. Tell all the first form to rise up and direct their faces to the wall.'

Miss Temple passed her handkerchief over her lips, as if to smooth away the involuntary smile that curled them; she gave the order, however, and when the first class could take in what was required of them, they obeyed. Leaning a little back on my bench, I could see the looks and grimaces with which they commented on this manœuvre: it was a pity Mr Brocklehurst could not see them too; he would perhaps have felt that, whatever he might do with the outside of the cup and platter, the inside was further beyond his interference than he imagined.

He scrutinized the reverse of these living medals some five minutes, then pronounced sentence. These words fell like the knell of doom:

'All those top-knots must be cut off.'

Miss Temple seemed to remonstrate.

'Madam,' he pursued, 'I have a Master to serve whose kingdom is not of this world; my mission is to mortify in these girls the lusts of the flesh; to teach them to clothe themselves with shamefacedness and sobriety, not with braided hair and costly apparel; and each of the young persons before us has a string of hair twisted in plaits which vanity itself might have woven: these, I repeat, must be cut off; think of the time wasted, of—'

Mr Brocklehurst was here interrupted; three other visitors, ladies, now entered the room. They ought to have come a little sooner to have heard his lecture on dress, for they were splendidly attired in velvet, silk, and furs. The two younger of the trio (fine girls of sixteen and seventeen) had grey beaver hats, then in fashion, shaded with ostrich plumes, and from under the brim of this graceful head-dress fell a profusion of light tresses, elaborately curled; the elder lady was enveloped in a costly velvet shawl trimmed with ermine, and she wore a false front of French curls.

These ladies were deferentially received by Miss Temple, as Mrs and Misses Brocklehurst, and conducted to seats of honour at the top of the room.

CHARLOTTE BRONTË, *Jane Eyre*, 1847

'Now let us see,' said Squeers. 'A letter for Cobbey. Stand up, Cobbey.'

Another boy stood up, and eyed the letter very hard while Squeers made a mental abstract of the same.

'Oh!' said Squeers: 'Cobbey's grandmother is dead, and his uncle John has took to drinking, which is all the news his sister sends, except eighteenpence, which will just pay for that broken square of glass. Mrs Squeers, my dear, will you take the money?'

The worthy lady pocketed the eighteenpence with a most business-like air, and Squeers passed on to the next boy, as coolly as possible.

'Graymarsh,' said Squeers, 'he's the next. Stand up, Graymarsh.'

Another boy stood up, and the schoolmaster looked over the letter as before.

'Graymarsh's maternal aunt,' said Squeers, when he had possessed himself of the contents, 'is very glad to hear he's so well and happy, and sends her respectful compliments to Mrs Squeers, and thinks she must be an angel. She likewise thinks Mr Squeers is too good for this world; but hopes he may long be spared to carry on the business. Would have sent the two pair of stockings as desired, but is short of money, so forwards a tract instead, and hopes Graymarsh will put his trust in Providence. Hopes, above all, that he will study in everything to please Mr and Mrs Squeers, and look upon them as his only friends; and that he will love Master Squeers; and not object to sleeping five in a bed, which no Christian should. Ah!' said Squeers, folding it up, 'a delightful letter. Very affecting indeed.'

It was affecting in one sense, for Graymarsh's maternal aunt was strongly supposed, by her more intimate friends, to be no other than his maternal parent; Squeers, however, without alluding to this part of the story (which would have sounded immoral before boys), proceeded with the business by calling out 'Mobbs,' whereupon another boy rose, and Graymarsh resumed his seat.

'Mobbs's mother-in-law,' said Squeers, 'took to her bed on hearing that he wouldn't eat fat, and has been very ill ever since. She wishes to know, by an early post, where he expects to go to, if he quarrels with his vittles; and with what feelings he could turn up his nose at the cow's liver broth, after his good master had asked a blessing on it. This was told her in the London newspapers—not by Mr Squeers, for he is too kind and too good to set anybody against anybody—and it has vexed her so much, Mobbs can't think. She is sorry to find he is discontented, which is sinful and horrid, and hopes Mr Squeers will flog him into a happier state of mind; with this view, she has also stopped his halfpenny a week pocket-money, and given a double-bladed knife with a corkscrew in it to the Missionaries, which she had bought on purpose for him.'

'A sulky state of feeling,' said Squeers, after a terrible pause, during which he had moistened the palm of his right hand again, 'won't do. Cheerfulness and contentment must be kept up. Mobbs, come to me!'

CHARLES DICKENS, *Nicholas Nickleby*, 1838–9

† *The bully Flashman is the tyrant of Rugby in* Tom Brown's Schooldays.

The sporting set . . . gathered round Tom. Public opinion wouldn't allow them actually to rob him of his ticket, but any humbug or intimidation by which he could be driven to sell the whole or part at an undervalue was lawful.

'Now, young Brown, come, what'll you sell me Harkaway for? I hear he isn't going to start. I'll give you five shillings for him,' begins the boy who had opened the ticket. Tom, remembering his good deed, and moreover in his forlorn state wishing to make a friend, is about to accept the offer, when another cries out, 'I'll give you seven shillings.' Tom hesitated, and looked from one to the other.

'No, no!' said Flashman, pushing in, 'leave me to deal with him; we'll draw lots for it afterwards. Now, sir, you know me—you'll sell Harkaway to us for five shillings, or you'll repent it.'

'I won't sell a bit of him,' answered Tom shortly.

'You hear that now!' said Flashman, turning to the others. 'He's the coxiest young blackguard in the house—I always told you so. We're to have all the trouble and risk of getting up the lotteries for the benefit of such fellows as he.'

Flashman forgets to explain what risk they ran, but he speaks to willing ears. Gambling makes boys selfish and cruel as well as men.

'That's true,—we always draw blanks,' cried one. 'Now, sir, you shall sell half at any rate.'

'I won't,' said Tom, flushing up to his hair, and lumping them all in his mind with his sworn enemy.

'Very well then, let's roast him,' cried Flashman, and catches hold of Tom by the collar: one or two boys hesitate, but the rest join in. East seizes Tom's arm and tries to pull him away, but is knocked back by one of the boys, and Tom is dragged along struggling. His shoulders are pushed against the mantelpiece, and he is held by main force before the fire, Flashman drawing his trousers tight by way of extra torture. Poor East, in more pain even than Tom, suddenly thinks of Diggs, and darts off to find him. 'Will you sell now for ten shillings?' says one boy who is relenting.

Tom only answers by groans and struggles.

'I say, Flashey, he has had enough,' says the same boy, dropping the arm he holds.

'No, no, another turn'll do it,' answers Flashman. But poor Tom is done already, turns deadly pale, and his head falls forward on his breast, just as Diggs, in frantic excitement, rushes into the Hall with East at his heels.

'You cowardly brutes!' is all he can say, as he catches Tom from them and supports him to the Hall table. 'Good God! he's dying. Here, get some cold water—run for the housekeeper.'

Flashman and one or two others slink away; the rest, ashamed and sorry, bend over Tom or run for water, while East darts off for the housekeeper. Water comes, and they throw it on his hands and face, and he begins to come to. 'Mother!'—the words came feebly and slowly—'it's very cold to-night.' Poor old Diggs is blubbering like a child. 'Where am I?' goes on Tom, opening his eyes. 'Ah! I remember now,' and he shut his eyes again and groaned.

'I say,' is whispered, 'we can't do any good, and the housekeeper will be here in a minute,' and all but one steal away; he stays with Diggs, silent and sorrowful, and fans Tom's face.

The housekeeper comes in with strong salts, and Tom soon recovers enough to sit up. There is a smell of burning; she examines his clothes, and looks up inquiringly. The boys are silent.

'How did he come so?' No answer.

'There's been some bad work here,' she adds, looking very serious, 'and I shall speak to the Doctor about it.' Still no answer.

THOMAS HUGHES, *Tom Brown's Schooldays*, 1857

On the very first morning after her arrival she was up and ringing her bell at cock-crow. When my mother came down to breakfast and was going to make the tea, Miss Murdstone gave her a kind of peck on the cheek, which was her nearest approach to a kiss, and said—

'Now, Clara, my dear, I am come here, you know, to relieve you of all the trouble I can. You're much too pretty and thoughtless'—my mother blushed but laughed, and seemed not to dislike this character—'to have any duties imposed upon you that can be undertaken by me. If you'll be so good as give me your keys, my dear, I'll attend to all this sort of thing in future.'

From that time, Miss Murdstone kept the keys in her own little jail all day, and under her pillow all night, and my mother had no more to do with them than I had.

My mother did not suffer her authority to pass from her without a shadow of protest. One night when Miss Murdstone had been developing certain household plans to her brother, of which he signified his approbation, my mother suddenly began to cry, and said she thought she might have been consulted.

'Clara!' said Mr Murdstone sternly. 'Clara! I wonder at you.'

'Oh, it's very well to say you wonder, Edward!' cried my mother, 'and it's very well for you to talk about firmness, but you wouldn't like it yourself.'

Firmness, I may observe, was the grand quality on which both Mr and Miss Murdstone took their stand. However I might have expressed my comprehension of it at that time, if I had been called upon, I nevertheless did clearly comprehend in my own way, that it was another name for tyranny; and for a certain gloomy, arrogant, devil's humour, that was in them both. The creed, as I should state it now, was this. Mr Murdstone was firm; nobody in his world was to be so firm as Mr Murdstone; nobody else in his world was to be firm at all, for everybody was to be bent to his firmness. Miss Murdstone was an exception. She might be firm, but only by relationship, and in an inferior and tributary degree. My mother was another exception.

She might be firm, and must be; but only in bearing their firmness, and firmly believing there was no other firmness upon earth.

'It's very hard,' said my mother, 'that in my own house—'

'*My* own house?' repeated Mr Murdstone. 'Clara!'

'*Our* own house, I mean,' faltered my mother, evidently frightened —'I hope you must know what I mean, Edward—it's very hard that in *your* own house I may not have a word to say about domestic matters. I am sure I managed very well before we were married. There's evidence,' said my mother sobbing; 'ask Peggotty if I didn't do very well when I wasn't interfered with!'

'Edward,' said Miss Murdstone, 'let there be an end of this. I go to-morrow.'

'Jane Murdstone,' said her brother, 'be silent! How dare you to insinuate that you don't know my character better than your words imply?'

CHARLES DICKENS, *David Copperfield*, 1849–50

† *The bullying sweep Mr Grimes is stuck inside a prison chimney, deprived of the consolations of tobacco and drink, and menaced by an animated truncheon. This is a fit payment for the ill-treatment he inflicted on Tom and all the other apprentices.*

A wicket in the door opened, and out looked a tremendous old brass blunderbuss charged up to the muzzle with slugs, who was the porter; and Tom started back a little at the sight of him.

'What case is this?' he asked in a deep voice; out of his broad bell mouth.

'If you please, sir, it is no case; only a young gentleman from her ladyship, who wants to see Grimes, the master-sweep.'

'Grimes?' said the blunderbuss. And he pulled in his muzzle, perhaps to look over his prison-lists.

'Grimes is up chimney No. 345,' he said from inside. 'So the young gentleman had better go on to the roof.'

Tom looked up at the enormous wall, which seemed at least ninety miles high, and wondered how he should ever get up: but, when he hinted that to the truncheon, it settled the matter in a moment. For it whisked round and gave him such a shove behind as sent him up to the roof in no time, with his little dog under his arm.

And there he walked along the leads, till he met another truncheon, and told him his errand.

'Very good,' it said. 'Come along: but it will be of no use. He is the most unremorseful, hard-hearted, foul-mouthed fellow I have in charge; and thinks about nothing but beer and pipes; which are not allowed here, of course.'

So they walked along over the leads, and very sooty they were, and Tom thought the chimneys must want sweeping very much. But he was surprised to see that the soot did not stick to his feet, or dirty them in the least.

And at last they came to chimney No. 345. Out of the top of it, his head and shoulders just showing, stuck poor Mr Grimes, so sooty, and bleared, and ugly, that Tom could hardly bear to look at him. And in his mouth was a pipe; but it was not alight; though he was pulling at it with all his might.

'Attention, Mr Grimes,' said the truncheon; 'here is a gentleman come to see you.'

But Mr Grimes only said bad words; and kept grumbling. 'My pipe won't draw. My pipe won't draw.'

'Keep a civil tongue, and attend!' said the truncheon; and popped up just like Punch, hitting Grimes such a crack over the head with itself, that his brains rattled inside like a dried walnut in its shell. He tried to get his hands out, and rub the place; but he could not, for they were stuck fast in the chimney. Now he was forced to attend.

'Hey!' he said, 'why, it's Tom! I suppose you have come here to laugh at me, you spiteful little atomy?'

Tom assured him he had not, but only wanted to help him.

'I don't want anything except beer, and that I can't get; and a light to this bothering pipe, and that I can't get either.'

'I'll get you one,' said Tom; and he took up a live coal (there were plenty lying about) and put it to Grimes' pipe: but it went out instantly.

'It's no use,' said the truncheon, leaning itself up against the chimney and looking on. 'I tell you, it is no use. His heart is so cold that it freezes everything that comes near him. You will see that presently, plain enough.'

'Oh, of course, it's my fault. Everything's always my fault,' said Grimes. 'Now don't go to hit me again' (for the truncheon started upright, and looked very wicked;) 'you know, if my arms were only free, you daren't hit me then.'

The truncheon leant back against the chimney, and took no notice of the personal insult, like a well-trained policeman as it was, though he was ready enough to avenge any transgression against morality or order.

CHARLES KINGSLEY, *The Water Babies*, 1863

Once I remember being taken to a town called Oxford and a street called Holywell, where I was shown an Ancient of Days who, I was told, was the Provost of Oriel; wherefore I never understood, but conceived him to be some sort of idol. And twice or thrice we went, all of us, to pay a day-long visit to an old gentleman in a house in the country near Havant. Here everything was wonderful and unlike my world, and he had an old lady sister who was kind, and I played in hot, sweet-smelling meadows and ate all sorts of things.

After such a visit I was once put through the third degree by the Woman and her son, who asked me if I had told the old gentleman that I was much fonder of him than was the Woman's son. It must have been the tail-end of some sordid intrigue or other—the old gentleman being of kin to that unhappy pair—but it was beyond my comprehension. My sole concern had been a friendly pony in the paddock. My dazed attempts to clear myself were not accepted and, once again, the pleasure that I was seen to have taken was balanced by punishments and humiliation—above all humiliation. That alternation was quite regular. I can but admire the infernal laborious ingenuity of it all. *Exempli gratia*. Coming out of church once I smiled. The Devil-Boy demanded why. I said I didn't know, which was child's truth. He replied that I *must* know. People didn't laugh for nothing. Heaven knows what explanation I put forward; but it was duly reported to the Woman as a 'lie.' Result, afternoon upstairs with the Collect to learn. I learned most of the Collects that way and a great deal of the Bible. The son after three or four years went into a Bank and was generally too tired on his return to torture me, unless things had gone wrong with him. I learned to know what was coming from his step into the house.

RUDYARD KIPLING, *Something of Myself*, 1937

'And then, you know,' said Ernest to me, when I asked him not long since to give me more of his childish reminiscences for the benefit of my story, 'we used to learn Mrs Barbauld's hymns; they were in prose, and there was one about the lion which began, "Come, and I will show you what is strong. The lion is strong; when he raiseth himself from his lair, when he shaketh his mane, when the voice of his roaring is heard the cattle of the field fly, and the beasts of the desert hide themselves, for he is very terrible." I used to say this to Joey and Charlotte about my father himself when I got a little older, but they were always didactic, and said it was naughty of me.

'One great reason why clergymen's households are generally unhappy is because the clergyman is so much at home or close about the house. The doctor is out visiting patients half his time: the lawyer and the merchant have offices away from home, but the clergyman has no official place of business which shall ensure his being away from home for many hours together at stated times. Our great days were when my father went for a day's shopping to Gildenham. We were some miles from this place, and commissions used to accumulate on my father's list till he would make a day of it and go and do the lot. As soon as his back was turned the air felt lighter; as soon as the hall door opened to let him in again, the law with its all-reaching "touch not, taste not, handle not" was upon us again. The worst of it was that I could never trust Joey and Charlotte; they would go a good way with me and then turn back, or even the whole way and then their consciences would compel them to tell papa and mamma. They liked running with the hare up to a certain point, but their instinct was towards the hounds.

'It seems to me,' he continued, 'that the family is a survival of the principle which is more logically embodied in the compound animal —and the compound animal is a form of life which has been found incompatible with high development. I would do with the family among mankind what nature has done with the compound animal, and confine it to the lower and less progressive races. Certainly there is no inherent love for the family system on the part of nature herself. Poll the forms of life and you will find it in a ridiculously small minority. The fishes know it not, and they get along quite nicely. The ants and the bees, who far outnumber man, sting their fathers to death as a matter of course, and are given to the atrocious mutilation of nine-tenths of the offspring committed to their charge, yet where shall we find communities more universally respected? Take the cuckoo again—is there any bird which we like better?'

SAMUEL BUTLER, *The Way of All Flesh*, 1903

† *Henry James's heiress, in* Washington Square, *is subjected to intolerable moral pressure from her tyrant father.*

Her father sat looking at her, and she was afraid he was going to break out into wrath, his eyes were so fine and cold.

'You are a dear, faithful child,' he said, at last. 'Come here to your father.' And he got up, holding out his hands toward her.

The words were a surprise, and they gave her an exquisite joy. She went to him, and he put his arm round her tenderly, soothingly; and then he kissed her. After this he said, 'Do you wish to make me very happy?'

'I should like to—but I am afraid I can't,' Catherine answered.

'You can if you will. It all depends on your will.'

'Is it to give him up?' said Catherine.

'Yes, it is to give him up.'

And he held her still, with the same tenderness, looking into her face and resting his eyes on her averted eyes. There was a long silence; she wished he would release her.

'You are happier than I, Father,' she said, at last.

'I have no doubt you are unhappy just now. But it is better to be unhappy for three months and get over it, than for many years and never get over it.'

'Yes, if that were so,' said Catherine.

'It would be so; I am sure of that.' She answered nothing, and he went on: 'Have you no faith in my wisdom, in my tenderness, in my solicitude for your future?'

'Oh, Father!' murmured the girl.

'Don't you suppose that I know something of men—their vices, their follies, their falsities?'

She detached herself, and turned upon him. 'He is not vicious—he is not false!'

Her father kept looking at her with his sharp, pure eye. 'You make nothing of my judgment, then?'

'I can't believe that!'

'I don't ask you to believe it, but to take it on trust.'

Catherine was far from saying to herself that this was an ingenious sophism; but she met the appeal none the less squarely. 'What has he done—what do you know?'

'He has never done anything—he is a selfish idler.'

'Oh, Father, don't abuse him!' she exclaimed, pleadingly.

'I don't mean to abuse him; it would be a great mistake. You may do as you choose,' he added, turning away.

'I may see him again?'

'Just as you choose.'

'Will you forgive me?'

'By no means.'

'It will only be for once.'

'I don't know what you mean by once. You must either give him up or continue the acquaintance.'

'I wish to explain—to tell him to wait.'

'To wait for what?'

'Till you know him better—till you consent.'

'Don't tell him any such nonsense as that. I know him well enough, and I shall never consent.'

'But we can wait a long time,' said poor Catherine, in a tone which was meant to express the humblest conciliation, but which had upon her father's nerves the effect of an iteration not characterized by tact.

The doctor answered, however, quietly enough: 'Of course; you can wait till I die, if you like.'

Catherine gave a cry of natural horror.

'Your engagement will have one delightful effect upon you; it will make you extremely impatient for that event.'

Catherine stood staring, and the doctor enjoyed the point he had made. It came to Catherine with the force—or rather with the vague impressiveness—of a logical axiom which it was not in her province to controvert; and yet, though it was a scientific truth, she felt wholly unable to accept it.

'I would rather not marry, if that were true,' she said.

'Give me a proof of it, then; for it is beyond a question that by engaging yourself to Morris Townsend you simply wait for my death.'

HENRY JAMES, *Washington Square*, 1881

† *After being orphaned in the flu epidemic of 1918, Mary McCarthy (then aged 7) and her brothers were transferred to the care of various relatives, some of whom were short on affection and understanding. The worst of the lot was Uncle Myers.*

When I was eight, I began writing poetry in school: 'Father Gaughan is our dear parish priest | And he is loved from west to east.' And 'Alas, Pope Benedict is dead, | The sorrowing people said.' Pope Benedict at that time was living, and, as far as I know, in good health; I had written this opening couplet for the rhyme and the sad idea; but then, very conveniently for me, about a year later he died, which gave me a feeling of fearsome power, stronger than a priest's power of loosing and binding. I came forward with my poem and it was beautifully copied out by our teacher and served as the school's elegy at a memorial service for the Pontiff. I dared not tell that I had had it ready in my desk. Not long afterward, when I was ten, I wrote an essay for a children's contest on 'The Irish in American History', which won first the City and then the State prize. Most of my facts I had cribbed from a series on Catholics in American history that was running in *Our Sunday Visitor*. I worked on the assumption that anybody who was Catholic must be Irish, and then, for good measure, I went over the signers of the Declaration of Independence and added any name that sounded Irish to my ears. . . . I believe that even Kosciusko figured as an Irishman *de cœur*. At any rate, there was a school ceremony, at which I was presented with the City prize (twenty-five dollars, I think, or perhaps that was the State prize); my aunt was in the audience in her best mallard-feathered hat, looking, for once, proud and happy. She spoke kindly to me as we walked home, but when we came to our ugly house, my uncle silently rose from his chair, led me into the dark downstairs lavatory, which always smelled of shaving cream, and furiously beat me with the razor strop—to teach me a lesson, he said, lest I become stuck-up. Aunt Margaret did not intervene. After her first look of discomfiture, her face settled into folds of approval; she had been too soft. This was the usual tribute she paid Myers's greater discernment—she was afraid of losing his love by weakness. The money was taken, 'to keep for me', and that, of course, was the end of it. Such was the fate of anything considered 'much too good for her', a category that was rivalled only by its pendant, 'plenty good enough'.

We were beaten all the time, as a matter of course, with the hair-brush across the bare legs for ordinary occasions, and with the razor strop across the bare bottom for special occasions, like the prize-winning. It was as though these ignorant people, at sea with four frightened children, had taken a Dickens novel—*Oliver Twist*, perhaps, or *Nicholas Nickleby*—for a navigation chart. Sometimes our punishments were earned, sometimes not; they were administered gratuitously, often, as preventive medicine. I was whipped more frequently than my brothers, simply by virtue of seniority; that is, every time one of them was whipped, I was whipped also, for not having set a better example, and this was true for all four of us in a descending line. Kevin was whipped for Preston's misdeeds and for Sheridan's, and Preston was whipped for Sheridan's, while Sheridan, the baby and the favourite, was whipped only for his own. This naturally made us fear and distrust each other, and only between Kevin and myself was there a kind of uneasy alliance. When Kevin ran away, as he did on one famous occasion, I had a feeling of joy and defiance, mixed with the fear of punishment for myself, mixed with something worse, a vengeful anticipation of the whipping *he* would surely get. I suppose that the two times I ran away, his feelings were much the same—envy, awe, fear, admiration, and a certain evil thrill, collusive with my uncle, at the thought of the strop ahead. Yet, strange to say, nobody was beaten on these historic days. The culprit, when found, took refuge at my grandmother's, and a fearful hush lay over the house on Blaisdell Avenue at the thought of the monstrous daring and deceitfulness of the runaway; Uncle Myers, doubtless, was shaking in his boots at the prospect of explanations to the McCarthy family council. The three who remained at home were sentenced to spend the day upstairs, in strict silence. But if my uncle's impartial application of punishment served to make us each other's enemies very often, it did nothing to establish discipline, since we had no incentive to behave well, not knowing when we might be punished for something we had not done or even for something that by ordinary standards would be considered good. We knew not when we would offend, and what I learned from this, in the main, was a policy of lying and concealment; for several years after we were finally liberated, I was a problem liar.

Despite Myers's quite justified hatred of the intellect, of reading and education (for he was right—it *was* an escape from him), my uncle, like all dictators, had one book that he enjoyed. It was *Uncle*

Remus, in a red cover—a book I detested—which he read aloud to us in his den over and over again in the evenings. It seemed to me that this reduction of human life to the level of talking animals and this corruption of language to dialect gave my uncle some very personal relish. He knew I hated it and he rubbed it in, trotting my brother Sheridan on his knee as he dwelt on some exploit of Br'er Fox's with many chuckles and repetitions. In *Uncle Remus* he had his hour, and to this day I cannot read anything in dialect or any fable without some degree of repugnance.

MARY MCCARTHY, *Memories of a Catholic Girlhood*, 1957

Autumn came and Mother was still dying in her room. It was peaceful in there because Father was frightened of her illness and never visited her. Each Monday morning he would ask for her purse. I would hand it to him, all black and thin and worn. He would put in four sovereigns and four half-crowns, and the purse would come alive again. He could hardly bear to touch it and would wash his hands in the surgery afterwards. He made me take away Mother's outdoor clothes, which hung on pegs in the hall; and the rather downtrodden slippers that lived under the kitchen dresser were thrown into the boiler as if they had been black beetles.

A young boy called Hank helped with the animals now because I had to do most of the cooking and all the shopping and see to Mother when Mrs Churchill had gone home. In spite of the boy's help, I didn't look after Father as well as Mother used to, and he often hit me because the bacon was burnt or the coffee weak. Once, when I had ironed a shirt badly, he suddenly rushed at me like a charging bull in a thunderstorm, seeming to toss the shirt in some way with his head. I held on to the kitchen sink, too afraid to move. He came right up to me, and I saw the whites of his eyes were all red. He was only wearing his vest and trousers and was dreadfully hairy. He seized the arms of the shirt and was trying to tie them round my neck with his great square hands when the parrot suddenly started to give one of its awful laughs. Father seemed to go all limp, and stumbled from the room, while the parrot went on laughing.

This was the only time Father got really fierce all the time Mother was ill. On the whole, he was rather subdued and stayed in the house as little as possible. He never asked after Mother. Sometimes the doctor would catch him in the hall, and then he would have to listen to him; but usually, when the doctor came, he would go out.

One morning a dreadful thing happened. A man came to measure Mother for her coffin as if she were dead already. He said Father had told him to come. Mrs Churchill sent him away, but Mother kept calling, 'Who was that? Who was that?' and we had to make excuses. In the afternoon she seemed worse, and wimpered and moaned and would not be comforted. The people waiting with their dogs and cats in the hall could hear her. It was like some awful symphony—Mother's sad sounds, and the screams and laughs of the parrot, and the howls and barks of the dogs, and in the background a plaintive chorus of mews from the cats. Father came out of the surgery, grey in the face, and hissed in my ear, 'Keep her quiet! I won't have that noise. I can't stand it, I tell you!'

BARBARA COMYNS, *The Vet's Daughter*, 1959

† *In George Orwell's fable, the liberated animals of Manor Farm gradually find themselves subjected to a dictatorship no less rigorous than the one they overthrew—only now it is a pig who is in the seat of office.*

For the next two days Boxer remained in his stall. The pigs had sent out a large bottle of pink medicine which they had found in the medicine chest in the bathroom, and Clover administered it to Boxer twice a day after meals. In the evenings she lay in his stall and talked to him, while Benjamin kept the flies off him. Boxer professed not to be sorry for what had happened. If he made a good recovery, he might expect to live another three years, and he looked forward to the peaceful days that he would spend in the corner of the big pasture. It would be the first time that he had had leisure to study and improve his mind. He intended, he said, to devote the rest of his life to learning the remaining twenty-two letters of the alphabet.

However, Benjamin and Clover could only be with Boxer after working hours, and it was in the middle of the day when the van came to take him away. The animals were all at work weeding turnips under the supervision of a pig, when they were astonished to see Benjamin come galloping from the direction of the farm buildings, braying at the top of his voice. It was the first time that they had ever seen Benjamin excited—indeed, it was the first time that anyone had ever seen him gallop. 'Quick, quick!' he shouted. 'Come at once! They're taking Boxer away!' Without waiting for orders from the pig, the animals broke off work and raced back to the farm buildings. Sure enough, there in the yard was a large closed van, drawn by two horses, with lettering on its side and a sly-looking man in a low-crowned bowler hat sitting on the driver's seat. And Boxer's stall was empty.

The animals crowded round the van. 'Good-bye, Boxer!' they chorused, 'good-bye!'

'Fools! Fools!' shouted Benjamin, prancing round them and stamping the earth with his small hoofs. 'Fools! Do you not see what is written on the side of that van?'

That gave the animals pause, and there was a hush. Muriel began to spell out the words. But Benjamin pushed her aside and in the midst of a deadly silence he read:

' "Alfred Simmonds, Horse Slaughterer and Glue Boiler, Willingdon. Dealer in Hides and Bone-Meal. Kennels Supplied." Do you not understand what that means? They are taking Boxer to the knacker's!'

A cry of horror burst from all the animals. At this moment the man on the box whipped up his horses and the van moved out of the yard at a smart trot. All the animals followed, crying out at the tops of their voices. Clover forced her way to the front. The van began to gather speed. Clover tried to stir her stout limbs to a gallop, and achieved a canter. 'Boxer!' she cried. 'Boxer! Boxer! Boxer!' And just at this moment, as though he had heard the uproar outside, Boxer's face, with the white stripe down his nose, appeared at the small window at the back of the van.

'Boxer!' cried Clover, in a terrible voice. 'Boxer! Get out! Get out quickly! They are taking you to your death!'

All the animals took up the cry of 'Get out, Boxer, get out!' But the van was already gathering speed and drawing away from them. It was uncertain whether Boxer had understood what Clover had said. But a moment later his face disappeared from the window and there was the sound of a tremendous drumming of hoofs inside the van. He was trying to kick his way out. The time had been when a few kicks from Boxer's hoofs would have smashed the van to matchwood. But alas! his strength had left him; and in a few moments the sound of drumming hoofs grew fainter and died away. In desperation the animals began appealing to the two horses which drew the van to stop. 'Comrades, comrades!' they shouted. 'Don't take your own brother to his death!' But the stupid brutes, too ignorant to realize what was happening, merely set back their ears and quickened their pace. Boxer's face did not reappear at the window. Too late, someone thought of racing ahead and shutting the five-barred gate; but in another moment the van was through it and rapidly disappearing down the road. Boxer was never seen again.

Three days later it was announced that he had died in the hospital at Willingdon, in spite of receiving every attention a horse could have. Squealer came to announce the news to the others. He had, he said, been present during Boxer's last hours.

'It was the most affecting sight I have ever seen!' said Squealer, lifting his trotter and wiping away a tear. 'I was at his bedside at the very last. And at the end, almost too weak to speak, he whispered in my ear that his sole sorrow was to have passed on before the windmill was finished. "Forward, comrades!" he whispered. "Forward in the name of the Rebellion. Long Live Animal Farm! Long live Comrade Napoleon! Napoleon is always right." Those were his very last words, comrades.'

Here Squealer's demeanour suddenly changed. He fell silent for a moment, and his little eyes darted suspicious glances from side to side before he proceeded.

It had come to his knowledge, he said, that a foolish and wicked rumour had been circulated at the time of Boxer's removal. Some of the animals had noticed that the van which took Boxer away was marked 'Horse Slaughterer', and had actually jumped to the conclusion that Boxer was being sent to the knacker's. It was almost unbelievable, said Squealer, that any animal could be so stupid. Surely, he cried indignantly, whisking his tail and skipping from side to side, surely they knew their beloved Leader, Comrade Napoleon, better than that? But the explanation was really very simple. The van had previously been the property of the knacker, and had been bought by the veterinary surgeon, who had not yet painted the old name out. That was how the mistake had arisen.

The animals were enormously relieved to hear this. And when Squealer went on to give further graphic details of Boxer's death bed, the admirable care he had received, and the expensive medicines for which Napoleon had paid without a thought as to the cost, their last doubts disappeared and the sorrow that they felt for their comrade's death was tempered by the thought that at least he had died happy.

Napoleon himself appeared at the meeting on the following Sunday morning and pronounced a short oration in Boxer's honour. It had not been possible, he said, to bring back their lamented comrade's remains for interment on the farm, but he had ordered a large wreath to be made from the laurels in the farmhouse garden and sent down to be placed on Boxer's grave. And in a few days' time the pigs intended to hold a memorial banquet in Boxer's honour. Napoleon ended his speech with a reminder of Boxer's two favourite maxims, 'I will work harder' and 'Comrade Napoleon is always right'—maxims, he said, which every animal would do well to adopt as his own.

On the day appointed for the banquet, a grocer's van drove up from Willingdon and delivered a large wooden crate at the farmhouse. That night there was the sound of uproarious singing, which was followed by what sounded like a violent quarrel and ended at about eleven o'clock with a tremendous crash of glass. No one stirred in the farmhouse before noon on the following day, and the word went round that from somewhere or other the pigs had acquired the money to buy themselves another case of whisky.

GEORGE ORWELL, *Animal Farm*, 1945

† *The tyranny of his Aunt Agatha is something strange and terrible. Bertie Wooster does his best to explain it.*

To people who don't know my Aunt Agatha I find it extraordinarily difficult to explain why it is that she has always put the wind up me to such a frightful extent. I mean, I'm not dependent on her financially, or anything like that. It's simply personality, I've come to the conclusion. You see, all through my childhood and when I was a kid at school she was always able to turn me inside out with a single glance, and I haven't come out from under the 'fluence yet. We run to height a bit in our family, and there's about five-foot-nine of Aunt Agatha, topped off with a beaky nose, an eagle eye, and a lot of grey hair, and the general effect is pretty formidable.

Her arrival in Roville at this juncture had made things more than a bit complicated for me. What to do? Leg it quick before she could get hold of me, would no doubt have been the advice most fellows would have given me. But the situation wasn't as simple as that. I was in much the same position as the cat on the garden wall who, when on the point of becoming matey with the cat next door, observes the boot-jack sailing through the air. If he stays where he is, he gets it in the neck; if he biffs, he has to start all over again where he left off. I didn't like the prospect of being collared by Aunt Agatha, but on the other hand I simply barred the notion of leaving Roville by the night-train and parting from Aline Hemmingway. Absolutely a man's crossroads, if you know what I mean.

I prowled about the neighbourhood all the afternoon and evening, then I had a bit of dinner at a quiet restaurant in the town and trickled cautiously back to the hotel. Jeeves was popping about in the suite.

'There is a note for you, sir,' he said, 'on the mantelpiece.'

The blighter's manner was still so cold and unchummy that I bit the bullet and had a dash at being airy.

'A note, eh?'

'Yes, sir. Mrs Gregson's maid brought it shortly after you had left.'

'Tra-la-la!' I said.

'Precisely, sir.'

I opened the note.

'She wants me to look in on her after dinner some time.'

'Yes, sir?'

'Jeeves,' I said, 'mix me a stiffish brandy-and-soda.'

'Yes, sir.'

'Stiffish, Jeeves. Not too much soda, but splash the brandy about a bit.'

'Very good, sir.'

He shimmered off into the background to collect the materials, and just at that moment there was a knock at the door.

I'm bound to say it was a shock. My heart stood still, and I bit my tongue.

'Come in,' I bleated.

P. G. WODEHOUSE, 'Aunt Agatha Takes the Count', 1923

ACKNOWLEDGEMENTS AND INDEXES

ACKNOWLEDGEMENTS

THE editor and publisher are grateful for permission to include the following copyright material in this volume:

Eric Ambler, from *Journey into Fear*. Copyright 1940 and renewed 1968 by Eric C. Ambler. Reprinted by permission of Hodder & Stoughton Ltd. and Alfred A. Knopf Inc.

Kingsley Amis, 'Nothing to Fear' from *Collected Poems* (Hutchinson). © 1967 Kingsley Amis. Reprinted by permission of Jonathan Clowes Ltd., London on behalf of Kingsley Amis and the Random Century Group Ltd. for the publisher.

W. H. Auden, 'Epitaph on a Tyrant' from *Collected Shorter Poems 1927–1957*. Reprinted by permission of Faber & Faber Ltd. Published in the USA by Random House Inc.

Luigi Barzini, from *The Italians* (1964). Reprinted by permission of Hamish Hamilton Ltd.

Hilaire Belloc, 'On Lady Poltargue, A Public Peril' from *Complete Verse* (Pimlico, a division of Random Century) Reprinted by permission of Peters Fraser & Dunlop Group Ltd.

Alan Bennett, from *An Englishman Abroad*. Reprinted by permission of Faber & Faber Ltd. and BBC Publications.

Beowulf, translated by David Wright (Penguin Classics, 1957). © David Wright 1957. Reprinted by permission of Penguin Books Ltd.

William Bolitho, from *Murder for Profit* (Cape, 1926).

Jorge Luis Borges, 'The Disinterested Killer Bill Harrigan' and 'Monk Eastman, Purveyor of Iniquities' from *A Universal History of Infamy*, translated by Norman Thomas di Giovanni, translation copyright © 1970, 1971, 1972 by Emece Editores, SA, and Norman Thomas di Giovanni. Used by permission of the publisher, Dutton, an imprint of New American Library, a division of Penguin Books USA Inc.

Elizabeth Bowen, from *The Heat of the Day*. Copyright 1948 by Elizabeth Bowen. Reprinted by permission of Alfred A. Knopf Inc. and the Random

Century Group Ltd., on behalf of the Estate of Elizabeth Bowen, and Jonathan Cape as UK publishers.

Bertolt Brecht, extracts from *The Threepenny Opera* translated by John Willett and Ralph Manheim. Reprinted by permission of Methuen London and Routledge, Chapman & Hall, Inc.

Francis X. Busch, 'The Loeb-Leopold Case' from 'Prisoners at the Bar' in *Notable American Trials* by Francis X. Busch (Arco, 1957).

James M. Cain, from *Double Indemnity* (published in the UK as *Three of a Kind*). Copyright 1936 and renewed 1954 by James M. Cain. Reprinted by permission of Robert Hale Ltd., and Alfred A. Knopf Inc.

Albert Camus, from *The Outsider* (1946). Reprinted by permission of Hamish Hamilton Ltd. Published and copyrighted in the USA by Alfred A. Knopf Inc.

Angela Carter, from *The Company of Wolves* (1979). Reprinted by permission of Victor Gollancz Ltd. Published and copyrighted in the USA by Harper-Collins, New York. From *Black Venus* (Chatto, 1985). Reprinted by permission of the Random Century Group Ltd. Published in the USA as *Saints and Strangers*, © 1985, 1986 by Angela Carter. Reprinted by permission of Viking Penguin.

Cassanova, extracts from *Cassanova's Memoirs*, translated by Arthur Machen (New York: Dover Publications, 1961).

Raymond Chandler, from *The High Window* (1942). Copyright 1942 by Raymond Chandler and renewed 1970 by Helga Greene, executrix of the Estate of Raymond Chandler. Reprinted by permission of Hamish Hamilton Ltd. and Alfred A. Knopf Inc.

Leslie Charteris, from *Enter the Saint* (1930). Reprinted by permission of Hodder & Stoughton Ltd.

Chaucer, from *The Canterbury Tales*, translated by David Wright. Reprinted by permission of the Peters Fraser & Dunlop Group Ltd.

Caryl Churchill, from *Serious Money*. Reprinted by permission of Methuen London.

Cicero: Selected Works, translated by Michael Grant (Penguin Classics, revised edition, 1971). © Michael Grant, 1960, 1965, 1971. Reprinted by permission of Penguin Books Ltd.

James Comyn, from *Irish at Law* (1981). Reprinted by permission of Martin Secker & Warburg Ltd. as publisher.

Barbara Comyns, from *The Vet's Daughter* (Heinemann, 1959). Reprinted by permission of John Johnson Ltd.

ACKNOWLEDGEMENTS

Alistair Cooke, from *A Generation on Trial* (Rupert Hart-Davis, 1950).

Tom Cullen, from *Autumn of Terror, Jack the Ripper* (Bodley Head, 1965).

F. M. Dostoevsky, from *Crime and Punishment*, translated by Jessie Coulson (1953). Reprinted by permission of Oxford University Press.

T. S. Eliot, 'Macavity: the Mystery Cat' from *Old Possum's Book of Practical Cats* (1939). Reprinted by permission of Faber & Faber Ltd. Copyright in the USA by Harcourt Brace Jovanovich Inc.

The Encyclopedia of American Crime extracts on 'Bordenmania', 'Al-Capone' and 'Cackle-Bladder'. © 1982 by Facts on File. Reprinted by permission of Facts on File Inc., New York.

D. J. Enright, 'Lucifer Broods' from *The Collected Poems of D. J. Enright* (OUP, 1987). Reprinted by permission of Watson, Little Ltd. as agent.

Gavin Ewart, 'The Clarissa Harlowe Poem' and 'Charles Augustus Milverton' from *The Collected Ewart 1922–1980* (Hutchinson). Reprinted by permission of the Random Century Group Ltd.

Ian Fleming, from *Dr No* (Cape, 1958). Reprinted by permission of the Random Century Group Ltd. Copyrighted in the USA by Glidrose Publications.

Dick Francis, from *Dead Cert* (1960). Reprinted by permission of John Johnson Ltd. and Michael Joseph Ltd.

J. H. Gaute and Robin Odell, 'Leopold and Loeb' from *The New Murderers' Who's Who*. Reprinted by permission of Virgin Publishing.

Maxim Gorky, from *Fragments from My Diary*, ch. XI, translated by Moira Budberg (Penguin Books Ltd.).

Robert Graves, from *Claudius the God*, and from *Suetonius: The Twelve Caesars*. Reprinted by permission of A. P. Watt Ltd. on behalf of the Trustees of the Robert Graves Copyright Trust.

Graham Greene, (1) from *The Third Man* (1950). Copyright 1950 Francis Greene. (2) From *Brighton Rock*. Copyright 1938 Francis Greene. (3) From *A Gun for Sale*. Copyright 1936 Francis Greene. All published by William Heinemann Ltd. and reprinted by permission of David Higham Associates Ltd.

Hermann Hesse, from *Steppenwolf*, translated by Basil Creighton (A. Lane/Penguin, 1974, 1990).

Patricia Highsmith, from *Strangers on a Train* and *Ripley Underground*. Reprinted by permission of William Heinemann Ltd. and Diogenes Verlag AG on behalf of the author.

ACKNOWLEDGEMENTS

Homer, from *The Odyssey* Books IX, X translated by E. V. Rieu. Reprinted by permission of Richard Rieu.

Richard Hughes, from *High Wind in Jamaica* (1929). Copyright 1928, 1929 by Richard Hughes © renewed 1956, 1957 by Richard Hughes. Reprinted by permission of the Random Century Group Ltd. on behalf of Chatto & Windus, and the Estate of Richard Hughes, and Harold Ober Associates Inc.

The Earl Jowitt, from *Some Were Spies* (Hodder, 1954).

James Joyce, from *The Dubliners.* Copyright 1916 by B. W. Heubsch. Definitive text © 1967 by the Estate of James Joyce. Used by permission of Viking Penguin, a division of Penguin Books USA Inc.

King Arthur's Death, translated by Brian Stone (Penguin Classics, 1988). © Brian Stone 1988. Reprinted by permission of Penguin Books Ltd.

Phillip Knightley, from *Philby* (Deutsch, 1988). Reprinted by permission of Andre Deutsch Ltd. and the Tessa Sayle Agency.

P. C. de Laclos, from *Les Liaisons dangereuses*, translated by Richard Aldington. Reprinted by permission of Routledge.

Mikhail Lermontov, from *A Hero of Our Time*, translated by Vladimir and Dmitri Nabokov (World's Classics, 1984). Reprinted by permission of Oxford University Press. Copyrighted in the USA by the Estate of Vladimir Nabokov.

Philip Lindsay, from *The Great Buccaneer* (Peter Nevill, 1950).

Christopher Logue, 'Mad Luck', 'Greek Mythology', and extract from *Private Eye* from *The Bumper Book of True Stories* (Private Eye in association with Andre Deutsch, 1980). Reprinted by permission of Christopher Logue.

Mrs Belloc Lowndes, from *The Lodger* (Ernest Benn, 1932).

Mary McCarthy, from *Memories of a Catholic Girlhood* (1957). Reprinted by permission of A. M. Heath on behalf of the Estate of the late Mary McCarthy.

John Masefield, from *The Box of Delights* (Heinemann, 1935). Reprinted by permission of The Society of Authors as the literary representatives of the Estate of John Masefield.

Somerset Maugham, from *Ashenden.* Reprinted by permission of A. P. Watt Ltd. on behalf of The Royal Literary Fund, and Wm. Heinemann Ltd.

Medieval English Verse ('Not long ago . . .'), translated by Brian Stone (Penguin Classics, 1964). © Brian Stone, 1964. Reprinted by permission of Penguin Books Ltd.

Arthur Miller, from *Time Bends* (1987). © 1987 by Arthur Miller. Reprinted by permission of Methuen London and ICM Inc.

Gladys Mitchell, from *The Rising of the Moon* (1945). Reprinted by permission of the Random Century Group on behalf of Chatto & Windus as publisher.

Naomi Mitchison, from *The Fourth Pig* (Constable, 1936). Reprinted by permission of David Higham Associates Ltd.

Molière, from 'Tartuffe' from *The Misanthrope and Other Plays*, translated by John Wood (Penguin Classics, 1959). © John Wood, 1959. From 'Don Juan' from *The Miser and Other Plays*, translated by John Wood (Penguin Classics, 1953). © John Wood 1953. Both reprinted by permission of Penguin Books Ltd.

Blake Morrison, from *The Ballad of the Yorkshire Ripper* (Chatto, 1987). Reprinted by permission of the Peters Fraser & Dunlop Group Ltd.

John Mortimer, from 'Rumpole and the Younger Generation' from *Rumpole of the Bailey*; from 'Rumpole and the Man of God' from *The Trials of Rumpole*; from 'Rumpole at Sea' from *Rumpole à la carte*. Reprinted by permission of the Peters Fraser & Dunlop Group Ltd.

Wolfgang Amadeus Mozart, from *Don Giovanni*, libretto by L. da Ponte, translated by Amanda and Anthony Holden (Deutsch, 1987). Reprinted by permission of Trafalgar Square Publishing and Andre Deutsch Ltd.

Robert Murray, 'The Four Guests Mystery' from *The Union Jack* (1932).

Notable British Trials, extracts from 'The Trial of Crippen' and 'The Trial of Captain Kidd'. Reprinted by permission of Wm. Hodge & Company Ltd.

Liam O'Flaherty, from *The Informer*. Copyright 1925 and renewed 1953 by Liam O'Flaherty. Reprinted by permission of the Random Century Group Ltd. on behalf of Jonathan Cape as publishers and Harcourt Brace Jovanovich Inc.

George Orwell, from *Animal Farm* (1945). Copyright 1946 by Harcourt Brace Jovanovich Inc. and renewed 1974 by Sonia Orwell. Reprinted by permission of A. M. Heath on behalf of the estate of the late Sonia Brownell Orwell and Martin Secker & Warburg Ltd., and Harcourt Brace Jovanovich Inc.

S. J. Perelman, 'Don't Blame Inspector Byrnes' from *Rogues' Gallery* by Inspector Byrnes (Caster, 1988). Reprinted by permission of the Peters Fraser & Dunlop Group Ltd.

Harold Pinter, from *The Dumb Waiter*. Reprinted by permission of Faber & Faber Ltd. and Grove Press Inc.

William Plomer, 'The Murder on the Downs' from *Collected Poems* (Cape,

1960). Reprinted by permission of the Random Century Group Ltd. on behalf of the Estate of William Plomer.

Ezra Pound, extract from 'Canto XLVI' from *The Cantos of Ezra Pound*. Copyright 1937 by Ezra Pound. Reprinted by permission of Faber & Faber Ltd., and New Directions Publishing Corporation.

J. B. Priestley, from *Blackout in Gretley* (1942). Reprinted by permission of the Peters Fraser & Dunlop Group Ltd.

Alexander Pushkin, from *The Queen of Spades and Other Stories*, translated by Rosemary Edmonds (Penguin Classics, 1962). © Rosemary Edmonds 1958, 1962. Reprinted by permission of Penguin Books Ltd.

Stephen Pyle, 'The Least Successful Attempt to Murder a Spouse', 'The Worst Burglar', 'The Least Successful Diamond Robbery' and 'The Least Successful Blackmailer' from *The Book of Heroic Failures* (1979).

William Sterne Randall, from *Benedict Arnold* (William Morrow, 1990).

Ruth Rendell, from *The Bridesmaid* (Hutchinson, 1989).

Riccini, extracts from *Tosca*, translated by Edmund Tracey. © 1980 Josef Weinberger Ltd. Reproduced by permission of the copyright owners.

Sax Rohmer, from *The Mystery of Dr Fu-Manchu* (Methuen, 1913). Reprinted by permission of A. P. Watt Ltd. on behalf of the Society of Authors and Authors' League of America.

Amanda McKittrick Ros, from *Helen Huddleson* (Chatto, 1969).

Damon Runyon, from 'The Snatching of Bookie Bob' and from 'Tobias the Terrible'. Reprinted by permission of Constable Publishers. 'Al Capone' from *Trials and Other Tribulations*.

Siegfried Sassoon, 'Base Details' from *Collected Poems* (Faber, 1956). Reprinted by permission of George Sassoon.

Sir Osbert Sitwell, from *Fee Fi Fo Fum* (Macmillan). Reprinted by permission of David Higham Associates Ltd.

Stevie Smith, 'Some are More Human than Others', 'Bag-snatching in Dublin', 'Lord Barrenstock' and 'Villains' from *The Collected Poems of Stevie Smith* (London: Penguin 20th Century Classics; New York: New Directions). Copyright © 1972 by Stevie Smith. Reprinted by permission of James MacGibbon and New Directions Publishing Corporation.

Laurie Taylor, from *In the Underworld*. Reprinted by permission of A. P. Watt Ltd. on behalf of the author.

Dylan Thomas, 'The Hand that Signed the Paper Felled a City' from

Collected Poems (Dent). Reprinted by permission of David Higham Associates Ltd.

Barbara Tuchman, from *The March of Folly* (1984). Reprinted by permission of Michael Joseph Ltd. and Random House Inc.

Stephen Tumin, from *Great Legal Disasters* (Arthur Barker Ltd., 1983). Reprinted by permission of the author.

Horace Annesley Vachell, from *The Hill* (1906). Reprinted by permission of John Murray (Publishers) Ltd.

David Ward, from *Kings of Lags: The Story of Charles Peace* (1989). Reprinted by permission of Souvenir Press Ltd.

Bernard Wasserstein, from *The Secret Lives of Trebitsch Lincoln*. Reprinted by permission of Yale University Press.

Evelyn Waugh, from *Decline and Fall*; from Waugh's review of *The Tichborne Claimant* by Douglas Woodruff from *The Essays, Articles and Reviews of Evelyn Waugh* (Methuen). Reprinted by permission of the Peters Fraser & Dunlop Group Ltd.

Rebecca West, from *The Meaning of Treason* (Macmillan).

P. G. Wodehouse, from *Do Butlers Burgle Banks?*; from *Aunt Agatha Takes the Count* and from *Louder and Funnier*. Reprinted by permission of the Random Century Group on behalf of Hutchinson as publisher, and of A. P. Watt Ltd. on behalf of The Trustees of the Wodehouse Estate.

Douglas Woodruff, from *The Tichborne Claimant: A Victorian Mystery* (Hollis & Carter, 1937).

W. B. Yeats, 'John Kinsella's Lament For Mrs Mary Moore', copyright 1940 by Georgie Yeats, renewed © 1968 by Bertha Georgie Yeats, Michael Butler Yeats and Anne Yeats; 'Leda and the Swan', copyright 1928 by Macmillan Publishing Company, renewed © 1956 by Georgie Yeats, both reprinted with permission of Macmillan Publishing Company from *The Poems of W. B. Yeats: A New Edition*, edited by Richard J. Finneran.

Although every effort has been made to locate and contact copyright holders prior to printing this has not always been possible. However if notified the publisher will be pleased to rectify any inadvertent errors or omissions at the earliest opportunity.

INDEX OF VILLAINS

NOTE. Villains not identified are entered under titles of texts. Those with only first names are generally identified by the texts.

INDEX OF AUTHORS

OXFORD BOOKS

Oxford Books began in 1900 with Sir Arthur Quiller-Couch ('Q')'s *Oxford Book of English Verse*. Since then over 60 superb anthologies of poetry, prose, and songs have appeared in a series that has a very special place in British publishing.

THE OXFORD BOOK OF ENGLISH GHOST STORIES

Chosen by Michael Cox and R. A. Gilbert

This anthology includes some of the best and most frightening ghost stories ever written, including M. R. James's 'Oh Whistle, and I'll Come to You, My Lad', 'The Monkey's Paw' by W. W. Jacobs, and H. G. Wells's 'The Red Room'. The important contribution of women writers to the genre is represented by stories such as Amelia Edwards's 'The Phantom Coach', Edith Wharton's 'Mr Jones', and Elizabeth Bowen's 'Hand in Glove'.

As the editors stress in their informative introduction, a good ghost story, though it may raise many profound questions about life and death, entertains as much as it unsettles us, and the best writers are careful to satisfy what Virginia Woolf called 'the strange human craving for the pleasure of feeling afraid'. This anthology, the first to present the full range of classic English ghost fiction, similarly combines a serious literary purpose with the plain intention of arousing pleasing fear at the doings of the dead.

'an excellent cross-section of familiar and unfamiliar stories and guaranteed to delight' *New Statesman*

Also in Oxford Paperbacks:

The Oxford Book of Short Stories edited by V. S. Pritchett
The Oxford Book of Political Anecdotes
edited by Paul Johnson
The Oxford Book of Ages
edited by Anthony and Sally Sampson
The Oxford Book of Dreams edited by Stephen Brock